Palm OS® Programming from the Ground Up

About the Author

Robert Mykland has been working with hardware, application design, and programming for many years. His experience includes object oriented design, MS-Windows applications, real-time embedded systems, SCSI hosts and targets, network servers and "groupware", UNIX applications, multitasking and multiprocessing kernels, Web and internet applications, and DCOM and ActiveX. His programming languages include C/C++, Pascal, Lisp, and a dozen other high-level languages. He is also fluent in assembler. Most recently he has been programming on the Palm platform and is familiar with all major versions of Palm OS. He created a graphical rapid application development environment for the Pilot/PalmIII for Computer Associates' Opal authoring tool. His SQL expertise involves working for the last couple years on (among other things) code that connected to the top databases (Oracle, Sybase, Informix, MS-SQL Server, Ingres, etc.) via ODBC, which is SQL-92 based.

Palm OS® Programming from the Ground Up

Robert Mykland

Osborne/**McGraw-Hill**

Berkeley   New York   St. Louis   San Francisco
Auckland   Bogotá   Hamburg   London   Madrid
Mexico City   Milan   Montreal   New Delhi   Panama City
Paris   São Paulo   Singapore   Sydney
Tokyo   Toronto

Osborne/**McGraw-Hill**
2600 Tenth Street
Berkeley, California 94710
U.S.A.

For information on translations or book distributors outside the U.S.A., or to arrange
bulk purchase discounts for sales promotions, premiums, or fund-raisers, please
contact Osborne/**McGraw-Hill** at the above address.

Palm OS® Programming from the Ground Up

234567890 DOC DOC 019876543210

Book P/N 0-07-212150-5   and   CD P/N 0-07-212151-3
parts of
ISBN 0-07-212152-1

Publisher	**Copy Editor**
Brandon A. Nordin	Claire Splan
Associate Publisher and Editor-in-Chief	**Proofreader**
Scott Rogers	John Gildersleeve
Acquisitions Editor	**Indexer**
Wendy Rinaldi	Claire Splan
Project Editor	**Computer Designers**
Mark Karmendy	Michelle Galicia
	Elizabeth Jang
Acquisitions Coordinator	**Illustrator**
Monika Faltiss	Michael Mueller
Technical Editor	**Series Design**
Geoffrey Bonser	Peter Hancik

This book was composed with Corel VENTURA ™ Publisher.

To my wife Terri,
whose infinite generosity, love, support,
and partnership in all things
allows me to live
the life of my dreams.

Contents

Contents

Acknowledgements

I'd like to thank my large, tireless, and gloriously nitpicky squad of technical reviewers. My technical editor Geoffrey Bonser of Vanteon, Inc., is probably the most knowledgeable and meticulous technical editor anyone has ever had. The support and guidance of Ryan Robertson of Palm Computing, Inc., was of invaluable assistance on dozens of occasions. Kevin O'Keefe of Vanteon, Inc., was a major technical contributor and organized a stellar review team at Vanteon that included Jeff Ishaq, Bill Kirby, Cathy Donovan, David Irvine, and Sudeep Narain—unparalleled Palm OS gurus all. Thanks also go to Mike Finneran of Applied Physics Systems as well as to John Lamb and Paul Anderson for their invaluable advice on various crucial sections of the book.

There were people who really made this book happen. First among these were my acquisitions editor Wendy Rinaldi, whose patience and good cheer would rival that of any saint, my acquistions coordinator Monika Faltiss who handled all the details so wonderfully, and my project editor Mark Karmendy, whose Herculean efforts severely curtailed my abuse of the English language. Thanks also to Tim Allen and John Baumgarten of

Vanteon, Inc., who allowed me free access to the world's finest team of Palm OS experts outside of Palm Computing itself. Lisa Rathjens at Palm Computing got me everything I needed to get through this book, for which I will always be thankful. I'd like to acknowledge Kelly Baker, Kim Harris, and Luis Quiroga of Metrowerks for their tireless support through two versions of CodeWarrior. Finally, I thank my literary agent Chris Van Buren, without whom none of this would ever have taken place.

There were people who contributed substantially to the result you see here. My wife Terri Mykland is largely responsible for several glorious sections of the book, especially in Chapter 10. Monty Boyer of Palm Computing, Inc., generously answered my questions on the early history and evolution of Palm Computing and Palm devices. Jeff Ishaq of Vanteon spent considerable time and effort teaching me some of the coolest aspects of Palm OS, for which I am thankful.

Introduction

Much of this book concerns the specifics of how to create Palm OS software applications. If your aim is to get started with this as soon as possible, begin with Chapter 2 and then skip back to Chapter 1 when you need a breather.

Only a few chapters diverge from the fundamental concern of this book, which is head-on, hands-on Palm OS application design. Chapters 2 through 9 lead you through the design and implementation of a simple contact manager for the Palm OS.

Part Two of the book begins with three chapters concerning topics other than straight application development. Chapter 10 covers application design, both in general and as it applies specifically to the Palm. It's a very useful reference chapter for polishing a Palm user interface design at any stage of development. Chapter 11 examines all the different hardware and software resources currently available for Palm developers, and how you can connect with these resources. Chapter 12 explores how to organize and document

Palm OS C code to make it easy to work with and reuse. The book ends with the design and implementation of a calculator for Palm OS, along with a discussion of how to reuse code, use shared libraries, and port existing software to the Palm OS.

PART I

Lithosphere

CHAPTER 1

About the Palm

Much of this book concerns the specifics of how to create Palm OS software applications. If your aim is to get started with this as soon as possible, I recommend you start with Chapter 2 and then skip back here when you need a breather.

Only a few chapters diverge from the fundamental concern of this book, which is head-on, hands-on Palm OS application design. This chapter gives you useful background on the nature of Palm devices: where they came from, why they might be so successful where other handheld devices have so spectacularly failed, details of the different versions of the operating system, and discussions of the actual Palm hardware and its quirks. You don't need to know any of this to get started programming, but it is all useful to know as you build your expertise as a Palm developer.

Three other chapters concern topics other than straight application development. Chapter 10 is all about application design, both in general and as it applies specifically to the Palm. It's a very useful reference chapter for polishing a Palm user interface design at any stage of development. Chapter 11 is about all the different hardware and software resources currently out there for Palm developers, and how you can connect with these resources. Chapter 12 is about how to organize and document Palm OS C code to make it easy to work with and reuse.

The Success of Palm Computing

The early '90s were strewn with the carcasses of countless pen computing devices that never made it. Just when everybody had finally given up on ever having large-scale commercial success with a pen-driven mobile device, Palm Computing launched the Pilot and made history. The Pilot's market grew faster than any other computing product in history, faster than the TV or the VCR. How could such enormous success come after so many had tried for so long and failed so miserably?

As you might imagine, there are countless opinions about this. My opinion rests upon something Jeff Hawkins, the inventor of the Pilot and Palm OS, calls "user experience." Upon meeting Jeff Hawkins, I was reminded of a Yankee craftsman of some bygone era. He's a thoughtful, precise kind of guy who values simplicity of design. He's a guy who puts himself in his user's shoes and can play with stuff as if he is a new user. This is a great skill to have. I've heard tales about him scrawling holes in pieces of paper in meetings while he was developing Graffiti. People thought him a little eccentric, but actually he was testing out Graffiti in a real user experience kind of way: "Can I sit in meetings and take notes with this?"

1

Another story is how he carried a block of wood around with him for quite some time, pressing fake buttons on it, talking to it, and so forth. Again, people thought him a little wacko. But that block of wood turned into the Pilot.

I think the Palm worked because Jeff Hawkins designed it with the total user experience in mind. He left out everything possible without leaving the user frustrated in some way, and thereby made it simple enough for anyone to use quickly and effortlessly. He also made it affordable at the same time.

The second big thing that Jeff did and continues to do at Handspring is to put himself in the developer's shoes. Having developed on countless platforms in my career, I can confidently say that Palm OS is the easiest and most fun operating system to develop on since the invention of personal computing. That ease and fun for developers is also by design, and it has led to countless free and innovative applications for the Palm.

The History of Palm Computing

As with anything of significance, the concept of the Palm didn't just appear overnight. Its development and the path it took to success is, I think, instructive not just to us Palm developers, but to designers working with any new technology.

Jeff Hawkins and Donna Dubinsky founded Palm Computing. Jeff had been at Grid before then. Grid was famous for those laptops that would survive a trip out a second-story window. Remember that back in those days most PCs were so delicate that if you bumped them while they were on, you destroyed all your data, because disk drives were so fragile. So we were all very impressed by Grid.

Palm Computing started off as a software company. Originally, they produced Graffiti, the shorthand style of data entry found on all Palm OS devices, and sold it as an add-on to Newtons and other early handhelds.

Despite the success of Graffiti itself, the pen computing market as a whole was tanking. Palm Computing collaborated heavily in the development of the Casio Zoomer, but this promising device went the way of countless other handhelds before it.

Jeff decided that the only way to save the pen computing market was to design the right hardware. In order to succeed at this, two things had to happen: The people at Palm would have to come up with the right design, and someone would have to be found who would provide the capital that would allow Palm to manufacture and sell the device.

So Jeff started carrying blocks of wood around. The early look and feel of Palm OS was developed on HyperCard. Some magnificent design took place. But even more remarkable was Palm's ability to convince someone to invest in the first Pilot right during the whole period the pen-based market was crashing and burning so badly.

In March 1996, the Pilot 1000 hit retail stores. Bankrolled by U.S. Robotics, which had acquired Palm Computing during the development of the Pilot, this first model had everything that was essential and nothing that was not essential, and sold for $299.

In 1997, U.S. Robotics was bought by 3Com, and Palm Computing became a 3Com company and moved onto the 3Com campus in Santa Clara. The very successful Palm III shipped in the spring of 1998. In late 1999, Palm Computing spun off once again into its own company, Palm Computing, Inc.

The Corporate Structure of Palm Computing

Palm Computing, which is no longer a division of 3Com but its own company, has a corporate structure that you as a developer need to know something about. Palm Computing is actually several businesses. Two groups you need to know about as a developer have historically been called the Platform Group and the Hardware Group.

The first business is the Platform Group. These are the people who bring you Palm OS. Their business is to license Palm OS to the world. They don't care about what the Hardware Group is building. They don't care what anyone is building. Their job is to develop and license Palm OS. If you want information about Palm OS software or tools, ask the Platform Group.

The second business is the Hardware Group. They are a Palm OS licensee like any other. They compete directly with the other hardware licensees. If you have questions about specific Palm Computing hardware, you must ask the Hardware Group.

The Palm OS

In this section, I'll talk about the different versions of Palm OS and what features can and can't be used if you want to support them.

Version 1.0

The Pilot 1000 shipped with version 1.0 of the Palm OS in March 1996, followed shortly by the Pilot 5000. The vast majority of Palm functions are unchanged from version 1.0, a credit to its design.

Version 2.0

The PalmPilot Personal and PalmPilot Professional shipped with version 2.0 of the Palm OS in February 1997. Later some relabeled units from IBM appeared on the market. The PalmPilot Professional sported a TCP/IP stack built in, which enabled it to communicate over TCP/IP networks given the appropriate connection.

Release 2.0 cleaned up and improved on the very lean version 1.0 in a conservative way. The major improvements were

◆ TCP/IP support was added.

◆ Scrollbars were added.

◆ Sorting and searching databases became easier.

◆ Functions were added to make fields easier to use.

◆ Functions were added to make categories easier to use.

◆ Functions were added to make events easier to manipulate.

◆ Lots of standard string-manipulation functions were added.

Version 3.0

The Palm III, sporting a 3Com logo, was the first Palm device to ship with version 3.0 of the operating system in March 1998. The primary motivation of this release was to add Infrared beaming to the repertoire of the Palm. Version 3.0.2 of the operating system is unique to the Symbol SPT1500 and is functionally identical to version 3.0. The major improvements were

◆ Infrared beaming and a full-featured infrared support library of functions were added.

◆ Grayscale colors were increased to four: black, dark gray, light gray, and white.

◆ The dynamic memory heap (used by running applications) was increased to 96K.

◆ More advanced sound capabilities were added.

◆ It became easier to make and use custom text fonts.

◆ A file system was added for those die-hard file-system people.

◆ Creating dynamic forms and controls was made easier.

◆ Progress dialogs were added.

◆   Each device can have a unique serial number. Only some 3.x devices
    support this feature.

◆   The Application Launcher became a full-fledged application.

Version 3.1

The Palm IIIx and Palm V shipped with version 3.1 of the Palm OS in March
1999. Shortly thereafter, IBM remarketed these units under their own brand,
though the units were still built by Palm Computing. The 3.1 release made
these improvements:

◆   There were minor changes to the ASCII table above 0x80.

◆   The DragonBall EZ processor, upon which the IIIx and the V are based,
    was supported.

Version 3.2

The Palm VII was released with version 3.2 of the Palm OS in May 1999.
Originally it was sold in the New York metropolitan area only, but went into
wider distribution later that year. Most of Symbol's latest units are also
based on 3.2.

Version 3.2 was primarily about wireless and Web clipping support. Also,
improved serial communications software was added. You must check to see
whether these features exist on a device with version 3.2, because they
need not be available if, for example, the device does not have the capability
of making a wireless connection.

Version 3.3

In Fall 1999, a plethora of new Palm OS units made by third parties shipped
with Palm OS 3.3, including the Visor and TRG Pro. Version 3.3 had many
internal clean-ups that allowed it to be more easily used by third parties.

Version 3.5

In February 2000, Palm announced the first color Palm, the IIIc, using version
3.5 of Palm OS. The really big thing about version 3.5 is color. Here are the
improvements:

- Color support was added from black and white through 256 colors, including grayscale support.
- Graphical buttons were added that have bitmaps defined for their selected and deselected looks.
- Slider controls were added.
- Dynamic menus were added.
- Gadgets or custom controls were made easier to program.

The Devices

Table 1-1 shows all past and current Palm OS based devices as of this writing.

The Pilot 1000 and Pilot 5000

These early units used version 1.0 of the operating system and had no backlight.

The PalmPilot Personal and PalmPilot Professional

These units, still the majority of the installed base, were physically very similar to the 5000. They came with version 2.0 of Palm OS and had backlighting.

Palm III

The Palm III was the first unit in the tapered plastic case, and the first unit with an infrared port. Version 3.0 of the operating system was originally for the Palm III.

Palm IIIx

The Palm IIIx is basically the same as a Palm III except with a better screen and more memory (4M instead of 2M).

Palm V

This design was physically a radical departure for Palm. This was the first sleek metal case. It was also the first rechargeable unit. The V has a unique form of contrast adjustment. You push a button on the side of the unit, and a slider bar appears on the screen that you can use to adjust the contrast. Otherwise, the V is a IIIx with 2M of memory.

As of February 2000, newer Palm V units ship with version 3.5 of Palm OS.

Device	OS	Memory	Heap	Screen	TCP/IP	IR	Shipped
Pilot 1000	1.0	128K	32K	Gray and green	No	No	March 1996
Pilot 5000	1.0	512K	32K	Gray and green	No	No	May 1996
PalmPilot Personal	2.0	512K	32K	Gray and green	No	No	March 1997
PalmPilot Professional	2.0	1M	64K	Gray and green	Yes	No	March 1997
IBM WorkPad (original)	2.0	1M	64K	Gray and green	Yes	Yes	May 1997
Palm III	3.0	2M	96K	Gray and green	Yes	Yes	March 1998
Symbol SPT1500	3.0.2	2M	96K	Gray and green	Yes	Yes	September 1998
Palm IIIx	3.1	4M	128K	Black and gray	Yes	Yes	February 1999
Palm V	3.1	2M	128K	Black and gray	Yes	Yes	February 1999
IBM WorkPad	3.1	4M	128K	Black and gray	Yes	Yes	March 1999
IBM WorkPad c3	3.1	2M	128K	Black and gray	Yes	Yes	March 1999

Table 1-1   The Features of Palm OS Devices

Device	OS	Memory	Heap	Screen	TCP/IP	IR	Shipped
Palm VII	3.2	2M	128K	Black and gray	Yes	Yes	May 1999
Palm IIIe	3.2	2M	128K	Black and gray	Yes	Yes	July 1999
Symbol SPT1700	3.2	2 or 8M	96K	Gray and green	Yes	Yes	August 1999
Symbol SPT1740	3.2	2 or 8M	96K	Gray and green	Yes	Yes	August 1999
Handspring Visor	3.3	2 or 8M	128K	Gray and green	Yes	Yes	September 1999
Qualcomm pdQ	3.0.2	2M	128K	Gray and green	Yes	Yes	October 1999
TRG TRGpro	3.3	8M	128K	Gray and green	Yes	Yes	October 1999
Palm Vx	3.3	8M	128K	Black and gray	Yes	Yes	January 2000
Palm IIIxe	3.5	8M	128K	Black and gray	Yes	Yes	February 2000
Palm IIIc	3.5	8M	128K	Color	Yes	Yes	February 2000

Table 1-1   The Features of Palm OS Devices *(continued)*

Palm VII

The Palm VII is the first and so far the only integrated wireless Palm OS device. It looks like a IIIx with a heavy top end. Other than that it has an antenna that, when flipped up, turns on the unit and displays the Palm.Net category of applications. It has 2M of memory.

Palm Vx

The Palm Vx is an 8M version of the Palm V. Originally, it shipped with version 3.3 of Palm OS, but as of February 2000, it ships with version 3.5 of Palm OS.

Palm IIIxe

The Palm IIIxe is basically an 8M version of the Palm IIIx. It runs version 3.5 of Palm OS.

Palm IIIc

The Palm IIIc is the first color Palm device. It can display 256 colors. It is a little thicker at the top than a IIIx, but it is basically like a IIIx in shape. Palm IIIc units can synchronize in regular III cradles, but of course they don't recharge. Palm III series units can synchronize in a IIIc cradle without damage. The IIIc has 8M of memory, which is good, because those color forms are bigger!

IBM Devices

IBM has always resold units that are identical functionally to their Palm counterparts. The original IBM WorkPad was exactly like a PalmPilot Professional. The new IBM WorkPad is exactly like a Palm IIIx, and the WorkPad c3 is exactly like a Palm V.

No news on whether IBM will start shipping the c3 with OS 3.5. However, since the ROM in the c3 and the V is upgradable, it is possible to download 3.5 onto any c3 unit anyway.

Symbol Devices

Symbol was the first successful Palm OS licensee outside of Palm Computing. The Symbol units are fun because they all contain bar-code readers. The SPT1500 is very much like a Palm VII in shape. There is some extra bulk above the screen that contains the bar-code reader hardware. The SPT1700 and 1740 are factory-hardened units and are practically indestructible. The 1740 contains a wireless radio network interface as well.

Both 1700 units are significantly larger than the standard Palm form factor.

The Handspring Visor

Jeff Hawkins and Donna Dubinsky now own a company called Handspring, and they are a Palm OS licensee. The Visor is much like a PalmPilot Professional in shape. It has the same screen as the earlier Palm units, which makes it difficult to read in bright sunlight. It has a modified Datebook application that is better than the standard Palm OS version. Its main advantage over the Palm series is that it has a proprietary expansion slot: the Springboard slot. There are already several cards that fit into this slot and enhance the Visor in various ways.

1

TRGpro

The TRGpro is an interesting unit. It looks and acts very much like a Palm III, except it has a standard CompactFlash card expansion slot. Since CompactFlash is an existing standard for digital cameras and a host of other small electronic devices, expansion options for the TRGpro are already broad and varied.

Developing Software for Palm OS

There are many ways to develop software for Palm OS. This section explores the various ways applications can be developed. There is much more detail about all the different tools and support services available in Chapter 11. This section is a brief overview that will give you the basic picture.

Choice of Languages

Palm OS was developed with a C API, so the most efficient and flexible software for the Palm is written in C. C++ is generally a problem on the Palm because C++ requires memory that does not relocate. Since memory is very constrained in the Palm OS dynamic heap, it is hard to develop a C++ application that is large enough to take real advantage of the power of C++ and that is efficient enough with memory to work well.

680x0 assembly language is also an option. It is hard to beat a good compiler these days in the long haul, especially GCC on the 68K. If you are intensely interested in making your application run fast, I recommend you write it initially in C and then use a good profiling tool to find out what functions are taking the most time. Then you can rewrite these functions in assembler until you achieve the performance you require.

Tools like Puma Satellite Forms allow you to rapidly develop very sophisticated applications. They don't allow you the flexibility and performance of C, however. Historically, one of the disadvantages of developing applications this way was the licensing restrictions on applications created with these tools.

Web clipping applications are a whole different kind of application you can write for the Palm VII. Palm Computing distributes free tools that make writing these applications easy.

Palm Device Hardware Details

Here are the in-depth details of the hardware inside Palm OS devices. Although you shouldn't need to know any of this to write good Palm applications, knowing it will help you use Palm devices more effectively.

RAM and ROM

Palm OS devices can have quite a bit of memory, theoretically. The largest Palm device today has 8MB built in. There are CompactFlash cards for the TRGpro that hold up to an additional 40MB of flash memory. The built-in memory is fast and effectively nonvolatile, kept alive with a trickle of current while the unit is off. This is why your batteries eventually wear down whether you use your unit or not, and also why it's so important to swap old batteries for new batteries as quickly as possible.

Palm OS defines a fairly small area of this memory for use as the dynamic heap. The stack, heap, and other dynamic portions of your program must fit into this dynamic-heap area. The dynamic-heap sizes for the various devices are shown in Table 1-1 above. For devices that have TCP/IP capability, 32K of the dynamic heap is taken up by the TCP/IP stack.

Flash memory, such as that found on a CompactFlash or other expansion card, is much slower than the built-in memory. Right now, only the Visor or TRGpro would have access to such memory. Remember that this memory would be on card 1 instead of card 0. Some Palm OS function calls require you to know what card the memory you're using is on.

Most of the recent Palm devices are equipped with flash ROM. This means that they can theoretically be upgraded to more recent versions of the operating system. The devices that can't upgrade their ROMs are all the devices before the Palm III, the Palm IIIe, the Visor, and the pdQ.

The Motorola 68328 "DragonBall"

The Motorola 68328 "DragonBall" and its successor, the 68EZ328 "DragonBall EZ," are the processors used by Palm devices. They are basically

68000 processors like those found in early Macintosh and Amiga computers. In addition to the usual stuff, they have a number of other useful things like timers, parallel ports, a pulse width modulation circuit to make sound with, an LCD display controller, and so forth. You should never touch any of this stuff directly, or you will mess up whatever the operating system is doing, and furthermore your code will not be very portable to new versions of Palm OS and Palm hardware.

Modes

Palm devices have three modes of operation: Sleep mode, Doze mode, and Active mode.

In Sleep mode, the device looks like it is off. The screen is blank and so forth. In fact, this is as "off" as Palm devices ever get. The Palm uses some power in this mode but very little. It mostly listens for someone pressing the green On button or for a timer (alarm) to go off.

Whenever Palm OS is in charge and there are no events like button clicks or pen taps to respond to, the device is in Doze mode. You can write software that doesn't allow for this mode. For example, you could repeatedly call **EvtGetEvent()** with a timeout of zero. This would prevent the unit from dozing and therefore use up the batteries much faster. If you do things that prevent the Palm OS from waiting indefinitely for events, make sure that you do these things as infrequently as possible in order to conserve battery life.

Connectivity

All Palm devices have a serial port built into their bottoms. This plugs into the cradle and allows you to synchronize the unit. You can also plug a modem or other hardware into this port.

In addition, recent Palm devices have an infrared port. Most units have this port right on the top, but some, like the Visor, have it on the side of the case. This port conforms to the IrDA standard, so you can use it, given the appropriate programming, to talk to many printers, TVs, VCRs, and other things that communicate with infrared.

The Palm VII has a wireless connection to the Internet, provided you sign up for the appropriate wireless service. You don't want to see the specific hardware in this case. I highly recommend that you use the Internet Library and the socket services. This makes your code easily portable to future wireless solutions and current solutions such as the Novatel wireless hardware and service.

Symbol devices contain an integrated bar-code scanner. This can be useful if you're developing an application for a business that uses bar codes. Symbol has a free and well-organized developer's kit that makes it easy to use this scanner if you have a need for it. Retail applications for this are probably a ways off, although I have heard of a supermarket chain over in Europe that is using Symbol devices to make shopping easier. There are a lot of bar codes around these days. Who knows?

One of the Symbol devices, the SPT1740, connects to Symbol's line of wireless LAN networks. You can use this connection to tap into your LAN using socket services over on the Palm device. I imagine you'll see more solutions like this on future Palm devices.

The Visor and the TRGpro have expansion slots that can hold all kinds of stuff. The Visor slot is a proprietary design called Springboard. It's a very nicely designed slot, but suffers at the moment by not being standard. The TRGpro has a CompactFlash slot. This architecture has limitations. Most other devices that use CompactFlash slots just want memory. Both Handspring and TRGpro have nice free development kits for their slots.

Clock and Timer

Inside the DragonBall is a real time clock that keeps the current time even when the device is in Sleep mode. There is a timer that goes off every 1/100th of a second. It is used by the operating system to poll the screen to see if it has been tapped or to track pen movements, and for various other tasks. This is the timer the system uses to hand control back to you after a specific wait period when you call **EvtGetEvent()**.

Screen

The Palm device screen is 160 by 160 pixels. All devices can do black and white (or some pair of shades representing black and white). All devices that have Palm OS 3.0 or higher can run four shades of gray. With variations in contrast due to heat and so forth, the two middle gradations are hard to count on except for graphics or games.

The Palm IIIc has a revolutionary active matrix TFT screen that allows for a 256-color palette. These colors are bright and nice.

Sound

Palm devices use a pulse width modulation (PWM) circuit built into the DragonBall to produce sounds. A PWM circuit is basically a really fast On/Off switch. By turning power to the speaker on and off very quickly using this circuit, you can make sort of hazy sound waves come out of the speaker.

The speaker itself is very tiny and is much louder producing high notes than low notes. You're not going to get much bass response from a Palm device.

Reset

There are three kinds of reset on Palm devices: soft, medium, and hard.

You can soft reset a Palm device by pressing a little button that lives in a little hole on the back of the device. If you use a metal stylus like the one that comes with the Palm III and similarly styled devices, it's handy to know that if you unscrew the top plastic part you'll find a tiny plastic rod on it that will fit in the reset hole. Paper clips also work. Soft reset will clear out the dynamic heap. We will be doing lots of soft resets after debugging examples in this book.

You can give the Palm a medium reset by pressing the Reset button and the Up arrow at the same time. This type of reset is called "Shift Reset" in the Palm documentation. If an application that responds to soft reset is crashing, the device won't really reset when you soft reset it. This is what medium reset is for. In the case of an application that is crashing on reset and taking Palm OS with it, you can issue a medium reset and delete the offending application. This is because medium reset does not notify applications that reset is happening.

You can hard reset a Palm device by pressing the Reset button and holding it down, pressing the On/Off button and holding it down, then releasing the Reset button, then releasing the On/Off button. You will be asked if you want to destroy all data. If you answer No, it will do a soft reset. If you answer Yes, the device is completely wiped, and it should be as it was when it came out of the box.

If things are still weird with your Palm, it doesn't hurt to leave the batteries out for five minutes and then put them back in. This should be at least as good as a hard reset.

CHAPTER 2

Creating a Palm
OS Application

This chapter is designed to get you programming Palm OS applications as quickly as possible whether you're a programming expert or a beginner. In it you will create a solid working development environment for yourself. A development environment is more than a collection of programming tools. It is a structure for clarity and success you create for yourself. Once you have even one computer program working in your development environment, you have a huge advantage. Thereafter, fixing future programs becomes at worst a matter of trial and error, of comparing what's working to what's not working.

After briefly going over the basic structure of Palm OS applications, you will create a robust programming environment for yourself. Then we will work through the essentials of resource programming and coding for the Palm OS. The product of these endeavors will be a simple but fully functional Palm OS application.

The Programming Environment

We will almost exclusively use the C programming language to write our applications. Palm OS was designed specifically to support applications written in C with a minimum of overhead. We will use Metrowerks CodeWarrior for most of the application examples in this book. Most of the time, we will assume you are using a Windows computer. We have included a free version of Metrowerks CodeWarrior Lite, which operates under Windows 95, 98, or NT, on the CD at the back of the book.

Using a Mac as Your Development Platform

If you are developing on a Mac exclusively and don't have access to a Windows machine, it will take a bit more work to follow along with the examples because they are written assuming you are using Windows. We have included a Macintosh version of CodeWarrior Lite on the CD-ROM. The Mac and Windows versions of CodeWarrior are very similar.

What You Need to Know About C

Before you start the exercises in this chapter, you need to know enough about the C programming language to write simple programs. I recommend that you invest in at least one good book about the C programming language if you don't already have one. *Teach Yourself C* by Herbert Schildt (Osborne/ McGraw-Hill, 1997) is an excellent book for gaining proficiency in C.

The Anatomy of a Palm OS Application

A Palm OS application in C is created in much the same way as other programs in C are. The source code is compiled and linked with libraries that allow you to manipulate the inner workings of the Palm Computing device. Figure 2-1 contains a diagram of how a Palm OS application executable is created from its various source components.

Additionally, there are resource files that are compiled separately and linked with your object files and libraries. These resource files describe the graphical elements in your program such as screens (which are called *forms* in Palm OS), buttons, edit boxes, and so forth. Many modern graphical application environments such as MacOS and Windows also make use of resource files to describe their user interfaces.

Each of your forms contains a number of buttons and other controls. Your resource file contains all the information about all the forms in your application. You can use a resource editor such as Metrowerks Constructor to edit this resource file and add, change, or remove forms or controls.

Palm OS Memory

Most computer systems spend a lot of time moving data from permanent storage on a hard disk or CD into RAM for actual use by the computer. It is taken for granted that memory comes in two basic flavors: fast volatile storage in RAM or slow permanent storage in a file on a hard disk.

The Palm Computing device vastly differs from most computer systems in this respect. It has only one type of storage: fast permanent storage in RAM. This dramatically changes the most efficient approach to manipulating data. For example, Palm Computing devices have no file system. What purpose would

IN DEPTH

What is a control? A *control* is an area of the screen that accepts some input from the user. It can range from a button, which the user taps with a finger or stylus to activate, to a complex table filled with many different kinds of other controls. You create and define controls using the resource editor.

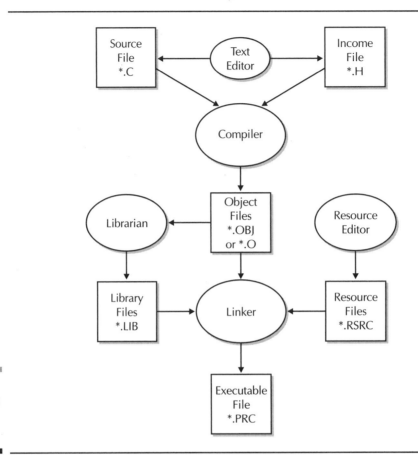

How a Palm
OS application
is created

Figure 2-1.

it serve? Instead, memory is organized into databases. Basically, everything in memory is a database. Even Palm OS applications are stored this way. Application databases contain records filled with executable code and other records that contain compiled resources from the resource editor.

With conventional computer applications, multiple copies of the same piece of data (for example, one copy in RAM, one copy on the hard disk) are an inevitable part of making your applications run fast. With Palm OS, moving data around and having multiple copies generally only waste time because you can look at and manipulate data directly no matter where it is in memory.

Palm OS Application Execution and Debugging

The Palm OS runs only one application at a time. An application can be started by selecting it from the application's home area or by pressing one of the four round silk-screened buttons at the bottom of the unit. Once an application is running, it is designed to continue to run until another application is selected. Turning off your device will stop execution, but when you turn your device on, execution will continue where it left off.

When you test your application, the CodeWarrior development environment will initiate communication with an application called Console that you will run on your Palm Computing device. CodeWarrior will download your code and other debugging information to the Console. Then CodeWarrior will use the Console to execute your program, step through it, set breakpoints, examine data, and so forth. When you are done debugging your program, it is always a good idea to reset your device by clicking on the X control on the PC debugger control panel or by pressing a push-pin or the end of a paper clip into the hole on the back of the device. When you do this you wipe away any cruft that may still be lingering around in working memory from the debugging session.

The Console is built into every Palm device as a hidden application. You need not load anything into your device to get the Console.

IN DEPTH

What is a debugger? A *debugger* is a computer application designed to help you find and fix problems in other computer applications. In the case of CodeWarrior and the Palm OS, the debugger resides on the PC and communicates with the Console application to allow you to examine your program as it is running. A debugger will allow you to watch your code and the variables it uses as it executes line by line. You can also set stopping places in the code called *breakpoints* that will allow you to see that you have reached a particular part of your program. When you reach a breakpoint, you can examine the values of the variables you are using to make sure your code is operating properly.

Installing Your Development Environment

Follow the directions contained on the CD to install CodeWarrior Lite off the CD. CodeWarrior Lite works exactly the same as regular CodeWarrior except that some limitations on the size and complexity of your program have been established in order to compel serious programmers to go out and buy the real thing. Since you are a serious programmer now (by definition, since you own this book), I encourage you to go out and buy full-blown CodeWarrior, if not immediately, then at least by the time you finish the book. The time you will use writing cool applications for your Palm device versus struggling with other inferior development environments will pay for itself in no time.

After installing CodeWarrior or CodeWarrior Lite on a Windows computer, you will notice a problem with Constructor. The fonts displayed in forms you are building will be way too large. You must perform the following steps in order for Constructor to work properly:

1. Locate the folder that contains your operating system. This is usually located on the C: drive and is usually called Windows.
2. Open your Windows folder.
3. Open the Fonts folder contained in this folder by double-clicking it.
4. Close the Fonts folder.
5. Close your Windows folder.

You're done. Constructor should work properly now.

IDEs and CodeWarrior

A programming environment is really anything you use to turn your programming ideas into reality. In the old days (defined for the purpose of this discussion as after punched cards went out of fashion but before Turbo Pascal), you usually built your own development environment out of a text editor, a compiler, and a linker, sometimes from three different companies. The free compiler for Palm OS, gcc, fits very much into this paradigm. You find your own text editor, create your files and resources, then use the gcc tools to separately compile, link, and debug your code.

In the early '90s, a new type of programming environment, called an Integrated Development Environment (IDE), became ubiquitous. This is a single application that allows you to edit, compile, link, and debug your code seamlessly. CodeWarrior is such an environment. These environments save a lot of time and effort because you don't have to keep switching applications to get the next thing done. Also, you spend less time setting up your environment because all the tools are designed to work together.

2

Testing Your Development Environment

It can save a lot of time in the future for you to have a method of ensuring that all your hardware and software is connected properly and happily. This is especially true of embedded environments like Palm OS where the compiling and linking is done on one computer and the program actually runs on another computer. As far as I'm concerned, there's nothing more harrowing than trying to debug a situation where I don't know whether the problem is in my environment, my hardware, or the code I've just written. I've been torture-trained over the years to eliminate all possible sources of uncertainty on the way in. Here's a step-by-step procedure for testing your environment:

1. If you haven't already, install the software that comes with your Palm Computing device on your development machine.
2. Make sure your Palm device synchronizes.

T IP: Some things to try if your device doesn't synchronize:

Make sure your cradle is plugged into the same serial port you have selected in HotSync.

Make sure that your serial port is working through some independent method (like plugging in a modem and calling someone).

Follow the directions in Help to examine whether you have a hardware conflict that might be preventing the serial port from working.

Try a different serial port if you have more than one serial port.

Try resetting your Palm device by pushing the reset button on the back of the device.

NOTE: If you use your Palm device for anything other than development, make sure it is synchronized before each debugging session. It is quite possible to trample all the data in your Palm device in the course of a debug session.

3. Exit HotSync by right-clicking on the HotSync icon in the Windows menu bar and selecting Exit from the pop-up menu. This is a necessary step because if HotSync is running, it owns the only connection to the Palm device. CodeWarrior won't be able to connect to the Palm device to download code or debug. However, if you forget to do this, the consequences are not severe. CodeWarrior will pop up a nice message telling you to kill HotSync.

4. Launch the CodeWarrior IDE.

5. Select File | New.

6. Select Palm OS 3.1 from the Project tab.

7. Set your directory location using the Set button and picking the directory you want.

8. Type the project name **Starter**.

NOTE: It is a good idea to store the sample app and your future apps in a folder separate from the CodeWarrior tree so that you can easily back them up and keep track of them. Also, if it hits the fan and you need to reinstall CodeWarrior, you won't inadvertently blow away your work along with CodeWarrior in your rush to get your system working again. And don't even ask why I thought of suggesting this, okay? It's not a happy story.

9. On the PC, select Project | Enable Debugger.

10. On the PC, select Project | Debug or hit F5 to compile and link the project and bring up the debugger.

11. On the Palm device, put your device in Console Mode. The easiest way I've found to do this is tap find, delete any text that is already there, and enter the shortcut symbol. The shortcut symbol looks like a cursive lowercase "l," and you draw a small cursive "l" in the letter portion of the graffiti pad to create it. After creating the shortcut symbol, write a period (by tapping twice in the graffiti area) and the number 2. If you do this correctly the Palm device will click and the writing will disappear. The graffiti strokes you need to make to put your Palm device in console mode are shown in Figure 2-2.

2

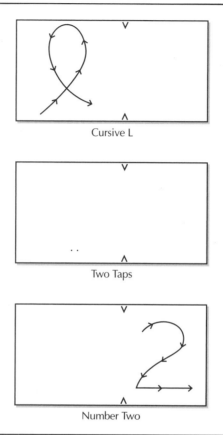

Cursive L

Two Taps

Number Two

The graffiti to
draw to put
your Palm
device into
console mode

Figure 2-2.

12. On the PC, click OK to download the application to the Palm device. The dialog box shown in Figure 2-3 should appear on your Palm device screen.

13. Click OK on the Palm device screen. Now you should be sitting in the CodeWarrior debugger at the first line of the function **PilotMain()** on your PC screen.

14. On the PC, hit the RIGHT ARROW or CTRL-R to run the application.

15. On the Palm device, play around with the application and make sure it is working. You should see a blank form. Push the menu icon to bring up the menu bar. There is a menu item that you can select. If you select it you will see another form with an OK button. You can click the OK button to return to the original form.

CodeWarrior
Lite's warning
message

Figure 2-3.

16. On the PC, press the X button at the top of the debugger window
    to reset the Palm device. (See Figure 2-4.) If your device has already
    powered down, power it up and then hit the X button. This resets the
    device and puts it in a known good state with the console off. You can
    also reset the device by sticking a push-pin or the end of a paper clip
    into the hole marked Reset on the back of the unit.

Now you know that your development and download environment is all
working with the Starter application. Keep this application around so that
in the future, when those strange download weirdnesses hit your machine
(and believe me, even for the luckiest of us, your turn will come), you can try
downloading the Starter application as a sanity check both for you and your
development environment.

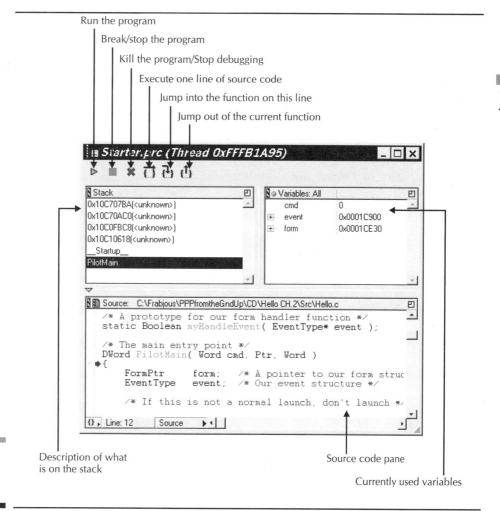

Run the program

Break/stop the program

Kill the program/Stop debugging

Execute one line of source code

Jump into the function on this line

Jump out of the current function

Description of what
is on the stack

Source code pane

Currently used variables

The debugger
window

Figure 2-4.

If you look in the Applications area of your Palm device, you'll notice a new application called Starter. For the Palm III or above, choosing Apps | Delete in the application area will blow away the downloaded application.

For earlier Palm devices such as the Pilot 1000, Pilot 5000, PalmPilot, or PalmPilot Pro, you can get rid of Starter by selecting the Delete Apps button at the bottom of the Memory form.

Creating Your Project

Now it's time for you to create your own Palm OS project. It will have just one button that says "Hello" on it. We'll do this by creating another Starter application, removing its source code and resources, and putting stuff you create in its place. You may want to play with the project settings automatically established by using this method. Many of these settings, though somewhat interesting, have only one right answer, and have been nicely set up for us in Starter. So, without further ado:

1. Launch the CodeWarrior IDE.
2. Select File | New.
3. Select Palm OS 3.1 from the Project tab.
4. Set your directory location by pressing the Set button and picking the directory your want.
5. Click OK.
6. Type the project name **Hello**.

NOTE: You can put useful documentation at the top level or in a special Docs category for easy reference by yourself and others. I often keep notes in a file called "ideas" when I have to set aside an application for later resurrection. To add such a file to the project, select Project | Add Files. Remember to change the file type to All Files so that you can see your document file.

7. Click on the AppSource tree to expand it.
8. Right-click on Starter.c and select Delete. This is the code for the starter application. You're going to replace it with your code later on.
9. Click on the AppResources tree to expand it.
10. Right-click on Starter.rsrc and select Delete. This is the file that contains the layout data for all the forms and controls for the Starter application. You'll also replace this file with one of your own making.
11. Go into Windows Explorer and find the project folder you just created. It should be named Hello. In this folder is another folder named Src. Open this folder. Select everything in the folder. Delete it. You have eliminated the old source files for the Starter application. In the next section you will start creating new source files for your Hello application. They will be stored in this folder.

Creating Your Resources

2

Palm OS resources are similar in nature to the resources you create for a Mac or Windows application, only simpler. This is quite literally so for the Mac in that the Palm OS resources grew out of the RezEdit resource format. The screens of a Palm OS application are referred to as Forms. In building this simple "Hello" application, you are going to create a single form with a button on it. Here's what to do:

1. Launch Constructor for Palm OS. This is Metrowerks' resource editing tool. You'll find it in the same menu as the CodeWarrior IDE.

2. Select File | New Project File. This will create a new empty resource file. The project properties here are fine pretty much as they stand. Later chapters will describe what other things can or should be done with them.

3. Change the Application Icon Name setting in the project settings to Hello.

4. Select the Forms line in the Resource Type and Name list box.

5. Select Edit | New Form Resource or press CTRL-K to create a new form resource. It will appear below the Forms line and will be named "untitled."

6. Click on the name and wait until it changes into an edit box. Change the name of the form to "Hello."

7. Double-click on this form to open it. In later chapters we'll get into what all these properties mean and how to use them.

8. Select Window | Catalog or press CTRL-Y to pop up the list of controls.

9. Drag a button on to the middle of the form. Now the properties of the button will replace the properties of the form on the left-hand side of the form dialog. Again, these properties are mostly fine for now. We'll get into them later. You can fool with the Left Origin and Top Origin properties if you have a desire to position the button exactly.

10. Click on the Label property and change it from OK to Hello.

11. Click on the form in the right-hand panel to get back the properties of the form.

12. Select Layout | Hide Object IDs. This will allow you to see that your button actually has the word "Hello" written on it. If the "Hello" looks too big for the face of the button, you are experiencing the weird font problem I mentioned in the installation section. To correct this problem, close Constructor, open the Fonts folder contained in your Windows folder, then reopen Constructor. Your Hello form should look like Figure 2-5.

13. Select File | Save to save the resource project. Save this project in the Src subfolder under your Hello project folder. Put it in the Src folder in your Hello folder. Name it hello.rsrc.

14. Now that you've created your new resource project, it's time to stick it into your overall project. This resource project will become a subproject in your overall application project. It contains all the descriptions of the graphical aspects of your user interface, such as the size, placement, and look of forms and controls.

15. Bring up the CodeWarrior IDE again and select File | Open Recent | hello.mcp.

16. Select Project | Add Files. View files of type All Files so that you can see your resource file. Find hello.rsrc and select Open.

17. Your resource file may now appear at the top level of the project. Drag it under the AppResources group just for neatness' sake. You do this by clicking the mouse and dragging the file icon until a line appears right under the AppResources group label, then dropping.

18. You're all done creating and adding your new resources.

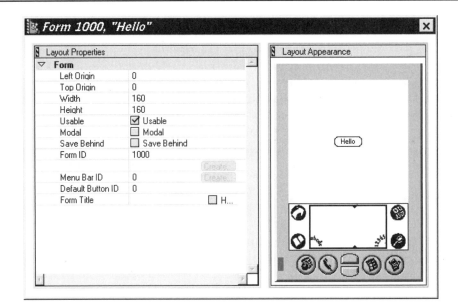

What your
Hello form
should
look like

Figure 2-5.

Creating the Code

In order for your application to work, it must also contain C source code. Here's what to do:

1. Create a new file to put your code in. You can do this by selecting File | New Text File.
2. Select File | Save As and save the file as hello.c.
3. Select the Project window, then select Project | Add Files. Find hello.c and add it to the project.
4. If it doesn't appear under the AppSource folder, move it there by dragging it under the folder. When you drag the file, you'll see a little line that allows you to insert the file where you want to put it.

Type the following code into your hello.c file. In the next section, we will go through the code line by line and understand it.

```c
/* The super-include for Palm OS */
#include <Pilot.h>

/* Our resource file */
#include "hello_res.h"

/* A prototype for our form handler function */
static Boolean myHandleEvent( EventType* event );

/* The main entry point */
DWord PilotMain( Word cmd, Ptr, Word )
{
    FormPtr    form;   /* A pointer to our form structure */
    EventType  event;  /* Our event structure */

    /* If this is not a normal launch, don't launch */
    if( cmd != sysAppLaunchCmdNormalLaunch )
        return( 0 );

    /* Initialize our form */
    form = FrmInitForm( HelloForm );
    FrmSetEventHandler( form, myHandleEvent );
    FrmSetActiveForm( form );
    FrmDrawForm( form );

    /* Our event loop */
    do
    {
```

```
    /* Get the next event */
    EvtGetEvent( &event, -1 );

    /* Handle system events */
    if( SysHandleEvent( &event ) )
        continue;

    /* Handle form events */
    FrmDispatchEvent( &event );
/* If it's a stop event, exit */
} while( event.eType != appStopEvent );

    /* We're done */
    return( 0 );
}

/* Our form handler function */
static Boolean myHandleEvent( EventType* event )
{
    /* Parse the event */
    if( event->eType == ctlSelectEvent )
        SndPlaySystemSound( sndAlarm );

    /* We're done */
    return( false );
}
```

Understanding the Code

This source code consists of two short function calls. It has only one form with one button that exits the application. Of course we'll have to add infrastructure as the applications you write get complex enough to do useful work.

Here's a line-by-line description of what is going on in the source code.

```
/* The super-include for Palm OS */
#include <Pilot.h>
```

Pilot.h includes all the likely include files for Palm OS library function calls.

```
/* Our resource file */
#include "hello_res.h"
```

You created this include file, hello_res.h, when you created your hello.rsrc resource project in Constructor. It contains the ID tag constants for your form and your button.

> **IN DEPTH**
>
> Notice that Pilot.h is enclosed in <> brackets and hello_res.h is enclosed in quotes. This tells the compiler to look for Pilot.h among the system includes in the Palm OS support folder. The quotes tell the compiler to start looking in our Hello\Src folder for hello_res.h.

NOTE: While you're at it, select hello_res.h and add it to your project. Having include files in your project doesn't cause problems for the CodeWarrior IDE (unlike some other IDEs I know). It allows you to conveniently view and edit them. To add the file, select Project | Add Files. Find hello_res.h and add the file. Then drag it and drop it into the AppSource folder.

```
/* A prototype for our form handler function */
static Boolean helloHandleEvent( EventType* event );
```

This is the prototype for the callback function that will handle events for the form and its controls. A callback function is a function in your application that the operating system calls in order to have you respond to an event such as someone tapping the button on your form with the stylus.

The Function PilotMain()

```
/* The main entry point */
DWord PilotMain( Word cmd, Ptr, Word )
{
```

PilotMain() is the function that gets called by the startup code. The variable *cmd* is the launch code that describes the reason why the application was activated. I'll tell you about what the other parameters do when we get into launch codes.

Here's some storage space for odds and ends:

```
FormPtr     form;    /* A pointer to our form structure */
```

Here is storage for the current event. This data structure, when filled, will contain all the information about what kind of event has been received.

```
EventType   event;  /* Our event structure */
```

PORTABILITY TIP: Normally, we would check here at the top of **PilotMain()** to make sure we exit gracefully if we find an earlier version of Palm OS. For simplicity's sake, I've left this code out. That's because this application will run on any Palm device anyway. However, if we were to include code to check the OS version here, it would look something like this:

```
DWord ROMVersion;

    // Get the ROM version
    ROMVersion = 0;
    FtrGet( sysFtrCreator, sysFtrNumROMVersion, &ROMVersion );

    // Alert and bail if the ROM version is too low
    if( ROMVersion < ROM_VERSION_MIN )
    {
        // Do something here that reports an error

// Palm OS 1.0 will continuously re-launch this app
    // unless we switch to another safe one
    if( ROMVersion < ROM_VERSION_2 )
    {
        AppLaunchWithCommand( sysFileCDefaultApp,
                sysAppLaunchCmdNormalLaunch, NULL );
    }
    return( 0 );
}
```

The call to **FtrGet()** retrieves the ROM version. You would then compare that version to the minimum version of Palm OS that your application could tolerate. Palm OS 1.0 will continuously relaunch your application unless you actively switch to another application. You must add the if statement and call to **AppLaunchWithCommand()** above to handle this situation and actually get out of the application.

This is where the launch code gets checked. You're checking to see whether you were launched under normal circumstances. We'll get into the other circumstances in a later chapter.

```
/* If this is not a normal launch, don't launch */
if( cmd != sysAppLaunchCmdNormalLaunch )
    return( 0 );
```

These are some calls to the Palm OS's built-in Form Manager ROM code. First we use **FrmInitForm()** to get our form ready for use. We attach our event handling function to the form using **FrmSetEventHandler()**. Then we are ready to set the form to be active with **FrmSetActiveForm()**. Finally, we draw the form with a call to **FrmDrawForm()**.

```
/* Initialize our form */
form = FrmInitForm( HelloForm );
FrmSetEventHandler( form, myHandleEvent );
FrmSetActiveForm( form );
FrmDrawForm( form );
```

Next the event loop begins.

```
/* Our event loop */
do
{
```

IN DEPTH

What is an event loop? An *event loop* is a program loop responsible for responding to the movements of the stylus, buttons being pressed, and so forth. Most modern graphical user interfaces, such as MacOS and Windows, are event-driven systems. Events are just a way for the operating system to communicate in an exact way with your application with regard to what the user is doing. Generally, as with Palm OS, the events are stored in their order of occurrence by the operating system, and you can ask for them and process them one at a time.

This function, a call to the Event Manager in ROM, pulls the oldest event off the queue, thus processing events in the same order Palm OS received them.

```
/* Get the next event */
EvtGetEvent( &event, -1 );
```

This call to the System Manager handles system events such as the silkscreen buttons.

```
/* Handle system events */
if( SysHandleEvent( &event ) )
    continue;
```

This function not only calls our callback function, but also performs a number of other duties. For example, it uses the penUpEvent and penDownEvent primitives to generate events like ctlSelectEvent, which we use in our form event handler function to determine that our button has been pressed. This is why we have to have a callback function instead of putting everything in one big happy event loop.

```
/* Handle form events */
FrmDispatchEvent( &event );
```

The code below handles the event the program would get if another application had been selected. In this case, there's nothing to clean up, so we can just stop executing by ending our do loop and exiting our application. This code appears at the end of our loop because we may want to do something about this event in our form event handler or elsewhere in our event handling code at some future time, so it's good to let this event trickle through the whole structure.

```
    /* If it's a stop event, exit */
    } while( event.eType != appStopEvent );

    /* We're done */
    return( 0 );
}
```

The Function helloHandleEvent()

This is the function that gets called by **FrmDispatchEvent()** to handle form events. Remember, we passed Palm OS the address of this function when we called **FrmSetEventHandler()**.

```
/* Our form handler function */
static Boolean helloHandleEvent( EventType* event )
{
```

This event is sent when the Hello button on our form gets pressed. In this case, we play the system alarm sound.

```
    /* The button was pressed */
    if( event->eType == ctlSelectEvent )
       SndPlaySystemSound( sndAlarm );
          break;
     /* We're done */
     return( false );
}
```

My C coding style has been honed over sixteen years of programming C applications as large as 500,000 lines. However, just because it works great for me doesn't mean it will work best for you. Like the rest of this book, adopt the ideas that work for you. Don't feel nervous about trying your own style. Writing the code examples your way will help you to really learn and notice what's going on inside them, so I encourage you to make the code your own.

Debugging: Getting It All Working

At this point you're ready to compile and link the project. To do that, select Project | Make. If you're like me (that is, not perfect in every way), you'll probably have bugs. Good luck with them.

Okay, okay, I'll try to be a little more helpful. You can probably whip compile-time bugs by comparing your code to mine if you get completely stopped. Link bugs might come up if you accidentally got rid of the library when we created the project. You can copy it back over from the Sample application we created earlier.

Stepping through the code line by line is the best way to catch runtime bugs. You can do this in the CodeWarrior IDE by performing the following steps:

1. On the PC, select Project | Debug or hit F5 to compile and link the project and bring up the debugger.

2. On the Palm device, put your device in Console Mode. The easiest way I've found to do this is tap find, delete any text that is already there and enter the shortcut symbol. The shortcut symbol looks like a small cursive "l," and you draw a small cursive "l" in the letter portion of the

graffiti pad to create it. After creating the shortcut symbol, write a period (by tapping twice in the graffiti area) and the number 2. If you do this correctly the device will click and the writing will disappear. The strokes you need to make in the graffiti area were shown earlier in Figure 2-2.

3. On the PC, click OK to download the application to the Palm device. Click OK to dismiss the warning on your Palm device. Now you should be sitting in the CodeWarrior debugger at the first line of the function **PilotMain()**.

4. On the PC, click on the button at the top of the debugger window that looks like an arrow pointing to the right and hitting a vertical line. This will step you one step into the program. To enter the function the cursor is pointing at, hit the button that looks like an arrow pointing down hitting a horizontal line. In this manner you can step through all the lines of code in all the functions in your program.

5. On the PC, press the X button at the top of the debug window to reset the Palm device. If your Palm device has already powered down, power it up and then press the X button. This resets the device and puts it in a known good state with the console off. You can also reset the Palm device by sticking a push-pin or the end of a paper clip into the hole marked Reset on the back of the unit.

Hopefully, my earlier source code comments will be of use to you as you're noodling out what the code is supposed to be doing. If your form doesn't appear at all, make sure you've linked in the correct resource (*.rsrc) file and make sure that **FrmDrawForm()** is getting called by setting a breakpoint at the function call and watching it execute.

You can set a breakpoint by right-clicking in the left margin of the line you want to break at and selecting Set Breakpoint. A red dot should appear in the margin, replacing a black dash. You can't set a breakpoint at a line of code with no black dash next to it. To remove a breakpoint, simply click on the red dot to turn it back into a black dash. Figure 2-6 shows what the application should look like if it's working.

When your Hello application is fully debugged, it should

◆ Appear as an icon labeled "Hello" in the applications area of your Palm device.

◆ When launched, show its form and button.

◆ Exit when the button is pressed.

◆ Exit when a real button or a permanent silkscreen button is pressed.

2

Figure 2-6.

Congratulations! You've just written your first Palm OS application. This is a good application to keep around for trying out code snippets that don't easily or safely fit into the application you're currently working on.

What Happened When You Ran Your Program

Now that you have a working Palm OS application, let's set a breakpoint and step through the program so that we can examine in further depth how it operates.

1. On the PC, start the debugger again. Select Project | Debug or press F5 to compile and link the project and bring up the debugger.

2. On the Palm device, put your device in Console Mode. Draw a small cursive "l" in the letter portion of the graffiti pad. After creating this

shortcut symbol, write a period (by tapping twice in the graffiti area) and the number 2. If you do this correctly the device will click and the writing will disappear. The strokes you need to make in the graffiti area were shown earlier in Figure 2-2.

3. On the PC, click OK to download the application to the Palm device. Now you should be sitting in the CodeWarrior debugger at the first line of the function **PilotMain()**.

4. On the PC, in the debugger window, find the line of your program that looks like this:

```
/* Parse the event */
if( spEvent->eType == ctlSelectEvent )
    SndPlaySystemSound( sndAlarm );
```

5. On the PC, set a breakpoint at the if statement by clicking on the line next to it in the margin of the debugger window.

6. Step through the program line by line by pressing this button (Execute one line of source code) repeatedly. Notice that the call to **FrmDispatchEvent()** causes you to end up at your breakpoint in your form event handler, but this is not a ctlSelectEvent, so the call to **SndPlaySystemSound()** is skipped this time. After this, the program just sits in **GetEvent()**, waiting for something to happen.

7. Tap the Hello button on the Palm device. Notice that **GetEvent()** returns right away. Your form event handler is called several more times, and finally, it is a ctlSelectEvent and **SndPlaySystemSound()** is called. You have just witnessed your code dispatching and handling several events.

8. On the PC, press the X button at the top of the debug window to reset the Palm device. If your device has already powered down, power it up and then press the X button. This resets the device and puts it in a known good state with the console off. You can also reset the Palm device by sticking a push-pin or the end of a paper clip into the hole marked Reset on the back of the unit.

Turning Projects into Stationary

We will use this application as a formal starting point for the application in Chapter 4. There is a way to make a particular project a template for future projects, called "Stationary" in CodeWarrior land. Please do this with your Hello application. Put a copy of your application in the Stationary subfolder of your CodeWarrior folder. Next time you select New Project it will appear there. You can copy the application in Windows Explorer by performing the following steps:

1. Launch Windows Explorer and find your Hello project folder.
2. Select the entire Hello project folder.
3. Press CTRL-C to copy it.
4. Select the entire Stationary folder. You can find it under your CodeWarrior folder.
5. Press CTRL-V to paste the Hello folder.

What's Next?

In the next chapter we're going to play with fields, entering text, and menus. Also, we'll start to examine how to allocate and manage chunks of Palm OS memory.

CHAPTER 3

Fun with Fields

In this chapter we'll hack up a copy of our Hello application from Chapter 2 and use it to play with fields and their attributes and events. We'll start to cover how fields use the Palm OS memory and how that relationship can be managed. We'll also spend time playing with things relating to fields such as:

◆ Graffiti shift indicators

◆ String resources

◆ The Edit menu in particular and menus in general

◆ Palm OS version compatibility code

◆ Error messages and alerts

What Are Fields Anyway?

Fields are edit boxes that you can use to get your user to enter text or numeric data. Let's just create a field and have some fun with it.

First create a new application in the CodeWarrior IDE:

1. Launch the CodeWarrior IDE.

2. Create a new project by selecting File | New Project.

3. Pick your Hello application from the project stationery choices. Name your new application Contacts.

4. Remove the resource file from the project. You can do this by right-clicking on Hello.rsrc and selecting Remove Selected Items.

5. Delete Hello.rsrc in the Src folder of your project folder.

6. Launch Constructor to create a new resource file.

7. Create a form named Contact Detail by selecting Forms in the resource list and pressing CTRL-K. Click on the default name to rename the form.

8. Open the form for editing by double-clicking on it.

9. Put a field on the form. You can do this by selecting Window | Catalog to open the catalog window. Then drag a field object from the catalog window and drop it on the form.

10. Name the field FirstName. You can do this by clicking on the field to display its attributes in the left-hand pane of the form's window. Click on the Object Identifier attribute and enter the word **FirstName**.

11. While you're at it, put a graffiti shift indicator on your form as well. Drag a graffiti shift indicator object over from the catalog window and drop it on your form. The standard location for this indicator is at the lower-right corner of the form.

12. When you're done, your form should look like Figure 3-1.

13. Go back to the CodeWarrior IDE and add the new resource file to your project. In the CodeWarrior IDE select Project I Add Files.

14. Compile and link your project by selecting Project I Make.

15. Take a look at it under the debugger. First enable the debugger by selecting Project I Enable Debugger.

16. Turn your Palm Computing device on. Make sure it is firmly seated in its cradle. HotSync the device and then turn HotSync off on the PC.

17. On the PC, select Project I Debug.

18. On your device, enter a cursive l, a period, and a 2 (*1.2*) to bring up the console.

19. On the PC, click OK to start the debugger.

20. Click the forward arrow in the debugger window to start your application.

3

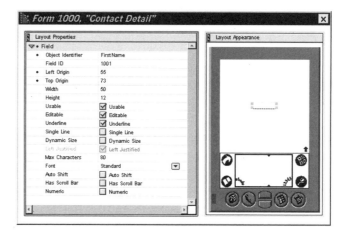

What your form should look like

Figure 3-1.

Play with the running application on your device. If you select the field, you'll be able to enter text and numbers into it using graffiti. If you do an upstroke for capitalization or a dot for symbols, the graffiti shift indicator you put on the form should show up as an arrow or a dot, respectively. Your application in action should look like this:

When you are done playing with the application, remember to click the X in the debugger window to reset your device and stop the console running. Leaving the console running can cause problems on your device.

If your graffiti shift indicator is working okay in the program you just wrote, this is really all you need to know about graffiti shift indicators. If your graffiti shift indicator is not working correctly, make sure you have not added anything to your code that would prevent field events from being processed by the operating system. You ought to put them on any form that you can use graffiti on. They always live at or near the lower-right corner of the form because that's where people expect them to be. No programming is required for them. Just put them on the form and they work.

You can see from the above example that a lot of things just work about fields, too. The code we're running with this form (hello.c) has nothing to do with the form, and yet we can edit, use graffiti, select and replace text, and do almost all the other things we would expect to do. Cut and paste commands don't work. For that we'll have to get to menus and shortcuts later in the chapter.

NOTE: If your device has been acting strange after some debugging sessions, it may be because it was never reset and the Console program is still running. To put your device in a known good state, use a push pin or the end of a paper clip to push the Reset button located in a hole on the back of the device.

3

Attributes

You can change a lot of things about how this field works just by fooling around with the field's attributes in Constructor. Bring up your Contact Detail form in Constructor by launching Constructor, selecting your project's .rsrc file, and double-clicking on the Contact Detail form. Click on the field, and its attributes will appear alongside it. All Palm OS UI objects share some of these attributes, like Left Origin and Top Origin. Table 3-1 is a list of all of the field's attributes and their implications. Play around with the attributes, then recompile and debug your application to experiment with how each of these attributes will affect the behavior of the field.

All the Field
Attributes and
What They
Mean
Table 3-1.

Name	Description
Object Identifier	A name you choose. The variables Constructor creates in the Contacts_res.h file will be derived from this name.
Field ID	The number the Palm OS uses to identify this specific UI object.
Left Origin	Defines the position of the left-hand side of the field in pixels. The entire screen is 160 pixels across.
Top Origin	Defines the position of the top of the field in pixels. The entire screen is 160 pixels from top to bottom.
Width	The width of the field in pixels.
Height	The height of the field in pixels. You'll have to increase this number to avoid chopping the heads off of some of the larger fonts.

Name	Description
Usable	Defines whether the field appears on the form at all. Fields that are not marked usable are not visible and not selectable until they are enabled with a function call. This setting is useful if you want to make fields appear or disappear without changing forms.
Editable	Defines whether the field can be selected and will accept graffiti input. This is checked for most fields.
Underline	Draws a dotted line underneath the field to indicate its position. Otherwise, nothing is drawn on the screen to indicate the presence of a blank field.
Single Line	Confines the text entered to a single line. The field won't scroll horizontally or accept Return or Tab characters.
Dynamic Size	Makes the field expandable as needed to display all the text that has been entered into it. You need to add code to make this happen, so don't worry about not seeing this effect just from changing this attribute.
Left Justified	Aligns text on the left. Being able to uncheck this is useful for displaying numbers so that the decimal places line up.
Max Characters	Defines the number of characters the Palm OS will allow you to enter before it starts ignoring input and beeping.
Font	The font in which text is displayed in the field. Note that you may have to change the height of the field manually based on the font you choose.
Auto Shift	Capitalizes the first character entered into the field.
Has Scroll Bar	This alone doesn't give the field its own scroll bar. This causes the Palm OS to send events that you can use to update a scroll bar.
Numeric	Confines the allowable characters to numbers.

All the Field
Attributes and
What They
Mean
(continued)

Table 3-1.

More About Events

As you saw in Chapter 2, Palm OS programs, like programs for MacOS or Windows, are event-driven programs. They don't do anything (for the most part) until they get some input from the user such as a button being pushed or the stylus or your finger touching the screen.

There are four events we care about when contemplating the use of fields. First, there are penDownEvent and penUpEvent. A penDownEvent is issued every time the device's screen is touched. Similarly, a penUpEvent is issued every time the stylus is raised off the screen.

For most Palm OS user interface elements, including fields, this raw information is interpreted further by the call to **FrmDispatchEvent()**. **FrmDispatchEvent()** generates three other events that concern fields: the fldEnterEvent, the fldChangedEvent, and the keyDownEvent. A fldEnterEvent is sent whenever a field is selected by tapping it. A fldChangedEvent is sent whenever the field does something to adjust its appearance, for example, when it scrolls horizontally. A keyDownEvent is sent whenever a graffiti character is recognized by the graffiti engine and sent to the field.

3

You need to be careful to return false in your event handler for events you don't handle. Otherwise, the wonderful automatic generating of the events I just described will not work. If you return true from your event handler, **FrmDispatchEvent()** just goes on to the next event. If you return false, **FrmDispatchEvent()** calls **FrmHandleEvent()**, which is the function that actually handles the generating of complex events from simple events. To handle the case of fields, **FrmHandleEvent()** calls **FldHandleEvent()** to create the field events we just discussed. I don't recommend calling either **FrmHandleEvent()** or **FldHandleEvent()** yourself except in very unusual circumstances. Just take care in returning false from your event handler when you want further processing to take place on a particular event.

Let's modify the code in our Contacts project to bring it up to date with the new resources we've created. Using Explorer, copy another copy of Hello.c into the Src folder of your Contacts project. Rename it to Contacts.c, then re-add it to the project by selecting Project | Add Files in the CodeWarrior IDE. Start using the new Contacts_res.h include file by modifying Contacts.c to include it instead of hello_res.h. When you do this, you'll have to change the reference from HelloForm to ContactDetailForm in order for the code to compile and link again successfully. Up until this point things have been working even though we've been using the wrong resource include file because the ID represented by HelloForm matched the ID for ContactDetailForm. Constructor always numbers its form IDs starting at 1,000.

The other thing to modify is the case statement that looks for the ctlSelectEvent that means a button has been pressed. This is the old version:

```
// CH.2 The button was pressed
case ctlSelectEvent:
    SndPlaySystemSound( sndAlarm );
    return( false );
```

In Contacts, this case statement has done nothing up until this point. Since our form has no buttons on it, there is no chance of receiving this event. Let's make things more exciting by changing the case statement to catch a penDownEvent. Replace the code above with:

```
// CH.3 The pen touched down
case penDownEvent:
    SndPlaySystemSound( sndAlarm );
    return( false );
```

Make and debug the modified code by selecting Project | Make followed by Project | Debug. Click the forward arrow in the debug window to start the modified application running. It should sound like you have an urgent appointment every time you tap the field. In fact, the alarm should sound no matter where you tap on the form. A penDownEvent is generated no matter where the pen comes down. Try replacing the penDownEvent with a penUpEvent. Make, debug, and run the application again. Now the alarm should instead sound whenever you lift your stylus off the screen.

Try replacing the constant penUpEvent with fldEnterEvent. Make, debug, and run the application again. Notice that now the pen has to come down inside the field for the alarm to sound. It's very handy to use these more refined events instead of having to decipher raw events like penDownEvent and penUpEvent. Not only is it easier, but it will give your user interfaces a feel that is much more consistent with other Palm OS applications. So penUpEvent and penDownEvent are good for you to know about, but my advice is only use them when more refined events aren't available.

Try replacing fldEnterEvent with fldChangedEvent. Make, debug, and run again. If you enter enough characters into the field to make the field scroll horizontally, the alarm should go off.

Try replacing fldEnterEvent with keyDownEvent. Make, debug, and run the application. Now the alarm should sound whenever you produce a valid glyph in the graffiti area. It's fun to see if you can lift your pen out of the graffiti area without the graffiti engine deciding you've entered something valid. It's not easy (at least not for me).

 NOTE: The technique of playing a sound when an event occurs is generally a good way to see exactly when a particular event is issued and under what circumstances. Since documentation is never absolutely complete, it's good to collect tricks that can help you determine the operating system's exact behavior experimentally.

Focus

There are well over 50 Palm OS function calls that allow you to manipulate fields and the data in them in various ways. In these next sections we will deal only with the most essential function calls you'll probably use most often (at least for fields that are not directly connected to database data). The field functions for cut, copy, delete, paste, and undo are popular too, but we will deal with these matters soon when we get into the use of menus and shortcuts.

At the moment you need to click on your field in order to start entering graffiti text. By tapping your stylus on the field you're establishing that this field should be the place that graffiti goes. In other words, the field becomes the focus of graffiti, or has focus.

Let's fix the need to tap on the field initially with a call to **FrmSetFocus()**. This call must come after we draw the form because the call will have no effect before the form is drawn. Therefore, a good place for it is right after **FrmDrawForm()** in **PilotMain()**. You will need to call **FrmGetObjectIndex()** first to get the object index of your field for use in the call to **FrmSetFocus()**. If you make, debug, and run your code after these modifications, you should see a blinking cursor at the edit field even before you click on it. The new code you add should look something like this:

```
// CH.3 Initialize our form
form = FrmInitForm( ContactDetailForm );
FrmSetEventHandler( form, myHandleEvent );
FrmSetActiveForm( form );
FrmDrawForm( form );

// CH.3 Get the index of our field
index = FrmGetObjectIndex( form, ContactDetailFirstNameField );

// CH.3 Set the focus to our field
FrmSetFocus( form, index );

// CH.2 Our event loop
do
{
```

Putting Text in Fields

Let's put some text in the field now. First you need to understand a little about how fields use Palm OS memory. Since much of the editing that is done in fields causes database memory to be edited directly, everything about fields is geared towards handing the field a piece of memory that it can manipulate and resize freely. In Palm OS terminology, these pieces of memory are called *chunks*.

Fields need to use these special data structures because of the problem of expanding the size of field text as users enter data. Consider the situation where we have allocated two chunks of memory for two data fields. Each chunk is, say, 80 bytes in size:

XXXXXXXXYYYYYYYY

Say that the first field needs to expand to 100 bytes in size. There is no room to just expand the chunk because the other chunk for the other field is right next to it. If we aren't going to just give up and limit fields to some small and inflexible amount of characters, something has to move.

To fight this problem, the concept of *memory handles* was developed. Instead of returning pointers directly to each piece of memory that is allocated, we are given a pointer into a list of pointers to memory. The operating system is then free to change the location of chunks of memory in order to allow for other chunks to expand:

XXXXXXXXXXXXYYYYYYYY

While we are actively using our memory, we forbid the operating system from moving it by locking it before we start and unlocking it after we're done.

In our simple field examples in earlier sections, when we started adding characters to our field, a chunk was automatically allocated and attached to our field by the Palm OS. If we want to start off the field with some text in it, we need to allocate a chunk, put our text into it, and give it to the field. Let's add some C code to Contacts.c that will do this. We can allocate and initialize the chunk near the beginning of Contacts.c:

```
// CH.3 Our field memory handle
static Handle htext;      // CH.3 Handle to the text in our edit field
#define HTEXT_SIZE 81     // CH.3 Size of our edit field

// CH.2 The main entry point
DWord PilotMain( Word cmd, Ptr, Word )
{
    FormPtr     form;     // CH.2 A pointer to our form structure
    CharPtr     ptext;    // CH.3 Points to the text in the edit field
    Word        index;    // CH.3 A general purpose index
    FieldPtr    field;    // CH.3 Used for manipulating fields
    EventType   event;    // CH.2 Our event structure

    // CH.2 If this is not a normal launch, don't launch
    if( cmd != sysAppLaunchCmdNormalLaunch )
        return( 0 );
```

```
// CH.3 Allocate our field chunk
htext = MemHandleNew( HTEXT_SIZE );
if( htext == NULL )
    return( 0 );

// CH.3 Lock the memory, get the pointer
ptext = MemHandleLock( htext );

// CH.3 Initialize it
StrCopy( ptext, "hello" );

// CH.3 Unlock the field's memory
MemHandleUnlock( htext );
```

3

In the code above you see four new Palm OS functions. **MemHandleNew()** allocates a chunk of memory for us. **MemHandleLock()** prevents the Palm OS from moving our memory while we're using it. **StrCopy()** is like the C library function **strcpy()**. It copies a zero-delimited string from one place in memory to another—in this case, from a constant into our chunk. **MemHandleUnlock()** tells the operating system we're done fooling with our chunk. Any use of ptext after this point would be dangerous, because our chunk could be moved at any time.

In the catastrophic event that the device is out of memory, **MemHandleNew()** will return a NULL handle. In this event the above code quietly exits the application, but this is far from an ideal solution. Later in the chapter you will learn how to send error messages to your users with Alerts.

All that's left to do is give our chunk to the field. We can do this before we draw the form:

```
// CH.3 Initialize our form
form = FrmInitForm( ContactDetailForm );
FrmSetEventHandler( form, myHandleEvent );
FrmSetActiveForm( form );

// CH.3 Get the index of our field
index = FrmGetObjectIndex( form, ContactDetailFirstNameField );

// CH.3 Get the pointer to our field
field = FrmGetObjectPtr( form, index );

// CH.3 Set the editable text
FldSetTextHandle( field, htext );

// CH.2 Draw the form
FrmDrawForm( form );
```

The function that does the trick is **FldSetTextHandle()**. In order to call this function you must have a pointer to the field you're passing the chunk to. You can get this pointer by calling **FrmGetObjectPtr()**. Notice that **FldSetTextHandle()** must be called before **FrmDrawForm()**, or else the text you put in the chunk won't be drawn along with the rest of the form. We could also fix this by calling **FldDrawField()** afterwards.

After you make the above code modifications to Contacts.c, make, debug, and run your project again. The initial value "hello" should show up in the field.

Using String Resources

Currently, we are initializing our field with a string that is hard-coded in our program. This is not a problem for such a small application, but for applications of significant size, it can cause nightmarish problems when you go to sell your software overseas and find that you need to make endless expensive code changes in order to translate it into other languages. One way to prevent this problem is to use string resources.

String resources are strings that are stored in your resource file along with your other user interface elements. Many translation companies these days are capable of translating your application into a foreign language if you simply give them the Constructor files, so this is a good way of assuring that your application can be translated into another language with a minimum of fuss.

To create a string resource in Constructor:

1. Launch Constructor and open Contacts.rsrc.
2. Select the string resource type from the resource list.
3. Press CTRL-K to create a new string resource. Name it FieldInit.
4. Double-click on the new string resource to open it. Type **hello**.

To use the string resource in your code, you must get it, lock it down, use it for whatever you're going to use it for, unlock it, and free it afterwards. Here is what it looks like in code:

```
// CH.2 If this is not a normal launch, don't launch
if( cmd != sysAppLaunchCmdNormalLaunch )
    return( 0 );

// CH.3 Get the initialization string resource handle
hsrc = DmGetResource( strRsc, FieldInitString );

// CH.3 Lock the resource, get the pointer
psrc = MemHandleLock( hsrc );
```

```
// CH.3 Allocate our field chunk
htext = MemHandleNew( HTEXT_SIZE );
if( htext == NULL )
    return( 0 );

// CH.3 Lock the memory, get the pointer
ptext = MemHandleLock( htext );

// CH.3 Initialize it
StrCopy( ptext, psrc );

// CH.3 Unlock the field's memory
MemHandleUnlock( htext );

// CH.3 Unlock the resource's memory
MemHandleUnlock( hsrc );

// CH.3 Release the string resource
DmReleaseResource( hsrc );
```

Make the above code modifications to Contacts.c. Make, debug, and run the result. The program shouldn't look any different, but now you're getting your initial string from a string resource instead of having it hard-coded into your C source file.

Menus

Now it is time to add an Edit menu to Contacts. The Palm OS user interface guidelines define a standard Edit menu that you should always provide whenever you provide a field that can be edited with graffiti. This menu is shown here:

First, build the resource part of the menu:

1. Launch Constructor and open Contacts.rsrc.
2. Click on the menu bar's resource type in the resource list. Press CTRL-K to create a menu bar. Name it Contact Detail.
3. Double-click on the Contact Detail menu bar resource to open it. Press CTRL-M to create a new menu.
4. Change the name on the menu bar from Untitled to Edit.
5. Press CTRL-K to create a new menu item. Type **Undo**. Press the TAB key to get to the shortcut area of the menu item. Type **U**. Continue this process to create each new menu item as shown in the previous illustration. You can use CTRL-hyphen (-) to create the separator bar between Select All and Keyboard.
6. When you're done creating the menu, double-click on the Contact Detail form to open it. Enter the ID of the menu bar (probably 1000) into the Menu Bar ID attribute of the form.
7. You're done. Your completed menu bar resource should look like the standard Edit menu in the previous illustration.

To use the menu you just created, you need to add some code to Contacts.c. In order to process menu events, you need to add a call to **MenuHandleEvent()** in the event loop to handle menu events. This call should happen after system events are handled.

```
// CH.2 Handle system events
if( SysHandleEvent( &event ) )
    continue;

// CH.3 Handle menu events
if( MenuHandleEvent( NULL, &event, &error ) )
    continue;

// CH.2 Handle form events
FrmDispatchEvent( &event );
```

In your event handler loop, replace your ctlSelectEvent if statement with a menuEvent if statement. Use it to call a function you'll write called

menuEventHandler(). Your new event handler function should now look like this:

```
// CH.2 Our form handler function
static Boolean myHandleEvent( EventType* event )
{
    // CH.3 Parse menu events
    if( event->eType == menuEvent )
        return( menuEventHandler( event ) );

    // CH.2 We're done
    return( false );
}
```

3

Now write the **menuEventHandler()** function. First, you need to signal to the user interface that the menu event has been received and the menu or shortcut display can therefore be wiped from the screen:

```
// CH.3 Handle menu events
Boolean menuEventHandler( EventPtr event )
{
    FormPtr     form;    // CH.3 A pointer to our form structure
    Word        index;   // CH.3 A general purpose control index
    FieldPtr    field;   // CH.3 Used for manipulating fields

    // CH.3 Get our form pointer
    form = FrmGetActiveForm();

    // CH.3 Erase the menu status from the display
    MenuEraseStatus( NULL );
```

Provide graffiti help separately. This is because graffiti help should be available even if a field isn't currently selected, whereas the other commands simply don't make sense if a field hasn't been selected.

```
// CH.3 Handle graffiti help
    if( event->data.menu.itemID == EditGraffitiHelp )
    {
        // CH.3 Pop up the graffiti reference based on
        // the graffiti state
```

```
        SysGraffitiReferenceDialog( referenceDefault );
        return( true );
    }
```

Next, you get the field pointer so that you can call those nice editing commands. The example below shows a more general way to get the field pointer than the method we used in handling the frmOpenEvent case. It will work no matter how many fields are on the form.

```
// CH.3 Get the index of our field
    index = FrmGetFocus( form );

    // CH.3 If there is no field selected, we're done
    if( index == noFocus )
        return( false );

    // CH.3 Get the pointer of our field
    field = FrmGetObjectPtr( form, index );
```

Now we can do the edit commands. They are very simple to call and they pretty much handle everything. To do the Select All command, you pass the whole length of the string to **FldSetSelection()**.

```
// CH.3 Do the edit command
switch( event->data.menu.itemID )
{
    // CH.3 Undo
    case EditUndo:
        FldUndo( field );
    break;

    // CH.3 Cut
    case EditCut:
        FldCut( field );
    break;

    // CH.3 Copy
    case EditCopy:
        FldCopy( field );
    break;

    // CH.3 Paste
    case EditPaste:
        FldPaste( field );
```

3

```
        break;

        // CH.3 Select All
        case EditSelectAll:
        {
            // CH.3 Get the length of the string in the field
            Word length = FldGetTextLength( field );

            // CH.3 Select the whole string
            FldSetSelection( field, 0, length );
        }
        break;

        // CH.3 Bring up the keyboard tool
        case EditKeyboard:
            SysKeyboardDialog( kbdDefault );
        break;
    }

    // CH.3 We're done
    return( true );
}
```

After making the above modifications, make, debug, and run your application again. You should be able to use the menu and shortcuts you have created.

Supporting the Various Versions of the Palm OS

The code above will actually crash on a Pilot 1000 or Pilot 5000 running the PalmOS version 1.0. That's because in version 1.0, **SysKeyboardDialog()** is a different call. There are several ways to fix this problem. The first is to just call **SysKeyboardDialogV10()**, which is always backwards-compatible. If you want to get the most out of the latest system calls, you can check for the OS version and do the right call based on the version of the OS.

We will get more sophisticated as we encounter more serious instances of OS version changes. For now, just replace this function call with **SysKeyboardDialogV10()**.

```
        // CH.3 Bring up the keyboard tool
        case EditKeyboard:
            SysKeyboardDialogV10();
        break;
```

Errors and Alerts

Contacts has grown to the extent that it's possible for users to do things to it that will cause error conditions. This seems an excellent time to talk about handling these error conditions.

If you play with the edit commands, you will notice that if you do something nonsensical like try to copy even though no selection has been made, the edit function will produce a warning beep for you. Not so with Select All because you're calling a generic function that does not beep if there is an error. To make Select All match the other functions in terms of beeping behavior, you can add a call to **SndPlaySystemSound()**, like this:

```
// CH.3 Select All
case EditSelectAll:
{
    // CH.3 Get the length of the string in the field
    Word length = FldGetTextLength( field );

    // CH.3 Sound an error if appropriate
    if( length == 0 )
    {
        SndPlaySystemSound( sndError );
        return( false );
    }

    // CH.3 Select the whole string
    FldSetSelection( field, 0, length );
}
```

Let's say you want to go above and beyond the call of duty and actually tell the user something about what they might have done wrong. There is a cool way to do this: alerts. *Alerts* are pre-made mini-forms controlled by the operating system. They're very convenient and easy to build and use.

Give it a try: build an alert resource that contains an error message for the Select All command:

1. Launch Constructor.
2. Select Alert from the resource types list.
3. Press CTRL-K to create a new alert.
4. Double-click on the alert to open it.

5. Change the message attribute to something like "There was no text to select."

6. Change the title attribute to Error.

7. Change the alert type attribute to Error.

To call up this alert from our code, we add a call to **FrmAlert()**. You can get the variable name for the alert ID from your Contacts_res.h file.

3

```
// CH.3 Pop up an error if appropriate
if( length == 0 )
{
    SndPlaySystemSound( sndError );
    FrmAlert( SelectAllErrorAlert );
    return( false );
}
```

After adding the above code, make, debug, and run your application. Note that there are two beeps: one from the call to **SndPlaySystemSound()** and one from the alert, since we set its alert type to Error.

Another place we might want to put an alert or at least a system beep is up where we check for focus. It's actually not possible for our field to not have focus because of how the rest of the application is set up, but in the general case we would want to signal an error to the user here, classically with a system beep.

Since errors in select all are not usually greeted by an alert, let's remove the alert resource and the code that brings it up. We will be using alerts in future chapters to signal various errors.

What's Next?

In the next chapter, we will investigate how to have multiple forms in your applications.

The Final Result

Here is the entire listing of Contacts.c for your perusal. The lines that have changed from hello.c are commented with // CH.3 comments.

```
// CH.2 The super-include for the Palm OS
#include <Pilot.h>
```

```
// CH.3 Our resource file
#include "Contacts_res.h"

// CH.2 Prototypes for our event handler functions
static Boolean myHandleEvent( EventPtr event );
static Boolean menuEventHandler( EventPtr event );

// CH.3 Our field memory handle
static Handle htext;     // CH.3 Handle to the text in our edit field
#define HTEXT_SIZE 81     // CH.3 Size of our edit field

// CH.2 The main entry point
DWord PilotMain( Word cmd, Ptr, Word )
{
    FormPtr     form;     // CH.2 A pointer to our form structure */
    Handle      hsrc;     // CH.3 Handle to the string resource
    CharPtr     psrc;     // CH.3 Points to the text in the resource
    CharPtr     ptext;    // CH.3 Points to the text in the edit field
    Word        index;    // CH.3 A general purpose index
    FieldPtr    field;    // CH.3 Used for manipulating fields
    EventType   event;    // CH.2 Our event structure
    Word        error;    // CH.3 Error word for menu event handler

    // CH.2 If this is not a normal launch, don't launch
    if( cmd != sysAppLaunchCmdNormalLaunch )
        return( 0 );

    // CH.3 Get the initialization string resource handle
    hsrc = DmGetResource( strRsc, FieldInitString );

    // CH.3 Lock the resource, get the pointer
    psrc = MemHandleLock( hsrc );

    // CH.3 Allocate our field chunk
    htext = MemHandleNew( HTEXT_SIZE );
    if( htext == NULL )
        return( 0 );

    // CH.3 Lock the memory, get the pointer
    ptext = MemHandleLock( htext );

    // CH.3 Initialize it
    StrCopy( ptext, psrc );

    // CH.3 Unlock the field's memory
    MemHandleUnlock( htext );

    // CH.3 Unlock the resource's memory
    MemHandleUnlock( hsrc );

    // CH.3 Release the string resource
```

```
            DmReleaseResource( hsrc );

            // CH.2 Initialize our form
            form = FrmInitForm( ContactDetailForm );
            FrmSetEventHandler( form, myHandleEvent );
            FrmSetActiveForm( form );

            // CH.3 Get the index of our field
            index = FrmGetObjectIndex( form, ContactDetailFirstNameField );

            // CH.3 Get the pointer to our field
            field = FrmGetObjectPtr( form, index );

            // CH.3 Set the editable text
            FldSetTextHandle( field, htext );

            // CH.2 Draw the form
            FrmDrawForm( form );

            // CH.3 Set the focus to our field
            FrmSetFocus( form, index );

            // CH.2 Our event loop
            do
            {
                // CH.2 Get the next event
                EvtGetEvent( &event, -1 );

                // CH.2 Handle system events
                if( SysHandleEvent( &event ) )
                    continue;

                // CH.3 Handle menu events
                if( MenuHandleEvent( NULL, &event, &error ) )
                    continue;

                // CH.2 Handle form events
                FrmDispatchEvent( &event );

            // CH.2 If it's a stop event, exit
            } while( event.eType != appStopEvent );

            // CH.2 We're done
            return( 0 );
        }

        // CH.2 Our form handler function
        static Boolean myHandleEvent( EventType* event )
        {
            // CH.3 Parse menu events
            if( event->eType == menuEvent )
```

3

```
            return( menuEventHandler( event ) );

        // CH.2 We're done
        return( false );
    }

// CH.3 Handle menu events
Boolean menuEventHandler( EventPtr event )
{
        FormPtr     form;     // CH.3 A pointer to our form structure
        Word        index;    // CH.3 A general purpose control index
        FieldPtr    field;    // CH.3 Used for manipulating fields

        // CH.3 Get our form pointer
        form = FrmGetActiveForm();

        // CH.3 Erase the menu status from the display
        MenuEraseStatus( NULL );

        // CH.3 Handle graffiti help
        if( event->data.menu.itemID == EditGraffitiHelp )
        {
            // CH.3 Pop up the graffiti reference based on
            // the graffiti state
            SysGraffitiReferenceDialog( referenceDefault );
            return( true );
        }

        // CH.3 Get the index of our field
        index = FrmGetFocus( form );

        // CH.3 If there is no field selected, we're done
        if( index == noFocus )
            return( false );

        // CH.3 Get the pointer of our field
        field = FrmGetObjectPtr( form, index );

        // CH.3 Do the edit command
        switch( event->data.menu.itemID )
        {
            // CH.3 Undo
            case EditUndo:
                FldUndo( field );
            break;

            // CH.3 Cut
            case EditCut:
                FldCut( field );
            break;
```

```
            // CH.3 Copy
            case EditCopy:
                FldCopy( field );
            break;

            // CH.3 Paste
            case EditPaste:
                FldPaste( field );
            break;

            // CH.3 Select All
            case EditSelectAll:
            {
                // CH.3 Get the length of the string in the field
                Word length = FldGetTextLength( field );

                // CH.3 Pop up an error if appropriate
                if( length == 0 )
                {
                    SndPlaySystemSound( sndError );
                    return( false );
                }

                // CH.3 Select the whole string
                FldSetSelection( field, 0, length );
            }
            break;

            // CH.3 Bring up the keyboard tool
            case EditKeyboard:
                SysKeyboardDialogV10();
            break;
    }

    // CH.3 We're done
    return( true );
}
```

3

CHAPTER 4

Applications
and Forms

In this chapter we'll continue to unfold the power and easy style of the Palm OS by adding an About form to last chapter's Contacts application. You'll learn how to create and lay out forms containing bitmaps, text, and buttons. You'll add a menu and code to Contacts that will allow you to reach this new form and return to the Contact Detail form.

We will begin the chapter with a tour of the fundamental application settings. We'll create big and small application icons for Contacts during the course of this investigation.

Application Settings

In this section we will look at and change some settings that affect our entire application. We will also create some application icons for Contacts.

First, make a backup copy of your application.

1. Launch Windows Explorer.
2. Locate your Contacts project folder.
3. Copy and Paste the Contacts project folder.
4. Rename the folder Contacts CH.3. This folder will be your backup copy of Contacts.

Creating Big and Small Application Icons

First look at the Project Settings in Constructor.

NOTE: The version of Constructor included in Code Warrior 6 has a bug in it that prevents creating and editing multibit icons. We have included a solution for you on the CD. Look for a file named icon.txt on the CD for directions to work around this problem.

1. Launch Constructor and open Contacts.rsrc.
2. Look at the project settings at the bottom of the Contacts.rsrc window. If there is only an arrow pointing to the right at the bottom of your window, click it and the project settings will appear. The only project settings you would usually want to change are the Application Icon Name, the Version String, and the Application Icon. In the last chapter you already changed the Application Icon Name to Contacts. Table 4-1 provides a list of all the settings and what they do.

Name	Description
Generate App Resources	Creates a version and application icon name resource for the application. I recommend that you always leave this checked.
Application Icon Name	The name of your application.
Version String	The version of your application. As you make significant revisions to your application, you should increase this number so that you can tell the different versions of your application apart.
Application Icon	Defines a black-and-white version of your "big" application icon. This was for application icons in Palm OS version 2.0 and earlier. Don't use this.
Auto Generate Header File	Makes Constructor automatically generate a header file for you. I recommend leaving this checked.
Header File Name	The name of the automatically generated header file. I recommend that you leave the filename at the default value.
Include Details in Header	Constructor will add comments to the header file. I recommend leaving this checked.
Keep IDs in Sync	Causes Constructor to automatically renumber IDs when form IDs change. If you are making a small ID change to a large application you might consider unchecking this. Otherwise, it's good to leave it checked.

Project Settings
in Constructor
Table 4-1.

4

3. Create a big application icon for Contacts. Select Multibit Icon from the resources list and press CTRL-K. Make sure that the resource ID is 1000. This step is critical. Note that if you click on the Create button next to the Application Icon property it will create a regular icon instead of a multibit icon. Although this will work for the big icon, it's not ideal.

4. Double-click on the new icon. An editor window will pop up and you can draw an icon in it. Make sure to create both a black-and-white and a 2-bit grayscale icon. You can select between the two by clicking on the real size versions of the icons at the right side of the editor window. The

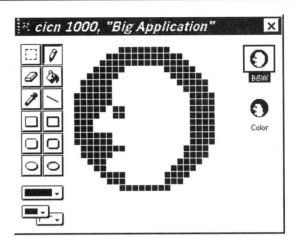

A possible big
application
icon for
Contacts

Figure 4-1.

controls in the editor are similar to those available in Paint and other
graphics programs. When you're done you can close the window by
clicking the X in the upper-right corner. Your big icon might look
something like the one I drew, which appears in Figure 4-1.

5. Create a small application icon for Contacts. This icon will only show up
   on devices running Palm OS 3.0 or higher. Select Multibit Icons in the
   Resource Type and Name panel at the top of the Contacts.rsrc window.

6. Press CTRL-K to create a new icon.

7. Click on the ID and change it to 1001. This step is critical.

8. Double-click on the new icon. This will bring up the icon editor
   window. Palm OS will only display the upper 9 pixels and the leftmost
   15 pixels of this icon, so design accordingly. The small icon I drew
   appears in Figure 4-2.

Project Settings in the CodeWarrior IDE

Here's how to find the settings for your application in the CodeWarrior IDE:

1. Launch the CodeWarrior IDE. Open the Contacts project.

2. Select Edit | Starter Settings. The settings are still called this because we
   have never changed the name of our application from the time we
   created the first project called Starter. You'll notice there are lots of
   settings in here. You'll never want to fool with most of them.

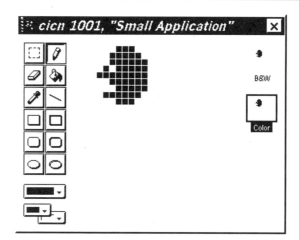

A possible small application icon for Contacts

Figure 4-2.

4

3. The left side of the Target Settings dialog is a tree structure of all the settings. Under Target, select Target Settings. Change the Target Name from Starter to Contacts. Save the settings. Now the CodeWarrior IDE will call your project Contacts.

4. Under Target select 68K Target. Change File Name from Starter.tmp to Contacts.tmp.

5. Under Linker choose PalmRez Post Linker. Change the Mac Resource Files setting from Starter.tmp to Contacts.tmp. Change the Output File setting from Stater.prc to Contacts.prc. Change the Database Name setting from being blank to Contacts-PPGU.

NOTE: As I mentioned earlier, everything is stored as a database on the Palm device, including your application. Each database on a Palm device must have a unique name or there is trouble. The name Contacts-PPGU is the application's name combined with its unique creator ID. This method of naming guarantees uniqueness. You will learn more about creator IDs in the next chapter.

There are many other settings under what is now called Contacts Settings. We will not need to start fooling with any of the rest of these until later on in the book. If you're curious about them now, you can find out more about these settings in the CodeWarrior documentation IDE Guide.

Multiple Forms

In this section we will add a second form to our Contacts application: an About form. We'll also change the code in Contacts.c to enable us to move between the two forms.

Additions to Contacts.rsrc

We will start by adding the About form to our resource file.

1. Launch Constructor and open Contacts.rsrc.
2. Create the About form. Select Forms from the resource list and press CTRL-K.
3. Name the About form. Click on the name Untitled and change it to About.
4. Double-click on the About form to open it.
5. Look at the form attributes in the left panel of the Form dialog. Table 4-2 shows a list of the attributes of a form and what they can be used for.
6. Now modify the form's attributes. Check Save Behind. Fill in the title **About Contacts**.

Adding a Bitmap

Create a bitmap to put on the About form. To accomplish this, follow these steps:

1. Select Bitmaps on the Resource Type and Name list.
2. Press CTRL-K to create a new bitmap.
3. In Constructor, select Options | Set Image Size. This allows you to set the size of the bitmap.
4. Make a bitmap that is 42 × 42.
5. Draw your bitmap. My bitmap looks like the one in Figure 4-3. Constructor's editor is hard to use for bitmaps this large. I used Paint and then cut and pasted my image into Constructor.
6. When you're done, close the bitmap editor by clicking on the X in the upper-right corner.
7. Add the bitmap to the Contacts form. To do this, open the Catalog window by selecting Window | Catalog. Drag a bitmap from the Catalog window and drop it on the About form.

4

Name	Description
Left Origin	The position of the left side of the form in pixels. The entire screen is 160 pixels across.
Top Origin	The position of the top of the form in pixels. The entire screen is 160 pixels from top to bottom.
Width	The width of the form in pixels. A form doesn't have to cover the entire screen.
Height	The height of the form in pixels.
Usable	Defines whether the form appears at all. Objects that are not marked usable are not displayed until they are marked usable. Forms should always be marked usable.
Modal	If this form is the active form and Modal is checked, pen events are ignored outside the boundaries of the form. Also, a Modal form shows its title centered across the top of the form. Modal forms also prevent interruption by system dialogs such as alarms, so they should be used sparingly.
Save Behind	If checked, the contents of the screen area behind the form are saved before the form is drawn and restored after the form is closed.
Form ID	The ID of the form. This ID uniquely identifies the form.
Help ID	If the form is Modal, you can put the ID of a string resource with a helpful message here and a little "i" icon will appear in the upper-right corner of the form. When the user clicks on this icon, your help message will be displayed to the user. You can see an example of this help in use in the Details form of the standard Date Book application.
Menu Bar ID	The ID of the menu bar associated with the form. We used this attribute in the last chapter to give our Contact Detail form a menu bar.
Default Button ID	If you supply an ID here and the user switches to another application, Palm OS will press this button before exiting the application. This is especially handy for modal forms. Often the button you'll want to press by default is Cancel.
Form Title	If you supply a title for your form, Palm OS creates a title bar and puts your title in it.

Form
Attributes
Table 4-2.

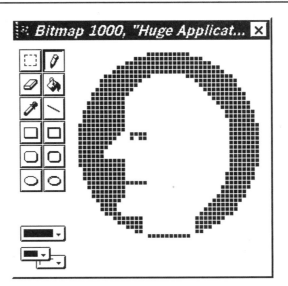

One possible
bitmap for the
About page

Figure 4-3.

8. Modify the bitmap attributes. The attributes of a bitmap are very
   straightforward. Table 4-3 lists all these attributes.

Bitmap
Attributes

Table 4-3.

Name	Description
Object ID	The unique ID of this bitmap on the form. This ID is unique across all objects in the application.
Object Identifier	The name of the bitmap.
Left Origin	The position of the left side of the bitmap in pixels. The entire screen is 160 pixels across.
Top Origin	The position of the top of the bitmap in pixels. The entire screen is 160 pixels from top to bottom.
Bitmap Resource ID	Defines what bitmap resource this bitmap is.
Usable	Defines whether the bitmap appears at all. Objects that are not marked usable are not displayed until they are marked usable.

9. Set the Bitmap Resource ID to the Resource ID of the bitmap you created previously. This ID is probably 1000. You should see your bitmap appear in place of the generic bitmap that was originally there.

10. Set the Left Origin and Top Origin to place the bitmap on the form. I gave my bitmap image a Left Origin of 59 (centering it on the form) and a Top Origin of 20 (placing it below the title bar).

Adding a Label

Now create a label that contains the information about Contacts. You can create a label by dragging and dropping a label from the Catalog window onto your form. Table 4-4 contains a list of label object attributes.

4

Name	Description
Object Identifier	The name you choose for the label. The variables Constructor creates in the Contacts_res.h file will be derived from this name.
Label ID	The number Palm OS uses to identify this specific UI object.
Left Origin	The position of the left side of the label in pixels. The entire screen is 160 pixels across. The width of the label is determined by the text contained in it.
Top Origin	The position of the top of the button in pixels. The entire screen is 160 pixels from top to bottom. The number of lines of text and the size of the font determines the height of the label.
Usable	Defines whether the label appears on the form at all. Controls that are not marked usable are not displayed. This setting is useful if you want to make controls appear or disappear without changing forms.
Font	The font that is used to display the text in the label. You can look at these fonts using the Windows Key Caps utility.
Text	The text that is displayed in the label.

Label
Attributes

Table 4-4.

Some things usually in the label of an About form are the application name, your or your company's name, a copyright notice, and the version of the application. I created two labels so that Contacts could be in a bigger font than the rest of the text. You can use as many labels as you wish.

Since bitmaps and labels aren't referred to in the code, there is no chance of your needing different code than what is in the listing due to more or different bitmaps or labels. I got the copyright symbol by looking at the Pilot Standard font in my Windows Key Caps utility. You can cut the character out of Key Caps and paste it into Constructor.

Adding a Button

Create a button and put it at the bottom of the About form. You can leave it saying OK or you can change the text to something different.

Once Contacts.c is modified, this button will close the About form and return control to the Contacts form. Since this is our first foray into buttons beyond the initial example, it's worth including a table of button attributes (Table 4-5).

Name	Description
Object Identifier	The name you choose for the button. The variables Constructor creates in the Contacts_res.h file will be derived from this name.
Button ID	The number Palm OS uses to identify this specific UI object.
Left Origin	The position of the left side of the button in pixels. The entire screen is 160 pixels across. The button border extends one pixel to the left of this origin, so the farthest left a button with an intact border can be placed is 1. Bold button frames extend two pixels.
Top Origin	The position of the top of the button in pixels. The entire screen is 160 pixels from top to bottom. The button border extends one pixel up the screen from this origin, so the highest on the screen a button with an intact border can be placed is 1. Bold button frames extend two pixels.
Width	The width of the button in pixels. For the actual width, border and all, add 2 for the border if it is non-bold, 4 if it is bold.

Button
Attributes
Table 4-5.

Name	Description
Height	The height of the button in pixels. For the actual height, border and all, add 2 for the border if it is non-bold, 4 if it is bold.
Usable	Defines whether the button appears on the form at all. Controls that are not marked usable are not displayed. This setting is useful if you want to make controls appear or disappear without changing forms.
Anchor Left	Controls how the button resizes itself if you change the length of the label while your application is running. If checked, the button will extend or shrink the right side of the button. If unchecked, the button will extend or shrink the left side of the button.
Frame	If checked, the button has a frame.
Non-Bold Frame	If checked, the button frame is 1 pixel wide. If unchecked, the button frame is 2 pixels wide.
Font	The font that is used to display the text in the button. You can look at these fonts using the Windows Key Caps utility.
Label	The text that is displayed in the button.

Button
Attributes
(continued)

Table 4-5.

4

Name the button OK. When you are done with your About form, it should look somewhat like Figure 4-4. The only thing the form absolutely needs is an OK button.

Adding a Menu
The About form will be accessible via a menu item choice on the Options menu. Create the Options menu and add it to Contacts's menu bar. Here are the steps:

1. Click Menus in the Resource Type and Name list and press CTRL-K to create a new menu.
2. Click on the name field and name it Options.
3. Double-click the Options menu to open it.

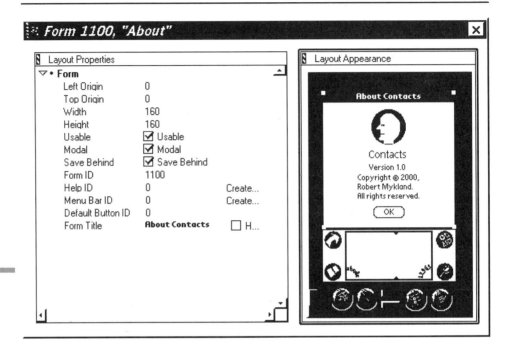

What your
form might
look like

Figure 4-4.

4. Change the title in the menu bar to Options.

5. Press CTRL-K to create a new menu item. Type in **About Contacts**.

6. Close the Options menu.

7. Double-click the Contact Detail menu bar to open it.

8. Drag the Options menu from the Resource Type and Name list and drop it onto the Contact Detail menu bar after the Edit menu. When you're done, your Contacts menu bar should look exactly like Figure 4-5.

9. Close and save Contacts.rsrc. You're done.

Additions to Contacts.c

In order for multiple forms to work, we need to add some code to Contacts.c and modify other parts. We're also adding an Options menu, so we need to add code to work that menu.

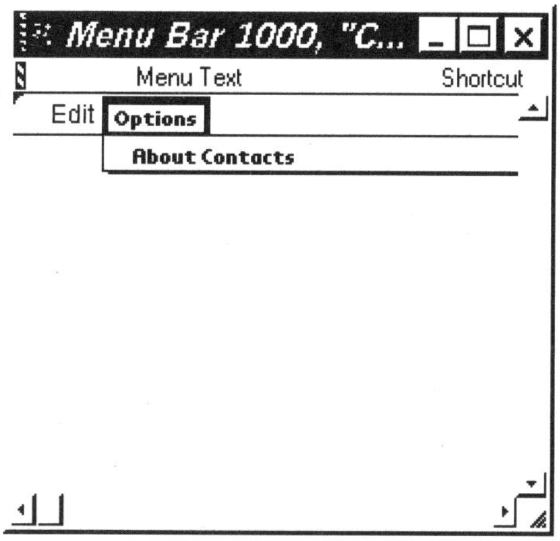

The Contact
Detail menu
bar after you're
done adding
the Options
menu

Figure 4-5.

4

Generalizing the Form-Loading Code

Since we are now going to be loading more than one form, it's time to make
our form-loading code more general purpose.

At the top of the file, change the name of **myHandleEvent()** to
contactDetailHandleEvent() because this event handler only really
applies to the Contact Detail form. Your prototype should look like this when
you're done:

```
// Prototype for our form handler function
static Boolean contactDetailHandleEvent( EventType* event );
```

You'll need to change the top of the **myHandleEvent()** function call
to match:

```
// Our Contact Detail form event handler function
static Boolean contactDetailHandleEvent( EventType* event )
{
```

Next, we handle a new event called *frmOpenEvent*. This event is sent when
you change from one form to another. I'll talk about how exactly to change

forms a bit later, after we have changed the event handler to make it possible to change forms.

```
Word        index;  // CH.3 A general purpose index
FieldPtr    field;  // CH.3 Used for manipulating fields

// CH.3 Get our form pointer
form = FrmGetActiveForm();

// CH.4 Parse events
switch( event->eType )
{
    // CH.4 Form open event
    case frmOpenEvent:
    {
        // CH.3 Get the index of our field
        index = FrmGetObjectIndex( form, ContactDetailFirstNameField );

        // CH.3 Get the pointer to our field
        field = FrmGetObjectPtr( form, index );

        // CH.3 Set the editable text
        FldSetTextHandle( field, htext );

        // CH.2 Draw the form */
        FrmDrawForm( form );

        // CH.3 Set the focus to our field
        FrmSetFocus( form, index );
    }
    break;
```

The code inside the *frmOpenEvent* block is cut from **PilotMain()** before the event loop. We put it here because now that we are traveling between forms, we want this code to be executed every time we start displaying this form, which could now be several times during the execution of the application.

It's a very good idea to steal our text handle back away from the field before we change forms. This is because all memory associated with the form (and therefore any fields in the form) is deallocated when we switch to a new form. If we return to the form expecting the handle to be good, we will instead be in big trouble.

The way we can accomplish stealing back our text handle is to respond to the *frmCloseEvent*. This event is sent before the current form is destroyed on the way to bringing up another form.

```
// CH.4 Form close event
case frmCloseEvent:
{
    // CH.3 Get the index of our field
    index = FrmGetObjectIndex( form, ContactDetailFirstNameField );

    // CH.3 Get the pointer to our field
    field = FrmGetObjectPtr( form, index );

    // CH.4 Unlink our handle from the field
    FrmSetTextHandle( field, NULL );
}
break;
```

Here all we're doing is getting a pointer to our field and setting its text handle to NULL. This prevents our text handle from being freed.

We need to replace the code we cut from **PilotMain()** with a call that will cause the *frmOpenEvent* to be sent. If we don't, nothing will happen. We will stare at a blank screen forever because the first form will never get loaded. The function you call to send the *frmLoadForm* and *frmOpenForm* events to switch forms is **FrmGotoForm()**. The code around **FrmGotoForm()** in **PilotMain()** now looks like this:

```
// CH.3 Release the string resource
DmReleaseResource( hsrc );

// CH.4 Go to our starting page
FrmGotoForm( ContactDetailForm );

// CH.2 Our event loop
do
{
```

The last bit of code we need to generalize the loading of forms is code to switch the event handler functions from one form to another. Each form

4

should have its own event handler. A good way to do this is to respond to the *frmLoadForm* event in the main event loop, like so:

```
// CH.3 Handle menu events
if( MenuHandleEvent( NULL, &event, &error ) )
    continue;

// CH.4 Handle form load events
if( event.eType == frmLoadEvent )
{
    // CH.4 Initialize our form
    switch( event.data.frmLoad.formID )
    {
        // CH.4 Contact Detail form
        case ContactDetailForm:
            form = FrmInitForm( ContactDetailForm );
            FrmSetEventHandler( form, contactDetailHandleEvent );
        break;

        // CH.4 About form
        case AboutForm:
            form = FrmInitForm( AboutForm );
            FrmSetEventHandler( form, aboutHandleEvent );
        break;
    }
    FrmSetActiveForm( form );
}

// CH.2 Handle form events
FrmDispatchEvent( &event );
```

For each form we want to load, we'll add a case to the switch statement that will initialize the form and set its specific event handler.

It's time to be a little more responsible for the memory we allocated in the last chapter. Although our text handle will be deallocated when our application is unloaded from memory, it's a good idea, since the closing form is no longer deallocating it, to deallocate it ourselves at the end of **PilotMain()**:

```
// CH.4 Deallocate memory
    MemHandleFree( htext );

    // CH.2 We're done
    return( 0 );
```

This is more of a neatness thing rather than something that will cause your application to crash. However, as your application gets more complex and as you move code around, being neat about allocating and deallocating memory can save you a lot of time that you would otherwise spend trying to figure out why your application is crashing.

Handling the Options Menu

We will use a menu item to get to the About form, as is customary. Since all menu IDs are unique, you can simply add a bit of code to the existing menu event handler code for Contacts:

```
// CH.3 Erase the menu status from the display
MenuEraseStatus( NULL );

// CH.4 Handle options menu
if( event->data.menu.itemID == OptionsAboutContacts )
{
    // CH.4 Pop up the About form as a Dialog
    FrmPopupForm( AboutForm );
    return( true );
}

// CH.3 Handle graffiti help
if( event->data.menu.itemID == EditGraffitiHelp )
{
    // CH.3 Pop up the graffiti reference based on
    // the graffiti state
    SysGraffitiReferenceDialog( referenceDefault );
    return( true );
}
```

The code added to **MenuEventHandler()** after the call to **MenuEraseStatus()** will work. You check for the item ID of the new selection and respond with a call to **FrmPopupForm()**. The function **FrmPopupForm()** is similar to **FrmGotoForm()** except that the old form never gets closed. This is appropriate in the case of the About form because we know we're going to return to the Contact Detail form from the About form. There isn't any other path.

This means that technically we don't have to do some of the general purpose form-changing work we did in the last section. However, it's just very practical

4

to have our form-changing code set up like this so we don't have to worry as we add forms that we might mess up the behavior of the Contact Detail form.

NOTE: Here we are handling the options menu in the middle of code originally intended to handle the edit menu. How can this work? Well, Constructor gives unique IDs to all menu items in all menus. Therefore, it is not necessary to handle one set of menu items separately from another.

Adding an Event Handler for the About Form

Each form should have its own event handler, so we need to add an event handler for the new About form. First, add a prototype for the new event handler function for the About form. Call it **aboutHandleEvent()**. Your prototypes should look like this when you're done:

```
// CH.3 Prototypes for our event handler functions
static Boolean contactDetailHandleEvent( EventPtr event );
static Boolean aboutHandleEvent( EventPtr event );
static Boolean menuEventHandler( EventPtr event );
```

Next, we have to add a bit of code to the portion of our event loop that handles the *frmLoadEvent*. This code will initialize the About form and install its event handler function as the target of **FrmDispatchEvent()**.

```
// CH.4 Initialize our form
switch( event.data.frmLoad.formID )
{
    // CH.4 Contact Detail form
    case ContactDetailForm:
        form = FrmInitForm( ContactDetailForm );
        FrmSetEventHandler( form, contactDetailHandleEvent );
    break;

    // CH.4 About form
    case AboutForm:
        form = FrmInitForm( AboutForm );
        FrmSetEventHandler( form, aboutHandleEvent );
    break;
}
```

All that's left is to add the event handler function **aboutHandleEvent()**:

```
// CH.4 Our About form event handler function
static Boolean aboutHandleEvent( EventPtr event )
{
    FormPtr                    form;        // CH.4 A pointer to our form structure

    // CH.4 Get our form pointer
    form = FrmGetActiveForm();

    // CH.4 Respond to the Open event
    if( event->eType == frmOpenEvent )
    {
        // CH.4 Draw the form
        FrmDrawForm( form );
    }

    // CH.4 Return to the calling form
    if( event->eType == ctlSelectEvent )
    {
        FrmReturnToForm( 0 );

        // CH.4 Always return true in this case
        return( true );
    }
}
```

The event handler responds to *frmOpenEvent* with the only essential call for displaying a form: **FrmDrawForm()**. It also responds to *ctlSelectEvent* as our very first Hello application did, except this time, instead of sounding an alarm, it calls **FrmReturnToForm(0)**, which causes the About form to be destroyed and the calling form (in our case, the Contact Detail form) to be reactivated.

NOTE: It is very important to return true in the case of returning to the calling form. This is because otherwise the Palm OS attempts to fully handle the ctlSelectEvent, which involves manipulating structures that have just been destroyed by you in the call to **FrmReturnToForm()**. To prevent these memory shenanigans, always return true after **FrmReturnToForm()** so the form is exited immediately.

Debugging It

It's time to debug again. Your Contact Detail form should look and work as it did before. Your About form should pop up if you select its item from the Options menu. It should return to the Contact Detail form when you press its OK button. The Contact Detail form should have a menu bar consisting of the original Edit menu along with the new Options menu. The About form should not have a menu bar since we haven't defined one for it.

As before, the program starts execution at **PilotMain()** and goes through its regular routine. When the *frmLoadEvent* gets picked up, it initializes the Contact Detail form's event handler function. After that, the *frmOpenEvent* is sent to the Contact Detail form's event handler function. There it is processed, the form is drawn, and the field is set up as before. Then the program sits there and waits for something to happen.

Figure 4-6 shows the application sitting in this state.

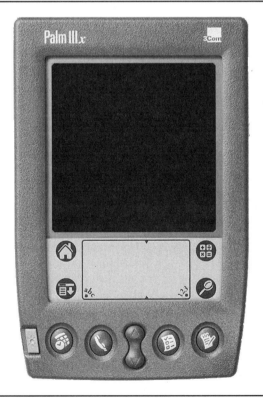

The Contact
Detail form
waiting for
input

Figure 4-6.

What's Next?

In the next chapter we'll continue to examine more of the Palm device's built-in controls.

Listing

Here is the new version of Contacts.c in its entirety:

```c
// CH.2 The super-include for PalmOS
#include <Pilot.h>

// CH.3 Our resource file
#include "Contacts_res.h"

// CH.3 Prototypes for our event handler functions
static Boolean contactDetailHandleEvent( EventPtr event );
static Boolean aboutHandleEvent( EventPtr event );
static Boolean menuEventHandler( EventPtr event );

// CH.3 Our field memory handle
static Handle htext;         // CH.3 Handle to the text in our edit field
#define HTEXT_SIZE 81        // CH.3 Size of our edit field

// CH.4 Constants for ROM revision
#define ROM_VERSION_2        0x02003000
#define ROM_VERSION_MIN      ROM_VERSION_2

// CH.2 The main entry point
DWord PilotMain( Word cmd, Ptr, Word )
{
    DWord               romVersion; // CH.4 ROM version
    FormPtr             form;       // CH.2 A pointer to our form structure
    Handle              hsrc;       // CH.3 Handle to the string resource
    CharPtr             psrc;       // CH.3 Points to the text in the resource
    CharPtr             ptext;      // CH.3 Points to the text in the edit field
    EventType           event;      // CH.2 Our event structure
    Word                error;      // CH.3 Error word

    // CH.4 Get the ROM version
    romVersion = 0;
    FtrGet( sysFtrCreator, sysFtrNumROMVersion, &romVersion );

    // CH.4 If we are below our minimum acceptable ROM revision
    if( romVersion < ROM_VERSION_MIN )
    {
        // CH.4 Display the alert
        FrmAlert( LowROMVersionErrorAlert );
```

```
    // CH.4 PalmOS 1.0 will continuously re-launch this app
    // unless we switch to another safe one
    if( romVersion < ROM_VERSION_2 )
    {
        AppLaunchWithCommand( sysFileCDefaultApp,
                sysAppLaunchCmdNormalLaunch, NULL );
    }
    return( 0 );
}

// CH.2 If this is not a normal launch, don't launch
if( cmd != sysAppLaunchCmdNormalLaunch )
    return( 0 );

// CH.3 Get the initialization string resource handle
hsrc = DmGetResource( strRsc, FieldInitString );

// CH.3 Lock the resource, get the pointer
psrc = MemHandleLock( hsrc );

// CH.3 Allocate our field chunk
htext = MemHandleNew( HTEXT_SIZE );
if( htext == NULL )
    return( 0 );

// CH.3 Lock the memory, get the pointer
ptext = MemHandleLock( htext );

// CH.3 Initialize it
StrCopy( ptext, psrc );

// CH.3 Unlock the field's memory
MemHandleUnlock( htext );

// CH.3 Unlock the resource's memory
MemHandleUnlock( hsrc );

// CH.3 Release the string resource
DmReleaseResource( hsrc );

// CH.4 Go to our starting page
FrmGotoForm( ContactDetailForm );

// CH.2 Our event loop
do
{
    // CH.2 Get the next event
    EvtGetEvent( &event, -1 );

    // CH.2 Handle system events
    if( SysHandleEvent( &event ) )
        continue;
```

```
            // CH.3 Handle menu events
            if( MenuHandleEvent( NULL, &event, &error ) )
                continue;

            // CH.4 Handle form load events
            if( event.eType == frmLoadEvent )
            {
                // CH.4 Initialize our form
                switch( event.data.frmLoad.formID )
                {
                    // CH.4 Contact Detail form
                    case ContactDetailForm:
                        form = FrmInitForm( ContactDetailForm );
                        FrmSetEventHandler( form, contactDetailHandleEvent );
                    break;

                    // CH.4 About form
                    case AboutForm:
                        form = FrmInitForm( AboutForm );
                        FrmSetEventHandler( form, aboutHandleEvent );
                    break;
                }
                FrmSetActiveForm( form );
            }

            // CH.2 Handle form events
            FrmDispatchEvent( &event );

        // CH.2 If it's a stop event, exit
        } while( event.eType != appStopEvent );

        // CH.4 Deallocate memory
        MemHandleFree( htext );

        // CH.2 We're done
        return( 0 );
}

// CH.4 Our Contacts form handler function
static Boolean contactDetailHandleEvent( EventPtr event )
{
    FormPtr      form;    // CH.3 A pointer to our form structure
    Word         index;   // CH.3 A general purpose index
    FieldPtr     field;   // CH.3 Used for manipulating fields

    // CH.3 Get our form pointer
    form = FrmGetActiveForm();

    // CH.4 Parse events
    switch( event->eType )
    {
        // CH.4 Form open event
        case frmOpenEvent:
        {
```

4

```
                // CH.3 Get the index of our field
                index = FrmGetObjectIndex( form, ContactDetailFirstNameField );

                // CH.3 Get the pointer to our field
                field = FrmGetObjectPtr( form, index );

                // CH.3 Set the editable text
                FldSetTextHandle( field, htext );

                // CH.2 Draw the form */
                FrmDrawForm( form );

                // CH.3 Set the focus to our field
                FrmSetFocus( form, index );
            }
            break;

            // CH.4 Form close event
            case frmCloseEvent:
            {
                // CH.3 Get the index of our field
                index = FrmGetObjectIndex( form, ContactDetailFirstNameField );

                // CH.3 Get the pointer to our field
                field = FrmGetObjectPtr( form, index );

                // CH.4 Unlink our handle from the field
                FrmSetTextHandle( field, NULL );
            }
            break;

            // CH.3 Parse menu events
            case menuEvent:
                return( menuEventHandler( event ) );
            break;
        }

    // CH.2 We're done
    return( false );
}

// CH.4 Our About form event handler function
static Boolean aboutHandleEvent( EventPtr event )
{
    FormPtr                    form;        // CH.4 A pointer to our form structure

    // CH.4 Get our form pointer
    form = FrmGetActiveForm();

    // CH.4 Respond to the Open event
    if( event->eType == frmOpenEvent )
    {
```

```
        // CH.4 Draw the form
        FrmDrawForm( form );
    }

    // CH.4 Return to the calling form
    if( event->eType == ctlSelectEvent )
    {
        FrmReturnToForm( 0 );

        // CH.4 Always return true in this case
        return( true );
    }

    // CH.4 We're done
    return( false );
}

// CH.3 Handle menu events
Boolean menuEventHandler( EventPtr event )
{
    FormPtr                 form;       // CH.3 A pointer to our form structure
    Word                    index;      // CH.3 A general purpose control index
    FieldPtr                field;      // CH.3 Used for manipulating fields

    // CH.3 Get our form pointer
    form = FrmGetActiveForm();

    // CH.3 Erase the menu status from the display
    MenuEraseStatus( NULL );

    // CH.4 Handle options menu
    if( event->data.menu.itemID == OptionsAboutContacts )
    {
        // CH.4 Pop up the About form as a Dialog
        FrmPopupForm( AboutForm );
        return( true );
    }

    // CH.3 Handle graffiti help
    if( event->data.menu.itemID == EditGraffitiHelp )
    {
        // CH.3 Pop up the graffiti reference based on
        // the graffiti state
        SysGraffitiReferenceDialog( referenceDefault );
        return( true );
    }

    // CH.3 Get the index of our field
    index = FrmGetFocus( form );

    // CH.3 If there is no field selected, we're done
    if( index == noFocus )
        return( false );
```

```
    // CH.3 Get the pointer of our field
    field = FrmGetObjectPtr( form, index );

    // CH.3 Do the edit command
    switch( event->data.menu.itemID )
    {
        // CH.3 Undo
        case EditUndo:
            FldUndo( field );
        break;

        // CH.3 Cut
        case EditCut:
            FldCut( field );
        break;

        // CH.3 Copy
        case EditCopy:
            FldCopy( field );
        break;

        // CH.3 Paste
        case EditPaste:
            FldPaste( field );
        break;

        // CH.3 Select All
        case EditSelectAll:
        {
            // CH.3 Get the length of the string in the field
            Word length = FldGetTextLength( field );

            // CH.3 Sound an error if appropriate
            if( length == 0 )
            {
                SndPlaySystemSound( sndError );
                return( false );
            }

            // CH.3 Select the whole string
            FldSetSelection( field, 0, length );
        }
        break;

        // CH.3 Bring up the keyboard tool
        case EditKeyboard:
            SysKeyboardDialogV10();
        break;
    }

    // CH.3 We're done
    return( true );
}
```

CHAPTER 5

Databases

Since pretty much everything in Palm OS memory is a database, it's about time to jump in and start learning to create and use databases. We will do this by continuing to build our Contacts application. We will put contacts into a database.

Cleaning Up

To prepare for adding a database to Contacts, you'll want to remove earlier code used for demonstration or educational purposes.

Making a Copy of the Contacts Application

First, make a copy of your current Contacts application. I named mine Contacts CH.4, and it is on the CD. To make a copy, perform the following steps:

1. Launch Windows Explorer.
2. Find and select your Contacts project folder.
3. Press CTRL-C to copy this folder.
4. Click on the folder you want to store the backup in.
5. Press CTRL-V to put a copy of your Contents project folder there.
6. Click on the name Contacts and change it to something more specific like Contacts CH.4.

Deleting Resources from the Resource File

There are some resources in the project we won't need any more. Perform the following steps to get rid of them:

1. Launch Constructor.
2. Open Contacts.rsrc in the Src folder of your Contacts project folder.
3. Select the FieldInit string resource and press DELETE to delete it.
4. Close and save Contacts.rsrc.

Cleaning Up the Code

We now need to remove and rearrange the code to work again without the resources we just deleted. Perform the following steps:

1. Launch the CodeWarrior IDE.

2. Open Contacts.mcp in your Contacts project folder.

3. Remove the following code from just above the start of **PilotMain()**:

```
// CH.3 Our field memory handle
static Handle htext;     // CH.3 Handle to the text in our edit field
#define HTEXT_SIZE 81    // CH.3 Size of our edit field
```

4. Remove the following code from near the top of **PilotMain()**:

```
    // CH.3 Get the initialization string resource handle
    hsrc = DmGetResource( strRsc, FieldInitString );

    // CH.3 Lock the resource, get the pointer
    psrc = MemHandleLock( hsrc );

    // CH.3 Allocate our field chunk
    htext = MemHandleNew( HTEXT_SIZE );
    if( htext == NULL )
        return( 0 );

    // CH.3 Lock the memory, get the pointer
    ptext = MemHandleLock( htext );

    // CH.3 Initialize it
    StrCopy( ptext, psrc );

    // CH.3 Unlock the field's memory
    MemHandleUnlock( htext );

    // CH.3 Unlock the resource's memory
    MemHandleUnlock( hsrc );

    // CH.3 Release the string resource
    DmReleaseResource( hsrc );
```

5. Remove the following code from the *frmOpenEvent* handling portion of **contactDetailEventHandler()**:

```
        // CH.3 Get the index of our field
        index = FrmGetObjectIndex( form, ContactDetailFirstNameField );

        // CH.3 Get the pointer to our field
        field = FrmGetObjectPtr( form, index );
```

5

```
// CH.3 Set the editable text
FldSetTextHandle( field, htext );

// CH.3 Set the focus to the First Name field
FrmSetFocus( form, index );
```

6. Remove the frmCloseEvent case from **contactDetailEventHandler()**.

7. Remove the call to **MemHandleFree()** at the end of **PilotMain()**.

Adding a Database

Now you'll attach a database to your fields. First, using Constructor, you will add some buttons to the Contact Detail form to allow you to navigate through the database records. You'll also add a help message and a new alert using Constructor. Then you'll add the code you need to create and edit your application's database.

Database Technology and Terminology

There are many different kinds of databases. There are also many confusing technical terms associated with databases. I'll take a crack at the basic terminology in this section and define other terms as we go along.

The basic unit of data storage in a database is a *record*, also called a *row*. A record usually consists of several pieces of data: for example, the name, address, and telephone number for one person. Each piece of data can be called a *field*, *cell*, or *column*. Usually the term "column" refers to similar pieces of information in all records: for example, all the first names in the database.

You can think of the information in a database being arranged in rows and columns. Each row represents an individual entry. Each column represents a specific type of data associated with each entry. For example, you might have a row in the database represent a person. In this case, the columns might be first name and last name. If your rows represented appointments, your columns might be the time of the appointment, the duration, and so forth.

Normally, you can only look at one row of a database at a time. The row you are currently looking at is often called the *cursor*. Palm OS calls this row the *index*. Moving from row to row in a database is sometimes called *navigation*.

The two most popular kinds of databases are flat-file databases and relational databases. *Flat-file databases* store information in a single list of rows and columns. Palm OS uses this simpler flat-file database model for its databases. *Relational databases* can have several different tables of rows and columns that can be related and associated in different ways. Most major databases today are relational databases. With some work, you can make several flat-file databases in Palm OS do the work of a relational database.

Databases allow you to look at a subset of data they contain based on restrictions you can establish. It's like asking the database a question and getting back all the information that validly answers that question. This database question is often called a *query*. The rows you receive in response to a query are called a *result set* or *solution set*.

In the Palm OS databases are more flexible than most flat-file databases because the records are just pointers to chunks of memory, and you can interpret them any way you want to. Thus, you can have a database full of records, each of which has a different format and length, if you want to.

Additions to Contacts.rsrc   5

In this case, it's a good thing to just jump in and build the application and allow these concepts to sort themselves out as you see them working. First, create the buttons you'll need to add and delete records and navigate the database on the Contact Detail form:

1. Launch Constructor.
2. Open Contacts.rsrc in the Src folder of your Contacts project folder.
3. Select the Contact Detail form and double-click on it to open it.
4. Select Window | Catalog to bring up the Catalog window.
5. Drag three labels over to the Contact Detail form. Set their attributes according to this table:

Left Origin	Top Origin	Text
20	15	First Name:
21	30	Last Name:
2	45	Phone Number:

NOTE: The way I came up with the Left Origin Numbers for these titles is I selected them all using SHIFT-left mouse click, then I selected Arrange | Align Right Edges from the Constructor menu.

6. Drag two more fields over to the Contact Detail form. Set all three fields' attributes according to this table:

Object Identifier	Left Origin	Top Origin	Width	Max Characters	Auto Shift
FirstName	80	15	79	15	Yes
LastName	80	30	79	15	Yes
PhoneNumber	80	45	79	15	No

7. Drag six buttons over to the Contact Detail form. Set their attributes according to this table:

Object Identifier	Left Origin	Top Origin	Width	Max Characters
First	1	130	28	First
Prev	45	130	28	Prev
Next	88	130	28	Next
Last	131	130	28	Last
Delete	103	146	36	Delete
New	53	146	36	New

NOTE: I used another trick to find out how to space the buttons horizontally. I selected the First, Prev, Next, and Last buttons using SHIFT-click, and then I selected Arrange | Spread Horizontally from the menu.

When you're done, your Contact Detail form should look like Figure 5-1.

Creating Some Alerts
You will need to add an alert to handle the case where the ROM revision of the Palm device is less than version 2.0 (Pilot 1000, Pilot 5000). Here are the steps:

1. Select the Alert resources and press CTRL-K to create a new alert.

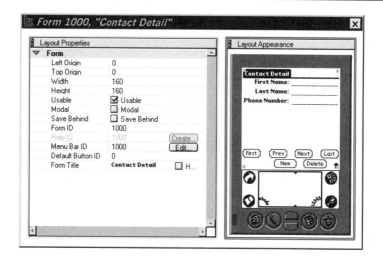

What your
Contact Detail
form should
look like after
adding all
the stuff

Figure 5-1.

5

2. Click on the name and change it from Untitled to
   LowROMVersionError.

3. Double-click on the new alert to open it.

4. Change the Alert Type attribute to Error.

5. Change the Title attribute to Fatal Error.

6. Change the Message attribute to "The version of Palm device you have
   can't run this software. Please upgrade your Palm device." Your new alert
   should look like the one in Figure 5-2.

You will also need to add an alert to handle the case where a new database
can't be created. Here are the steps:

1. Select the Alert resources and press CTRL-K to create a new alert.

2. Click on the name and change it from untitled to DBCreationError.

3. Double-click on the new alert to open it.

4. Change the Alert Type attribute to Error.

5. Change the Title attribute to Fatal Error.

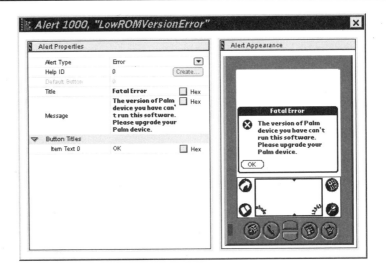

The LowROM-
VersionError
alert

Figure 5-2.

6. Change the Message attribute to "The Contacts database could not be created. Please free up some memory." Your new alert should look like the one in Figure 5-3.

7. Close and save Contacts.rsrc.

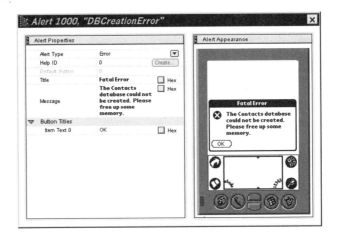

The
DBCreation-
Error alert

Figure 5-3.

Additions to Contacts.c

I'll go though the additions and changes to Contacts.c to support the new database one by one. A complete modified listing appears at the end of this section.

First we have some definitions for a ROM version check we're going to put into **PilotMain()**. The new code will make sure the version of the Palm OS we are running is high enough.

```
// CH.5 Constants for ROM revision
#define ROM_VERSION_2      0x02003000
#define ROM_VERSION_MIN    ROM_VERSION_2
```

 NOTE: I found out what number to use for ROM_VERSION_2 in the Palm OS SDK Reference (Reference.pdf in your CodeWarrior Documentation folder). The information is on page 1012. This particular document is a very handy reference for practically everything in this book.

5

The prototypes for six new utility functions appear at the top of the file. The function **newRecord()** creates a new record for the database. The function **getObject()** is a combination of **FrmGetObjectIndex()** and **FrmGetObjectPtr()**. The function **setFields()** copies the contents of a database record to the three fields on the Contact Detail form. The function **getFields()** fills a database record from the same fields. The function **setText()** sets the text in a field. The function **getText()** gets text from a field and puts it in a locked database record. We will walk through each of these functions and understand them completely later on.

```
// CH.4 Prototypes for utility functions
static void     newRecord( void );
static VoidPtr  getObject( FormPtr, Word );
static void     setFields( void );
static void     getFields( void );
static void     setText( FieldPtr, CharPtr );
static void     getText( FieldPtr, VoidPtr, Word );
```

Five new variables support our use of the database. The variable *contactsDB* allows us to operate on the database once it is open. The variable *numRecords* is the current number of records in the database. The variable *cursor* identifies the current record shown on the Contact Detail form. The variable *isDirty* defines whether the current record has been modified. This allows us to mark the record for synchronizing without marking records that haven't been modified. The variable *hrecord* contains the handle to our current record if there is one.

```
// CH.5 Our open database reference
static DmOpenRef   contactsDB;
static ULong       numRecords;
static UInt        cursor;
static Boolean     isDirty;
static VoidHand    hrecord;
```

The database record length of our database is fixed (although it need not be in Palm OS). The starting point of each field in the record must be carefully defined in order for data to be stored in the record correctly. To make this task easier, a number of constants have been defined.

```
// CH.5 Constants that define the database record
#define DB_ID_START            0
#define DB_ID_SIZE             (sizeof( ULong ))
#define DB_DATE_TIME_START     (DB_ID_START +\
                               DB_ID_SIZE)
#define DB_DATE_TIME_SIZE      (sizeof( DateTimeType ))
#define DB_FIRST_NAME_START    (DB_DATE_TIME_START +\
                               DB_DATE_TIME_SIZE)
#define DB_FIRST_NAME_SIZE     16
#define DB_LAST_NAME_START     (DB_FIRST_NAME_START +\
                               DB_FIRST_NAME_SIZE)
#define DB_LAST_NAME_SIZE      16
#define DB_PHONE_NUMBER_START  (DB_LAST_NAME_START +\
                               DB_LAST_NAME_SIZE)
#define DB_PHONE_NUMBER_SIZE   16
#define DB_RECORD_SIZE         (DB_PHONE_NUMBER_START +\
                               DB_PHONE_NUMBER_SIZE)
```

As you can see, each field in the database record has a starting point and a size defined. In addition, a size is defined for the entire record.

At the top of **PilotMain()**, where we used to allocate the memory chunk we played with in earlier chapters, we now create and initialize the database. Before that code, however, we need to add code that checks the version of the Palm device we're operating on.

Several of the database functions, especially the ones for sorting, are changed from version 1.0 of the Palm OS. For this reason, we want to add code that will limit us to operating on version 2.0 or above devices.

```
// CH.5 Get the ROM version
romVersion = 0;
FtrGet( sysFtrCreator, sysFtrNumROMVersion, &romVersion );

// CH.5 If we are below our minimum acceptable ROM revision
if( romVersion < ROM_VERSION_MIN )
{
    // CH.5 Display the alert
    FrmAlert( LowROMVersionErrorAlert );

    // CH.5 Palm OS 1.0 will continuously re-launch this app
    // unless we switch to another safe one
    if( romVersion < ROM_VERSION_2 )
    {
        AppLaunchWithCommand( sysFileCDefaultApp,
                sysAppLaunchCmdNormalLaunch, NULL );
    }
    return( 0 );
}

// CH.2 If this is not a normal launch, don't launch
if( cmd != sysAppLaunchCmdNormalLaunch )
    return( 0 );
```

First comes the attempt to create the database. This call insures that there is a database to open below. Here is where we make the call to the new alert that reports a database creation error. If a database already exists, we move on.

```
// CH.5 Create a new database in case there isn't one
if( ((error = DmCreateDatabase( 0, "ContactsDB", 'PPGU',
        'ctct',
        false )) != dmErrAlreadyExists) &&
        (error != 0) )
{
    // CH.5 Handle db creation error
    FrmAlert( DBCreationErrorAlert );
    return( 0 );
}

// CH.5 Open the database
contactsDB = DmOpenDatabaseByTypeCreator( 'ctct', 'PPGU',
        dmModeReadWrite );
```

IN DEPTH

Creator IDs

The two constants you see in the call to **DmCreateDatabase()** have special significance. They are meant to uniquely identify your application's databases so that other applications don't try to open and modify them by accident.

The main ID is the first one: 'PPGU,' called the Creator ID. This identifies the application or group of applications that created the database. The second ID can be anything you want. I chose 'ctct' to stand for "Contacts."

Note the single quotes around both these constants. Mac programmers will be familiar with this type of constant, but it's unknown in the Windows world. Mac resources are identified using these four character constants, and Palm OS creator IDs follow this same pattern. These four bytes are turned into a single 32-bit number by the compiler.

To make sure the creator ID you use for your applications is unique, you must register your creator ID on Palm Computing's Web site at **http://www.palm.com/devzone/crid/cridsub.html**. I registered the creator ID 'PPGU' for use by the examples in this book. You can feel free to use this creator ID until you register one of your own.

The new or existing database is opened by this call. It is guaranteed to work because if we get here it means a database exists. We store the database reference *contactsDB* for future calls involving the database.

```
// CH.5 Get the number of records in the database
numRecords = DmNumRecords( contactsDB );

// CH.5 Initialize the record number
cursor = 0;

// CH.5 If there are no records, create one
if( numRecords == 0 )
    newRecord();
```

Accessing nonexistent records will crash Palm OS, so you must keep careful track of the records and insure in your code that you are always referring to a legitimate record in your database. One way to do this is shown above. The *numRecords* variable is initialized. This gives you the boundaries within which you can address records. The first record in a database is always record zero, so we initialize *cursor* to zero to insure that we are sitting on a good record, even if we only have one record in the database. In case there are no records, a record is created with a call to **newRecord()**.

```
// CH.5 Close all open forms
FrmCloseAllForms();

// CH.5 Close the database
DmCloseDatabase( contactsDB );
```

5

On the way out of the application, records should be freed and the database should be closed for proper future operation. To release the last record, we now respond to the *frmCloseEvent* again in the Contact Detail event handler function. This event is usually sent whenever we change forms. To make sure it is sent for any still-open forms, it is a very good idea to put a call to **FrmCloseAllForms()** in the ending code.

Once this call is made, we can be sure that all database records have been released. We then call **DmCloseDatabase()** to close our database.

The newRecord() Function

Now let's jump down past the event handler routines and examine the new utility functions that have been added. The function **newRecord()** adds a new record to the database at the current index position defined by the variable *cursor*.

```
// CH.5 This function creates and initializes a new record
static void newRecord( void )
{
    VoidPtr     precord;     // CH.5 Pointer to the record

    // CH.5 Create the database record and get a handle to it
    hrecord = DmNewRecord( contactsDB, &cursor, DB_RECORD_SIZE );

    // CH.5 Lock down the record to modify it
    precord = MemHandleLock( hrecord );

    // CH.5 Clear the record
```

```
DmSet( precord, 0, DB_RECORD_SIZE, 0 );

// CH.5 Unlock the record
MemHandleUnlock( hrecord );

// CH.5 Clear the busy bit and set the dirty bit
DmReleaseRecord( contactsDB, cursor, true );

// CH.5 Increment the total record count
numRecords++;

// CH.5 Set the dirty bit
isDirty = true;

// CH.5 We're done
return;
}
```

The function starts with a call to **DmNewRecord()**, which actually creates the record in the database. The record may be filled with garbage at this point, however. It needs to be initialized so that the fields display a blank string instead of garbage. So, as we did in Chapter 2 with the memory chunk we allocated, we lock down the record and set its initial value. In this case we fill the record with zeroes. Note that we use a special function call **DmSet()** to write to this memory instead of writing the zeroes literally or using **StrCopy()**. This is because storage memory, where databases live, is specially protected against corruption and can only be changed using functions like **DmSet()**. To write a specific string into this record instead of all zeroes you could have used **DmWrite()**.

The return value of **DmNewRecord()** should always be checked to make sure that it is not zero, although we aren't checking it in this example. A value of zero would mean that the Palm device was out of memory. I will correct this oversight in Chapter 7 where I will introduce a comprehensive fatal-error handling strategy.

The call to **DmReleaseRecord()**, as it did in the *frmCloseEvent* handler earlier, frees the record for a subsequent **DmGetRecord() or DmQueryRecord()**. The variable *numRecords* is incremented because a record was just added to the database. The *isDirty* bit is set here so that we can set up the field for immediate data entry in the **attachFields()** call you'll see below.

The getObject() Function

The **getObject()** function is a time-saving function that just combines **FrmGetObjectIndex()** and **FrmGetObjectPtr()**, both of which we have seen before. Since we need pointers to fields and other controls a lot, this utility function will make our present and future code smaller and therefore, hopefully, easier to read.

```
// CH.5 A time saver: Gets object pointers based on their ID
static VoidPtr getObject( FormPtr form, Word objectID )
{
    Word    index;  // CH.5 The object index

    // CH.5 Get the index
    index = FrmGetObjectIndex( form, objectID );

    // CH.5 Return the pointer
    return( FrmGetObjectPtr( form, index ) );
}
```

Fields and Database Records

Most computer systems have RAM, where temporary data is stored, and a hard disk, where data is stored permanently. Since RAM is much faster than the hard disk, much of the programmer's job involves reading things efficiently off of the hard disk and writing new or modified information back on to the hard disk.

Since everything in the Palm device is always in memory, and therefore equally fast to access, it saves the most time to move things around as little as possible. Ideally, nothing would ever be moved in Palm memory because everything can be read with equal speed, so there is no advantage to moving data to any particular place in order to access it more quickly, as there is in most other computers.

On a personal computer, we would handle databases by allocating memory in RAM for a new record, then saving that record in the database on the hard disk when we were done with it. The efficient thing for us to do on a Palm device is to allocate a record in permanent storage and write directly into it. Palm OS makes it easy to extend this paradigm to visual controls by providing function calls like **FldSetText()** that allow you to directly attach a portion of a database record to an edit field. This is called editing in place.

Unfortunately, as of the latest revision of Palm OS, there are two major restrictions to editing in place. First of all, you can only attach one field to a given record at any given time. If you attach more than one field to a single record, it seems to work for a while, but eventually your application will lock up. Secondly, any portions of your record that come after a field that you edit in place will be zeroed out occasionally. This can be a mystifying thing to track down in your code, so when you are designing your database record, remember to put your edit-in-place field at the end of the record.

Given the extremely restrictive nature of editing in place in Palm OS, we can't use it for the work we must do in Contacts. However, keep it (and especially its restrictions) in mind if you have a single large edit field such as the one found in the built-in application Memo Pad.

The setFields() Function

In the **setFields()** function, the current database record is copied into the three edit fields we have on the Contact Detail form.

```
// CH.5 Gets the current database record and displays it
// in the detail fields
static void setFields( void )
{
    FormPtr     form;        // CH.5 The contact detail form
    CharPtr     precord;     // CH.5 A record pointer
    Word        index;       // CH.5 The object index

    // CH.5 Get the contact detail form pointer
    form = FrmGetActiveForm();

    // CH.5 Get the current record
    hrecord = DmQueryRecord( contactsDB, cursor );
    precord = MemHandleLock( hrecord );

    // CH.5 Set the text for the First Name field
    setText( getObject( form, ContactDetailFirstNameField ),
            precord + DB_FIRST_NAME_START );

    // CH.5 Set the text for the Last Name field
    setText( getObject( form, ContactDetailLastNameField ),
            precord + DB_LAST_NAME_START );

    // CH.5 Set the text for the Phone Number field
    setText( getObject( form, ContactDetailPhoneNumberField ),
            precord + DB_PHONE_NUMBER_START );
```

```
MemHandleUnlock( hrecord );

// CH.5 If the record is already dirty, it's new, so set the focus
if( isDirty )
{
        // CH.3 Get the index of our field
                index = FrmGetObjectIndex( form,
                ContactDetailFirstNameField );

        // CH.3 Set the focus to the First Name field
        FrmSetFocus( form, index );

        // CH.5 Set upper shift on
        GrfSetState( false, false, true );
}

// CH.5 We're done
return;
}
```

First, we get the active form and the record. For each of the three fields, **setText()** is called to copy the appropriate portion of the database record to the field.

TIP: Getting a record. There are two ways you can get an existing record. One is by using the function **DmGetRecord()** and the other is by using **DmQueryRecord()**. The problem with **DmGetRecord()** is that you have to remember to call **DmReleaseRecord()** when you are done with the record, so it is harder to use. If you forget to call **DmReleaseRecord()**, the next time you try to get a handle to that record, you'll get zero instead.

For the special case of a new record, which we can tell because the dirty bit is already set, we want to set up the cursor in the First Name field. We set focus here just as we did in Chapter 3. We must add a call to **SetGrfState()** to set upper shift on. This is because if we set focus to this field, it will not set the upper shift on even if we've marked its Auto Shift attribute to get it to capitalize the first letter. In order to call **SetGrfState()**, we'll have to include the file for the graffiti manager just below the include for Pilot.h:

```
// CH.5 Added for the call to GrfSetState()
#include <Graffiti.h>
```

The getFields() Function

The function **getFields()** collects the data that may have been entered in the fields and transfers it to the current database record.

```
// CH.5 Wipes out field references to the record and releases it
static void detachFields( void )
{
    FormPtr form;    // CH.5 The contact detail form

    // CH.5 Get the contact detail form pointer
    form = FrmGetActiveForm();

    // CH.5 Turn off focus
    FrmSetFocus( form, -1 );

    // CH.5 If the record has been modified
    if( isDirty )
    {
        CharPtr    precord;    // CH.5 Points to the DB record

        // CH.5 Lock the record
        precord = MemHandleLock( hrecord );

        // CH.5 Get the text for the First Name field
        getText( getObject( form, ContactDetailFirstNameField ),
                precord, DB_FIRST_NAME_START );

        // CH.5 Get the text for the Last Name field
        getText( getObject( form, ContactDetailLastNameField ),
                precord, DB_LAST_NAME_START );

        // CH.5 Get the text for the Phone Number field
        getText( getObject( form, ContactDetailPhoneNumberField ),
                precord, DB_PHONE_NUMBER_START );

        // CH.5 Unlock the record
        MemHandleUnlock( hrecord );
    }

    // CH.5 Reset the dirty bit
    isDirty = false;

    // CH.5 We're done
    return;
}
```

First, we remove focus from the field it is on. This means that the user will have to tap on a field and thus mark the record dirty if an edit occurs.

Next, we gather the data from the fields and put it in our database record provided it has been changed.

After this, we clear the *isDirty* bit. Otherwise, all records would be marked dirty after the first modified record. The dirty bit will be set again only by the user tapping in an edit field or by **newRecord()**.

The setText() Function

The function **setText()** gets passed a string and a field pointer and puts that string in the field much as we put the string resource in the field in Chapter 3.

5

```
// CH.5 Set the text in a field
static void setText( FieldPtr field, CharPtr text )
{
    VoidHand    hfield; // CH.5 Handle of field text
    CharPtr     pfield; // CH.5 Pointer to field text

    // CH.5 Get the current field handle
    hfield = FldGetTextHandle( field );

    // CH.5 If we have a handle
    if( hfield != NULL )
    {
        // CH.5 Resize it
        MemHandleResize( hfield, StrLen( text ) + 1 );
    }

    else
    // CH.5 Allocate a handle for the string
        hfield = MemHandleNew( StrLen( text ) + 1 );

    // CH.5 Lock it
    pfield = MemHandleLock( hfield );

    // CH.5 Copy the string
    StrCopy( pfield, text );

    // CH.5 Unlock it
    MemHandleUnlock( hfield );

    // CH.5 Give it to the field
    FldSetTextHandle( field, hfield );
```

```
// CH.5 Draw the field
FldDrawField( field );

// CH.5 We're done
return;
}
```

First we get the field's handle. If the field has a handle, we resize it to fit the string. If it doesn't have a handle, we allocate one for it of the appropriate size. It is dangerous to resize or allocate memory without checking for success, so we are doing something bad here just as we are in **newRecord()**. We will fix this lack of error checking in Chapter 7 when we talk about the Error Manager.

After we have a handle of the correct size, we go through some code you've seen before. We lock down the handle, copy the string, unlock the handle, and give it to the field. Finally we draw the field so that it will reflect the change.

The getText() Function
The function getText() copies the contents of a field to a database record.

```
// CH.5 Get the text from a field
static void getText( FieldPtr field, VoidPtr precord, Word offset )
{
    CharPtr    pfield; // CH.5 Pointer to field text

    // CH.5 Get the text pointer
    pfield = FldGetTextPtr( field );

    // CH.5 Copy it
    DmWrite( precord, offset, pfield, StrLen( pfield ) );

    // CH.5 We're done
    return;
}
```

First we get a pointer to the field string. This is the field's internal pointer, so don't unlock it! We use DmWrite() to copy the field string into the database record at the given offset. We know this copy will work because we have limited the number of characters that can be entered into the field and we have sized each entry in the record accordingly. That's why there is no further error checking.

Additions to the contactDetailHandleEvent() Function

In the first case statement, the *frmOpenEvent* case statement, add a call to **setFields()** after **FrmDrawForm()** to copy the current record to the fields. This should happen after **FrmDrawForm()** only because you wouldn't want to draw the fields before you draw the rest of the form. Drawing controls before the form can cause trouble.

```
// CH.4 Form open event
case frmOpenEvent:
{
    // CH.2 Draw the form
    FrmDrawForm( form );

    // CH.5 Draw the database fields
    setFields();
}
break;
```

There are a several new events being handled. The first new one is *frmCloseEvent*.

```
// CH.5 Form close event
case frmCloseEvent:
{
    // CH.5 Store away any modified fields
    getFields();
}
break;
```

This gets any last-minute modifications to the fields before they are destroyed by the closure of the form.

Next, we deal with the button event we have seen in the past: *ctlSelectEvent*. This time we need to know which of many possible buttons was pressed. To tell the buttons apart we use a switch statement and case statements depending on the *controlID* found in the *event* data structure.

```
// CH.5 Parse the button events
case ctlSelectEvent:
{

    // CH.5 Store any field changes
    getFields();

    switch( event->data.ctlSelect.controlID )
```

5

```
{
    // CH.5 First button
    case ContactDetailFirstButton:
    {
        // CH.5 Set the cursor to the first record
        if( cursor > 0 )
            cursor = 0;
    }
    break;
```

The first button we handle is, appropriately, the First button. This button should make us go to the first record in the database. For all button commands, we call **getFields()** to make sure the current record contains all the changes before potentially moving on to a new record. In the case statement, we set *cursor* to the first record. After all the case statements, we will call **setFields()**, which will get the new current record and copy it to the fields.

The next button we tackle is the Previous button—that is, the button that takes the user back one record.

```
    // CH.5 Previous button
    case ContactDetailPrevButton:
    {
        // CH.5 Move the cursor back one record
        if( cursor > 0 )
            cursor--;
    }
    break;
```

Again there is a check to make sure we're not on the first record, which would preclude going back any more. Then we move back one record and attach this new record to the fields.

After that we handle the Next button.

```
    // CH.5 Next button
    case ContactDetailNextButton:
    {
        // CH.5 Move the cursor up one record
        if( cursor < (numRecords - 1) )
            cursor++;
    }
    break;
```

This block of code is similar to the previous button handlers. This time we check to make sure we're not on the last record, which would prevent us from moving up a record. If everything is okay, we move up a record.

The reason why so much care is taken to validate the variable *cursor* is that if you do a **DmQueryRecord()** call on a nonexistent record, it's an immediate crash situation. Therefore, you need to make sure the variable you use for indexing always contains a valid value.

Now we'll look at the code for the Last button, the button that makes us go to the last record in the database.

```
// CH.5 Last button
case ContactDetailLastButton:
{
    // CH.5 Move the cursor to the last record
    if( cursor < (numRecords - 1) )
        cursor = numRecords - 1;
}
break;
```

This code is very similar to the previous navigation buttons. Note that the last record has the actual index of *numRecords* minus one since the first record starts at zero.

The Delete button is next:

```
// CH.5 Delete button
case ContactDetailDeleteButton:
{
    // CH.5 Remove the record from the database
    DmRemoveRecord( contactsDB, cursor );

    // CH.5 Decrease the number of records
    numRecords--;

    // CH.5 Place the cursor at the first record
    cursor = 0;

    // CH.5 If there are no records left, create one
    if( numRecords == 0 )
        newRecord();
}
break;
```

You must also make sure at least one record remains in the database so that **DmQueryRecord()** can succeed and not crash when we call it inside **setFields()**. Therefore, the code checks to see if there are any records left, and if there aren't, it calls **newRecord()** to create one.

It is possible to write an application where a database can validly have no records in it. In this case, you would have to make sure that **DmQueryRecord()** is never called in the case where there are no records.

Finally, we respond to the New button:

```
// CH.5 New button
case ContactDetailNewButton:
{
    // CH.5 Create a new record
    newRecord();
}
break;
}

// CH.5 Sync the current record to the fields
setFields();
}
break;
```

The New button code looks almost like navigation. However, instead of going to another existing record in the database as the navigation buttons do, we create a new record at the current cursor and go to that record. As a result, the record that was at the cursor and any records after it are shifted up by one.

At the end of all the button commands there is a call to **setFields()**. This call gets and copies the current record (which may be a new record or the same old record) to the fields.

There is one more event to look at. We want the database record marked dirty if it is modified. One way to guess that the record has been modified is if an edit field has been selected.

```
// CH.5 Respond to field tap
case fldEnterEvent:
    isDirty = true;
break;
```

Here we set the *isDirty* variable if a field has been tapped.

Debugging

Once you have made all the necessary changes to Contacts.c, you are ready to debug your application:

1. Open the CodeWarrior IDE.
2. Open Contacts.mcp in your Contacts project folder.
3. Select Project | Make. If your code fails to compile or link, check your code against the code listing at the end of the chapter. If you have problems with certain named resources, remember to check in Contacts_res.h to make sure the names match.
4. Synchronize your Palm device so you don't lose any data if you have to reset your device after debugging.
5. Exit HotSync.
6. Once your code is compiling and linking, select Project | Debug. Follow the directions in the dialog to bring up the debugger.

5

Step through your code line by line. You do this by clicking the button at the top of the Debug window that looks like an arrow pointing to a wall to the right. The first time you run, the ContactsDB database will be created, so **DmCreateDatabase()** will return zero. Subsequently, **DmCreateDatabase()** will return 537, which is *dmErrAlreadyExists*.

Set up breakpoints at all the individual button events by clicking on the dash next to the first line inside their respective case statements. These dashes should turn into red dots as you do this. Click the forward arrow to allow the application to free run.

The Contact Detail form should appear. Enter some data into the fields and then click New to get a new record. You should hit the breakpoint you set for the New button.

Step into the **newRecord()** function by stepping to it and then clicking the down arrow button at the top of the Debug window to enter the function. Step through the function and make sure it's working okay. Then hit the run button.

Create a few more records until you have four records in your database. Now test your navigation buttons. As you step through them and assure yourself they're working fine, you can click on the breakpoint red dots again to turn them off and allow your debugged code to run through those areas without stopping.

When your navigation controls, First, Previous, Next, and Last, are all working, try the Delete button. Step through the Delete button code. Delete all the records and make sure a new record is created so that there is always at least one record in the database.

What's Next?

In Chapter 6 we will continue to build the Contacts application. We will add date and time fields and forms to the Contact Detail form, thereby using many new kinds of controls.

Listing

Here is the whole Contacts.c file with all the changes. The additions made in this chapter have comments with CH.5 in them.

```
// CH.2 The super-include for Palm OS
#include <Pilot.h>

// CH.5 Added for the call to GrfSetState()
#include <Graffiti.h>

// CH.3 Our resource file
#include "Contacts_res.h"

// CH.4 Prototypes for our event handler functions
static Boolean          contactDetailHandleEvent( EventPtr event );
static Boolean          aboutHandleEvent( EventPtr event );
static Boolean          menuEventHandler( EventPtr event );

// CH.4 Constants for ROM revision
#define ROM_VERSION_2    0x02003000
#define ROM_VERSION_MIN  ROM_VERSION_2

// CH.5 Prototypes for utility functions
static void             newRecord( void );
static VoidPtr          getObject( FormPtr, Word );
static void             setFields( void );
static void             getFields( void );
static void             setText( FieldPtr, CharPtr );
static void             getText( FieldPtr, VoidPtr, Word );

// CH.5 Our open database reference
static DmOpenRef        contactsDB;
static ULong            numRecords;
static UInt             cursor;
static Boolean          isDirty;
static VoidHand         hrecord;
```

```
// CH.5 Constants that define the database record
#define DB_ID_START              0
#define DB_ID_SIZE               (sizeof( ULong ))
#define DB_DATE_TIME_START       (DB_ID_START +\
                                 DB_ID_SIZE)
#define DB_DATE_TIME_SIZE        (sizeof( DateTimeType ))
#define DB_FIRST_NAME_START      (DB_DATE_TIME_START +\
                                 DB_DATE_TIME_SIZE)
#define DB_FIRST_NAME_SIZE       16
#define DB_LAST_NAME_START       (DB_FIRST_NAME_START +\
                                 DB_FIRST_NAME_SIZE)
#define DB_LAST_NAME_SIZE        16
#define DB_PHONE_NUMBER_START    (DB_LAST_NAME_START +\
                                 DB_LAST_NAME_SIZE)
#define DB_PHONE_NUMBER_SIZE     16
#define DB_RECORD_SIZE           (DB_PHONE_NUMBER_START +\
                                 DB_PHONE_NUMBER_SIZE)

// CH.2 The main entry point
DWord PilotMain( Word cmd, Ptr, Word )
{
    DWord       romVersion;  // CH.5 ROM version
    FormPtr     form;        // CH.2 A pointer to our form structure
    EventType   event;       // CH.2 Our event structure
    Word        error;       // CH.3 Error word

    // CH.5 Get the ROM version
    romVersion = 0;
    FtrGet( sysFtrCreator, sysFtrNumROMVersion, &romVersion );

    // CH.5 If we are below our minimum acceptable ROM revision
    if( romVersion < ROM_VERSION_MIN )
    {
        // CH.5 Display the alert
        FrmAlert( LowROMVersionErrorAlert );

        // CH.5 Palm OS 1.0 will continuously re-launch this app
        // unless we switch to another safe one
        if( romVersion < ROM_VERSION_2 )
        {
            AppLaunchWithCommand( sysFileCDefaultApp,
                    sysAppLaunchCmdNormalLaunch, NULL );
        }
        return( 0 );
    }

    // CH.2 If this is not a normal launch, don't launch
    if( cmd != sysAppLaunchCmdNormalLaunch )
        return( 0 );
```

```
// CH.5 Create a new database in case there isn't one
if( ((error = DmCreateDatabase( 0, "ContactsDB-PPGU", 'PPGU', 'ctct',
        false )) != dmErrAlreadyExists) && (error != 0) )
{
    // CH.5 Handle db creation error
    FrmAlert( DBCreationErrorAlert );
    return( 0 );
}

// CH.5 Open the database
contactsDB = DmOpenDatabaseByTypeCreator( 'ctct', 'PPGU',
        dmModeReadWrite );

// CH.5 Get the number of records in the database
numRecords = DmNumRecords( contactsDB );

// CH.5 Initialize the record number
cursor = 0;

// CH.5 If there are no records, create one
if( numRecords == 0 )
    newRecord();

// CH.4 Go to our starting page
FrmGotoForm( ContactDetailForm );

// CH.2 Our event loop
do
{
    // CH.2 Get the next event
    EvtGetEvent( &event, -1 );

    // CH.2 Handle system events
    if( SysHandleEvent( &event ) )
        continue;

    // CH.3 Handle menu events
    if( MenuHandleEvent( NULL, &event, &error ) )
        continue;

    // CH.4 Handle form load events
    if( event.eType == frmLoadEvent )
    {
        // CH.4 Initialize our form
        switch( event.data.frmLoad.formID )
        {
            // CH.4 Contact Detail form
            case ContactDetailForm:
                form = FrmInitForm( ContactDetailForm );
                FrmSetEventHandler( form, contactDetailHandleEvent );
            break;
```

```
                    // CH.4 About form
                    case AboutForm:
                        form = FrmInitForm( AboutForm );
                        FrmSetEventHandler( form, aboutHandleEvent );
                    break;
                }
                FrmSetActiveForm( form );
            }

            // CH.2 Handle form events
            FrmDispatchEvent( &event );

        // CH.2 If it's a stop event, exit
        } while( event.eType != appStopEvent );

        // CH.5 Close all open forms
        FrmCloseAllForms();

        // CH.5 Close the database
        DmCloseDatabase( contactsDB );

        // CH.2 We're done
        return( 0 );
    }

// CH.4 Our Contact Detail form handler function
static Boolean contactDetailHandleEvent( EventPtr event )
{
    FormPtr     form;          // CH.3 A pointer to our form structure

    // CH.3 Get our form pointer
    form = FrmGetActiveForm();

    // CH.4 Parse events
    switch( event->eType )
    {
        // CH.4 Form open event
        case frmOpenEvent:
        {
            // CH.2 Draw the form
            FrmDrawForm( form );

            // CH.5 Draw the database fields
            setFields();
        }
        break;

        // CH.5 Form close event
        case frmCloseEvent:
        {
```

```
        // CH.5 Store away any modified fields
        getFields();
}
break;

// CH.5 Parse the button events
case ctlSelectEvent:
{
        // CH.5 Store any field changes
        getFields();

        switch( event->data.ctlSelect.controlID )
        {
            // CH.5 First button
            case ContactDetailFirstButton:
            {
                // CH.5 Set the cursor to the first record
                if( cursor > 0 )
                    cursor = 0;
            }
            break;

            // CH.5 Previous button
            case ContactDetailPrevButton:
            {
                // CH.5 Move the cursor back one record
                if( cursor > 0 )
                    cursor—;
            }
            break;

            // CH.5 Next button
            case ContactDetailNextButton:
            {
                // CH.5 Move the cursor up one record
                if( cursor < (numRecords - 1) )
                    cursor++;
            }
            break;

            // CH.5 Last button
            case ContactDetailLastButton:
            {
                // CH.5 Move the cursor to the last record
                if( cursor < (numRecords - 1) )
                    cursor = numRecords - 1;
            }
            break;

            // CH.5 Delete button
            case ContactDetailDeleteButton:
```

```
                        {
                            // CH.5 Remove the record from the database
                            DmRemoveRecord( contactsDB, cursor );

                            // CH.5 Decrease the number of records
                            numRecords-;

                            // CH.5 Place the cursor at the first record
                            cursor = 0;

                            // CH.5 If there are no records left, create one
                            if( numRecords == 0 )
                                newRecord();
                        }
                        break;

                        // CH.5 New button
                        case ContactDetailNewButton:
                        {
                            // CH.5 Create a new record
                            newRecord();
                        }
                        break;
                    }

                    // CH.5 Sync the current record to the fields
                    setFields();
                }
                break;

                // CH.5 Respond to field tap
                case fldEnterEvent:
                    isDirty = true;
                break;

                // CH.3 Parse menu events
                case menuEvent:
                    return( menuEventHandler( event ) );
                break;
        }

    // CH.2 We're done
    return( false );
}

// CH.4 Our About form event handler function
static Boolean aboutHandleEvent( EventPtr event )
{
    FormPtr        form;        // CH.4 A pointer to our form structure

    // CH.4 Get our form pointer
```

```
    form = FrmGetActiveForm();

    // CH.4 Respond to the Open event
    if( event->eType == frmOpenEvent )
    {
        // CH.4 Draw the form
        FrmDrawForm( form );
    }

    // CH.4 Return to the calling form
    if( event->eType == ctlSelectEvent )
    {
        FrmReturnToForm( 0 );

        // CH.4 Always return true in this case
        return( true );
    }

    // CH.4 We're done
    return( false );
}

// CH.3 Handle menu events
Boolean menuEventHandler( EventPtr event )
{
    FormPtr     form;       // CH.3 A pointer to our form structure
    Word        index;      // CH.3 A general purpose control index
    FieldPtr    field;      // CH.3 Used for manipulating fields

    // CH.3 Get our form pointer
    form = FrmGetActiveForm();

    // CH.3 Erase the menu status from the display
    MenuEraseStatus( NULL );

    // CH.4 Handle options menu
    if( event->data.menu.itemID == OptionsAboutContacts )
    {
        // CH.4 Pop up the About form as a Dialog
        FrmPopupForm( AboutForm );
        return( true );
    }

    // CH.3 Handle graffiti help
    if( event->data.menu.itemID == EditGraffitiHelp )
    {
        // CH.3 Pop up the graffiti reference based on
        // the graffiti state
        SysGraffitiReferenceDialog( referenceDefault );
        return( true );
    }
```

```c
// CH.3 Get the index of our field
index = FrmGetFocus( form );

// CH.3 If there is no field selected, we're done
if( index == noFocus )
    return( false );

// CH.3 Get the pointer of our field
field = FrmGetObjectPtr( form, index );

// CH.3 Do the edit command
switch( event->data.menu.itemID )
{
    // CH.3 Undo
    case EditUndo:
        FldUndo( field );
    break;

    // CH.3 Cut
    case EditCut:
        FldCut( field );
    break;

    // CH.3 Copy
    case EditCopy:
        FldCopy( field );
    break;

    // CH.3 Paste
    case EditPaste:
        FldPaste( field );
    break;

    // CH.3 Select All
    case EditSelectAll:
    {
        // CH.3 Get the length of the string in the field
        Word length = FldGetTextLength( field );

        // CH.3 Sound an error if appropriate
        if( length == 0 )
        {
            SndPlaySystemSound( sndError );
            return( false );
        }

        // CH.3 Select the whole string
        FldSetSelection( field, 0, length );
    }
    break;
```

```
        // CH.3 Bring up the keyboard tool
        case EditKeyboard:
            SysKeyboardDialogV10();
        break;
    }

    // CH.3 We're done
    return( true );
}

// CH.5 This function creates and initializes a new record
static void newRecord( void )
{
    VoidPtr      precord;      // CH.5 Pointer to the record

    // CH.5 Create the database record and get a handle to it
    hrecord = DmNewRecord( contactsDB, &cursor, DB_RECORD_SIZE );

    // CH.5 Lock down the record to modify it
    precord = MemHandleLock( hrecord );

    // CH.5 Clear the record
    DmSet( precord, 0, DB_RECORD_SIZE, 0 );

    // CH.5 Unlock the record
    MemHandleUnlock( hrecord );

    // CH.5 Clear the busy bit and set the dirty bit
    DmReleaseRecord( contactsDB, cursor, true );

    // CH.5 Increment the total record count
    numRecords++;

    // CH.5 Set the dirty bit
    isDirty = true;

    // CH.5 We're done
    return;
}

// CH.5 A time saver: Gets object pointers based on their ID
static VoidPtr getObject( FormPtr form, Word objectID )
{
    Word         index;        // CH.5 The object index

    // CH.5 Get the index
    index = FrmGetObjectIndex( form, objectID );

    // CH.5 Return the pointer
    return( FrmGetObjectPtr( form, index ) );
```

```
    }

    // CH.5 Gets the current database record and displays it
    // in the detail fields
    static void setFields( void )
    {
        FormPtr     form;        // CH.5 The contact detail form
        CharPtr     precord;     // CH.5 A record pointer
        Word        index;       // CH.5 The object index

        // CH.5 Get the contact detail form pointer
        form = FrmGetActiveForm();

        // CH.5 Get the current record
        hrecord = DmQueryRecord( contactsDB, cursor );
        precord = MemHandleLock( hrecord );

        // CH.5 Set the text for the First Name field
        setText( getObject( form, ContactDetailFirstNameField ),
                precord + DB_FIRST_NAME_START );

        // CH.5 Set the text for the Last Name field
        setText( getObject( form, ContactDetailLastNameField ),
                precord + DB_LAST_NAME_START );

        // CH.5 Set the text for the Phone Number field
        setText( getObject( form, ContactDetailPhoneNumberField ),
                precord + DB_PHONE_NUMBER_START );
        MemHandleUnlock( hrecord );

        // CH.5 If the record is already dirty, it's new, so set the focus
        if( isDirty )
        {
            // CH.3 Get the index of our field
            index = FrmGetObjectIndex( form, ContactDetailFirstNameField );

            // CH.3 Set the focus to the First Name field
            FrmSetFocus( form, index );

            // CH.5 Set upper shift on
            GrfSetState( false, false, true );
        }

        // CH.5 We're done
        return;
    }

    // CH.5 Wipes out field references to the record and releases it
    void getFields( void )
    {
        FormPtr     form;        // CH.5 The contact detail form
```

```
    // CH.5 Get the contact detail form pointer
    form = FrmGetActiveForm();

    // CH.5 Turn off focus
    FrmSetFocus( form, -1 );
    // CH.5 If the record has been modified
    if( isDirty )
    {
        CharPtr     precord;     // CH.5 Points to the DB record

        // CH.5 Lock the record
        precord = MemHandleLock( hrecord );

        // CH.5 Get the text for the First Name field
        getText( getObject( form, ContactDetailFirstNameField ),
                precord, DB_FIRST_NAME_START );

        // CH.5 Get the text for the Last Name field
        getText( getObject( form, ContactDetailLastNameField ),
                precord, DB_LAST_NAME_START );

        // CH.5 Get the text for the Phone Number field
        getText( getObject( form, ContactDetailPhoneNumberField ),
                precord, DB_PHONE_NUMBER_START );

        // CH.5 Unlock the record
        MemHandleUnlock( hrecord );
    }

    // CH.5 Reset the dirty bit
    isDirty = false;

    // CH.5 We're done
    return;
}
// CH.5 Set the text in a field
static void setText( FieldPtr field, CharPtr text )
{
    VoidHand    hfield; // CH.5 Handle of field text
    CharPtr     pfield; // CH.5 Pointer to field text

    // CH.5 Get the current field handle
    hfield = FldGetTextHandle( field );

    // CH.5 If we have a handle
    if( hfield != NULL )
    {
        // CH.5 Resize it
        MemHandleResize( hfield, StrLen( text ) + 1 );
    }
```

```
        else
        // CH.5 Allocate a handle for the string
            hfield = MemHandleNew( StrLen( text ) + 1 );

        // CH.5 Lock it
        pfield = MemHandleLock( hfield );

        // CH.5 Copy the string
        StrCopy( pfield, text );

        // CH.5 Unlock it
        MemHandleUnlock( hfield );

        // CH.5 Give it to the field
        FldSetTextHandle( field, hfield );

        // CH.5 Draw the field
        FldDrawField( field );

        // CH.5 We're done
        return;
    }

// CH.5 Get the text from a field
static void getText( FieldPtr field, VoidPtr precord, Word offset )
{
    CharPtr     pfield; // CH.5 Pointer to field text

    // CH.5 Get the text pointer
    pfield = FldGetTextPtr( field );

    // CH.5 Copy it
    DmWrite( precord, offset, pfield, StrLen( pfield ) );

    // CH.5 We're done
    return;
}
```

5

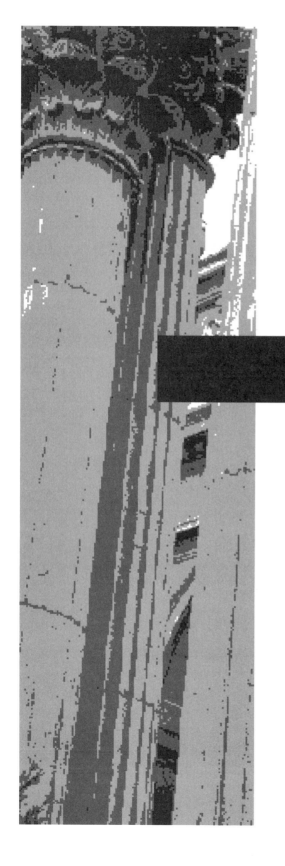

CHAPTER 6

Controls

In this chapter we will extend our Contact Detail form to display and set a date and time. We will add a form that allows us to set the time. This date and time represent an optional date and time to next communicate with the given contact.

You will be using four new resources to make these additions: selector triggers, push buttons, repeating buttons, and checkboxes. These resources, along with buttons, are known collectively as *controls* in Palm OS. Their attributes are similar, and they send the same events when interacted with. They all can have labels. They are all activated with a tap. They all change appearance when tapped, but some only change momentarily.

Save a Copy of Your Project

Before you start modifying your project, it's a good idea to save a copy of it as it stands. If you run into problems you can start again from your stored-away version. Here are the steps:

1. Launch Windows Explorer.
2. Find the folder that your project is stored in.
3. Select it and press CTRL-C to copy the folder.
4. Select a folder to save the copy in.
5. Press CTRL-V to paste a copy of your project into your backup folder.
6. Rename the project to something you will remember. I named mine Contacts CH.5.

Additions to Contacts.rsrc

In this section we'll modify the Contact Detail form to add controls to display the date and time. We will also build a separate form for changing the time. For changing the date, we'll use a standard system dialog provided by Palm OS.

Adding Date and Time Selector Triggers to the Contact Detail Form

Start out by adding two more labels and two selector triggers to the Contact Detail form. You will use these selector triggers to display the date and time of the next call to a given contact in the database. Selector triggers are very much like buttons in terms of the events they send but have a different appearance.

They surround a label with a dotted square. As with buttons, this dotted border or frame surrounds the control with one extra pixel of width and height on all sides that must be accounted for in order for controls to look aligned on the form. The attributes of selector triggers are listed in Table 6-1.

Now add these controls to the form:

1. Launch Constructor.
2. Open the resource file Contacts.rsrc. It is located in the Src folder inside your project folder.
3. Double-click on the Contact Detail form.
4. Bring up the palette of controls by selecting Window | Catalog.

6

Name	Description
Object Identifier	The name Constructor uses for the constant representing the resource ID in the resource include file.
Selector Trigger ID	The resource ID of the selector trigger.
Left Origin	The horizontal position of the left edge of the selector trigger.
Top Origin	The vertical position of the top edge of the selector trigger.
Width	The maximum width of the selector trigger. This is rarely used because the right border shrinks to fit the label text.
Height	The height of the control.
Usable	Defines whether the control is visible and active. If this is not checked, you can subsequently make the control usable via a function call.
Anchor Left	Defines whether the left edge or the right edge of the control shrinks to fit the text if it is changed by a function call at runtime.
Font	The font used to draw the label.
Label	The text of the label itself.

Selector
Trigger
Attributes
Table 6-1.

5. Drag and drop a label onto the Contact Detail form. Change the label text to Next Call Date. Place it under the Phone Number label. A Left Origin of 0 and a Top Origin of 60 work well for this label. Make the text bold.

6. Drag and drop a selector trigger onto the Contact Detail form. Set the Object Identifier to Date. Set the Left Origin to 81 and the Top Origin to 60. Set the Width to 78. Put ten spaces in the label. This will make the selector trigger wide enough by default to be tapped with a finger.

7. Drag and drop another label onto the Contact Detail form. Change the label text to Next Call Time. Place it under the Next Call Date label. A Left Origin of 12 and a Top Origin of 80 work well. Make the text bold.

8. Drag and drop another selector trigger onto the Contact Detail form. Set the Object Identifier to Time. Set the Left Origin to 81 and the Top Origin to 80. Set the Width to 78. Put ten spaces in this label as well.

9. The Contact Detail form should look like the one shown in Figure 6-1. Click on the X in the upper-right corner to close the Contact Detail form. You're done modifying it for now.

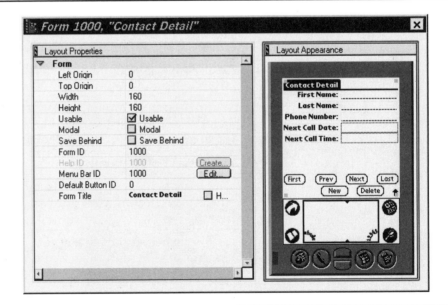

The Contact Detail form

Figure 6-1.

Creating the Enter Time Form

Now create a form for entering the time:

1. Click Forms in the resource list and press CTRL-K to create a new form.
2. Click on the name and rename the form to Enter Time.
3. Double-click on the Enter Time form to open it for editing.
4. First set the form attributes. Check the Modal and Save Behind attributes. We will launch this form as a pop-up form just like the About form.
5. This form will be our first form that doesn't fill the whole screen. Change its Width to 156 and its Height to 53.
6. To make the modal borders visible, we need to leave two pixels between the edge of the form and the edge of the screen, thus the Width of 156. Place the Left Origin at 2 and the Top Origin at 105. This allows two pixels on all sides.
7. Change the Form Title attribute to Enter Time.

6

Adding Push Buttons to the Enter Time Form

Push buttons are square buttons with a solid border that can express an "on" state by showing a dark face and light text instead of the usual light face and dark text. We use them here to show the hours, minutes, and AM/PM. Push buttons always have borders that are one pixel wide that you must account for when positioning them. The attributes of push buttons are shown in Table 6-2.

Add some push buttons to the Enter Time form:

1. Drag and drop a push button onto the Enter Time form.
2. Since this push button will display the hours, make the Object Identifier Hours. Place the push button at Left Origin = 5 and Top Origin = 17. Give it a Width of 18. Give it a Group ID of 1. Give it a Bold font. Erase the Label text.
3. Duplicate the Hours push button. Select it and press CTRL-D to duplicate it. Change this push button's Object Identifier to MinuteTens. Place it at Left Origin = 34 and Top Origin = 17. Give it a Width of 12 because it will be holding only one digit.
4. Duplicate the MinuteTens push button. Select it and press CTRL-D to duplicate it. Change the Object Identifier to MinuteOnes. Place it at Left Origin = 50 and Top Origin = 17.

5. Drag and drop another push button onto the Enter Time form. Change the Object Identifier to AM. Place it at Left Origin = 109 and Top Origin = 17. Make its Width 20. Change its Group ID to 2. Make the Label AM.

6. Duplicate the AM push button by pressing CTRL-D. Change the Object Identifier of the new push button to PM. Place it at Left Origin = 130 and Top Origin = 17. Note that the borders of the AM and PM buttons overlap so that there is only a one-pixel-wide border between them. This is how related push buttons should normally be grouped. Change the label to PM.

Name	Description
Object Identifier	The name Constructor uses for the constant representing the resource ID in the resource include file.
Push Button ID	The resource ID of the push button.
Left Origin	The horizontal position of the left edge of the push button.
Top Origin	The vertical position of the top edge of the push button.
Width	The width of the push button.
Height	The height of the push button.
Usable	Defines whether the control is visible and active. If this is not checked, you can subsequently make the control visible and usable via a function call.
Group ID	Affects whether the push button remains highlighted when selected. If this number is zero, the push button toggles between "on" and "off" states when tapped. If the number is nonzero, the push button stays selected when tapped. The number you use for each group should be unique in case you need to use the group numbers in your code.
Font	The font used to draw the label.
Label	The text of the label itself.

Push Button Attributes

Table 6-2.

Adding Repeating Buttons to the Enter Time Form

Repeating buttons send continuous *ctlRepeatEvent* events if the stylus is held down on them for more than half a second. After the first half second, a *ctlRepeatEvent* is sent about every tenth of a second. We will use repeating buttons to make up and down arrows for adjusting the time. Repeating buttons can have a border that surrounds the control and makes it larger just like with buttons. In our example, we won't use borders for these buttons, and in this case, they align like labels and fields. The attributes of repeating buttons are shown in Table 6-3.

Name	Description
Object Identifier	The name Constructor uses for the constant representing the resource ID in the resource include file.
Button ID	The resource ID of the repeating button.
Left Origin	The horizontal position of the left edge of the repeating button.
Top Origin	The vertical position of the top edge of the repeating button.
Width	The width of the repeating button.
Height	The height of the repeating button.
Usable	Defines whether the control is visible and active. If this is not checked, you can subsequently make the control visible and usable via a function call.
Anchor Left	If the button is resized programmatically, it will extend to the right if this attribute is checked.
Frame	If checked, the button will have a border.
Non-Bold Frame	If checked, the border will be one pixel wide instead of two.
Font	The font used to draw the label.
Label	The text of the label itself.

Repeating
Button
Attributes

Table 6-3.

Add an up and a down repeating button to the Enter Time form.

1. Drag and drop a repeating button onto the Enter Time form. Change the Object Identifier to TimeUp. A good position for it is Left Origin = 89 and Top Origin = 15. A good size for it is Width = 11 and Height = 8. Uncheck Frame.

2. Choose a Font of Symbol 7, and check the Hex box on the label. Type in **01**. This will show as blank in the label and on the form, but when you run the code, it will show as an up arrow. Don't be confused by hex 21, which does show up correctly in Constructor. When you run, hex 21 shows up as a little box instead.

3. Duplicate the repeating button by selecting it and pressing CTRL-D. Change the Object Identifier to TimeDown. This one should be placed at Left Origin = 69 and Top Origin = 25. Change the label to hex 02, which will show as a down arrow when you run the program.

Adding a Checkbox to the Enter Time Form

Checkboxes have a little box on the left that can be checked to indicate something. In the case of the Enter Time form, the checkbox will let the user choose not to enter a time at all. Checkboxes have no border, so their alignment is similar to that of a field. The attributes of checkbox controls are shown in Table 6-4.

Now add a checkbox to the Enter Time form:

1. Drag and drop a checkbox from the Catalog window onto the Enter Time form.

2. Change the Object Identifier attribute to NoTime. A good position for this control is Left Origin = 53 and Top Origin = 37. Make the Width 50. Check Selected. Leave the Group ID zero because this checkbox is not grouped. Make the Label NoTime.

Finishing Touches for the Enter Time Form

Now let's add some familiar controls:

1. The hours and minutes look nicer with a colon between them. Drag and drop a label from the Catalog window onto the Enter Time form. Put it at Left Origin = 27 and Top Origin = 17. Make the Font Bold. Add a colon.

Name	Description
Object Identifier	The name Constructor uses for the constant representing the resource ID in the resource include file.
Checkbox ID	The resource ID of the checkbox.
Left Origin	The horizontal position of the left edge of the checkbox.
Top Origin	The vertical position of the top edge of the checkbox.
Width	The width of the checkbox.
Height	The height of the checkbox.
Usable	Defines whether the control is visible and active. If this is not checked, you can subsequently make the control visible and usable via a function call.
Selected	If checked, the checkbox is also checked by default when drawn.
Group ID	Affects whether the checkbox remains checked when selected. If this number is zero, the checkbox toggles between checked and unchecked states when tapped. If the number is nonzero, the checkbox stays checked when tapped. The number you use for each group should be unique in case you need to use the group numbers in your code.
Font	The font used to draw the label.
Label	The text of the label itself.

Checkbox
Attributes
Table 6-4.

2. Every dialog box needs an OK button. Drag and drop a button from the Catalog window onto the Enter Time form. Place it at Left Origin = 5 and Top Origin = 37. Note that a Left Origin of 5 aligns the button with the push buttons above it and gives a left margin of 4 pixels.

3. It's nice to provide a Cancel button. Drag and drop another button onto the form. Change the Object Identifier to Cancel. This one fits at Left Origin = 115 and Top Origin = 37. Change the Label to Cancel.

4. Make the Cancel button the default button for the form. Remember the Button ID of the Cancel button. Display the Enter Time form attributes by clicking anywhere on the background of the form. Type the Button ID of the Cancel Button into the Default Button ID attribute of the form.

You're done making the Enter Time form. Your form should look like the one shown in Figure 6-2. Click on the X in the upper-right corner to close the form. Select File | Save to save your changes.

Additions to Contacts.c

Now we will add code to Contacts.c to support the date and time in the database, the controls, and the new form we just added.

Initializing and Saving the Date and Time in the Database

You will need some variables and constant definitions in order to store and define the date and time and its different states internally and in the database.

```
// CH.6 Storage for the record's date and time in expanded form
static DateTimeType dateTime;
static Word         timeSelect;
#define NO_DATE      0
#define NO_TIME      0x7fff
```

The variable *dateTime* stores the date and time of the record currently being worked on. The Enter Time form will use the variable *timeSelect*. The constants NO_TIME and NO_DATE allow us to use the same variable *dateTime* to express that no date or no time or both are the current choices.

In the function **newRecord()**, add code to set the date and time to an initial state of no date and no time.

```
// CH.6 Initialize the date and time
MemSet( &dateTime, sizeof( dateTime ), 0 );
dateTime.year = NO_DATE;
dateTime.hour = NO_TIME;
DmWrite( precord, DB_DATE_TIME_START, &dateTime,
        sizeof( DateTimeType ) );
```

Notice that we zero out the entire record using **MemSet()**. If we didn't do this, all the fields would have garbage in them and the field functions might even crash because we aren't sending them zero-delimited strings like they'd like to see. Then we use the variable *dateTime* as a temporary variable to initialize the record.

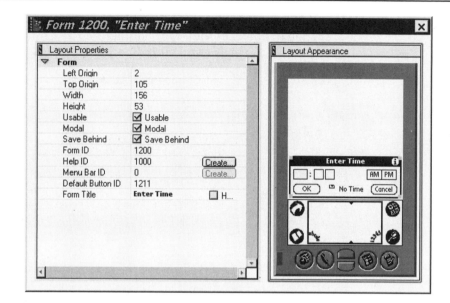

In the function **setFields()**, load the *dateTime* variable from the record.

```
// CH.6 Initialize the date and time variable
precord = MemHandleLock( hrecord );
MemMove( &dateTime, precord + DB_DATE_TIME_START,
         sizeof( dateTime ) );
```

Also, set the appearance of the date and time selector triggers. We will
examine these functions when we talk about the selector triggers.

```
// CH.6 Initialize the date control
setDateTrigger();
```

```
// CH.6 Initialize the time control
setTimeTrigger();
```

6

Supporting the Date and Time Selector Triggers

The first code to add is in the event handler for the Contact Detail form itself. For the date selector trigger you add something like this to your existing button parsing of the *ctlSelectEvent*:

```
// CH.6 Date selector trigger
case ContactDetailDateSelTrigger:
{
    // CH.6 Initialize the date if necessary
    if( dateTime.year == NO_DATE )
    {
        DateTimeType currentDate;

        // CH.6 Get the current date
        TimSecondsToDateTime( TimGetSeconds(),
                &currentDate );

        // CH.6 Copy it
        dateTime.year = currentDate.year;
        dateTime.month = currentDate.month;
        dateTime.day = currentDate.day;
    }

    // CH.6 Pop up the system date selection form
    SelectDay( selectDayByDay, &(dateTime.month),
            &(dateTime.day), &(dateTime.year),
            "Enter Date" );

    // CH.6 Get the record
    hrecord = DmQueryRecord( contactsDB, cursor );

    // CH.6 Lock it down
    precord = MemHandleLock( hrecord );

    // CH.6 Write the date time field
    DmWrite( precord, DB_DATE_TIME_START, &dateTime,
            sizeof( DateTimeType ) );

    // CH.6 Unlock the record
    MemHandleUnlock( hrecord );

    // CH.6 Mark the record dirty
    isDirty = true;
}
break;
```

If no date has been previously defined, define the date to be the current day. The current day is obtained by calling **TimGetSeconds()** and converting its output to a date with a call to **TimSecondsToDateTime()**. These calls are part of the time manager, which is described in the Palm OS literature in Reference.pdf.

Once some starting time is established, you can call the function **SelectDay()** to bring up the Palm OS built-in controls for selecting a date. Once a date has been selected, we lock down the current database record and write the new day value into it.

Selecting a time is somewhat different. There are no Palm OS built-in controls for selecting a single time, so we made our own. We need to pop up our Enter Time form and have it get a time from the user.

```
// CH.6 Time selector trigger
case ContactDetailTimeSelTrigger:
{
    // CH.6 Pop up our selection form
    FrmPopupForm( EnterTimeForm );
}
break;
```

6

All we do in the Contact Detail form event handler is pop up the Enter Time form. The Enter Time form will have to take care of modifying the database record and so forth.

The function **setDateTrigger()** is called to update the appearance of the date selection trigger.

```
// CH.6 Set the Contact Detail date selector trigger
static void setDateTrigger( void )
{
    FormPtr form;    // CH.5 The contact detail form

    // CH.6 Get the contact detail form pointer
    form = FrmGetActiveForm();

    // CH.6 If there is no date
    if( dateTime.year == NO_DATE )
    {
        CtlSetLabel( getObject( form, ContactDetailDateSelTrigger ),
                "              " );
    }

    else
    // CH.6 If there is a date
    {
        Char dateString[dateStringLength];
```

```
        // CH.6 Get the date string
        DateToAscii( dateTime.month, dateTime.day, dateTime.year,
                (DateFormatType)PrefGetPreference( prefDateFormat ),
                dateString );

        // CH.6 Set the selector trigger label
        CtlSetLabel( getObject( form, ContactDetailDateSelTrigger ),
                dateString );
    }

    // CH.6 We're done
    return;
}
```

If there is no time, we put ten spaces into the control. Since a selector trigger resizes itself to its label, this causes the trigger to be large enough to be selected with a finger. Remember that you must insure that the number of characters in a control label, including a selector trigger label, doesn't exceed what you originally defined in Constructor.

If there is a date, we get a date string. The system preferences define for us what format the date should be in. We get the date preference with a call to **PrefGetPreference()** with the parameter *prefDateFormat*. We need to typecast this to the type *DateFormatType* because **PrefGetPreference()** returns the values of many different preferences, so its return type is generic.

The function **DateToAscii()** converts our date variables into the short date format we specify, which is where we pass in the preferences value given by the system. Once we have the date string, we set the selector trigger label with it.

The function **SetTimeTrigger()** is called to set the time selector trigger. It is identical to **setDateTrigger()** except that it uses the corresponding function calls for time.

Supporting the Push Buttons

As you did in the Contact Detail event handler, build a switch statement in **enterTimeHandleEvent()** inside the case statement for the *ctlSelectEvent*. Have case statements based on the various values of *buttonID*, which is really a control ID in that it might represent the ID of any of the controls we have in the Enter Time form.

First, handle the hours and minutes push buttons:

```
                        // CH.6 Hours button
                        case EnterTimeHoursPushButton:
                        // CH.6 Minute Tens button
                        case EnterTimeMinuteTensPushButton:
                        // CH.6 Minute Ones button
                        case EnterTimeMinuteOnesPushButton:
                        {
                            // CH.6 If no time was set
                            if( dateTime.hour == NO_TIME )
                            {
                                // CH.6 Set the time to 12 PM
                                dateTime.hour = 12;
                                dateTime.minute = 0;

                                // CH.6 Set the controls
                                setTimeControls();
                            }

                            // CH.6 Clear the old selection if any
                            if( timeSelect )
                                CtlSetValue( getObject( form, timeSelect ),
                                        false );

                            // CH.6 Set the new selection
                            CtlSetValue( getObject( form, buttonID ), true );
                            timeSelect = buttonID;
                        }
                        break;
```

These buttons show their values on their labels. They show which digit
is subject to the up and down arrow buttons based on which one is
highlighted. If any of the push buttons is selected and there is no time
displayed, a value of 12 PM is set and shown. If there was a control
previously selected (in which case, *timeSelect* is nonzero), we clear that
selection. Finally we select the button that was just tapped.

In the function **setTimeControls()** you can see how push button labels
are set. They are set exactly like the label of any control:

```
                    // CH.6 Update the hour
                    hour = dateTime.hour % 12;
                    if( hour == 0 )
                        hour = 12;
                    CtlSetLabel( hourButton,
                            StrIToA( labelString, hour ) );
```

```
// CH.6 Update the minute tens
CtlSetLabel( minuteTensButton,
        StrIToA( labelString, dateTime.minute / 10 ) );

// CH.6 Update the minute ones
CtlSetLabel( minuteOnesButton,
        StrIToA( labelString, dateTime.minute % 10 ) );
```

Time is stored in 24-hour format, which we need to convert to 12-hour time format to show correctly on the controls.

In the function **enterTimeHandleEvent()** there are also two push buttons grouped together to act as an AM/PM setting. Their event code looks like this:

```
// CH.6 AM button
case EnterTimeAMPushButton:
{
    // CH.6 If no time was set
    if( dateTime.hour == NO_TIME )
    {
        // CH.6 Set the time to 12 AM
        dateTime.hour = 0;
        dateTime.minute = 0;

        // CH.6 Set the controls
        setTimeControls();
    }

    // CH.6 If it is PM
    if( dateTime.hour > 11 )
    {
        // CH.6 Change to AM
        dateTime.hour -= 12;

        // CH.6 Set the controls
        setTimeControls();
    }
}
break;
```

In the AM case, if there is no time, we set the time to 12 AM. If the time is PM, we subtract 12 from the 24-hour time to get to AM.

The PM control has similar event code associated with it.

In **setTimeControls()** we display AM and PM with the following code:

```
// CH.6 Update AM
CtlSetValue( amButton, (dateTime.hour < 12) );
```

```
        // CH.6 Update PM
        CtlSetValue( pmButton, (dateTime.hour > 11) );
```

It's a good trick to replace Boolean constants with logical arguments where Boolean values need to be passed.

Supporting the Repeating Buttons

The repeating buttons allow hours and minutes to be incremented and decremented. In order to get the repeating effect, we must respond to the *ctlRepeatEvent* as well as the *ctlSelectEvent*. In the function **enterTimeHandleEvent()** we must also return false from the event handler, or subsequent button processing will not create repeating events.

```
// CH.6 Up button
case EnterTimeTimeUpRepeating:
{
    // CH.6 If there's no time, do nothing
    if( dateTime.hour == NO_TIME )
        break;

    // CH.6 Based on what push button is selected
    switch( timeSelect )
    {
        // CH.6 Increase hours
        case EnterTimeHoursPushButton:
        {
            // CH.6 Increment hours
            dateTime.hour++;

            // CH.6 If it was 11 AM, make it 12 AM
            if( dateTime.hour == 12 )
                dateTime.hour = 0;

            // CH.6 If it was 11 PM, make it 12 PM
            if( dateTime.hour == 24 )
                dateTime.hour = 12;
        }
        break;

        // CH.6 Increase tens of minutes
        case EnterTimeMinuteTensPushButton:
        {
            // CH.6 Increment minutes
            dateTime.minute += 10;

            // CH.6 If it was 5X, roll over
            if( dateTime.minute > 59 )
```

6

```
                                    dateTime.minute -= 60;
            }
            break;

            // CH.6 Increase minutes
            case EnterTimeMinuteOnesPushButton:
            {
                // CH.6 Increment minutes
                dateTime.minute++;

                // CH.6 If it is zero, subtract ten
                if( (dateTime.minute % 10) == 0 )
                    dateTime.minute -= 10;
            }
            break;
        }

        // Revise the controls
        setTimeControls();
    }
    break;
```

If there is no time displayed, the arrows appropriately do nothing. If time is displayed, based on which push button is selected, the arrow increments hours, tens of minutes, or minutes. Rollover is also handled in these cases.

The down arrow similarly decrements the controls.

Supporting the Checkbox

The checkbox is handled like any other button. When it is tapped, you get a *ctlSelectEvent*.

```
// CH.6 No Time checkbox
case EnterTimeNoTimeCheckbox:
{
    // CH.6 If we are unchecking the box
    if( dateTime.hour == NO_TIME )
    {
        // CH.6 Set the time to 12 PM
        dateTime.hour = 12;
        dateTime.minute = 0;

        // CH.6 Set the controls
        setTimeControls();

        // CH.6 Set the push button
        timeSelect = EnterTimeHoursPushButton;
        CtlSetValue( getObject( form, timeSelect ),
                true );
    }
```

```
            else
            // CH.6 If we are checking the box
                dateTime.hour = NO_TIME;

            // CH.6 Set the controls
            setTimeControls();
        }
        break;
```

As a convenience, if we are unchecking the box, we select the hours push button. Everything else is handled in **setTimeControls()**, where we appropriately clear all the controls if we are checking the checkbox or set all the controls if we are unchecking the checkbox.

Finishing Up the Enter Time Form

There are a few other details to handling the form. Handle the *frmOpenEvent* in **enterTimeHandleEvent()**:

```
    // CH.6 Initialize the form
    case frmOpenEvent:
    {
        // CH.6 Store the time value
        oldTime = dateTime;

        // CH.6 Draw it
        FrmDrawForm( form );

        // CH.6 Set the time controls
        setTimeControls();
    }
    break;
```

When we open the form, we call **setTimeControls()** to initialize the form. We also save the current time value so that we can restore it if we cancel.

```
            // CH.6 Cancel button
            case EnterTimeCancelButton:
            {
                // CH.6 Restore time
                dateTime = oldTime;

                // CH.6 Return to calling form
                FrmReturnToForm( 0 );
            }

                // CH.6 Always return true
            return( true );
```

The Cancel button just restores the old time and returns to the Contact Detail form.

The OK button is somewhat more complicated. Here we must update the database record and update the Contact Detail form visually with the new time value.

```
// CH.6 OK button
case EnterTimeOKButton:
{
    VoidPtr precord;     // CH.6 Points to the record

    // CH.6 Lock it down
    precord = MemHandleLock( hrecord );

    // CH.6 Write the date time field
    DmWrite( precord, DB_DATE_TIME_START, &dateTime,
             sizeof( DateTimeType ) );

    // CH.6 Unlock the record
    MemHandleUnlock( hrecord );

    // CH.6 Mark the record dirty
    isDirty = true;

    // CH.6 Return to the Contact Details form
    FrmReturnToForm( 0 );

    // CH.6 Update the field
    setTimeTrigger();
}

    // CH.6 Always return true
return( true )
```

There are a couple of important points here. This code block is why the *hrecord* variable is shared among the functions. Here we know that *hrecord* is valid, and therefore we can use it to write the new time value to the record.

Notice that **setTimeTrigger()**, which operates on the Contact Detail form's time selector trigger, is called after **FrmReturnToForm()**. This can happen because after **FrmReturnToForm()** the active form is again the calling form. This makes the space after **FrmReturnToForm()** an excellent window of opportunity to transfer data from the form that was popped up to the calling form.

Always return true after calling **FrmReturnToForm()**. This is because the structure of the old form is gone after this point, yet Palm OS will want to access these button structures to do more stuff if you return false. The form won't be there, so your application will crash if you return false.

Debugging

First, you'll need to make sure that database records are not being created or modified improperly. Hopefully, the display functions you added will be working well enough to show this. Your existing records will show no date and a time of 12 AM, but should not be dangerous.

The next step is to get the selector triggers in the Contact Detail form working as you want them to. This should be easy for the date control.

For the time control, you'll have to debug the Enter Time form. Debug each of the controls in turn until the entire form is working reliably. After the form is working, you can verify that the database record and the selector trigger are being properly modified.

What's Next

Next, we will add a contact list form to our Contacts application. We will also modify our code so that we can sort the database records by first name, last name, or date and time.

Listing

Here is a complete listing of the code as it stands:

```
// CH.2 The super-include for the Palm OS
#include <Pilot.h>

// CH.5 Added for the call to GrfSetState()
#include <Graffiti.h>

// CH.3 Our resource file
#include "Contacts_res.h"

// CH.4 Prototypes for our event handler functions
static Boolean   contactDetailHandleEvent( EventPtr event );
static Boolean   aboutHandleEvent( EventPtr event );
static Boolean   enterTimeHandleEvent( EventPtr event );
static Boolean   menuEventHandler( EventPtr event );

// CH.4 Constants for ROM revision
#define ROM_VERSION_2    0x02003000
#define ROM_VERSION_MIN ROM_VERSION_2
```

6

```
// CH.5 Prototypes for utility functions
static void     newRecord( void );
static VoidPtr  getObject( FormPtr, Word );
static void     setFields( void );
static void     getFields( void );
static void     setText( FieldPtr, CharPtr );
static void     getText( FieldPtr, VoidPtr, Word );
static void     setDateTrigger( void );
static void     setTimeTrigger( void );
static void     setTimeControls( void );

// CH.5 Our open database reference
static DmOpenRef    contactsDB;
static ULong        numRecords;
static UInt         cursor;
static Boolean      isDirty;
static VoidHand     hrecord;

// CH.5 Constants that define the database record
#define DB_ID_START             0
#define DB_ID_SIZE              (sizeof( ULong ))
#define DB_DATE_TIME_START      (DB_ID_START +\
                                DB_ID_SIZE)
#define DB_DATE_TIME_SIZE       (sizeof( DateTimeType ))
#define DB_FIRST_NAME_START     (DB_DATE_TIME_START +\
                                DB_DATE_TIME_SIZE)
#define DB_FIRST_NAME_SIZE      16
#define DB_LAST_NAME_START      (DB_FIRST_NAME_START +\
                                DB_FIRST_NAME_SIZE)
#define DB_LAST_NAME_SIZE       16
#define DB_PHONE_NUMBER_START   (DB_LAST_NAME_START +\
                                DB_LAST_NAME_SIZE)
#define DB_PHONE_NUMBER_SIZE    16
#define DB_RECORD_SIZE          (DB_PHONE_NUMBER_START +\
                                DB_PHONE_NUMBER_SIZE)

// CH.6 Storage for the record's date and time in expanded form
static DateTimeType dateTime;
static Word         timeSelect;
#define NO_DATE     0
#define NO_TIME     0x7fff

// CH.2 The main entry point
DWord PilotMain( Word cmd, Ptr, Word )
{
    DWord       romVersion; // CH.4 ROM version
    FormPtr     form;       // CH.2 A pointer to our form structure
    EventType   event;      // CH.2 Our event structure
    Word        error;      // CH.3 Error word
```

```
// CH.4 Get the ROM version
romVersion = 0;
FtrGet( sysFtrCreator, sysFtrNumROMVersion, &romVersion );

// CH.4 If we are below our minimum acceptable ROM revision
if( romVersion < ROM_VERSION_MIN )
{
    // CH.4 Display the alert
    FrmAlert( LowROMVersionErrorAlert );

    // CH.4 PalmOS 1.0 will continuously re-launch this app
    // unless we switch to another safe one
    if( romVersion < ROM_VERSION_2 )
    {
        AppLaunchWithCommand( sysFileCDefaultApp,
                sysAppLaunchCmdNormalLaunch, NULL );
    }
    return( 0 );
}

// CH.2 If this is not a normal launch, don't launch
if( cmd != sysAppLaunchCmdNormalLaunch )
    return( 0 );

// CH.5 Create a new database in case there isn't one
if( ((error = DmCreateDatabase( 0, "ContactsDB-PPGU", 'PPGU', 'ctct',
        false )) != dmErrAlreadyExists) && (error != 0) )
{
    // CH.5 Handle db creation error
    FrmAlert( DBCreationErrorAlert );
    return( 0 );
}

// CH.5 Open the database
contactsDB = DmOpenDatabaseByTypeCreator( 'ctct', 'PPGU',
        dmModeReadWrite );

// CH.5 Get the number of records in the database
numRecords = DmNumRecords( contactsDB );

// CH.5 Initialize the record number
cursor = 0;

// CH.5 If there are no records, create one
if( numRecords == 0 )
    newRecord();

// CH.4 Go to our starting page
FrmGotoForm( ContactDetailForm );

// CH.2 Our event loop
```

```
do
{
    // CH.2 Get the next event
    EvtGetEvent( &event, -1 );

    // CH.2 Handle system events
    if( SysHandleEvent( &event ) )
        continue;

    // CH.3 Handle menu events
    if( MenuHandleEvent( NULL, &event, &error ) )
        continue;

    // CH.4 Handle form load events
    if( event.eType == frmLoadEvent )
    {
        // CH.4 Initialize our form
        switch( event.data.frmLoad.formID )
        {
            // CH.4 Contact Detail form
            case ContactDetailForm:
                form = FrmInitForm( ContactDetailForm );
                FrmSetEventHandler( form, contactDetailHandleEvent );
            break;

            // CH.4 About form
            case AboutForm:
                form = FrmInitForm( AboutForm );
                FrmSetEventHandler( form, aboutHandleEvent );
            break;

            // CH.6 Enter Time form
            case EnterTimeForm:
                form = FrmInitForm( EnterTimeForm );
                FrmSetEventHandler( form, enterTimeHandleEvent );
            break;
        }
        FrmSetActiveForm( form );
    }

    // CH.2 Handle form events
    FrmDispatchEvent( &event );

// CH.2 If it's a stop event, exit
} while( event.eType != appStopEvent );

// CH.5 Close all open forms
FrmCloseAllForms();

// CH.5 Close the database
DmCloseDatabase( contactsDB );
```

```
        // CH.2 We're done
        return( 0 );
}

// CH.4 Our Contact Detail form handler function
static Boolean contactDetailHandleEvent( EventPtr event )
{
    FormPtr form;        // CH.3 A pointer to our form structure
    VoidPtr precord;     // CH.6 Points to a database record

    // CH.3 Get our form pointer
    form = FrmGetActiveForm();

    // CH.4 Parse events
    switch( event->eType )
    {
        // CH.4 Form open event
        case frmOpenEvent:
        {
            // CH.2 Draw the form
            FrmDrawForm( form );

            // CH.5 Draw the database fields
            setFields();
        }
        break;

        // CH.5 Form close event
        case frmCloseEvent:
        {
            // CH.5 Store away any modified fields
            getFields();
        }
        break;

        // CH.5 Parse the button events
        case ctlSelectEvent:
        {
            // CH.5 Store any field changes
            getFields();

            switch( event->data.ctlSelect.controlID )
            {
                // CH.5 First button
                case ContactDetailFirstButton:
                {
                    // CH.5 Set the cursor to the first record
                    if( cursor > 0 )
                        cursor = 0;
                }
```

```
        break;

        // CH.5 Previous button
        case ContactDetailPrevButton:
        {
            // CH.5 Move the cursor back one record
            if( cursor > 0 )
                cursor—;
        }
        break;

        // CH.5 Next button
        case ContactDetailNextButton:
        {
            // CH.5 Move the cursor up one record
            if( cursor < (numRecords - 1) )
                cursor++;
        }
        break;

        // CH.5 Last button
        case ContactDetailLastButton:
        {
            // CH.5 Move the cursor to the last record
            if( cursor < (numRecords - 1) )
                cursor = numRecords - 1;
        }
        break;

        // CH.5 Delete button
        case ContactDetailDeleteButton:
        {
            // CH.5 Remove the record from the database
            DmRemoveRecord( contactsDB, cursor );

            // CH.5 Decrease the number of records
            numRecords—;

            // CH.5 Place the cursor at the first record
            cursor = 0;

            // CH.5 If there are no records left, create one
            if( numRecords == 0 )
                newRecord();
        }
        break;

        // CH.5 New button
        case ContactDetailNewButton:
        {
            // CH.5 Create a new record
```

```
            newRecord();
    }
    break;

    // CH.6 Date selector trigger
    case ContactDetailDateSelTrigger:
    {
        // CH.6 Initialize the date if necessary
        if( dateTime.year == NO_DATE )
        {
            DateTimeType currentDate;

            // CH.6 Get the current date
            TimSecondsToDateTime( TimGetSeconds(),
                    &currentDate );

            // CH.6 Copy it
            dateTime.year = currentDate.year;
            dateTime.month = currentDate.month;
            dateTime.day = currentDate.day;
        }

        // CH.6 Pop up the system date selection form
        SelectDay( selectDayByDay, &(dateTime.month),
                &(dateTime.day), &(dateTime.year),
                "Enter Date" );

        // CH.6 Get the record
        hrecord = DmQueryRecord( contactsDB, cursor );

        // CH.6 Lock it down
        precord = MemHandleLock( hrecord );

        // CH.6 Write the date time field
        DmWrite( precord, DB_DATE_TIME_START, &dateTime,
                sizeof( DateTimeType ) );

        // CH.6 Unlock the record
        MemHandleUnlock( hrecord );

        // CH.6 Mark the record dirty
        isDirty = true;
    }
    break;

    // CH.6 Time selector trigger
    case ContactDetailTimeSelTrigger:
    {
        // CH.6 Pop up our selection form
        FrmPopupForm( EnterTimeForm );
    }
```

6

```
                    break;
                }

                // CH.5 Sync the current record to the fields
                setFields();
            }
            break;

            // CH.5 Respond to field tap
            case fldEnterEvent:
                isDirty = true;
            break;

            // CH.3 Parse menu events
            case menuEvent:
                return( menuEventHandler( event ) );
            break;
        }

        // CH.2 We're done
        return( false );
}

// CH.4 Our About form event handler function
static Boolean aboutHandleEvent( EventPtr event )
{
        FormPtr form;    // CH.4 A pointer to our form structure

        // CH.4 Get our form pointer
        form = FrmGetActiveForm();

        // CH.4 Respond to the Open event
        if( event->eType == frmOpenEvent )
        {
            // CH.4 Draw the form
            FrmDrawForm( form );
        }

        // CH.4 Return to the calling form
        if( event->eType == ctlSelectEvent )
        {
            FrmReturnToForm( 0 );

            // CH.4 Always return true in this case
            return( true );
        }

        // CH.4 We're done
        return( false );
}
```

```
// CH.6 Our Enter Time form event handler function
static Boolean enterTimeHandleEvent( EventPtr event )
{
    FormPtr              form;        // CH.6 A form structure pointer
    static DateTimeType oldTime;     // CH.6 The original time

    // CH.6 Get our form pointer
    form = FrmGetActiveForm();

    // CH.6 Switch on the event
    switch( event->eType )
    {
        // CH.6 Initialize the form
        case frmOpenEvent:
        {
            // CH.6 Store the time value
            oldTime = dateTime;

            // CH.6 Draw it
            FrmDrawForm( form );

            // CH.6 Set the time controls
            setTimeControls();
        }
        break;

        // CH.6 If a button was repeated
        case ctlRepeatEvent:
        // CH.6 If a button was pushed
        case ctlSelectEvent:
        {
            Word     buttonID;   // CH.6 The ID of the button

            // CH.6 Set the ID
            buttonID = event->data.ctlSelect.controlID;

            // CH.6 Switch on button ID
            switch( buttonID )
            {
                // CH.6 Hours button
                case EnterTimeHoursPushButton:
                // CH.6 Minute Tens button
                case EnterTimeMinuteTensPushButton:
                // CH.6 Minute Ones button
                case EnterTimeMinuteOnesPushButton:
                {
                    // CH.6 If no time was set
                    if( dateTime.hour == NO_TIME )
                    {
                        // CH.6 Set the time to 12 PM
                        dateTime.hour = 12;
```

```
            dateTime.minute = 0;

            // CH.6 Set the controls
            setTimeControls();
        }

        // CH.6 Clear the old selection if any
        if( timeSelect )
            CtlSetValue( getObject( form, timeSelect ),
                    false );

        // CH.6 Set the new selection
        CtlSetValue( getObject( form, buttonID ), true );
        timeSelect = buttonID;
    }
    break;

    // CH.6 Up button
    case EnterTimeTimeUpRepeating:
    {
        // CH.6 If there's no time, do nothing
        if( dateTime.hour == NO_TIME )
            break;

        // CH.6 Based on what push button is selected
        switch( timeSelect )
        {
            // CH.6 Increase hours
            case EnterTimeHoursPushButton:
            {
                // CH.6 Increment hours
                dateTime.hour++;

                // CH.6 If it was 11 AM, make it 12 AM
                if( dateTime.hour == 12 )
                    dateTime.hour = 0;

                // CH.6 If it was 11 PM, make it 12 PM
                if( dateTime.hour == 24 )
                    dateTime.hour = 12;
            }
            break;

            // CH.6 Increase tens of minutes
            case EnterTimeMinuteTensPushButton:
            {
                // CH.6 Increment minutes
                dateTime.minute += 10;

                // CH.6 If it was 5X, roll over
                if( dateTime.minute > 59 )
```

```
                                        dateTime.minute -= 60;
                        }
                        break;

                        // CH.6 Increase minutes
                        case EnterTimeMinuteOnesPushButton:
                        {
                            // CH.6 Increment minutes
                            dateTime.minute++;

                            // CH.6 If it is zero, subtract ten
                            if( (dateTime.minute % 10) == 0 )
                                dateTime.minute -= 10;
                        }
                        break;
                }

                // Revise the controls
                setTimeControls();
            }
            break;

            // CH.6 Down button
            case EnterTimeTimeDownRepeating:
            {

                // CH.6 If there's no time, do nothing
                if( dateTime.hour == NO_TIME )
                    break;

                // CH.6 Based on what push button is selected
                switch( timeSelect )
                {
                    // CH.6 Decrease hours
                    case EnterTimeHoursPushButton:
                    {
                        // CH.6 Decrement hours
                        dateTime.hour—;

                        // CH.6 If it was 12 AM, make it 11 AM
                        if( dateTime.hour == -1 )
                            dateTime.hour = 11;

                        // CH.6 If it was 12 PM, make it 11 PM
                        if( dateTime.hour == 11 )
                            dateTime.hour = 23;
                    }
                    break;

                    // CH.6 Decrease tens of minutes
                    case EnterTimeMinuteTensPushButton:
```

6

```
        {
            // CH.6 Decrement minutes
            dateTime.minute -= 10;

            // CH.6 If it was 0X, roll over
            if( dateTime.minute < 0 )
                dateTime.minute += 60;
        }
        break;

        // CH.6 Decrease minutes
        case EnterTimeMinuteOnesPushButton:
        {
            // CH.6 Decrement minutes
            dateTime.minute—;

            // CH.6 If it is 9, add ten
            if( (dateTime.minute % 10) == 9 )
                dateTime.minute += 10;

            // CH.6 If less than zero, make it 9
            if( dateTime.minute < 0 )
                dateTime.minute = 9;
        }
        break;
    }

    // CH.6 Revise the controls
    setTimeControls();
}
break;

// CH.6 AM button
case EnterTimeAMPushButton:
{
    // CH.6 If no time was set
    if( dateTime.hour == NO_TIME )
    {
        // CH.6 Set the time to 12 AM
        dateTime.hour = 0;
        dateTime.minute = 0;

        // CH.6 Set the controls
        setTimeControls();
    }

    // CH.6 If it is PM
    if( dateTime.hour > 11 )
    {
        // CH.6 Change to AM
        dateTime.hour -= 12;
```

```
            // CH.6 Set the controls
            setTimeControls();
        }
    }
    break;

    // CH.6 PM button
    case EnterTimePMPushButton:
    {
        // CH.6 If no time was set
        if( dateTime.hour == NO_TIME )
        {
            // CH.6 Set the time to 12 PM
            dateTime.hour = 12;
            dateTime.minute = 0;

            // CH.6 Set the controls
            setTimeControls();
        }

        // CH.6 If it is AM
        if( dateTime.hour < 12 )
        {
            // CH.6 Change to PM
            dateTime.hour += 12;

            // CH.6 Set the controls
            setTimeControls();
        }
    }
    break;

    // CH.6 No Time checkbox
    case EnterTimeNoTimeCheckbox:
    {
        // CH.6 If we are unchecking the box
        if( dateTime.hour == NO_TIME )
        {
            // CH.6 Set the time to 12 PM
            dateTime.hour = 12;
            dateTime.minute = 0;

            // CH.6 Set the controls
            setTimeControls();

            // CH.6 Set the new selection
            timeSelect = EnterTimeHoursPushButton;
            CtlSetValue( getObject( form, timeSelect ),
                    true );
        }
```

6

```
                    else
                    // CH.6 If we are checking the box
                        dateTime.hour = NO_TIME;

                    // CH.6 Set the controls
                    setTimeControls();
                }
                break;

                // CH.6 Cancel button
                case EnterTimeCancelButton:
                {
                    // CH.6 Restore time
                    dateTime = oldTime;

                    // CH.6 Return to calling form
                    FrmReturnToForm( 0 );
                }
                // CH.6 Always return true
                return( true );

                // CH.6 OK button
                case EnterTimeOKButton:
                {
                    VoidPtr precord;      // CH.6 Points to the record

                    // CH.6 Lock it down
                    precord = MemHandleLock( hrecord );

                    // CH.6 Write the date time field
                    DmWrite( precord, DB_DATE_TIME_START, &dateTime,
                            sizeof( DateTimeType ) );

                    // CH.6 Unlock the record
                    MemHandleUnlock( hrecord );

                    // CH.6 Mark the record dirty
                    isDirty = true;

                    // CH.6 Return to the Contact Details form
                    FrmReturnToForm( 0 );

                    // CH.6 Update the field
                    setTimeTrigger();
                }
                // CH.6 Always return true
                return( true );
            }
        }
        break;
    }
```

```
    // CH.6 We're done
    return( false );
}

// CH.3 Handle menu events
static Boolean menuEventHandler( EventPtr event )
{
    FormPtr     form;    // CH.3 A pointer to our form structure
    Word        index;   // CH.3 A general purpose control index
    FieldPtr    field;   // CH.3 Used for manipulating fields

    // CH.3 Get our form pointer
    form = FrmGetActiveForm();

    // CH.3 Erase the menu status from the display
    MenuEraseStatus( NULL );

    // CH.4 Handle options menu
    if( event->data.menu.itemID == OptionsAboutContacts )
    {
        // CH.4 Pop up the About form as a Dialog
        FrmPopupForm( AboutForm );
        return( true );
    }

    // CH.3 Handle graffiti help
    if( event->data.menu.itemID == EditGraffitiHelp )
    {
        // CH.3 Pop up the graffiti reference based on
        // the graffiti state
        SysGraffitiReferenceDialog( referenceDefault );
        return( true );
    }

    // CH.3 Get the index of our field
    index = FrmGetFocus( form );

    // CH.3 If there is no field selected, we're done
    if( index == noFocus )
        return( false );

    // CH.3 Get the pointer of our field
    field = FrmGetObjectPtr( form, index );

    // CH.3 Do the edit command
    switch( event->data.menu.itemID )
    {
        // CH.3 Undo
        case EditUndo:
            FldUndo( field );
```

6

```
        break;

        // CH.3 Cut
        case EditCut:
            FldCut( field );
        break;

        // CH.3 Copy
        case EditCopy:
            FldCopy( field );
        break;

        // CH.3 Paste
        case EditPaste:
            FldPaste( field );
        break;

        // CH.3 Select All
        case EditSelectAll:
        {
            // CH.3 Get the length of the string in the field
            Word length = FldGetTextLength( field );

            // CH.3 Sound an error if appropriate
            if( length == 0 )
            {
                SndPlaySystemSound( sndError );
                return( false );
            }

            // CH.3 Select the whole string
            FldSetSelection( field, 0, length );
        }
        break;

        // CH.3 Bring up the keyboard tool
        case EditKeyboard:
            SysKeyboardDialogV10();
        break;
    }

    // CH.3 We're done
    return( true );
}

// CH.5 This function creates and initializes a new record
static void newRecord( void )
{
    VoidPtr precord;     // CH.5 Pointer to the record

    // CH.5 Create the database record and get a handle to it
```

```
    hrecord = DmNewRecord( contactsDB, &cursor, DB_RECORD_SIZE );

    // CH.5 Lock down the record to modify it
    precord = MemHandleLock( hrecord );

    // CH.5 Clear the record
    DmSet( precord, 0, DB_RECORD_SIZE, 0 );

    // CH.6 Initialize the date and time
    MemSet( &dateTime, sizeof( dateTime ), 0 );
    dateTime.year = NO_DATE;
    dateTime.hour = NO_TIME;
    DmWrite( precord, DB_DATE_TIME_START, &dateTime,
            sizeof( DateTimeType ) );

    // CH.5 Unlock the record
    MemHandleUnlock( hrecord );

    // CH.5 Clear the busy bit and set the dirty bit
    DmReleaseRecord( contactsDB, cursor, true );

    // CH.5 Increment the total record count
    numRecords++;

    // CH.5 Set the dirty bit
    isDirty = true;

    // CH.5 We're done
    return;
}

// CH.5 A time saver: Gets object pointers based on their ID
static VoidPtr getObject( FormPtr form, Word objectID )
{
    Word    index;  // CH.5 The object index

    // CH.5 Get the index
    index = FrmGetObjectIndex( form, objectID );

    // CH.5 Return the pointer
    return( FrmGetObjectPtr( form, index ) );
}

// CH.5 Gets the current database record and displays it
// in the detail fields
static void setFields( void )
{
    FormPtr form;       // CH.5 The contact detail form
    CharPtr precord;    // CH.5 A record pointer
    Word    index;      // CH.5 The object index
```

```
    // CH.5 Get the contact detail form pointer
    form = FrmGetActiveForm();

    // CH.5 Get the current record
    hrecord = DmQueryRecord( contactsDB, cursor );

    // CH.6 Initialize the date and time variable
    precord = MemHandleLock( hrecord );
    MemMove( &dateTime, precord + DB_DATE_TIME_START,
            sizeof( dateTime ) );

    // CH.6 Initialize the date control
    setDateTrigger();

    // CH.6 Initialize the time control
    setTimeTrigger();

    // CH.5 Set the text for the First Name field
    setText( getObject( form, ContactDetailFirstNameField ),
            precord + DB_FIRST_NAME_START );

    // CH.5 Set the text for the Last Name field
    setText( getObject( form, ContactDetailLastNameField ),
            precord + DB_LAST_NAME_START );

    // CH.5 Set the text for the Phone Number field
    setText( getObject( form, ContactDetailPhoneNumberField ),
            precord + DB_PHONE_NUMBER_START );
    MemHandleUnlock( hrecord );

    // CH.5 If the record is already dirty, it's new, so set focus
    if( isDirty )
    {
        // CH.3 Get the index of our field
        index = FrmGetObjectIndex( form, ContactDetailFirstNameField );

        // CH.3 Set the focus to the First Name field
        FrmSetFocus( form, index );

        // CH.5 Set upper shift on
        GrfSetState( false, false, true );
    }

    // CH.5 We're done
    return;
}

// CH.5 Puts any field changes in the record
void getFields( void )
{
    FormPtr form;    // CH.5 The contact detail form
```

```
        // CH.5 Get the contact detail form pointer
        form = FrmGetActiveForm();

        // CH.5 Turn off focus
        FrmSetFocus( form, -1 );

        // CH.5 If the record has been modified
        if( isDirty )
        {
            CharPtr precord;     // CH.5 Points to the DB record

            // CH.5 Lock the record
            precord = MemHandleLock( hrecord );

            // CH.5 Get the text for the First Name field
            getText( getObject( form, ContactDetailFirstNameField ),
                    precord, DB_FIRST_NAME_START );

            // CH.5 Get the text for the Last Name field
            getText( getObject( form, ContactDetailLastNameField ),
                    precord, DB_LAST_NAME_START );

            // CH.5 Get the text for the Phone Number field
            getText( getObject( form, ContactDetailPhoneNumberField ),
                    precord, DB_PHONE_NUMBER_START );

            // CH.5 Unlock the record
            MemHandleUnlock( hrecord );
        }

        // CH.5 Reset the dirty bit
        isDirty = false;

        // CH.5 We're done
        return;
    }

// CH.5 Set the text in a field
static void setText( FieldPtr field, CharPtr text )
{
    VoidHand     hfield; // CH.5 Handle of field text
    CharPtr      pfield; // CH.5 Pointer to field text

    // CH.5 Get the current field handle
    hfield = FldGetTextHandle( field );

    // CH.5 If we have a handle
    if( hfield != NULL )
    {
        // CH.5 Resize it
```

```
        MemHandleResize( hfield, StrLen( text ) + 1 );
    }

    else
    // CH.5 Allocate a handle for the string
        hfield = MemHandleNew( StrLen( text ) + 1 );

    // CH.5 Lock it
    pfield = MemHandleLock( hfield );

    // CH.5 Copy the string
    StrCopy( pfield, text );

    // CH.5 Unlock it
    MemHandleUnlock( hfield );

    // CH.5 Give it to the field
    FldSetTextHandle( field, hfield );

    // CH.5 Draw the field
    FldDrawField( field );

    // CH.5 We're done
    return;
}

// CH.5 Get the text from a field
static void getText( FieldPtr field, VoidPtr precord, Word offset )
{
    CharPtr pfield; // CH.5 Pointer to field text

    // CH.5 Get the text pointer
    pfield = FldGetTextPtr( field );

    // CH.5 Copy it
    DmWrite( precord, offset, pfield, StrLen( pfield ) );

    // CH.5 We're done
    return;
}

// CH.6 Set the Contact Detail date selector trigger
static void setDateTrigger( void )
{
    FormPtr form;    // CH.5 The contact detail form

    // CH.6 Get the contact detail form pointer
    form = FrmGetActiveForm();

    // CH.6 If there is no date
    if( dateTime.year == NO_DATE )
```

```
        {
            CtlSetLabel( getObject( form, ContactDetailDateSelTrigger ),
                    "              " );
        }

        else
        // CH.6 If there is a date
        {
            Char dateString[dateStringLength];

            // CH.6 Get the date string
            DateToAscii( dateTime.month, dateTime.day, dateTime.year,
                    (DateFormatType)PrefGetPreference( prefDateFormat ),
    dateString );

            // CH.6 Set the selector trigger label
            CtlSetLabel( getObject( form, ContactDetailDateSelTrigger ),
                    dateString );
        }

        // CH.6 We're done
        return;
    }

// CH.6 Set the Contact Detail time selector trigger
static void setTimeTrigger( void )
{
    FormPtr          form;          // CH.5 The contact detail form

    // CH.6 Get the contact detail form pointer
    form = FrmGetActiveForm();

    // CH.6 If there's no time
    if( dateTime.hour == NO_TIME )
    {
        CtlSetLabel( getObject( form, ContactDetailTimeSelTrigger ),
                "              " );
    }

    else
    // CH.6 If there is a time
    {
        Char timeString[timeStringLength];

        // CH.6 Get the time string
        TimeToAscii( dateTime.hour, dateTime.minute,
                (TimeFormatType)PrefGetPreference( prefTimeFormat ),
    timeString );

        // CH.6 Set the selector trigger label
        CtlSetLabel( getObject( form, ContactDetailTimeSelTrigger ),
```

```
                    timeString );

        }

        // CH.6 We're done
        return;
    }

    // CH.6 Set the controls in the Enter Time form based on dateTime
    static void setTimeControls( void )
    {
        FormPtr     form;
        ControlPtr  hourButton;
        ControlPtr  minuteTensButton;
        ControlPtr  minuteOnesButton;
        ControlPtr  amButton;
        ControlPtr  pmButton;
        ControlPtr  noTimeCheckbox;
        Char        labelString[3];
        SWord       hour;

        // CH.6 Get the form
        form = FrmGetActiveForm();

        // CH.6 Get the control pointers
        hourButton = getObject( form, EnterTimeHoursPushButton );
        minuteTensButton = getObject( form,
                EnterTimeMinuteTensPushButton );
        minuteOnesButton = getObject( form,
                EnterTimeMinuteOnesPushButton );
        amButton = getObject( form, EnterTimeAMPushButton );
        pmButton = getObject( form, EnterTimePMPushButton );
        noTimeCheckbox = getObject( form, EnterTimeNoTimeCheckbox );

        // CH.6 If there is a time
        if( dateTime.hour != NO_TIME )
        {
            // CH.6 Update the hour
            hour = dateTime.hour % 12;
            if( hour == 0 )
                hour = 12;
            CtlSetLabel( hourButton,
                    StrIToA( labelString, hour ) );

            // CH.6 Update the minute tens
            CtlSetLabel( minuteTensButton,
                    StrIToA( labelString, dateTime.minute / 10 ) );

            // CH.6 Update the minute ones
            CtlSetLabel( minuteOnesButton,
                    StrIToA( labelString, dateTime.minute % 10 ) );
```

```
        // CH.6 Update AM
        CtlSetValue( amButton, (dateTime.hour < 12) );

        // CH.6 Update PM
        CtlSetValue( pmButton, (dateTime.hour > 11) );

        // CH.6 Uncheck the no time checkbox
        CtlSetValue( noTimeCheckbox, false );
    }

    else
    // If there is no time
    {
        // CH.6 Update the hour
        CtlSetValue( hourButton, false );
        CtlSetLabel( hourButton, "" );

        // CH.6 Update the minute tens
        CtlSetValue( minuteTensButton, false );
        CtlSetLabel( minuteTensButton, "" );

        // CH.6 Update the minute ones
        CtlSetValue( minuteOnesButton, false );
        CtlSetLabel( minuteOnesButton, "" );

        // CH.6 Update AM
        CtlSetValue( amButton, false );

        // CH.6 Update PM
        CtlSetValue( pmButton, false );

        // CH.6 Uncheck the no time checkbox
        CtlSetValue( noTimeCheckbox, true );
    }

    // CH.6 We're done
    return;
}
```

CHAPTER 7

Lists and Sorting

In this chapter we'll work with some new controls and some new database tricks. We will create a form that displays all the records in our contact database. We'll create a pop-up list that allows you to select sort criteria. Then we'll add the code to sort the records as you specify. We'll also add code to sort records created or modified in the Contact Detail form into the list in the correct position.

Save a Copy of Your Project

You know the routine. Here are the steps:

1. Launch Windows Explorer.
2. Find the folder that your project is stored in.
3. Select it and press CTRL-C to copy the folder.
4. Select a folder to save the copy in.
5. Press CTRL-V to paste a copy of your project into your backup folder.
6. Rename the project to something you will remember. I named mine Contacts CH.6.

Lists

Lists display several text strings and allow you to select from among these items. Each item is on its own line that you can scroll through and select from. You can also call functions that will scroll through a list or select an item. If you want to, you can draw the list items yourself. By default, they are drawn by the Palm OS.

Additions to Contacts.rsrc

In this section you'll add a new form to the Contacts application. The form will display your database as a list and allow you to scroll through the records and choose one. Selecting an item will bring up the Contact Detail form with that record displayed.

Additions to the Contact Detail Form

Since the Contact Detail form will now be launched from and return to the Contact List form, we need to add a Done button to the form. Here are the steps to do that:

1. Launch Constructor.

2. Open the resource file Contacts.rsrc. It is located in the Src folder inside your project folder.

3. Double-click on the Contact Detail form to open it.

4. Bring up the palette of controls by selecting Windows | Catalog.

5. Drag a button from the Catalog window onto the Contact Detail form.

6. Change the button's Object Identifier to Done. Put it at a Left Origin of 1 and a Top Origin of 147. Make the Label Done.

7. You are done modifying this form. It should look like the one shown next. Close the Contact Details form by clicking on the X in the upper-right corner of the form editor.

7

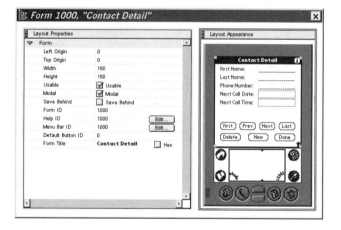

Creating a Menu Bar for the Contact List Form

Before you create the Contact List form itself, you might as well create the menu bar for it so you are prepared with a menu bar ID when you are modifying form attributes.

1. Click on Menu Bars in the Resource Type and Name list and press CTRL-K. A new menu bar resource will appear in the list. Click on the new menu bar and name it Contact List.

2. Double-click on the menu bar to open it.

3. Drag the Options menu over to the Contact List menu bar.

4. Your completed menu bar should look like the one shown next. Click on the X in the upper-right corner to close the menu bar.

Creating the Contact List Form

Now it's time to create the new Contact List form. Here are the steps for that:

1. Click on the Forms heading and press CTRL-K to create a new form.

2. Click on the form name. Rename the form Contact List.

3. Open the Contact List form in the form editor by double-clicking on it.

4. Add a form title of Contact List. Set the Menu Bar ID to match the ID of the Contact List menu bar.

Creating a List

1. Drag a List from the Catalog window and drop it on the form. The attributes of a list are shown in Table 7-1.

2. Make the Object Identifier List. Set the Left Origin at 0 and the Top Origin at 12. Set the Width to 160. Set the Visible Items to 12.

Name	Description
Object Identifier	The name Constructor uses for the constant representing the resource ID in the resource include file.
List ID	The resource ID of the list.
Left Origin	The horizontal position of the left edge of the list.
Top Origin	The vertical position of the top edge of the list.
Width	The width of the list.
Usable	Defines whether the control is visible and active. If this is not checked, you can subsequently make the control usable via a function call.
Font	The font used to draw the list items.
Visible Items	The number of rows displayed by the list. Note that the actual number of list members can be larger or smaller than this number.
List Items	A dynamic list of items that the list is initialized with. To add items to the list, press CTRL-K.

List Attributes
Table 7-1.

7

3. You're done creating the Contact List form. It should look like the one shown next. Click on the X in the upper-right corner to close the Contact List form. Select File | Save to save your changes.

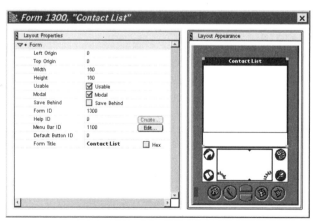

Adding a Memory Error Alert

We will be improving our handling of memory errors this chapter. We need an alert that will report our application is out of memory.

1. Click on Alerts in the Resource Type and Name list and press CTRL-K to create a new alert.
2. Click on the alert's name and change it to MemoryError.
3. Double-click on the alert to open it in the editor.
4. Change the Alert Type to Error. Change the title to Fatal Error. Change the message to "I have run out of memory."
5. When you are done editing the alert, it should look like the one shown next.

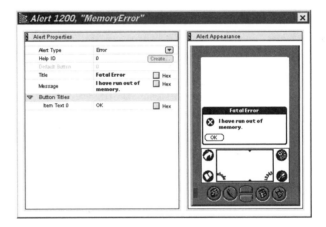

Additions to Contacts.c

Now let's add the code that will make our new form work. First, though, I'd like to correct my earlier omissions with regard to handling errors.

Improving Error Handling

In this chapter you are going to be adding many more ways to run out of memory. Therefore, it is about time to get serious about error handling in our application. The way that we will do this is by using the facilities of the Error Manager that is documented in *The Palm OS SDK Reference*.

First, above **PilotMain()**, we define the error exit macro:

```
// CH.7 The error exit macro
#define errorExit(alert) { ErrThrow( alert ); }
```

The Error Manager function **ErrThrow()** is an unusual one. It works in conjunction with the macros **ErrTry** and **ErrCatch()** to provide an exception handling mechanism similar to those found in C++ and Java. If any code surrounded by an **ErrTry** block calls the **ErrThrow()** function, control is given immediately to the **ErrCatch()** block of code. Let's go through the modifications to **PilotMain()** and you'll see what I mean.

We'll add the **ErrTry** macro above the start of the event loop.

```
// CH.7 Begin the try block
ErrTry {

// CH.2 Our event loop
do
{
```

We will complete the **ErrTry** block and put the **ErrCatch()** block below the event loop.

```
// CH.7 End the try block and do the catch block
}
ErrCatch( errorAlert )
{
    // CH.7 Display the appropriate alert
    FrmAlert( errorAlert );
} ErrEndCatch
```

This code displays the alert represented by the resource ID passed into **ErrCatch()** by **ErrThrow()**. After that, the application continues to exit normally after the catch block, executing the lines of code that close the database and so forth, and then **PilotMain()** returns control to the Palm OS.

Getting to the Contact List Form

Next, we'll add code that will allow us to get to the contact list form from the Contact Detail form. In **PilotMain()**, change the statement that initially loads the Contact Detail form to the following:

```
// CH.7 Choose our starting page
// CH.5 If there are no records, create one
if( numRecords == 0 )
{
    newRecord();
    FrmGotoForm( ContactDetailForm );
}
else
    FrmGotoForm( ContactListForm );
```

If there are no records, a record is created, and you initially jump to the Contact Detail form. If there are records, which will normally be the case, you jump directly to the Contact List form.

So that the Contact List form will be properly initialized, you need to add a case statement for the Contact List form in the *frmLoadEvent* handling code in the event loop.

```
// CH.7 Contact List form
case ContactListForm:
    form = FrmInitForm( ContactListForm );
    FrmSetEventHandler( form,
            contactListHandleEvent );
    break;
```

Here is the code to handle the Done button in the Contact Detail form's event handler:

```
// CH.7 Done button
case ContactDetailDoneButton:
{
    // CH.7 Load the contact list
    FrmGotoForm( ContactListForm );
}
break;
```

To travel among forms that are not pop-up forms, use **FrmGotoForm()** as we are all ready to load the initial form. This function sends a *frmCloseEvent* to the previous form and a *frmLoadEvent* and *frmOpenEvent* to the new form.

The Contact List Form Event Handler Function

The next step is writing an event handler function for the new Contact List form. First, you place a prototype at the top of the file.

```
static Boolean  contactListHandleEvent( EventPtr event );
```

You'll also need a couple of variables to hold handles to memory you will allocate to fill your list.

```
// CH.7 Contact list variables
static VoidHand  hchoices;   // CH.7 Handle to packed choices
static VoidHand  hpchoices;  // CH.7 Handle to pointers
```

Next, you add the function itself.

```
// CH.7 Our Contact List form event handler function
static Boolean contactListHandleEvent( EventPtr event )
{
    FormPtr form;    // CH.7 A form structure pointer

    // CH.7 Get our form pointer
    form = FrmGetActiveForm();

    // CH.7 Parse events
    switch( event->eType )
    {
        // CH.7 Form open event
        case frmOpenEvent:
        {
            // CH.7 Draw the form
            FrmDrawForm( form );

            // CH.7 Build the list
            buildList();
        }
        break;

        // CH.7 Form close event
        case frmCloseEvent:
        {
            // CH.7 Unlock and free things here
            MemHandleUnlock( hpchoices );
            MemHandleFree( hpchoices );
            MemHandleUnlock( hchoices );
```

7

```
            MemHandleFree( hchoices );
            hchoices = 0;
        }
        break;

        // CH.7 Respond to a list selection
        case lstSelectEvent:
        {
            // CH.7 Set the database cursor to the selected contact
            cursor = event->data.lstSelect.selection;

            // CH.7 Go to contact details
            FrmGotoForm( ContactDetailForm );
        }
        break;

        // CH.7 Respond to a menu event
        case menuEvent:
            return( menuEventHandler( event ) );

    }    // CH.7 End of the event switch statement

    // CH.7 We're done
    return( false );
}
```

The event handler function starts in a very standard way, establishing the form pointer variable. It responds to the *frmOpenEvent*, drawing the form and calling a new function, **buildList()**, that we will look at later.

This time we actively use the *frmCloseEvent* to free the memory we're going to use to store the list. We are freeing it in the close event because the Palm OS will be using this memory as long as the list is visible and the form is active. This is a peculiar part of using lists in Palm OS versus other controls. Usually controls handle their own memory, but in the case of lists, you need to provide the list with memory that you manage.

Next, the handler responds to an event we have never discussed before, *lstSelectEvent*. This is the event that is sent if an item is selected on a list. The variable *selection* tells you which list item, counting from zero at the top of the list, was selected. This is perfect for your uses because you can just set the current record equal to that list selection and jump to the Contact Detail form. That form will use the variable *cursor* that you set to bring up the right record.

Last, we handle menu events here exactly as the Contact Detail handler does. That's all we need to run the Contact List form.

The Function buildList()

Now we get to the fairly meaty function, **buildList()**. This function moves through the database, building a text string from each record. It uses these strings to fill the List object with items to select, one for each record in order.

```
// CH.7 Builds the contact list
static void buildList( void )
{
    FormPtr form;           // CH.6 A form structure pointer
    Int     choice;         // CH.7 The list choice we're doing
    CharPtr precord;        // CH.7 Pointer to a record
    Char    listChoice[dateStringLength + 1 +   // CH.7 We
                    timeStringLength + 1 +       // build
                    DB_FIRST_NAME_SIZE +         // list
                    DB_LAST_NAME_SIZE];          // choices here
                               // CH.7 The current list choice
    CharPtr pchoices;       // CH.7 Pointer to packed choices
    UInt    offset;         // CH.7 Offset into packed strings
    VoidPtr ppchoices;      // CH.7 Pointer to pointers to choices

    // CH.6 Get our form pointer
    form = FrmGetActiveForm();
```

After the variables are declared, the function does the conventional call to get the form pointer. The most interesting variable is the char array that will hold successive list strings. You can use the Palm OS constants dateStringLength and timeStringLength to make sure that the array is big enough to hold any date and time the palm OS sends back to you.

```
    // CH.7 Put the list choices in a packed string
    for( choice = 0; choice < numRecords; choice++ )
    {
        // CH.7 Get the record
        hrecord = DmQueryRecord( contactsDB, choice );
        precord = MemHandleLock( hrecord );

        // CH.7 Get the date and time
        MemMove( &dateTime, precord + DB_DATE_TIME_START,
                sizeof( dateTime ) );
```

We go through each record in the database. Here we get the record and set the variable *dateTime* with the date and time we find in the record. Note that we use **DmQueryRecord()** to get the record handle. This function will give us a read-only copy of the record (which is all we need here) even if the record is busy.

Next, we create the string that represents the record.

```
    // CH.7 Clear the list choice string
*listChoice = '\0';

// CH.7 Add the date string if any
if( dateTime.year != NO_DATE )
{
    DateToAscii( dateTime.month, dateTime.day,
            dateTime.year,
            (DateFormatType)PrefGetPreference(
            prefDateFormat ), listChoice );
    StrCat( listChoice, " " );
}

// CH.7 Add the time string if any
if( dateTime.hour != NO_TIME )
{
    TimeToAscii( dateTime.hour, dateTime.minute,
            (TimeFormatType)PrefGetPreference(
            prefTimeFormat ), listChoice +
            StrLen( listChoice ) );
    StrCat( listChoice, " " );
}

// CH.7 Append the first name
StrCat( listChoice, precord + DB_FIRST_NAME_START );
StrCat( listChoice, " " );

// CH.7 Append the last name
StrCat( listChoice, precord + DB_LAST_NAME_START );
```

Here we put the date, time, first name, and last name into the string. Note that the functions **DateToAscii()** and **TimeToAscii()** take a lot of time to execute. These functions are fine for this example program. If you are interested in handling a lot of records quickly, you may want to consider storing the date and time strings in each record to speed things up.

Next, we allocate memory in which to store a packed list of strings. You need to do this because this is the format in which List objects accept new items.

```
// CH.7 Allocate memory for the list entry string
    // CH.7 If this is the first choice
    if( hchoices == 0 )
    {
        // CH.7 Allocate the storage for the choice
        if( (hchoices = MemHandleNew(
                StrLen( listChoice ) + 1 )) == 0 )
            errorExit( MemoryErrorAlert );

        // CH.7 Initial offset points to the start
        offset = 0;
    }
```

This is the case when the packed list of strings needs to be created. We allocate memory for the string. If we fail, we use our cool new error handling macro. Then we set the initial offset telling where to write the string to zero.

Next is the case where we have already created the packed list.

7

```
    else
    // CH.7 If this is a subsequent choice
    {
        // CH.7 Unlock
        MemHandleUnlock( hchoices );

        // CH.7 Resize
        if( MemHandleResize( hchoices, offset +
                StrLen( listChoice ) + 1 ) )
            errorExit( MemoryErrorAlert );
    }
```

Here we unlock the locked memory and grow it to accommodate the next string.

Next, we write the string into the packed list of strings.

```
        // CH.7 Lock
        pchoices = MemHandleLock( hchoices );

        // CH.7 Copy the string into the memory
```

```
        StrCopy( pchoices + offset, listChoice );
        offset += StrLen( listChoice ) + 1;

        // CH.7 Unlock the record
        MemHandleUnlock( hrecord );
    }
```

First, we lock the chunk, then we copy the string we built locally into
the chunk. We are done with the record and the loop, so we unlock the
database record handle we were using. Note that we don't have to do a
DmReleaseRecord() here because we used **DmQueryRecord()** instead
of **DmGetRecord()**.

After the loop executes, we have a packed list of strings that describe each
database record. Now it's time to send these choices to the List object to
be displayed.

```
        // CH.7 Create a pointer array from the packed string list
        if( (hpchoices = SysFormPointerArrayToStrings( pchoices,
                numRecords )) == 0 )
            errorExit( MemoryErrorAlert );
            ppchoices = MemHandleLock( hpchoices );

        // CH.7 Set the list choices
        LstSetListChoices( getObject( form, ContactListListList ),
                ppchoices, numRecords );

        // CH.7 Draw the list
        LstDrawList( getObject( form, ContactListListList ) );

        // CH.7 We're done
        return;
    }
```

You can build a list of pointers to your packed strings by calling the pretty
handy special purpose function **SysFormPointerArrayToStrings()**
function. This function allocates and fills a list with pointers to the strings in
a packed list that you pass to it. Thus, we pass in our packed list and get a list
of pointers to them.

The function **LstSetListChoices()** needs this list of pointers to strings to fill
its items. Note that this function call clears out any items that were already

there. You always have to send this function the complete list of items you want to appear in the List.

Remember that we are ultimately going to free up all this memory we just used in the form close event.

Finally, we draw the list and we're done.

Debugging

In this round of debugging, or any round for that matter, it's a good idea to step through the new code and make sure it's working properly. The largest bit of new code you're likely to run into first is the new function **buildList()**. Set a breakpoint at the top of this function and walk through it, making especially sure that the memory that you allocate is being freed.

Select a record from the list and make sure that the Contact Detail form appears with the correct record in it. Return to the Contact List form with the Done button, verifying this works. Go back to the Contact Detail form, add a record using New, fill it in, and then return to the Contact List and make sure it appears in the list.

7

Sorting

This section introduces new controls, namely pop-up triggers and pop-up lists, as well as sorting. You'll add a pop-up list to the Contact List form and use it to select among sorting choices. Choosing an item on the pop-up list will cause the list of contacts to sort using these criteria. Finally, we will add code that causes contact records created or modified in the Contact Detail form to be inserted into the list at the correct position given the current sort strategy.

Pop-up Triggers

Pop-up triggers are controls like buttons. They have a label and respond to control events like buttons do. They are special controls in the sense that you can specify a list that is associated with the pop-up trigger. If the pop-up trigger is selected, it will display the list. Selecting an item on the list will generate the unique event *popSelectEvent*. You also cannot associate a list with the pop-up trigger and intercept its more fundamental events to use it for some other purpose.

Additions to Contacts.rsrc

You will now add a pop-up list to the Contact List form. This pop-up list will allow you to select among three sort strategies: sort by date and time, sort by first name, or sort by last name.

1. Launch Constructor.

2. Open the resource file Contacts.rsrc. It is located in the Src folder inside your project folder.

3. Double-click on the Contact List form to open it.

4. Bring up the palette of controls by selecting Window | Catalog.

5. Drag a Label object from the Catalog window onto the form. Place it at a Left Origin of 0 and a Top Origin of 149. Set its Label to Sort By:.

6. Drag a List object from the Catalog window onto the form. Change the Object Identifier to SortList. Place the list at a Left Origin of 40 and a Top Origin of 125. You will see that this positioning will align it with the Pop-up Trigger object we will create later. Set the Visible Items to 3.

7. Click on List Items to select it and then press CTRL-K to create the first list item. Change Item Text 1 to Date and Time.

8. Click on Item Text 1 to select it and then press CTRL-K to create the second list item. Change Item Text 2 to First Name.

9. Click on Item Text 2 to select it and press CTRL-K to create the third list item. Change Item Text 3 to Last Name.

Creating a Pop-up Trigger

1. Drag a pop-up trigger from the Catalog window onto the Contact List form. The attributes of pop-up triggers are shown in Table 7-2.

2. Change the Object Identifier to Trigger. Place the trigger at a Left Origin of 40 and a Top Origin of 149. Make its Width 80. Make the Label Date and Time. Fill in the ID of the list you just created in the List ID attribute.

3. You're done with modifications to the Contact List form. The form should now look like the one shown next. Click on the X in the upper-right corner of the form editor window to close the Contact List form. Select File | Save from the menu to save your changes.

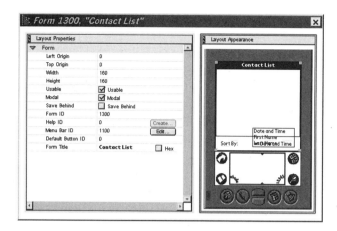

Name	Description
Object Identifier	The name Constructor uses for the constant representing the resource ID in the resource include file.
Popup ID	The resource ID of the pop-up trigger.
Left Origin	The horizontal position of the left edge of the pop-up trigger.
Top Origin	The vertical position of the top edge of the pop-up trigger.
Width	The width of the pop-up trigger.
Height	The height of the pop-up trigger.
Usable	Defines whether the control is visible and active. If this is not checked, you can subsequently make the control usable via a function call.
Anchor Left	As with a button, this attribute defines whether the pop-up trigger expands to the left or to the right if its label is changed. If checked, the control expands to the right.
Font	The font used to draw the label.
Label	The text that is initially displayed on the face of the pop-up trigger.
List ID	The resource ID of the List object the pop-up trigger should pop up.

Pop-up Trigger
Attributes
Table 7-2.

7

Additions to Contacts.c

First, add some variables and constants at the top of the file to support sorting:

```
// CH.7 The sort order variable and constants
static Int   sortBy;
// CH.7 NOTE: These items match the popup list entries!
#define SORTBY_DATE_TIME   0
#define SORTBY_FIRST_NAME  1
#define SORTBY_LAST_NAME   2
```

The variable *sortBy* defines which of the three sort algorithms is currently in effect. The three constants stand for the position of the sort choices in the pop-up list, so this set of constants must match that pop-up list you created.

The Initial Sort

In order to establish a criterion by which to sort the records, we will add code to handle the *popSelectEvent*. This is the event that the pop-up list creates when a list selection is tapped. Everything else is handled automatically for you in this control. This code will sort based on the criterion that was just selected.

```
// CH.7 Respond to the popup trigger
case popSelectEvent:
{
    // CH.7 If there is no change, we're done
    if( sortBy == event->data.popSelect.selection )
        return( true );

    // CH.7 Modify sort order variable
    sortBy = event->data.popSelect.selection;

    // CH.7 Sort the contact database by the new criteria
    DmQuickSort( contactsDB, (DmComparF*)sortFunc, sortBy );

    // CH.7 Rebuild the list
    buildList();
}
break;
```

First, we avoid doing anything if we don't change how we're sorting. This check could be skipped. Then we save the sort order because we'll need it in the Contact Detail form to sort in new records or records that have been edited in a way that has caused their sort order to change. We call **DmQuickSort()**, which calls back our function **sortFunc()** and passes it the criterion *sortBy*. After the database is sorted, we rebuild the list and display it.

Let's examine **sortFunc()**. This function is called by the Palm OS to resolve which of two items appears before the other. We are handed two of our own database records and we return an integer. If the integer is greater than zero, the first record should go first. If the integer is less than zero, the second record should go first. If the integer is zero, the records match.

7

```
// CH.7 This function is called by Palm OS to sort records
static Int sortFunc( CharPtr precord1, CharPtr precord2, Int sortBy )
{
    Int sortResult;

    // CH.7 Switch based on sort criteria
    switch( sortBy )
    {
        // CH.7 Sort by date and time
        case SORTBY_DATE_TIME:
        {
            DateTimePtr pdateTime1;
            DateTimePtr pdateTime2;
            Long        lDiff;

            pdateTime1 = (DateTimePtr)(precord1 +
                    DB_DATE_TIME_START);
            pdateTime2 = (DateTimePtr)(precord2 +
                    DB_DATE_TIME_START);

            // CH.7 Compare the dates and times
            lDiff = (Long)(TimDateTimeToSeconds( pdateTime1 ) / 60 )-
                    (Long)(TimDateTimeToSeconds( pdateTime2 ) / 60 );

            // CH.7 Date/time #1 is later
            if( lDiff > 0 )
                sortResult = 1;

            else
            // CH.7 Date/time #2 is later
            if( lDiff < 0 )
                sortResult = -1;

            else
            // CH.7 They are equal
                sortResult = 0;            }
        break;
```

Here we extract the two date and time structures from the two records we're passed. Then we convert each structure to seconds and compare the two. This algorithm will also put records with no date at the top of the list, but items with no time will go to the bottom of their given day. Since the number of seconds might overflow a 16-bit integer, we need to use a 32-bit-long integer to do the actual comparison and then set our 16-bit variable *sortResult* accordingly.

```
        // CH.7 Sort by first name
        case SORTBY_FIRST_NAME:
        {
            sortResult = StrCompare( precord1 +
DB_FIRST_NAME_START,
                    precord2 + DB_FIRST_NAME_START );
        }
        break;

        // CH.7 Sort by last name
        case SORTBY_LAST_NAME:
        {
            sortResult = StrCompare( precord1 + DB_LAST_NAME_START,
                    precord2 + DB_LAST_NAME_START );
        }
        break;
    }

    // CH.7 We're done
    return( sortResult );
}
```

Sorting by first name and last name is accomplished with a call to **StrCompare()**, a Palm OS string manager function defined in *Developing Palm OS 3.0 Applications Part II: System Management*. The function compares the two strings for us much like the ANSI C function **strcmp()**. It returns an integer that we can pass directly back to the Palm OS.

Sorting Records into the List

The function **getFields()** gets called whenever we are going to move on to another record or leave the Contact Detail form, so it makes sense to put the code that sorts any record that is new or has been modified into this function.

This code, inserted after the record is released but before the dirty bit is cleared, should serve our need.

```
// CH.5 If the record has been modified
if( isDirty )
{
    CharPtr precord;      // CH.5 Points to the DB record

    // CH.7 Detach the record from the database
    DmDetachRecord( contactsDB, cursor, &hrecord );

    // CH.5 Lock the record
    precord = MemHandleLock( hrecord );

    // CH.5 Get the text for the First Name field
    getText( getObject( form, ContactDetailFirstNameField ),
            precord, DB_FIRST_NAME_START );

    // CH.5 Get the text for the Last Name field
    getText( getObject( form, ContactDetailLastNameField ),
            precord, DB_LAST_NAME_START );

    // CH.5 Get the text for the Phone Number field
    getText( getObject( form, ContactDetailPhoneNumberField ),
            precord, DB_PHONE_NUMBER_START );

    // CH.7 Find the proper position
    cursor = DmFindSortPosition( contactsDB, precord, NULL,
            (DmComparF*)sortFunc, sortBy );

    // CH.5 Unlock the record
    MemHandleUnlock( hrecord );

    // CH.7 Reattach the record
    DmAttachRecord( contactsDB, &cursor, hrecord, NULL );
}
```

7

Since we only want to do this if the record may have been modified, we use the *isDirty* bit to determine that at least the record may have been modified. For dirty records, we detach the record temporarily from the database, lock it down, and call **DmFindSortPosition()** to determine where it should be located in the list. This function requires the list to already be sorted to work properly. Since we are only changing or adding one record at the time, this condition is met. We end the job by unlocking the record and inserting it into the database at the new location.

Debugging

Set breakpoints at the top of the case statement for *popSelectEvent*, the top of the new function **sortBy()**, and the top of the if statement you added to **getFields()**. Walk through the new code and convince yourself that it is working properly. Here are some functional tests you might also perform:

◆　Sort the list by all three criteria. Make sure that you have items in your database that will show you that the list has been resorted properly.

◆　Add a record to the database and verify that it is sorted to the correct spot.

◆　Modify an existing record and verify that it ends up in the proper spot.

What's Next?

Next, we will add more new kinds of controls, such as tables and scrollbars, to our application. We used a list to display our contact record information, which is good training, but what you want to use in practice for things like this is a table. We will make this correction and other improvements as we move forward.

Listing

Here we are at the end of the chapter. Your version of Contacts.c should look something like the listing below.

```
// CH.2 The super-include for the Palm OS
#include <Pilot.h>

// CH.5 Added for the call to GrfSetState()
#include <Graffiti.h>

// CH.3 Our resource file
#include "Contacts_res.h"

// CH.4 Prototypes for our event handler functions
static Boolean  contactDetailHandleEvent( EventPtr event );
static Boolean  aboutHandleEvent( EventPtr event );
```

```
static Boolean  enterTimeHandleEvent( EventPtr event );
static Boolean  contactListHandleEvent( EventPtr event );
static Boolean  menuEventHandler( EventPtr event );

// CH.4 Constants for ROM revision
#define ROM_VERSION_2    0x02003000
#define ROM_VERSION_MIN ROM_VERSION_2

// CH.5 Prototypes for utility functions
static void     newRecord( void );
static VoidPtr  getObject( FormPtr, Word );
static void     setFields( void );
static void     getFields( void );
static void     setText( FieldPtr, CharPtr );
static void     getText( FieldPtr, VoidPtr, Word );
static void     setDateTrigger( void );
static void     setTimeTrigger( void );
static void     setTimeControls( void );
static void     buildList( void );
static Int      sortFunc( CharPtr, CharPtr, Int );

// CH.5 Our open database reference
static DmOpenRef    contactsDB;
static ULong        numRecords;
static UInt         cursor;
static Boolean      isDirty;
static VoidHand     hrecord;

// CH.5 Constants that define the database record
#define DB_ID_START             0
#define DB_ID_SIZE              (sizeof( ULong ))
#define DB_DATE_TIME_START      (DB_ID_START +\
                                DB_ID_SIZE)
#define DB_DATE_TIME_SIZE       (sizeof( DateTimeType ))
#define DB_FIRST_NAME_START     (DB_DATE_TIME_START +\
                                DB_DATE_TIME_SIZE)
#define DB_FIRST_NAME_SIZE      16
#define DB_LAST_NAME_START      (DB_FIRST_NAME_START +\
                                DB_FIRST_NAME_SIZE)
#define DB_LAST_NAME_SIZE       16
#define DB_PHONE_NUMBER_START   (DB_LAST_NAME_START +\
                                DB_LAST_NAME_SIZE)
#define DB_PHONE_NUMBER_SIZE    16
#define DB_RECORD_SIZE          (DB_PHONE_NUMBER_START +\
                                DB_PHONE_NUMBER_SIZE)
```

```
// CH.6 Storage for the record's date and time in expanded form
static DateTimeType dateTime;
static Word         timeSelect;
#define NO_DATE      0
#define NO_TIME      0x7fff

// CH.7 The error exit macro
#define errorExit(alert) { ErrThrow( alert ); }

// CH.7 Contact list variables
static VoidHand  hchoices;    // CH.7 Handle to packed choices
static VoidHand  hpchoices;   // CH.7 Handle to pointers

// CH.7 The sort order variable and constants
static Int sortBy;
// CH.7 NOTE: These items match the popup list entries!
#define SORTBY_DATE_TIME    0
#define SORTBY_FIRST_NAME   1
#define SORTBY_LAST_NAME    2

// CH.2 The main entry point
DWord PilotMain( Word cmd, Ptr, Word )
{
    DWord       romVersion; // CH.4 ROM version
    FormPtr     form;       // CH.2 A pointer to our form structure
    EventType   event;      // CH.2 Our event structure
    Word        error;      // CH.3 Error word

    // CH.4 Get the ROM version
    romVersion = 0;
    FtrGet( sysFtrCreator, sysFtrNumROMVersion, &romVersion );

    // CH.4 If we are below our minimum acceptable ROM revision
    if( romVersion < ROM_VERSION_MIN )
    {
        // CH.4 Display the alert
        FrmAlert( LowROMVersionErrorAlert );

        // CH.4 PalmOS 1.0 will continuously re-launch this app
        // unless we switch to another safe one
        if( romVersion < ROM_VERSION_2 )
        {
            AppLaunchWithCommand( sysFileCDefaultApp,
                    sysAppLaunchCmdNormalLaunch, NULL );
```

```
        }
        return( 0 );
    }


    // CH.2 If this is not a normal launch, don't launch
    if( cmd != sysAppLaunchCmdNormalLaunch )
        return( 0 );


    // CH.5 Create a new database in case there isn't one
    if( ((error = DmCreateDatabase( 0, "ContactsDB-PPGU", 'PPGU',
            'ctct', false )) != dmErrAlreadyExists) && (error != 0) )
    {
        // CH.5 Handle db creation error
        FrmAlert( DBCreationErrorAlert );
        return( 0 );
    }


    // CH.5 Open the database
    contactsDB = DmOpenDatabaseByTypeCreator( 'ctct', 'PPGU',
            dmModeReadWrite );


    // CH.5 Get the number of records in the database
    numRecords = DmNumRecords( contactsDB );


    // CH.5 Initialize the record number
    cursor = 0;


    // CH.7 Choose our starting page
    // CH.5 If there are no records, create one
    if( numRecords == 0 )
    {
        newRecord();
        FrmGotoForm( ContactDetailForm );
    }
    else
        FrmGotoForm( ContactListForm );


    // CH.7 Begin the try block
    ErrTry {


    // CH.2 Our event loop
    do
    {
        // CH.2 Get the next event
        EvtGetEvent( &event, -1 );
```

7

```
// CH.2 Handle system events
if( SysHandleEvent( &event ) )
    continue;

// CH.3 Handle menu events
if( MenuHandleEvent( NULL, &event, &error ) )
    continue;

// CH.4 Handle form load events
if( event.eType == frmLoadEvent )
{
    // CH.4 Initialize our form
    switch( event.data.frmLoad.formID )
    {
        // CH.4 Contact Detail form
        case ContactDetailForm:
            form = FrmInitForm( ContactDetailForm );
            FrmSetEventHandler( form,
                    contactDetailHandleEvent );
        break;

        // CH.4 About form
        case AboutForm:
            form = FrmInitForm( AboutForm );
            FrmSetEventHandler( form, aboutHandleEvent );
        break;

        // CH.6 Enter Time form
        case EnterTimeForm:
            form = FrmInitForm( EnterTimeForm );
            FrmSetEventHandler( form, enterTimeHandleEvent );
        break;

        // CH.7 Contact List form
        case ContactListForm:
            form = FrmInitForm( ContactListForm );
            FrmSetEventHandler( form,
            contactListHandleEvent );
        break;
    }
    FrmSetActiveForm( form );
}

// CH.2 Handle form events
FrmDispatchEvent( &event );
```

```
        // CH.2 If it's a stop event, exit
        } while( event.eType != appStopEvent );

        // CH.7 End the try block and do the catch block
        }
        ErrCatch( errorAlert )
        {
            // CH.7 Display the appropriate alert
            FrmAlert( errorAlert );
        } ErrEndCatch

        // CH.5 Close all open forms
        FrmCloseAllForms();

        // CH.5 Close the database
        DmCloseDatabase( contactsDB );

        // CH.2 We're done
        return( 0 );
}

// CH.4 Our Contact Detail form handler function
static Boolean contactDetailHandleEvent( EventPtr event )
{
    FormPtr form;       // CH.3 A pointer to our form structure
    VoidPtr precord;    // CH.6 Points to a database record

    // CH.3 Get our form pointer
    form = FrmGetActiveForm();

    // CH.4 Parse events
    switch( event->eType )
    {
        // CH.4 Form open event
        case frmOpenEvent:
        {
            // CH.2 Draw the form
            FrmDrawForm( form );

            // CH.5 Draw the database fields
            setFields();
        }
        break;

        // CH.5 Form close event
        case frmCloseEvent:
```

```
{
    // CH.5 Store away any modified fields
    getFields();
}
break;

// CH.5 Parse the button events
case ctlSelectEvent:
{
    // CH.5 Store any field changes
    getFields();

    switch( event->data.ctlSelect.controlID )
    {
        // CH.5 First button
        case ContactDetailFirstButton:
        {
            // CH.5 Set the cursor to the first record
            if( cursor > 0 )
                cursor = 0;
        }
        break;

        // CH.5 Previous button
        case ContactDetailPrevButton:
        {
            // CH.5 Move the cursor back one record
            if( cursor > 0 )
                cursor--;
        }
        break;

        // CH.5 Next button
        case ContactDetailNextButton:
        {
            // CH.5 Move the cursor up one record
            if( cursor < (numRecords - 1) )
                cursor++;
        }
        break;

        // CH.5 Last button
        case ContactDetailLastButton:
        {
            // CH.5 Move the cursor to the last record
```

```
        if( cursor < (numRecords - 1) )
            cursor = numRecords - 1;
}
break;

// CH.5 Delete button
case ContactDetailDeleteButton:
{
    // CH.5 Remove the record from the database
    DmRemoveRecord( contactsDB, cursor );

    // CH.5 Decrease the number of records
    numRecords--;

    // CH.5 Place the cursor at the first record
    cursor = 0;

    // CH.5 If there are no records left, create one
    if( numRecords == 0 )
        newRecord();
}
break;

// CH.5 New button
case ContactDetailNewButton:
{
    // CH.5 Create a new record
    newRecord();
}
break;

// CH.7 Done button
case ContactDetailDoneButton:
{
    // CH.7 Load the contact list
    FrmGotoForm( ContactListForm );
}
break;

// CH.6 Date selector trigger
case ContactDetailDateSelTrigger:
{
    // CH.6 Initialize the date if necessary
    if( dateTime.year == NO_DATE )
    {
        DateTimeType currentDate;
```

```
            // CH.6 Get the current date
            TimSecondsToDateTime( TimGetSeconds(),
                    &currentDate );

            // CH.6 Copy it
            dateTime.year = currentDate.year;
            dateTime.month = currentDate.month;
            dateTime.day = currentDate.day;
        }

        // CH.6 Pop up the system date selection form
        SelectDay( selectDayByDay, &(dateTime.month),
                &(dateTime.day), &(dateTime.year),
                "Enter Date" );

        // CH.6 Get the record
        hrecord = DmQueryRecord( contactsDB, cursor );

        // CH.6 Lock it down
        precord = MemHandleLock( hrecord );

        // CH.6 Write the date time field
        DmWrite( precord, DB_DATE_TIME_START, &dateTime,
                sizeof( DateTimeType ) );

        // CH.6 Unlock the record
        MemHandleUnlock( hrecord );

        // CH.6 Mark the record dirty
        isDirty = true;
    }
    break;

    // CH.6 Time selector trigger
    case ContactDetailTimeSelTrigger:
    {
        // CH.6 Pop up our selection form
        FrmPopupForm( EnterTimeForm );
    }
    break;
}

// CH.5 Sync the current record to the fields
setFields();
```

```
        }
        break;

        // CH.5 Respond to field tap
        case fldEnterEvent:
            isDirty = true;
        break;

        // CH.3 Parse menu events
        case menuEvent:
            return( menuEventHandler( event ) );
        break;
    }

    // CH.2 We're done
    return( false );
}

// CH.4 Our About form event handler function
static Boolean aboutHandleEvent( EventPtr event )
{
    FormPtr form;    // CH.4 A pointer to our form structure

    // CH.4 Get our form pointer
    form = FrmGetActiveForm();

    // CH.4 Respond to the Open event
    if( event->eType == frmOpenEvent )
    {
        // CH.4 Draw the form
        FrmDrawForm( form );
    }

    // CH.4 Return to the calling form
    if( event->eType == ctlSelectEvent )
    {
        FrmReturnToForm( 0 );

        // CH.4 Always return true in this case
        return( true );
    }

    // CH.4 We're done
    return( false );
}
```

7

```
// CH.6 Our Enter Time form event handler function
static Boolean enterTimeHandleEvent( EventPtr event )
{
    FormPtr             form;        // CH.6 A form structure pointer
    static DateTimeType oldTime;     // CH.6 The original time

    // CH.6 Get our form pointer
    form = FrmGetActiveForm();

    // CH.6 Switch on the event
    switch( event->eType )
    {
        // CH.6 Initialize the form
        case frmOpenEvent:
        {
            // CH.6 Store the time value
            oldTime = dateTime;

            // CH.6 Draw it
            FrmDrawForm( form );

            // CH.6 Set the time controls
            setTimeControls();
        }
        break;

        // CH.6 If a button was repeated
        case ctlRepeatEvent:
        // CH.6 If a button was pushed
        case ctlSelectEvent:
        {
            Word    buttonID;    // CH.6 The ID of the button

            // CH.6 Set the ID
            buttonID = event->data.ctlSelect.controlID;

            // CH.6 Switch on button ID
            switch( buttonID )
            {
                // CH.6 Hours button
                case EnterTimeHoursPushButton:
                // CH.6 Minute Tens button
                case EnterTimeMinuteTensPushButton:
```

```
// CH.6 Minute Ones button
case EnterTimeMinuteOnesPushButton:
{
    // CH.6 If no time was set
    if( dateTime.hour == NO_TIME )
    {
        // CH.6 Set the time to 12 PM
        dateTime.hour = 12;
        dateTime.minute = 0;

        // CH.6 Set the controls
        setTimeControls();
    }

    // CH.6 Clear the old selection if any
    if( timeSelect )
        CtlSetValue( getObject( form, timeSelect ),
                false );

    // CH.6 Set the new selection
    CtlSetValue( getObject( form, buttonID ), true );
    timeSelect = buttonID;
}
break;

// CH.6 Up button
case EnterTimeTimeUpRepeating:
{
    // CH.6 If there's no time, do nothing
    if( dateTime.hour == NO_TIME )
        break;

    // CH.6 Based on what push button is selected
    switch( timeSelect )
    {
        // CH.6 Increase hours
        case EnterTimeHoursPushButton:
        {
            // CH.6 Increment hours
            dateTime.hour++;

            // CH.6 If it was 11 AM, make it 12 AM
            if( dateTime.hour == 12 )
                dateTime.hour = 0;
```

```
            // CH.6 If it was 11 PM, make it 12 PM
            if( dateTime.hour == 24 )
                dateTime.hour = 12;
        }
        break;

        // CH.6 Increase tens of minutes
        case EnterTimeMinuteTensPushButton:
        {
            // CH.6 Increment minutes
            dateTime.minute += 10;

            // CH.6 If it was 5X, roll over
            if( dateTime.minute > 59 )
                dateTime.minute -= 60;
        }
        break;

        // CH.6 Increase minutes
        case EnterTimeMinuteOnesPushButton:
        {
            // CH.6 Increment minutes
            dateTime.minute++;

            // CH.6 If it is zero, subtract ten
            if( (dateTime.minute % 10) == 0 )
                dateTime.minute -= 10;
        }
        break;
    }

    // Revise the controls
    setTimeControls();
}
break;

// CH.6 Down button
case EnterTimeTimeDownRepeating:
{

    // CH.6 If there's no time, do nothing
    if( dateTime.hour == NO_TIME )
        break;

    // CH.6 Based on what push button is selected
    switch( timeSelect )
```

```
    {
        // CH.6 Decrease hours
        case EnterTimeHoursPushButton:
        {
            // CH.6 Decrement hours
            dateTime.hour--;

            // CH.6 If it was 12 AM, make it 11 AM
            if( dateTime.hour == -1 )
                dateTime.hour = 11;

            // CH.6 If it was 12 PM, make it 11 PM
            if( dateTime.hour == 11 )
                dateTime.hour = 23;
        }
        break;

        // CH.6 Decrease tens of minutes
        case EnterTimeMinuteTensPushButton:
        {
            // CH.6 Decrement minutes
            dateTime.minute -= 10;

            // CH.6 If it was 0X, roll over
            if( dateTime.minute < 0 )
                dateTime.minute += 60;
        }
        break;

        // CH.6 Decrease minutes
        case EnterTimeMinuteOnesPushButton:
        {
            // CH.6 Decrement minutes
            dateTime.minute--;

            // CH.6 If it is 9, add ten
            if( (dateTime.minute % 10) == 9 )
                dateTime.minute += 10;

            // CH.6 If less than zero, make it 9
            if( dateTime.minute < 0 )
                dateTime.minute = 9;
        }
        break;
    }
```

7

```
        // CH.6 Revise the controls
        setTimeControls();
    }
    break;

    // CH.6 AM button
    case EnterTimeAMPushButton:
    {
        // CH.6 If no time was set
        if( dateTime.hour == NO_TIME )
        {
            // CH.6 Set the time to 12 AM
            dateTime.hour = 0;
            dateTime.minute = 0;

            // CH.6 Set the controls
            setTimeControls();
        }

        // CH.6 If it is PM
        if( dateTime.hour > 11 )
        {
            // CH.6 Change to AM
            dateTime.hour -= 12;

            // CH.6 Set the controls
            setTimeControls();
        }
    }
    break;

    // CH.6 PM button
    case EnterTimePMPushButton:
    {
        // CH.6 If no time was set
        if( dateTime.hour == NO_TIME )
        {
            // CH.6 Set the time to 12 PM
            dateTime.hour = 12;
            dateTime.minute = 0;

            // CH.6 Set the controls
            setTimeControls();
        }
```

```
    // CH.6 If it is AM
    if( dateTime.hour < 12 )
    {
        // CH.6 Change to PM
        dateTime.hour += 12;

        // CH.6 Set the controls
        setTimeControls();
    }
}
break;

// CH.6 No Time checkbox
case EnterTimeNoTimeCheckbox:
{
    // CH.6 If we are unchecking the box
    if( dateTime.hour == NO_TIME )
    {
        // CH.6 Set the time to 12 PM
        dateTime.hour = 12;
        dateTime.minute = 0;

        // CH.6 Set the controls
        setTimeControls();

        // CH.6 Set the new selection
        timeSelect = EnterTimeHoursPushButton;
        CtlSetValue( getObject( form, timeSelect ),
                true );
    }

    else
    // CH.6 If we are checking the box
        dateTime.hour = NO_TIME;

    // CH.6 Set the controls
    setTimeControls();
}
break;

// CH.6 Cancel button
case EnterTimeCancelButton:
{
    // CH.6 Restore time
    dateTime = oldTime;
```

```
                        // CH.6 Return to calling form
                        FrmReturnToForm( 0 );
                }
                // CH.6 Always return true
                return( true );

                // CH.6 OK button
                case EnterTimeOKButton:
                {
                        VoidPtr precord;      // CH.6 Points to the record

                        // CH.6 Lock it down
                        precord = MemHandleLock( hrecord );

                        // CH.6 Write the date time field
                        DmWrite( precord, DB_DATE_TIME_START, &dateTime,
                                sizeof( DateTimeType ) );

                        // CH.6 Unlock the record
                        MemHandleUnlock( hrecord );

                        // CH.6 Mark the record dirty
                        isDirty = true;

                        // CH.6 Return to the Contact Details form
                        FrmReturnToForm( 0 );

                        // CH.6 Update the field
                        setTimeTrigger();
                }
                // CH.6 Always return true
                return( true );
            }
        }
        break;
    }

    // CH.6 We're done
    return( false );
}

// CH.7 Our Contact List form event handler function
static Boolean contactListHandleEvent( EventPtr event )
{
    FormPtr form;    // CH.7 A form structure pointer
```

```
// CH.7 Get our form pointer
form = FrmGetActiveForm();

// CH.7 Parse events
switch( event->eType )
{
    // CH.7 Form open event
    case frmOpenEvent:
    {
        // CH.7 Draw the form
        FrmDrawForm( form );

        // CH.7 Build the list
        buildList();
    }
    break;

    // CH.7 Form close event
    case frmCloseEvent:
    {
        // CH.7 Unlock and free things here
        MemHandleUnlock( hpchoices );
        MemHandleFree( hpchoices );
        MemHandleUnlock( hchoices );
        MemHandleFree( hchoices );
        hchoices = 0;
    }
    break;

    // CH.7 Respond to a list selection
    case lstSelectEvent:
    {
        // CH.7 Set the database cursor to the selected contact
        cursor = event->data.lstSelect.selection;

        // CH.7 Go to contact details
        FrmGotoForm( ContactDetailForm );
    }
    break;

    // CH.7 Respond to a menu event
    case menuEvent:
        return( menuEventHandler( event ) );

    // CH.7 Respond to the popup trigger
    case popSelectEvent:
    {
```

```
            // CH.7 If there is no change, we're done
            if( sortBy == event->data.popSelect.selection )
                return( true );

            // CH.7 Modify sort order variable
            sortBy = event->data.popSelect.selection;

            // CH.7 Sort the contact database by the new criteria
            DmQuickSort( contactsDB, (DmComparF*)sortFunc, sortBy );

            // CH.7 Rebuild the list
            buildList();
        }
        break;

    }     // CH.7 End of the event switch statement

    // CH.7 We're done
    return( false );
}

// CH.3 Handle menu events
Boolean menuEventHandler( EventPtr event )
{
    FormPtr      form;    // CH.3 A pointer to our form structure
    Word         index;   // CH.3 A general purpose control index
    FieldPtr     field;   // CH.3 Used for manipulating fields

    // CH.3 Get our form pointer
    form = FrmGetActiveForm();

    // CH.3 Erase the menu status from the display
    MenuEraseStatus( NULL );

    // CH.4 Handle options menu
    if( event->data.menu.itemID == OptionsAboutContacts )
    {
        // CH.4 Pop up the About form as a Dialog
        FrmPopupForm( AboutForm );
        return( true );
    }

    // CH.3 Handle graffiti help
    if( event->data.menu.itemID == EditGraffitiHelp )
    {
```

```
    // CH.3 Pop up the graffiti reference based on
    // the graffiti state
    SysGraffitiReferenceDialog( referenceDefault );
    return( true );
}

// CH.3 Get the index of our field
index = FrmGetFocus( form );

// CH.3 If there is no field selected, we're done
if( index == noFocus )
    return( false );

// CH.3 Get the pointer of our field
field = FrmGetObjectPtr( form, index );

// CH.3 Do the edit command
switch( event->data.menu.itemID )
{
    // CH.3 Undo
    case EditUndo:
        FldUndo( field );
    break;

    // CH.3 Cut
    case EditCut:
        FldCut( field );
    break;

    // CH.3 Copy
    case EditCopy:
        FldCopy( field );
    break;

    // CH.3 Paste
    case EditPaste:
        FldPaste( field );
    break;

    // CH.3 Select All
    case EditSelectAll:
    {
        // CH.3 Get the length of the string in the field
        Word length = FldGetTextLength( field );
```

7

```
        // CH.3 Sound an error if appropriate
        if( length == 0 )
        {
            SndPlaySystemSound( sndError );
            return( false );
        }

        // CH.3 Select the whole string
        FldSetSelection( field, 0, length );
    }
    break;

    // CH.3 Bring up the keyboard tool
    case EditKeyboard:
        SysKeyboardDialogV10();
    break;
}

// CH.3 We're done
return( true );
}

// CH.5 This function creates and initializes a new record
static void newRecord( void )
{
    VoidPtr precord;    // CH.5 Pointer to the record

    // CH.7 Create the database record and get a handle to it
    if( (hrecord = DmNewRecord( contactsDB, &cursor,
            DB_RECORD_SIZE )) == NULL )
        errorExit( MemoryErrorAlert );

    // CH.5 Lock down the record to modify it
    precord = MemHandleLock( hrecord );

    // CH.5 Clear the record
    DmSet( precord, 0, DB_RECORD_SIZE, 0 );

    // CH.6 Initialize the date and time
    MemSet( &dateTime, sizeof( dateTime ), 0 );
    dateTime.year = NO_DATE;
    dateTime.hour = NO_TIME;
    DmWrite( precord, DB_DATE_TIME_START, &dateTime,
            sizeof( DateTimeType ) );
```

```
        // CH.5 Unlock the record
        MemHandleUnlock( hrecord );

        // CH.5 Clear the busy bit and set the dirty bit
        DmReleaseRecord( contactsDB, cursor, true );

        // CH.5 Increment the total record count
        numRecords++;

        // CH.5 Set the dirty bit
        isDirty = true;

        // CH.5 We're done
        return;
    }

// CH.5 A time saver: Gets object pointers based on their ID
static VoidPtr getObject( FormPtr form, Word objectID )
{
    Word    index;   // CH.5 The object index

    // CH.5 Get the index
    index = FrmGetObjectIndex( form, objectID );

    // CH.5 Return the pointer
    return( FrmGetObjectPtr( form, index ) );
}

// CH.5 Gets the current database record and displays it
// in the detail fields
static void setFields( void )
{
    FormPtr form;         // CH.5 The contact detail form
    CharPtr precord;      // CH.5 A record pointer
    Word    index;        // CH.5 The object index

    // CH.5 Get the contact detail form pointer
    form = FrmGetActiveForm();

    // CH.5 Get the current record
    hrecord = DmQueryRecord( contactsDB, cursor );

    // CH.6 Initialize the date and time variable
    precord = MemHandleLock( hrecord );
    MemMove( &dateTime, precord + DB_DATE_TIME_START,
            sizeof( dateTime ) );
```

7

```
    // CH.6 Initialize the date control
    setDateTrigger();

    // CH.6 Initialize the time control
    setTimeTrigger();

    // CH.5 Set the text for the First Name field
    setText( getObject( form, ContactDetailFirstNameField ),
            precord + DB_FIRST_NAME_START );

    // CH.5 Set the text for the Last Name field
    setText( getObject( form, ContactDetailLastNameField ),
            precord + DB_LAST_NAME_START );

    // CH.5 Set the text for the Phone Number field
    setText( getObject( form, ContactDetailPhoneNumberField ),
            precord + DB_PHONE_NUMBER_START );
    MemHandleUnlock( hrecord );

    // CH.5 If the record is already dirty, it's new, so set focus
    if( isDirty )
    {
        // CH.3 Get the index of our field
        index = FrmGetObjectIndex( form,
                ContactDetailFirstNameField );

        // CH.3 Set the focus to the First Name field
        FrmSetFocus( form, index );

        // CH.5 Set upper shift on
        GrfSetState( false, false, true );
    }

    // CH.5 We're done
    return;
}

// CH.5 Puts any field changes in the record
void getFields( void )
{
    FormPtr form;    // CH.5 The contact detail form

    // CH.5 Get the contact detail form pointer
    form = FrmGetActiveForm();
```

```
        // CH.5 Turn off focus
        FrmSetFocus( form, -1 );

        // CH.5 If the record has been modified
        if( isDirty )
        {
            CharPtr precord;     // CH.5 Points to the DB record

            // CH.7 Detach the record from the database
            DmDetachRecord( contactsDB, cursor, &hrecord );

            // CH.5 Lock the record
            precord = MemHandleLock( hrecord );

            // CH.5 Get the text for the First Name field
            getText( getObject( form, ContactDetailFirstNameField ),
                    precord, DB_FIRST_NAME_START );

            // CH.5 Get the text for the Last Name field
            getText( getObject( form, ContactDetailLastNameField ),
                    precord, DB_LAST_NAME_START );

            // CH.5 Get the text for the Phone Number field
            getText( getObject( form, ContactDetailPhoneNumberField ),
                    precord, DB_PHONE_NUMBER_START );

            // CH.7 Find the proper position
            cursor = DmFindSortPosition( contactsDB, precord, NULL,
                    (DmComparF*)sortFunc, sortBy );

            // CH.5 Unlock the record
            MemHandleUnlock( hrecord );

            // CH.7 Reattach the record
            DmAttachRecord( contactsDB, &cursor, hrecord, NULL );
        }

        // CH.5 Reset the dirty bit
        isDirty = false;

        // CH.5 We're done
        return;
    }
```

```
// CH.5 Set the text in a field
static void setText( FieldPtr field, CharPtr text )
{
    VoidHand    hfield; // CH.5 Handle of field text
    CharPtr     pfield; // CH.5 Pointer to field text

    // CH.5 Get the current field handle
    hfield = FldGetTextHandle( field );

    // CH.5 If we have a handle
    if( hfield != NULL )
    {
        // CH.5 Resize it
        if( MemHandleResize( hfield, StrLen( text ) + 1 ) != 0 )
            errorExit( MemoryErrorAlert );
    }

    else
    // CH.5 Allocate a handle for the string
    {
        hfield = MemHandleNew( StrLen( text ) + 1 );
        if( hfield == NULL )
            errorExit( MemoryErrorAlert );
    }

    // CH.5 Lock it
    pfield = MemHandleLock( hfield );

    // CH.5 Copy the string
    StrCopy( pfield, text );

    // CH.5 Unlock it
    MemHandleUnlock( hfield );

    // CH.5 Give it to the field
    FldSetTextHandle( field, hfield );

    // CH.5 Draw the field
    FldDrawField( field );

    // CH.5 We're done
    return;
}
```

```
// CH.5 Get the text from a field
static void getText( FieldPtr field, VoidPtr precord, Word offset )
{
    CharPtr pfield; // CH.5 Pointer to field text

    // CH.5 Get the text pointer
    pfield = FldGetTextPtr( field );

    // CH.5 Copy it
    DmWrite( precord, offset, pfield, StrLen( pfield ) );

    // CH.5 We're done
    return;
}

// CH.6 Set the Contact Detail date selector trigger
static void setDateTrigger( void )
{
    FormPtr form;    // CH.5 The contact detail form

    // CH.6 Get the contact detail form pointer
    form = FrmGetActiveForm();

    // CH.6 If there is no date
    if( dateTime.year == NO_DATE )
    {
        CtlSetLabel( getObject( form, ContactDetailDateSelTrigger ),
                "            " );
    }

    else
    // CH.6 If there is a date
    {
        Char    dateString[dateStringLength];

        // CH.6 Get the date string
        DateToAscii( dateTime.month, dateTime.day, dateTime.year,
                (DateFormatType)PrefGetPreference( prefDateFormat ),
                dateString );

        // CH.6 Set the selector trigger label
        CtlSetLabel( getObject( form, ContactDetailDateSelTrigger ),
                dateString );

    }
```

7

```
    // CH.6 We're done
    return;
}

// CH.6 Set the Contact Detail time selector trigger
static void setTimeTrigger( void )
{
    FormPtr form;    // CH.5 The contact detail form

    // CH.6 Get the contact detail form pointer
    form = FrmGetActiveForm();

    // CH.6 If there's no time
    if( dateTime.hour == NO_TIME )
    {
        CtlSetLabel( getObject( form, ContactDetailTimeSelTrigger ),
                "           " );
    }

    else
    // CH.6 If there is a time
    {
        Char    timeString[timeStringLength];

        // CH.6 Get the time string
        TimeToAscii( dateTime.hour, dateTime.minute,
                (TimeFormatType)PrefGetPreference( prefTimeFormat ),
                timeString );

        // CH.6 Set the selector trigger label
        CtlSetLabel( getObject( form, ContactDetailTimeSelTrigger ),
                timeString );

    }

    // CH.6 We're done
    return;
}

// CH.6 Set the controls in the Enter Time form based on dateTime
static void setTimeControls( void )
{
    FormPtr     form;
    ControlPtr  hourButton;
    ControlPtr  minuteTensButton;
```

```
ControlPtr   minuteOnesButton;
ControlPtr   amButton;
ControlPtr   pmButton;
ControlPtr   noTimeCheckbox;
Char         labelString[3];
SWord        hour;

// CH.6 Get the form
form = FrmGetActiveForm();

// CH.6 Get the control pointers
hourButton = getObject( form, EnterTimeHoursPushButton );
minuteTensButton = getObject( form,
        EnterTimeMinuteTensPushButton );
minuteOnesButton = getObject( form,
        EnterTimeMinuteOnesPushButton );
amButton = getObject( form, EnterTimeAMPushButton );
pmButton = getObject( form, EnterTimePMPushButton );
noTimeCheckbox = getObject( form, EnterTimeNoTimeCheckbox );

// CH.6 If there is a time
if( dateTime.hour != NO_TIME )
{
    // CH.6 Update the hour
    hour = dateTime.hour % 12;
    if( hour == 0 )
        hour = 12;
    CtlSetLabel( hourButton,
            StrIToA( labelString, hour ) );

    // CH.6 Update the minute tens
    CtlSetLabel( minuteTensButton,
            StrIToA( labelString, dateTime.minute / 10 ) );

    // CH.6 Update the minute ones
    CtlSetLabel( minuteOnesButton,
            StrIToA( labelString, dateTime.minute % 10 ) );

    // CH.6 Update AM
    CtlSetValue( amButton, (dateTime.hour < 12) );

    // CH.6 Update PM
    CtlSetValue( pmButton, (dateTime.hour > 11) );
```

7

```
            // CH.6 Uncheck the no time checkbox
            CtlSetValue( noTimeCheckbox, false );
        }

        else
        // If there is no time
        {
            // CH.6 Update the hour
            CtlSetValue( hourButton, false );
            CtlSetLabel( hourButton, "" );

            // CH.6 Update the minute tens
            CtlSetValue( minuteTensButton, false );
            CtlSetLabel( minuteTensButton, "" );

            // CH.6 Update the minute ones
            CtlSetValue( minuteOnesButton, false );
            CtlSetLabel( minuteOnesButton, "" );

            // CH.6 Update AM
            CtlSetValue( amButton, false );

            // CH.6 Update PM
            CtlSetValue( pmButton, false );

            // CH.6 Uncheck the no time checkbox
            CtlSetValue( noTimeCheckbox, true );
        }

        // CH.6 We're done
        return;
}

// CH.7 Builds the contact list
static void buildList( void )
{
    FormPtr form;         // CH.6 A form structure pointer
    Int     choice;       // CH.7 The list choice we're doing
    CharPtr precord;      // CH.7 Pointer to a record
    Char    listChoice[dateStringLength + 1 +   // CH.7 We
                timeStringLength + 1 +       // build
                DB_FIRST_NAME_SIZE +         // list
                DB_LAST_NAME_SIZE];          // choices here
                            // CH.7 The current list choice
    CharPtr pchoices;     // CH.7 Pointer to packed choices
    UInt    offset;       // CH.7 Offset into packed strings
    VoidPtr ppchoices;    // CH.7 Pointer to pointers to choices
```

```
// CH.6 Get our form pointer
form = FrmGetActiveForm();

// CH.7 Put the list choices in a packed string
for( choice = 0; choice < numRecords; choice++ )
{
    // CH.7 Get the record
    hrecord = DmQueryRecord( contactsDB, choice );
    precord = MemHandleLock( hrecord );

    // CH.7 Get the date and time
    MemMove( &dateTime, precord + DB_DATE_TIME_START,
            sizeof( dateTime ) );

    // CH.7 Clear the list choice string
    *listChoice = '\0';

    // CH.7 Add the date string if any
    if( dateTime.year != NO_DATE )
    {
        DateToAscii( dateTime.month, dateTime.day,
                dateTime.year,
                (DateFormatType)PrefGetPreference(
                prefDateFormat ), listChoice );
        StrCat( listChoice, " " );
    }

    // CH.7 Add the time string if any
    if( dateTime.hour != NO_TIME )
    {
        TimeToAscii( dateTime.hour, dateTime.minute,
                (TimeFormatType)PrefGetPreference(
                prefTimeFormat ), listChoice +
                StrLen( listChoice ) );
        StrCat( listChoice, " " );
    }

    // CH.7 Append the first name
    StrCat( listChoice, precord + DB_FIRST_NAME_START );
    StrCat( listChoice, " " );

    // CH.7 Append the last name
    StrCat( listChoice, precord + DB_LAST_NAME_START );
```

7

```
// CH.7 Allocate memory for the list entry string
// CH.7 If this is the first choice
if( hchoices == 0 )
{
    // CH.7 Allocate the storage for the choice
    if( (hchoices = MemHandleNew(
            StrLen( listChoice ) + 1 )) == 0 )
        errorExit( MemoryErrorAlert );

    // CH.7 Initial offset points to the start
    offset = 0;
}

else
// CH.7 If this is a subsequent choice
{
    // CH.7 Unlock
    MemHandleUnlock( hchoices );

    // CH.7 Resize
    if( MemHandleResize( hchoices, offset +
            StrLen( listChoice ) + 1 ) )
        errorExit( MemoryErrorAlert );

}

    // CH.7 Lock
    pchoices = MemHandleLock( hchoices );

    // CH.7 Copy the string into the memory
    StrCopy( pchoices + offset, listChoice );
    offset += StrLen( listChoice ) + 1;

    // CH.7 Unlock the record
    MemHandleUnlock( hrecord );
}

// CH.7 Create a pointer array from the packed string list
if( (hpchoices = SysFormPointerArrayToStrings( pchoices,
        numRecords )) == 0 )
    errorExit( MemoryErrorAlert );
    ppchoices = MemHandleLock( hpchoices );

// CH.7 Set the list choices
LstSetListChoices( getObject( form, ContactListListList ),
        ppchoices, numRecords );
```

```
    // CH.7 Draw the list
    LstDrawList( getObject( form, ContactListListList ) );

    // CH.7 We're done
    return;
}

// CH.7 This function is called by Palm OS to sort records
static Int sortFunc( CharPtr precord1, CharPtr precord2, Int sortBy )
{
    Int sortResult;

    // CH.7 Switch based on sort criteria
    switch( sortBy )
    {
        // CH.7 Sort by date and time
        case SORTBY_DATE_TIME:
        {
            DateTimePtr pdateTime1;
            DateTimePtr pdateTime2;
            Long        lDiff;

            pdateTime1 = (DateTimePtr)(precord1 +
                    DB_DATE_TIME_START);
            pdateTime2 = (DateTimePtr)(precord2 +
                    DB_DATE_TIME_START);

            // CH.7 Compare the dates and times
            lDiff = (Long)(TimDateTimeToSeconds( pdateTime1 ) / 60 )-
                    (Long)(TimDateTimeToSeconds( pdateTime2 ) / 60 );

            // CH.7 Date/time #1 is later
            if( lDiff > 0 )
                sortResult = 1;

            else
            // CH.7 Date/time #2 is later
            if( lDiff < 0 )
                sortResult = -1;

            else
            // CH.7 They are equal
                sortResult = 0;
        }
        break;
```

7

```
    // CH.7 Sort by first name
    case SORTBY_FIRST_NAME:
    {
        sortResult = StrCompare( precord1 + DB_FIRST_NAME_START,
                precord2 + DB_FIRST_NAME_START );
    }
    break;

    // CH.7 Sort by last name
    case SORTBY_LAST_NAME:
    {
        sortResult = StrCompare( precord1 + DB_LAST_NAME_START,
                precord2 + DB_LAST_NAME_START );
    }
    break;
}

// CH.7 We're done
return( sortResult );
}
```

CHAPTER 8

Tables and
Scrolling

In this chapter we will cover two of the most important UI elements available in the Palm OS: tables and scrollbars. Tables can be used to display and edit a wide range of variable sized data. You can see them in use all over the built-in applications. Scrollbars are cool, but they can only be used if you don't want to support the original Pilot 1000 and 5000, since scrollbars aren't supported by version 1.0 of the Palm OS. We will add both scroll buttons (which can be used by all Palm devices) and a scrollbar. (Don't do this in a real application! Talk about overkill!) If that wasn't enough, we will also show how to support the PAGE UP and PAGE DOWN hard keys.

Save a Copy of Your Project

You get the idea by now. Perhaps this has already saved you some time and frustration. Here are the steps:

1. Launch Windows Explorer.
2. Find the folder that your project is stored in.
3. Select it and press CTRL-C to copy the folder.
4. Select a folder to save the copy in.
5. Press CTRL-V to paste a copy of your project into your backup folder.
6. Rename the project to something you will remember. I named mine Contacts CH.7.

Remove Old Resources

We're replacing the big list on the Contact List form with a table, so first we need to get rid of the list.

1. Launch Metrowerks Constructor.
2. Open the resource file Contacts.rsrc. It is located in the Src folder inside your project folder.
3. Double-click on the Contact List form to open it.
4. Click on the list resource we have previously named List. Press the DELETE key to delete the resource.
5. The Contact List form should now look like Figure 8-1.

Rip Out the Old Code

Since the big list is gone, the functions **buildList()** and **deleteList()** are no longer needed. Find and delete them and all references to them. You can do

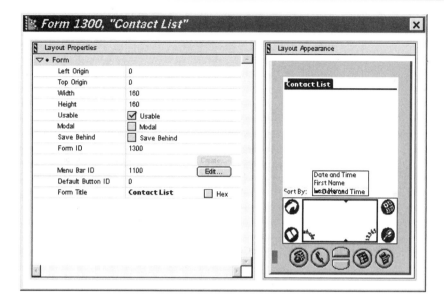

The Contact
List form
after the list
resource has
been deleted

Figure 8-1.

this by placing your cursor at the top of the file, selecting Search | Find, and
typing in **buildList**. After you've found and deleted all things related to
buildList(), you can go back and do the same thing for **deleteList()**.

8

Additionally, wipe out the code that responds to a lstSelectEvent in the
Contact List event handler function. The code to delete looks like this:

```
// CH.7 Respond to a list selection
case lstSelectEvent:
{
    // CH.7 Set the database cursor to the selected contact
    cursor = event->data.lstSelect.selection;

    // CH.7 Go to contact details
    FrmGotoForm( ContactDetailForm );
}
break;
```

Tables

Tables are containers for other UI elements. The UI elements in tables aren't
exactly like the UI elements available in Palm OS outside of tables. Each cell

(row + column) in a table can have a different style, that is, support a different kind of UI element. These styles are described in the following section.

Tables also use different ways of capturing events and of passing data to the various UI elements in the cells. There are several generic functions particular to tables for performing these functions. Tables look a lot like the rest of Palm OS, but the rules are just different enough to warrant careful and separate consideration of each type of UI element available.

Unfortunately, many of the UI elements available in tables have been too specialized to serve my purposes in my applications. I generally end up making my own custom-drawn cells, a technique I will also show you in this chapter.

Item Styles

Each cell of a table can have its own style. For example, the cell could act like a field resource or a checkbox resource. You define these styles at runtime. Table 8-1 has a rundown of these styles and what you can do with them.

Style	Uses
CheckboxTableItem	This kind of cell works the same as a regular checkbox resource, except that there is no label associated with the box, only the box by itself. You can check or uncheck the checkbox by calling **TblSetItemInt()** to 0 for no check or 1 for a check.
CustomTableItem	This is the most useful style of cell. You must define a custom-drawing function for any table column in which this style is specified. You'll see more about how to handle this style as the chapter unfolds. This style can be made editable with some work.
dateTableItem	This displays a date in the cell given the date in *DateType* format. You use the function **TblSetItemPtr()** to pass a pointer to a *DateType* to the table. The bad news about this format is that it always prints an exclamation point after any date in the past. This is sometimes a good thing but sometimes it forces you to customize the date display. This style by itself is not editable.

Table Item
Styles and
Their Uses

Table 8-1.

Style	Uses
labelTableItem	This displays a label. Use the function **TblSetItemPtr()** to pass a string to the table. The bad news is that the table always adds a colon (:) to the end of whatever string you pass, and the text is always right-justified. This is why we are using the custom style in our example in this chapter. This style is not editable.
numericTableItem	This displays a right-justified number. This style works fine and does not add weird things, making it one of the more useful styles. You set the number by calling **TblSetItemInt()**. This style is not editable.
popupTriggerTableItem	This style behaves similarly to the pop-up trigger object. Use **TblSetItemPtr()** to pass a pointer to the list object to display. Use **TblSetItemInt()** to set which selection on the list, starting with zero, is displayed as the current selection.
textTableItem	This style is analogous to a field object. It can be edited. The length of the field can change and wrap. Use TblSetLoadDataProcedure() to define a custom load function for passing the handle of the field to the table. Use TblSetSaveDataProcedure() to define a custom save function for the data in the handle. You'll have to also write these two custom functions to support fields in your table.
textWithNoteTableItem	This style adds a little note icon to the right of the regular text table item. The note icon will look like it is selected separately. When the cell is selected, you'll have to look to see whether the field is in edit mode by calling **TblEditing()**. If not, the note icon has been selected and you should jump to your note form to handle that.

8

Table Item
Styles and
Their Uses
(*continued*)
Table 8-1.

Style	Uses
narrowTextTableItem	This is like a regular text table item, except you can use **TblSetItemInt()** to define the size of a gap at the end of the field for other things to fit. For example, the Date Book application uses this style to provide room to put the little alarm clock icons and so forth to the right of items on the day calendar form.

Because of the specialized nature of the styles available, you'll find yourself writing custom styles fairly often to get exactly what you want.

Table Attributes

You'll find a description of a table's attributes in Table 8-2.

These, like the attributes of other resources, are editable in Constructor when you select the table resource in the Form view.

Name	Description
Object Identifier	Constructor will use this to name the constant representing the resource ID in the resource include file.
Table ID	The resource ID of the table.
Left Origin	The horizontal position of the left edge of the table in pixels.
Top Origin	The vertical position of the top edge of the table in pixels.
Width	The width of the table in pixels.
Height	The height of the table in pixels.
Editable	This defines whether the editable data in the table will accept user input.
Rows	The number of visible rows in the table.
Column Widths	The width in pixels of each column. To define a new column, press CTRL-K.

Adding a Table Resource

Now we will add the table to the Contact List.

1. Launch Metrowerks Constructor.
2. Open the resource file Contacts.rsrc. It is located in the Src folder inside your project folder.
3. Double-click on the Contact List form to open it.
4. Open the Catalog by selecting Window | Catalog from the menu.
5. Drag and drop a table resource onto the form.
6. Change the table's Object Identifier to Table. Put the Left Origin at 0, the Top Origin at 15, the Width at 153, and the Height at 130. This gives enough room for ten rows, so change Rows to 10. It also leaves enough room at the right side of the form to put a scrollbar there later.
7. Define the Column Widths. Set Column Width 1 to 40. Select Column Width 1 and press CTRL-K to create a new column. Set that column width, Column Width 2, to 40 as well. Select Column Width 2 and press CTRL-K to create a third column. Set the Column Width 3 to 73.
8. The Contact List form should now look like Figure 8-2.

8

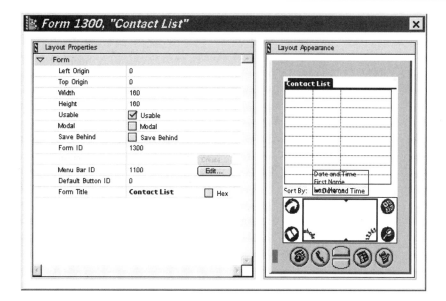

The Contact List form after the addition of a table

Figure 8-2.

Displaying Records in Your Table

We will add table functionality primarily in two new functions:
drawTable() and **drawCell()**. The function **drawTable()**draws the table
given the current state of the cursor and so forth. The function **drawCell()**
is our custom field drawing function that gets called each time Palm OS
needs to draw an entry in our table. Let's add prototypes for these functions.

```
static void     drawTable( void );
static void     drawCell( VoidPtr table, Word row,
                Word column, RectanglePtr bounds );
```

The prototype of **drawCell()** must match the callback function prototype for
custom field drawing functions. This prototype is defined in the description for
TblSetCustomDrawProcedure() in the Palm OS documentation.

For neatness' sake, it's good to define a few constants at the top of the file.

```
// CH.8 Table constants
#define TABLE_NUM_COLUMNS    3
#define TABLE_NUM_ROWS       10
#define TABLE_COLUMN_DATE    0
#define TABLE_COLUMN_TIME    1
#define TABLE_COLUMN_NAME    2
#define BLACK_UP_ARROW       "\x01"
#define BLACK_DOWN_ARROW     "\x02"
#define GRAY_UP_ARROW        "\x03"
#define GRAY_DOWN_ARROW      "\x04"
```

The constants TABLE_NUM_COLUMNS and TABLE_NUM_ROWS define the
visible size of the table on the form, which is relevant to many calculations
and iterations we'll make. The next three constants, TABLE_COLUMN_DATE,
TABLE_COLUMN_TIME, and TABLE_COLUMN_NAME, define which
column will hold what kind of information. The last four constants,
BLACK_UP_ARROW, BLACK_DOWN_ARROW, GRAY_UP_ARROW, and
GRAY_DOWN_ARROW, define the ASCII character values in the Palm OS
Symbol 7 font that represent these images. We will use these to appropriately
gray out the arrows when we reach the top or bottom of scrolling. It is worth
noting that this is the only control in Palm OS that is routinely grayed out.

Changes to the Function contactListHandleEvent()

Jumping down to the event handler function for the Contact List form, **contactListHandleEvent()**, you'll need to add a call to **drawTable()** to the open event:

```
// CH.7 Form open event
case frmOpenEvent:
{
    // CH.7 Draw the form
    FrmDrawForm( form );

    // CH.8 Populate and draw the table
    drawTable();
}
break;
```

Next, handle a table selection, which should call up the Contact Detail form for that record. Note the similarity of this code to the original code that handled list selections. We set the variable *cursor* so that the Contact Detail form presents the proper record.

```
// CH.7 Respond to a list selection
case tblSelectEvent:
{
    // CH.7 Set the database cursor to the selected contact
    cursor += event->data.tblSelect.row;

    // CH.7 Go to contact details
    FrmGotoForm( ContactDetailForm );
}
break;
```

Every time the database is sorted with different criteria, we'll have to redraw the table to reflect the new order of the records. To do this, add a call to **drawTable()** after the **DmQuickSort()** call in the code that responds to the *popSelectEvent*.

```
// CH.7 Sort the contact database by the new criteria
DmQuickSort( contactsDB, (DmComparF*)sortFunc, sortBy );

// CH.8 Rebuild the table
```

8

```
        drawTable();
    }
    break;
```

That's all we need to do to existing functions.

Adding the Function drawTable()

Next, add the function **drawTable()**. We start off defining a few variables and getting a pointer to the table object.

```
// CH.8 Draw our list of choices using a table object
static void drawTable( void )
{
    FormPtr     form;
    TablePtr    table;
    Int         column;
    Int         count;
    ControlPtr  upArrow;
    ControlPtr  downArrow;

    // CH.8 Get the form pointer
    form = FrmGetActiveForm();

    // CH.8 Get the table pointer
    table = getObject( form, ContactListTableTable );
```

We iterate through the columns to do a couple of things. First, each column can have a custom-draw routine. Even though item styles are set on a cell-by-cell basis, if cells are custom-drawn, every cell in a particular column must use the same routine. In our case, we will make one custom-drawing routine, **drawCell()**, that we'll use for every cell in our table.

The other issue we need to handle here is making the columns visible. Columns are invisible by default and need to be set visible to be displayed.

```
    // CH.8 For all columns
    for( column = 0; column < TABLE_NUM_COLUMNS; column++ )
    {
        // CH.8 Set the draw routine
        TblSetCustomDrawProcedure( table, column, drawCell );

        // CH.8 Make the column visible
        TblSetColumnUsable( table, column, true );
    }
```

Next, we iterate through the rows of the table. Every cell in the table needs a style defined for it, so we iterate through the columns, too. There's no need to do this for unused rows of the visible table. If our database contains fewer records than we have visible rows, we turn the unused rows off. This is important. If we don't turn off these unused rows, the way our code is written, we would try to draw records that don't exist, and this would crash the device. Since the number of records in the table may vary, we need to make sure that this code marks rows usable when there is data and unusable when there is no data.

```
// CH.8 Initialize the table styles
for( count = 0; count < TABLE_NUM_ROWS; count++ )
{
    // CH.8 If there is data
    if( count < numRecords )
    {
        // CH.8 Show the row
        TblSetRowUsable( table, count, true );

        // CH.8 Set the cell styles
        for( column = 0; column < TABLE_NUM_COLUMNS; column++ )
        {
            TblSetItemStyle( table, count, column,
            customTableItem );
        }
    }

    else
    // CH.8 Hide unused rows if any
        TblSetRowUsable( table, count, false );
}

// CH.8 Draw the table
TblDrawTable( table );
```

Once our table's styles and so forth are determined, we draw the table with a call to **TblDrawTable()**.

It's worth noting that you can use **TblSetRowUsable()** to write code that scrolls a table by hiding and showing sections of a table that has one row for every record in your database. The downside to this method is that it uses more memory than the method we'll use later in this chapter.

Adding the Function drawCell()

We have set things up so that the Palm OS will call our custom-draw function, **drawCell()**, every time it goes to draw an item in the table. The function begins like this:

```
// CH.8 The custom drawing routine for a table cell
static void drawCell( VoidPtr table, Word row, Word column,
        RectanglePtr bounds )
{
    Int     record;
    CharPtr precord;
    Char    string[DB_FIRST_NAME_SIZE + DB_LAST_NAME_SIZE];
    SWord   width;
    SWord   len;
    Boolean noFit;
```

The parameters and return value for the function are determined by the fact that it is a callback function set by calling **TblSetCustomDrawProcedure()**. We get a pointer to the table object, the row and column of the cell to be drawn, and the bounding rectangle of this cell on the form.

```
// CH.8 Calculate our record
    record = cursor + row;

    // CH.8 Get our record
    hrecord = DmQueryRecord( contactsDB, record );
    precord = MemHandleLock( hrecord );

    // CH.8 Get the date and time
    MemMove( &dateTime, precord + DB_DATE_TIME_START,
            sizeof( dateTime ) );
```

First, we get the record associated with the row, and further extract the date and time info for easier access.

```
// CH.8 Switch on the column
    switch( column )
    {
        // CH.8 Handle dates
        case TABLE_COLUMN_DATE:
        {
```

```
            if( dateTime.year != NO_DATE )
            {
                DateToAscii( dateTime.month, dateTime.day,
                        dateTime.year,
                        (DateFormatType)PrefGetPreference(
                        prefDateFormat ), string );
            }
            else
                StrCopy( string, "-" );
        }
        break;
```

Depending on the column, we create the string we want to display. For the date, we use the same function we used for displaying the date in the big list in the last chapter. Otherwise, we will print a dash to represent that no date has been selected.

```
// CH.8 Handle times
        case TABLE_COLUMN_TIME:
        {
            if( dateTime.hour != NO_TIME )
            {
                TimeToAscii( dateTime.hour, dateTime.minute,
                        (TimeFormatType)PrefGetPreference(
                        prefTimeFormat ), string );
            }
            else
                StrCopy( string, "-" );
        }
        break;
```

The next column displays the time selected. As with the date, we use the same function we used for the list, or we use a dash if there is no time selected.

```
// CH.8 Handle names
        case TABLE_COLUMN_NAME:
        {
            StrCopy( string, precord + DB_FIRST_NAME_START );
            StrCat( string, " " );
            StrCat( string, precord + DB_LAST_NAME_START );
        }
        break;
    }
```

8

The third and final column contains the first and last names. Next, we draw the text we have created for the cell.

```
// CH.8 Unlock the record
MemHandleUnlock( hrecord );
```

We can unlock the record now that we have built the appropriate text string. Notice that this method doesn't use any memory permanently to store cell data. No matter how many records are in the database, this function will still work well. Because of this, custom drawing is really the way to display data in both tables and lists.

```
// CH.8 Set the text mode
WinSetUnderlineMode( noUnderline );
FntSetFont( stdFont );

// CH.8 Truncate the string if necessary
width = bounds->extent.x;
len = StrLen( string );
noFit = false;
FntCharsInWidth( string, &width, &len, &noFit );
```

Next, we want to make sure the text mode is set up properly so that **WinDrawChars()** will do what we expect it to do. The names may not entirely fit in the space we have on the screen, so we check and make sure that the string is not too long to fit in the cell. If it is, we just chop it off. In reality, you would probably want to get more fancy and figure out how to put ellipses (…) at the end of the string and have it fit.

```
// CH.8 Draw the cell
    WinEraseRectangle( bounds, 0 );
    WinDrawChars( string, len, bounds->topLeft.x, bounds->topLeft.y );

    // CH.8 We're done
    return;
}
```

Finally, we draw the string after first erasing anything else that might have been hanging out in that part of the screen beforehand. This is all there is to the custom-drawing functions. They are easy to write and the ultimate in flexibility.

Debugging Tables

It's a good idea to step through **drawTable()** and **drawCell()** when you run them the first time. Your application will crash if you don't turn off rows you're not using because **drawCell()** will try to access records that don't exist. Remember to test the table both by going back and forth between detail and list, but also by re-sorting using the pop-up list.

The Contact List form in your application should look something like Figure 8-3.

Three Kinds of Scrolling

There are three kinds of scrolling generally used in Palm OS applications. The first kind is scroll buttons, which are the pair of up and down repeating buttons we have already used in the Enter Time form. You can use these in

8

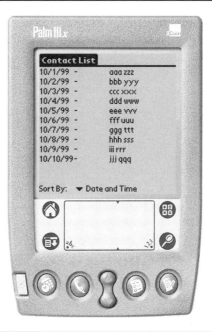

The table
in action

Figure 8-3.

all versions of Palm OS. The second kind is scrollbars, which can't be used with the early Pilot 1000 or Pilot 5000 but can be used everywhere else. The third kind is the PAGE UP and PAGE DOWN hard keys.

In the following sections we will add resources and code to support all three of these kinds of scrolling to the Contact List form. This would not normally be a good idea.

Scrollbar Attributes

Table 8-3 describes the attributes of a scrollbar.

Name	Description
Object Identifier	Constructor will use this to name the constant representing the resource ID in the resource include file.
Scrollbar ID	The resource ID of the scrollbar.
Left Origin	The horizontal position of the left edge of the scrollbar in pixels.
Top Origin	The vertical position of the top edge of the scrollbar in pixels.
Width	The width of the scrollbar in pixels.
Height	The height of the scrollbar in pixels.
Usable	This defines whether the scrollbar can be seen and tapped on.
Value	The initial scroll value of the scrollbar.
Minimum Value	The minimum value that the scrollbar can be set to.
Maximum Value	The maximum value that the scrollbar can be set to.
Page Size	The size of one page of table rows or note lines or whatever the scrollbar is keeping track of. This is used to set the size of the box in the scrollbar.
Orientation	This defines whether the scrollbar is horizontal or vertical.

Scrollbar
Attributes
Table 8-3.

Adding Scroll Buttons and a Scrollbar Resource

Add two scroll buttons and a scrollbar to support two of our three types of scrolling.

1. Launch Metrowerks Constructor.
2. Open the resource file Contacts.rsrc. It is located in the Src folder inside your project folder.
3. Double-click on the Contact List form to open it.
4. Open the Catalog by selecting Window | Catalog from the menu.
5. Drag and drop a scrollbar resource onto the form.
6. Change the scrollbar's Object Identifier to Scrollbar. Put the Left Origin at 153, the Top Origin at 15, the Width at 7, and the Height at 130. This puts the scrollbar just to the right of the table against the right edge of the form.
7. Add scroll buttons. You can steal the scroll buttons you made for the Enter Time form. Open the Enter Time form. Drag the scroll buttons from the Enter Time form onto the Contact List form. Place the up arrow at a Left Origin of 149 and a Top Origin of 145. Change its Object Identifier to RecordUp. Place the down arrow at a Left origin of 149 and a Top Origin of 152. Change its Object Identifier to RecordDown.
8. The Contact List form should now look like Figure 8-4.

Getting the Scroll Buttons Working

In our case, the object of the game is to set the variable cursor equal to where we want the top of the table to be. We also want to make sure the up arrow turns gray at the top record and the down button turns gray at the bottom record. We start by adding code to **contactListHandleEvent()**:

```
// CH.8 Respond to arrows
case ctlRepeatEvent:
{
    switch( event->data.ctlRepeat.controlID )
    {
        // CH.8 Up arrow
        case ContactListRecordUpRepeating:
```

```
                if( cursor > 0 )
                ....cursor--;
            break;

            // CH.8 Down arrow
            case ContactListRecordDownRepeating:
                if( (numRecords > TABLE_NUM_ROWS) &&
                        (cursor < numRecords - TABLE_NUM_ROWS)
)

                    cursor++;
            break;
        }

        // CH.8 Now refresh the table
        drawTable();
    }
    return( true );
```

This is straightforward code. Note that these are repeating buttons, so we look for *ctlRepeatEvent*. For the up arrow we subtract one from the cursor. For the down arrow we add one to the cursor. For both arrows we draw the table.

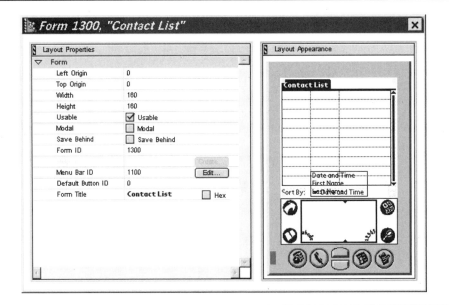

The Contact List form after adding a scrollbar and scroll buttons

Figure 8-4.

To make it safe, we check to make sure the cursor can move that far. You'll see that in drawing the table we also redisplay and appropriately disable the buttons.

To accomplish this, we add the following code to the bottom of **drawTable()**:

```
// CH.8 Get pointers to the arrow buttons
upArrow = getObject( form, ContactListRecordUpRepeating );
downArrow = getObject( form, ContactListRecordDownRepeating );

// CH.8 Update the arrow buttons and scrollbars
if( numRecords > TABLE_NUM_ROWS )
{
    // CH.8 Show the up arrow
    if( cursor > 0 )
    {
        CtlSetLabel( upArrow, BLACK_UP_ARROW );
        CtlSetEnabled( upArrow, true );
    }
    else
    {
        CtlSetLabel( upArrow, GRAY_UP_ARROW );
        CtlSetEnabled( upArrow, false );
    }
    CtlShowControl( upArrow );

    // CH.8 Show the down arrow
    if( cursor >= numRecords - TABLE_NUM_ROWS )
    {
        CtlSetLabel( downArrow, GRAY_DOWN_ARROW );
        CtlSetEnabled( downArrow, false );
    }
    else
    {
        CtlSetLabel( downArrow, BLACK_DOWN_ARROW );
        CtlSetEnabled( downArrow, true );
    }
    CtlShowControl( downArrow );
}
else
{
    // CH.8 Hide the arrows
    CtlHideControl( upArrow );
    CtlHideControl( downArrow );
}
```

8

```
    // CH.8 We're done
    return;
}
```

If the table is at the beginning or end of its extent, we gray out and disable the appropriate repeating button. This prevents the cursor from being set to a bad value. It also looks nice.

This is all you need to do to support repeating buttons as scrolling arrows.

Adding Support for the PAGE UP and PAGE DOWN Hard Keys

To catch the PAGE UP and PAGE DOWN hard keys, you need to first look for the *keyDownEvent.*

The math gets a little tricky for these buttons. When you page up or page down, it's a good idea to leave at least one familiar line on the page. Instead of moving TABLE_NUM_ROWS, we want to move TABLE_NUM_ROWS – 1. Also, since we can't turn off these buttons, we have to make sure that pressing them can't put the cursor out of range. Furthermore, both the cursor and *numRecords* are unsigned, so we need to check them before we do any math on them that might cause them to go negative and thus turn into garbage values. Again, these changes are to **contactListHandleEvent()**:

```
        // CH.8 Respond to up and down arrow hard keys
        case keyDownEvent:
        {
            switch( event->data.keyDown.chr )
            {
                // CH.8 Up arrow hard key
                case pageUpChr:
                    if( cursor > TABLE_NUM_ROWS - 1 )
                        cursor -= TABLE_NUM_ROWS - 1;
                    else
                        cursor = 0;
                break;
```

For page up, the calculation is fairly simple. If paging up won't cause us to go below zero, then we page up a full page. Otherwise, we go to zero.

```
                    // CH.8 Down arrow hard key
                    case pageDownChr:
                        if( (numRecords > 2 * TABLE_NUM_ROWS - 1) &&
                                (cursor < numRecords -
                                2 * TABLE_NUM_ROWS - 1) )
                            cursor += TABLE_NUM_ROWS - 1;
                        else
                            cursor = numRecords - TABLE_NUM_ROWS;
                        break;
                }

                // CH.8 Now refresh the table
                drawTable();
            }
            break;
```

For page down, we need to remember that we are effectively at the end of the records when the value of the cursor is *numRecords* minus TABLE_NUM_ROWS (remember the cursor is zero based). So first we look to see if we are more than a page away from the end of the records. First, we check to make sure that there are enough records in the table so that subtracting this from *numRecords* will yield a positive number. Then we see if the cursor is before the next-to-last page. If it is, we page down a whole page. If it isn't, we page down to the bottom.

At the bottom, as with the scroll buttons, we must redraw the table. This completes all it takes to support the hard keys.

8

Programming Scrollbars

Scrollbars require a snippet of code in the event handler and a snippet of code in whatever drawing routine, in our case, **drawTable()**. First look at the event handling code:

```
            // CH.8 Respond to scrollbar events
            case sclRepeatEvent:
                cursor = event->data.sclExit.newValue;
                drawTable();
            break;
```

We respond to the repeating scroll event by setting the cursor equal to the new value of the scrollbar we're given. If we set the bounds of the scrollbar correctly we can guarantee this never results in us getting a bad value for the cursor. Once we set the cursor, we redraw the table and scroll controls, as with the other scrolling.

Next, look at the code we added to the **drawTable()** function. After the scroll-button code in the if(*numRecords* > TABLE_NUM_ROWS) statement:

```
// CH.8 Show the scrollbar
FrmShowObject( form, FrmGetObjectIndex( form,
        ContactListScrollbarScrollBar ) );
SclSetScrollBar( getObject( form,
        ContactListScrollbarScrollBar ), cursor, 0,
        numRecords - TABLE_NUM_ROWS, TABLE_NUM_ROWS );
```

Here we show the scrollbar and set it to the appropriate values. Because we know we have more records than visible rows, we know that *numRecords* – TABLE_NUM_ROWS won't yield a garbage result.

In the else statement, which means we have fewer records than visible rows, we want to hide the scrollbar:

```
// CH.8 Hide the scrollbar
FrmHideObject( form, FrmGetObjectIndex( form,
        ContactListScrollbarScrollBar ) );
```

This is all you need to support scrollbars.

Debugging Scrollbars

As always, walk through the code you've added. Additionally, make all the controls end up on the exact first and last records at the extents, not too few (some records are never displayed) or too many (crash!).

The Contact List form should now look something like Figure 8-5.

What's Next?

In the next chapter we will wrap up the fundamental section of the book by adding several cool features to Contacts, including system find, categories, and secret records.

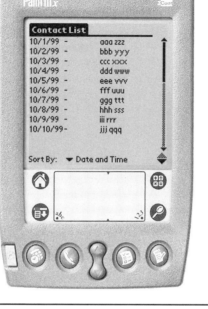

The scrolling
things in action
Figure 8-5.

8

Listing

Here is Contacts.c after it has received all the modifications in this chapter:

```
// CH.2 The super-include for the Palm OS
#include <Pilot.h>

// CH.5 Added for the call to GrfSetState()
#include <Graffiti.h>

// CH.3 Our resource file
#include "Contacts_res.h"

// CH.4 Prototypes for our event handler functions
static Boolean   contactDetailHandleEvent( EventPtr event );
static Boolean   aboutHandleEvent( EventPtr event );
static Boolean   enterTimeHandleEvent( EventPtr event );
static Boolean   contactListHandleEvent( EventPtr event );
static Boolean   menuEventHandler( EventPtr event );
```

```
// CH.4 Constants for ROM revision
#define ROM_VERSION_2    0x02003000
#define ROM_VERSION_MIN ROM_VERSION_2

// CH.5 Prototypes for utility functions
static void     newRecord( void );
static VoidPtr  getObject( FormPtr, Word );
static void     setFields( void );
static void     getFields( void );
static void     setText( FieldPtr, CharPtr );
static void     getText( FieldPtr, VoidPtr, Word );
static void     setDateTrigger( void );
static void     setTimeTrigger( void );
static void     setTimeControls( void );
static Int      sortFunc( CharPtr, CharPtr, Int );
static void     drawTable( void );
static void     drawCell( VoidPtr table, Word row,
                          Word column, RectanglePtr bounds );

// CH.5 Our open database reference
static DmOpenRef    contactsDB;
static ULong        numRecords;
static UInt         cursor;
static Boolean      isDirty;
static VoidHand     hrecord;

// CH.5 Constants that define the database record
#define DB_ID_START             0
#define DB_ID_SIZE              (sizeof( ULong ))
#define DB_DATE_TIME_START      (DB_ID_START +\
                                DB_ID_SIZE)
#define DB_DATE_TIME_SIZE       (sizeof( DateTimeType ))
#define DB_FIRST_NAME_START     (DB_DATE_TIME_START +\
                                DB_DATE_TIME_SIZE)
#define DB_FIRST_NAME_SIZE      16
#define DB_LAST_NAME_START      (DB_FIRST_NAME_START +\
                                DB_FIRST_NAME_SIZE)
#define DB_LAST_NAME_SIZE       16
#define DB_PHONE_NUMBER_START   (DB_LAST_NAME_START +\
                                DB_LAST_NAME_SIZE)
#define DB_PHONE_NUMBER_SIZE    16
#define DB_RECORD_SIZE          (DB_PHONE_NUMBER_START +\
                                DB_PHONE_NUMBER_SIZE)

// CH.6 Storage for the record's date and time in expanded form
```

```
static DateTimeType dateTime;
static Word         timeSelect;
#define NO_DATE     0
#define NO_TIME     0x7fff


// CH.7 The error exit macro
#define errorExit(alert) { ErrThrow( alert ); }


// CH.7 The sort order variable and constants
static Int sortBy;
// CH.7 NOTE: These items match the popup list entries!
#define SORTBY_DATE_TIME    0
#define SORTBY_FIRST_NAME   1
#define SORTBY_LAST_NAME    2


// CH.8 Table constants
#define TABLE_NUM_COLUMNS   3
#define TABLE_NUM_ROWS      11
#define TABLE_COLUMN_DATE   0
#define TABLE_COLUMN_TIME   1
#define TABLE_COLUMN_NAME   2
#define BLACK_UP_ARROW      "\x01"
#define BLACK_DOWN_ARROW    "\x02"
#define GRAY_UP_ARROW       "\x03"
#define GRAY_DOWN_ARROW     "\x04"

// CH.2 The main entry point
DWord PilotMain( Word cmd, Ptr, Word )
{
    DWord       romVersion; // CH.4 ROM version
    FormPtr     form;       // CH.2 A pointer to our form structure
    EventType   event;      // CH.2 Our event structure
    Word        error;      // CH.3 Error word
    // CH.4 Get the ROM version
    romVersion = 0;
    FtrGet( sysFtrCreator, sysFtrNumROMVersion, &romVersion );

    // CH.4 If we are below our minimum acceptable ROM revision
    if( romVersion < ROM_VERSION_MIN )
    {
        // CH.4 Display the alert
        FrmAlert( LowROMVersionErrorAlert );

        // CH.4 PalmOS 1.0 will continuously re-launch this app
        // unless we switch to another safe one
```

```
    if( romVersion < ROM_VERSION_2 )
    {
        AppLaunchWithCommand( sysFileCDefaultApp,
                sysAppLaunchCmdNormalLaunch, NULL );
    }
    return( 0 );
}


// CH.2 If this is not a normal launch, don't launch
if( cmd != sysAppLaunchCmdNormalLaunch )
    return( 0 );

// CH.5 Create a new database in case there isn't one
if( ((error = DmCreateDatabase( 0, "ContactsDB-PPGU", 'PPGU',
        'ctct', false )) != dmErrAlreadyExists) && (error != 0)
)
{
    // CH.5 Handle db creation error
    FrmAlert( DBCreationErrorAlert );
    return( 0 );
}

// CH.5 Open the database
contactsDB = DmOpenDatabaseByTypeCreator( 'ctct', 'PPGU',
        dmModeReadWrite );

// CH.5 Get the number of records in the database
numRecords = DmNumRecords( contactsDB );

// CH.5 Initialize the record number
cursor = 0;

// CH.7 Choose our starting page
// CH.5 If there are no records, create one
if( numRecords == 0 )
{
    newRecord();
    FrmGotoForm( ContactDetailForm );
}
else
    FrmGotoForm( ContactListForm );

// CH.7 Begin the try block
ErrTry {
```

```
// CH.2 Our event loop
do
{
    // CH.2 Get the next event
    EvtGetEvent( &event, -1 );

    // CH.2 Handle system events
    if( SysHandleEvent( &event ) )
        continue;

    // CH.3 Handle menu events
    if( MenuHandleEvent( NULL, &event, &error ) )
        continue;

    // CH.4 Handle form load events
    if( event.eType == frmLoadEvent )
    {
        // CH.4 Initialize our form
        switch( event.data.frmLoad.formID )
        {
            // CH.4 Contact Detail form
            case ContactDetailForm:
                form = FrmInitForm( ContactDetailForm );
                FrmSetEventHandler( form,
                        contactDetailHandleEvent );
            break;

            // CH.4 About form
            case AboutForm:
                form = FrmInitForm( AboutForm );
                FrmSetEventHandler( form, aboutHandleEvent );
            break;

            // CH.6 Enter Time form
            case EnterTimeForm:
                form = FrmInitForm( EnterTimeForm );
                FrmSetEventHandler( form, enterTimeHandleEvent );
            break;

            // CH.7 Contact List form
            case ContactListForm:
                form = FrmInitForm( ContactListForm );
                FrmSetEventHandler( form,
                        contactListHandleEvent );
break;
```

8

```
            }
            FrmSetActiveForm( form );
        }

        // CH.2 Handle form events
        FrmDispatchEvent( &event );

    // CH.2 If it's a stop event, exit
    } while( event.eType != appStopEvent );

    // CH.7 End the try block and do the catch block
    }
    ErrCatch( errorAlert )
    {
        // CH.7 Display the appropriate alert
        FrmAlert( errorAlert );
    } ErrEndCatch

    // CH.5 Close all open forms
    FrmCloseAllForms();

    // CH.5 Close the database
    DmCloseDatabase( contactsDB );

    // CH.2 We're done
    return( 0 );
}

// CH.4 Our Contact Detail form handler function
static Boolean contactDetailHandleEvent( EventPtr event )
{
    FormPtr form;       // CH.3 A pointer to our form structure
    VoidPtr precord;    // CH.6 Points to a database record

    // CH.3 Get our form pointer
    form = FrmGetActiveForm();

    // CH.4 Parse events
    switch( event->eType )
    {
        // CH.4 Form open event
        case frmOpenEvent:
        {
            // CH.2 Draw the form
            FrmDrawForm( form );
```

```
        // CH.5 Draw the database fields
        setFields();
    }
    break;

    // CH.5 Form close event
    case frmCloseEvent:
    {
        // CH.5 Store away any modified fields
        getFields();
    }
    break;

    // CH.5 Parse the button events
    case ctlSelectEvent:
    {
        // CH.5 Store any field changes
        getFields();

        switch( event->data.ctlSelect.controlID )
        {
            // CH.5 First button
            case ContactDetailFirstButton:
            {
                // CH.5 Set the cursor to the first record
                if( cursor > 0 )
                    cursor = 0;
            }
            break;

            // CH.5 Previous button
            case ContactDetailPrevButton:
            {
                // CH.5 Move the cursor back one record
                if( cursor > 0 )
                    cursor—;
            }
            break;

            // CH.5 Next button
            case ContactDetailNextButton:
            {
                // CH.5 Move the cursor up one record
                if( cursor < (numRecords - 1) )
```

```
            cursor++;
    }
    break;

    // CH.5 Last button
    case ContactDetailLastButton:
    {
        // CH.5 Move the cursor to the last record
        if( cursor < (numRecords - 1) )
            cursor = numRecords - 1;
    }
    break;

    // CH.5 Delete button
    case ContactDetailDeleteButton:
    {
        // CH.5 Remove the record from the database
        DmRemoveRecord( contactsDB, cursor );

        // CH.5 Decrease the number of records
        numRecords—;

        // CH.5 Place the cursor at the first record
        cursor = 0;

        // CH.5 If there are no records left, create one
        if( numRecords == 0 )
            newRecord();
    }
    break;

    // CH.5 New button
    case ContactDetailNewButton:
    {
        // CH.5 Create a new record
        newRecord();
    }
    break;

    // CH.7 Done button
    case ContactDetailDoneButton:
    {
        // CH.7 Load the contact list
        FrmGotoForm( ContactListForm );
    }
```

```
        break;

        // CH.6 Date selector trigger
        case ContactDetailDateSelTrigger:
        {
            // CH.6 Initialize the date if necessary
            if( dateTime.year == NO_DATE )
            {
                DateTimeType currentDate;

                // CH.6 Get the current date
                TimSecondsToDateTime( TimGetSeconds(),
                        &currentDate );

                // CH.6 Copy it
                dateTime.year = currentDate.year;
                dateTime.month = currentDate.month;
                dateTime.day = currentDate.day;
            }

            // CH.6 Pop up the system date selection form
            SelectDay( selectDayByDay, &(dateTime.month),
                    &(dateTime.day), &(dateTime.year),
                    "Enter Date" );

            // CH.6 Get the record
            hrecord = DmQueryRecord( contactsDB, cursor );

            // CH.6 Lock it down
            precord = MemHandleLock( hrecord );

            // CH.6 Write the date time field
            DmWrite( precord, DB_DATE_TIME_START, &dateTime,
                    sizeof( DateTimeType ) );

            // CH.6 Unlock the record
            MemHandleUnlock( hrecord );

            // CH.6 Mark the record dirty
            isDirty = true;
        }
        break;

        // CH.6 Time selector trigger
        case ContactDetailTimeSelTrigger:
```

8

```
                {
                        // CH.6 Pop up our selection form
                        FrmPopupForm( EnterTimeForm );
                    }
                    break;
                }

                // CH.5 Sync the current record to the fields
                setFields();
            }
            break;

            // CH.5 Respond to field tap
            case fldEnterEvent:
                isDirty = true;
            break;

            // CH.3 Parse menu events
            case menuEvent:
                return( menuEventHandler( event ) );
            break;
        }

    // CH.2 We're done
    return( false );
}

// CH.4 Our About form event handler function
static Boolean aboutHandleEvent( EventPtr event )
{
    FormPtr form;    // CH.4 A pointer to our form structure

    // CH.4 Get our form pointer
    form = FrmGetActiveForm();

    // CH.4 Respond to the Open event
    if( event->eType == frmOpenEvent )
    {
        // CH.4 Draw the form
        FrmDrawForm( form );
    }

    // CH.4 Return to the calling form
    if( event->eType == ctlSelectEvent )
    {
```

8

```
        FrmReturnToForm( 0 );

        // CH.4 Always return true in this case
        return( true );
    }

    // CH.4 We're done
    return( false );
}

// CH.6 Our Enter Time form event handler function
static Boolean enterTimeHandleEvent( EventPtr event )
{
    FormPtr             form;        // CH.6 A form structure pointer
    static DateTimeType oldTime;     // CH.6 The original time

    // CH.6 Get our form pointer
    form = FrmGetActiveForm();

    // CH.6 Switch on the event
    switch( event->eType )
    {
        // CH.6 Initialize the form
        case frmOpenEvent:
        {
            // CH.6 Store the time value
            oldTime = dateTime;

            // CH.6 Draw it
            FrmDrawForm( form );

            // CH.6 Set the time controls
            setTimeControls();
        }
        break;

        // CH.6 If a button was repeated
        case ctlRepeatEvent:
        // CH.6 If a button was pushed
        case ctlSelectEvent:
        {
            Word    buttonID;   // CH.6 The ID of the button

            // CH.6 Set the ID
            buttonID = event->data.ctlSelect.controlID;
```

```
// CH.6 Switch on button ID
switch( buttonID )
{
    // CH.6 Hours button
    case EnterTimeHoursPushButton:
    // CH.6 Minute Tens button
    case EnterTimeMinuteTensPushButton:
    // CH.6 Minute Ones button
    case EnterTimeMinuteOnesPushButton:
    {
        // CH.6 If no time was set
        if( dateTime.hour == NO_TIME )
        {
            // CH.6 Set the time to 12 PM
            dateTime.hour = 12;
            dateTime.minute = 0;

            // CH.6 Set the controls
            setTimeControls();
        }

        // CH.6 Clear the old selection if any
        if( timeSelect )
            CtlSetValue( getObject( form, timeSelect ),
                    false );

        // CH.6 Set the new selection
        CtlSetValue( getObject( form, buttonID ), true );
        timeSelect = buttonID;
    }
    break;

    // CH.6 Up button
    case EnterTimeTimeUpRepeating:
    {
        // CH.6 If there's no time, do nothing
        if( dateTime.hour == NO_TIME )
            break;

        // CH.6 Based on what push button is selected
        switch( timeSelect )
        {
            // CH.6 Increase hours
```

```
                case EnterTimeHoursPushButton:
                {
                    // CH.6 Increment hours
                    dateTime.hour++;

                    // CH.6 If it was 11 AM, make it 12 AM
                    if( dateTime.hour == 12 )
                        dateTime.hour = 0;

                    // CH.6 If it was 11 PM, make it 12 PM
                    if( dateTime.hour == 24 )
                        dateTime.hour = 12;
                }
                break;

                // CH.6 Increase tens of minutes
                case EnterTimeMinuteTensPushButton:
                {
                    // CH.6 Increment minutes
                    dateTime.minute += 10;

                    // CH.6 If it was 5X, roll over
                    if( dateTime.minute > 59 )
                        dateTime.minute -= 60;
                }
                break;

                // CH.6 Increase minutes
                case EnterTimeMinuteOnesPushButton:
                {
                    // CH.6 Increment minutes
                    dateTime.minute++;

                    // CH.6 If it is zero, subtract ten
                    if( (dateTime.minute % 10) == 0 )
                        dateTime.minute -= 10;
                }
                break;
            }

            // Revise the controls
            setTimeControls();
        }
        break;
```

8

```
// CH.6 Down button
case EnterTimeTimeDownRepeating:
{

    // CH.6 If there's no time, do nothing
    if( dateTime.hour == NO_TIME )
        break;

    // CH.6 Based on what push button is selected
    switch( timeSelect )
    {
        // CH.6 Decrease hours
        case EnterTimeHoursPushButton:
        {
            // CH.6 Decrement hours
            dateTime.hour—;

            // CH.6 If it was 12 AM, make it 11 AM
            if( dateTime.hour == -1 )
                dateTime.hour = 11;

            // CH.6 If it was 12 PM, make it 11 PM
            if( dateTime.hour == 11 )
                dateTime.hour = 23;
        }
        break;

        // CH.6 Decrease tens of minutes
        case EnterTimeMinuteTensPushButton:
        {
            // CH.6 Decrement minutes
            dateTime.minute -= 10;

            // CH.6 If it was 0X, roll over
            if( dateTime.minute < 0 )
                dateTime.minute += 60;
        }
        break;

        // CH.6 Decrease minutes
        case EnterTimeMinuteOnesPushButton:
        {
            // CH.6 Decrement minutes
            dateTime.minute—;
```

```
                    // CH.6 If it is 9, add ten
                    if( (dateTime.minute % 10) == 9 )
                        dateTime.minute += 10;

                    // CH.6 If less than zero, make it 9
                    if( dateTime.minute < 0 )
                        dateTime.minute = 9;
                }
                break;
        }

        // CH.6 Revise the controls
        setTimeControls();
    }
    break;

    // CH.6 AM button
    case EnterTimeAMPushButton:
    {
        // CH.6 If no time was set
        if( dateTime.hour == NO_TIME )
        {
            // CH.6 Set the time to 12 AM
            dateTime.hour = 0;
            dateTime.minute = 0;

            // CH.6 Set the controls
            setTimeControls();
        }

        // CH.6 If it is PM
        if( dateTime.hour > 11 )
        {
            // CH.6 Change to AM
            dateTime.hour -= 12;

            // CH.6 Set the controls
            setTimeControls();
        }
    }
    break;

    // CH.6 PM button
    case EnterTimePMPushButton:
    {
```

8

```
        // CH.6 If no time was set
        if( dateTime.hour == NO_TIME )
        {
            // CH.6 Set the time to 12 PM
            dateTime.hour = 12;
            dateTime.minute = 0;

            // CH.6 Set the controls
            setTimeControls();
        }

        // CH.6 If it is AM
        if( dateTime.hour < 12 )
        {
            // CH.6 Change to PM
            dateTime.hour += 12;

            // CH.6 Set the controls
            setTimeControls();
        }
    }
    break;

    // CH.6 No Time checkbox
    case EnterTimeNoTimeCheckbox:
    {
        // CH.6 If we are unchecking the box
        if( dateTime.hour == NO_TIME )
        {
            // CH.6 Set the time to 12 PM
            dateTime.hour = 12;
            dateTime.minute = 0;

            // CH.6 Set the controls
            setTimeControls();

            // CH.6 Set the new selection
            timeSelect = EnterTimeHoursPushButton;
            CtlSetValue( getObject( form, timeSelect ),
                    true );
        }

        else
        // CH.6 If we are checking the box
```

```
            dateTime.hour = NO_TIME;

      // CH.6 Set the controls
      setTimeControls();
}
break;

// CH.6 Cancel button
case EnterTimeCancelButton:
{
      // CH.6 Restore time
      dateTime = oldTime;

      // CH.6 Return to calling form
      FrmReturnToForm( 0 );
}
// CH.6 Always return true
return( true );

// CH.6 OK button
case EnterTimeOKButton:
{
      VoidPtr precord;    // CH.6 Points to the record

      // CH.6 Lock it down
      precord = MemHandleLock( hrecord );

      // CH.6 Write the date time field
      DmWrite( precord, DB_DATE_TIME_START, &dateTime,
             sizeof( DateTimeType ) );

      // CH.6 Unlock the record
      MemHandleUnlock( hrecord );

      // CH.6 Mark the record dirty
      isDirty = true;

      // CH.6 Return to the Contact Details form
      FrmReturnToForm( 0 );

      // CH.6 Update the field
      setTimeTrigger();
}
// CH.6 Always return true
```

```
                    return( true );
                }
            }
        break;
    }

    // CH.6 We're done
    return( false );
}

// CH.7 Our Contact List form event handler function
static Boolean contactListHandleEvent( EventPtr event )
{
    FormPtr form;    // CH.7 A form structure pointer

    // CH.7 Get our form pointer
    form = FrmGetActiveForm();

    // CH.7 Parse events
    switch( event->eType )
    {
        // CH.7 Form open event
        case frmOpenEvent:
        {
            // CH.7 Draw the form
            FrmDrawForm( form );

            // CH.8 Populate and draw the table
            drawTable();
        }
        break;

        // CH.7 Respond to a list selection
        case tblSelectEvent:
        {
            // CH.7 Set the database cursor to the selected contact
            cursor += event->data.tblSelect.row;

            // CH.7 Go to contact details
            FrmGotoForm( ContactDetailForm );
        }
        break;

        // CH.7 Respond to a menu event
        case menuEvent:
```

```
            return( menuEventHandler( event ) );

        // CH.7 Respond to the popup trigger
        case popSelectEvent:
        {
            // CH.7 If there is no change, we're done
            if( sortBy == event->data.popSelect.selection )
                return( true );

            // CH.7 Modify sort order variable
            sortBy = event->data.popSelect.selection;

            // CH.7 Sort the contact database by the new criteria
            DmQuickSort( contactsDB, (DmComparF*)sortFunc, sortBy );

            // CH.8 Rebuild the table
            drawTable();
        }
        break;

        // CH.8 Respond to arrows
        case ctlRepeatEvent:
        {
            switch( event->data.ctlRepeat.controlID )
            {
                // CH.8 Up arrow
                case ContactListRecordUpRepeating:
                    if( cursor > 0 )
                        cursor—;
                break;

                // CH.8 Down arrow
                case ContactListRecordDownRepeating:
                    if( (numRecords > TABLE_NUM_ROWS) &&
                            (cursor < numRecords - TABLE_NUM_ROWS) )
                        cursor++;
                break;
            }

            // CH.8 Now refresh the table
            drawTable();
        }
        return( true );

        // CH.8 Respond to up and down arrow hard keys
```

```
        case keyDownEvent:
            {
                switch( event->data.keyDown.chr )
                {
                    // CH.8 Up arrow hard key
                    case pageUpChr:
                        if( cursor > TABLE_NUM_ROWS - 1 )
                            cursor -= TABLE_NUM_ROWS - 1;
                        else
                            cursor = 0;
                    break;

                    // CH.8 Down arrow hard key
                    case pageDownChr:
                        if( (numRecords > 2 * TABLE_NUM_ROWS - 1) &&
                                (cursor < numRecords -
                                2 * TABLE_NUM_ROWS - 1) )
                            cursor += TABLE_NUM_ROWS - 1;
                        else
                            cursor = numRecords - TABLE_NUM_ROWS;
                    break;
                }

                // CH.8 Now refresh the table
                drawTable();
            }
            break;

            // CH.8 Respond to scrollbar events
            case sclRepeatEvent:
                cursor = event->data.sclExit.newValue;
                drawTable();
            break;

        }    // CH.7 End of the event switch statement

        // CH.7 We're done
        return( false );
    }

// CH.3 Handle menu events
Boolean menuEventHandler( EventPtr event )
{
    FormPtr     form;      // CH.3 A pointer to our form structure
    Word        index;     // CH.3 A general purpose control index
    FieldPtr    field;     // CH.3 Used for manipulating fields
```

8

```
// CH.3 Get our form pointer
form = FrmGetActiveForm();

// CH.3 Erase the menu status from the display
MenuEraseStatus( NULL );

// CH.4 Handle options menu
if( event->data.menu.itemID == OptionsAboutContacts )
{
    // CH.4 Pop up the About form as a Dialog
    FrmPopupForm( AboutForm );
    return( true );
}

// CH.3 Handle graffiti help
if( event->data.menu.itemID == EditGraffitiHelp )
{
    // CH.3 Pop up the graffiti reference based on
    // the graffiti state
    SysGraffitiReferenceDialog( referenceDefault );
    return( true );
}

// CH.3 Get the index of our field
index = FrmGetFocus( form );

// CH.3 If there is no field selected, we're done
if( index == noFocus )
    return( false );

// CH.3 Get the pointer of our field
field = FrmGetObjectPtr( form, index );

// CH.3 Do the edit command
switch( event->data.menu.itemID )
{
    // CH.3 Undo
    case EditUndo:
        FldUndo( field );
    break;

    // CH.3 Cut
    case EditCut:
        FldCut( field );
```

```
        break;

        // CH.3 Copy
        case EditCopy:
            FldCopy( field );
        break;

        // CH.3 Paste
        case EditPaste:
            FldPaste( field );
        break;

        // CH.3 Select All
        case EditSelectAll:
        {
            // CH.3 Get the length of the string in the field
            Word length = FldGetTextLength( field );

            // CH.3 Sound an error if appropriate
            if( length == 0 )
            {
                SndPlaySystemSound( sndError );
                return( false );
            }

            // CH.3 Select the whole string
            FldSetSelection( field, 0, length );
        }
        break;

        // CH.3 Bring up the keyboard tool
        case EditKeyboard:
            SysKeyboardDialogV10();
        break;
    }

    // CH.3 We're done
    return( true );
}
// CH.5 This function creates and initializes a new record
static void newRecord( void )
{
    VoidPtr precord;    // CH.5 Pointer to the record

    // CH.7 Create the database record and get a handle to it
```

```
        if( (hrecord = DmNewRecord( contactsDB, &cursor,
                DB_RECORD_SIZE )) == NULL )
            errorExit( MemoryErrorAlert );

        // CH.5 Lock down the record to modify it
        precord = MemHandleLock( hrecord );

        // CH.5 Clear the record
        DmSet( precord, 0, DB_RECORD_SIZE, 0 );

        // CH.6 Initialize the date and time
        MemSet( &dateTime, sizeof( dateTime ), 0 );
        dateTime.year = NO_DATE;
        dateTime.hour = NO_TIME;
        DmWrite( precord, DB_DATE_TIME_START, &dateTime,
                sizeof( DateTimeType ) );

        // CH.5 Unlock the record
        MemHandleUnlock( hrecord );

        // CH.5 Clear the busy bit and set the dirty bit
        DmReleaseRecord( contactsDB, cursor, true );

        // CH.5 Increment the total record count
        numRecords++;

        // CH.5 Set the dirty bit
        isDirty = true;

        // CH.5 We're done
        return;
    }


// CH.5 A time saver: Gets object pointers based on their ID
static VoidPtr getObject( FormPtr form, Word objectID )
{
    Word    index;  // CH.5 The object index

    // CH.5 Get the index
    index = FrmGetObjectIndex( form, objectID );

    // CH.5 Return the pointer
    return( FrmGetObjectPtr( form, index ) );
}
```

8

```
// CH.5 Gets the current database record and displays it
// in the detail fields
static void setFields( void )
{
    FormPtr form;          // CH.5 The contact detail form
    CharPtr precord;       // CH.5 A record pointer
    Word    index;         // CH.5 The object index

    // CH.5 Get the contact detail form pointer
    form = FrmGetActiveForm();

    // CH.5 Get the current record
    hrecord = DmQueryRecord( contactsDB, cursor );

    // CH.6 Initialize the date and time variable
    precord = MemHandleLock( hrecord );
    MemMove( &dateTime, precord + DB_DATE_TIME_START,
            sizeof( dateTime ) );

    // CH.6 Initialize the date control
    setDateTrigger();

    // CH.6 Initialize the time control
    setTimeTrigger();

    // CH.5 Set the text for the First Name field
    setText( getObject( form, ContactDetailFirstNameField ),
            precord + DB_FIRST_NAME_START );

    // CH.5 Set the text for the Last Name field
    setText( getObject( form, ContactDetailLastNameField ),
            precord + DB_LAST_NAME_START );

    // CH.5 Set the text for the Phone Number field
    setText( getObject( form, ContactDetailPhoneNumberField ),
            precord + DB_PHONE_NUMBER_START );
    MemHandleUnlock( hrecord );

    // CH.5 If the record is already dirty, it's new, so set focus
    if( isDirty )
    {
        // CH.3 Get the index of our field
        index = FrmGetObjectIndex( form,
                ContactDetailFirstNameField );
```

```
                // CH.3 Set the focus to the First Name field
                FrmSetFocus( form, index );

                // CH.5 Set upper shift on
                GrfSetState( false, false, true );
        }

        // CH.5 We're done
        return;
}

// CH.5 Puts any field changes in the record
static void getFields( void )
{
        FormPtr form;      // CH.5 The contact detail form

        // CH.5 Get the contact detail form pointer
        form = FrmGetActiveForm();

        // CH.5 Turn off focus
        FrmSetFocus( form, -1 );

        // CH.5 If the record has been modified
        if( isDirty )
        {
                CharPtr record; // CH.5 Points to the DB record

                // CH.7 Detach the record from the database
                DmDetachRecord( contactsDB, cursor, &hrecord );

                // CH.5 Lock the record
                precord = MemHandleLock( hrecord );

                // CH.5 Get the text for the First Name field
                getText( getObject( form, ContactDetailFirstNameField ),
                        precord, DB_FIRST_NAME_START );

                // CH.5 Get the text for the Last Name field
                getText( getObject( form, ContactDetailLastNameField ),
                        precord, DB_LAST_NAME_START );

                // CH.5 Get the text for the Phone Number field
                getText( getObject( form, ContactDetailPhoneNumberField ),
                        precord, DB_PHONE_NUMBER_START );
```

8

```
        // CH.7 Find the proper position
        cursor = DmFindSortPosition( contactsDB, precord, NULL,
                (DmComparF*)sortFunc, sortBy );

        // CH.5 Unlock the record
        MemHandleUnlock( hrecord );

        // CH.7 Reattach the record
        DmAttachRecord( contactsDB, &cursor, hrecord, NULL );
    }

    // CH.5 Reset the dirty bit
    isDirty = false;

    // CH.5 We're done
    return;
}

// CH.5 Set the text in a field
static void setText( FieldPtr field, CharPtr text )
{
    VoidHand    hfield; // CH.5 Handle of field text
    CharPtr     pfield; // CH.5 Pointer to field text

    // CH.5 Get the current field handle
    hfield = FldGetTextHandle( field );

    // CH.5 If we have a handle
    if( hfield != NULL )
    {
        // CH.5 Resize it
        if( MemHandleResize( hfield, StrLen( text ) + 1 ) != 0 )
            errorExit( MemoryErrorAlert );
    }

    else
    // CH.5 Allocate a handle for the string
    {
        hfield = MemHandleNew( StrLen( text ) + 1 );
        if( hfield == NULL )
            errorExit( MemoryErrorAlert );
    }

    // CH.5 Lock it
    pfield = MemHandleLock( hfield );
```

```
        // CH.5 Copy the string
        StrCopy( pfield, text );

        // CH.5 Unlock it
        MemHandleUnlock( hfield );

        // CH.5 Give it to the field
        FldSetTextHandle( field, hfield );

        // CH.5 Draw the field
        FldDrawField( field );

        // CH.5 We're done
        return;
}

// CH.5 Get the text from a field
static void getText( FieldPtr field, VoidPtr precord, Word offset )
{
    CharPtr pfield; // CH.5 Pointer to field text

    // CH.5 Get the text pointer
    pfield = FldGetTextPtr( field );

    // CH.5 Copy it
    DmWrite( precord, offset, pfield, StrLen( pfield ) );

    // CH.5 We're done
    return;
}

// CH.6 Set the Contact Detail date selector trigger
static void setDateTrigger( void )
{
    FormPtr form;    // CH.5 The contact detail form

    // CH.6 Get the contact detail form pointer
    form = FrmGetActiveForm();

    // CH.6 If there is no date
    if( dateTime.year == NO_DATE )
    {
        CtlSetLabel( getObject( form, ContactDetailDateSelTrigger ),
                    "              " );
```

8

```
        }

    else
    // CH.6 If there is a date
    {
        Char dateString[dateStringLength];

        // CH.6 Get the date string
        DateToAscii( dateTime.month, dateTime.day, dateTime.year,
                (DateFormatType)PrefGetPreference( prefDateFormat ),
                dateString );

        // CH.6 Set the selector trigger label
        CtlSetLabel( getObject( form, ContactDetailDateSelTrigger ),
                dateString );

    }

    // CH.6 We're done
    return;
}

// CH.6 Set the Contact Detail time selector trigger
static void setTimeTrigger( void )
{
    FormPtr form;     // CH.5 The contact detail form

    // CH.6 Get the contact detail form pointer
    form = FrmGetActiveForm();

    // CH.6 If there's no time
    if( dateTime.hour == NO_TIME )
    {
        CtlSetLabel( getObject( form, ContactDetailTimeSelTrigger ),
                "                " );
    }

    else
    // CH.6 If there is a time
    {
        Char timeString[timeStringLength];

        // CH.6 Get the time string
        TimeToAscii( dateTime.hour, dateTime.minute,
```

```
                    (TimeFormatType)PrefGetPreference( prefTimeFormat ),
                    timeString );

           // CH.6 Set the selector trigger label
           CtlSetLabel( getObject( form, ContactDetailTimeSelTrigger ),
                    timeString );

    }

    // CH.6 We're done
    return;
}

// CH.6 Set the controls in the Enter Time form based on dateTime
static void setTimeControls( void )
{
    FormPtr     form;
    ControlPtr  hourButton;
    ControlPtr  minuteTensButton;
    ControlPtr  minuteOnesButton;
    ControlPtr  amButton;
    ControlPtr  pmButton;
    ControlPtr  noTimeCheckbox;
    Char        labelString[3];
    SWord       hour;

    // CH.6 Get the form
    form = FrmGetActiveForm();

    // CH.6 Get the control pointers
    hourButton = getObject( form, EnterTimeHoursPushButton );
    minuteTensButton = getObject( form,
            EnterTimeMinuteTensPushButton );
    minuteOnesButton = getObject( form,
            EnterTimeMinuteOnesPushButton );
    amButton = getObject( form, EnterTimeAMPushButton );
    pmButton = getObject( form, EnterTimePMPushButton );
    noTimeCheckbox = getObject( form, EnterTimeNoTimeCheckbox );

    // CH.6 If there is a time
    if( dateTime.hour != NO_TIME )
    {
        // CH.6 Update the hour
```

8

```
    hour = dateTime.hour % 12;
    if( hour == 0 )
        hour = 12;
    CtlSetLabel( hourButton,
            StrIToA( labelString, hour ) );

    // CH.6 Update the minute tens
    CtlSetLabel( minuteTensButton,
            StrIToA( labelString, dateTime.minute / 10 ) );

    // CH.6 Update the minute ones
    CtlSetLabel( minuteOnesButton,
            StrIToA( labelString, dateTime.minute % 10 ) );

    // CH.6 Update AM
    CtlSetValue( amButton, (dateTime.hour < 12) );

    // CH.6 Update PM
    CtlSetValue( pmButton, (dateTime.hour > 11) );

    // CH.6 Uncheck the no time checkbox
    CtlSetValue( noTimeCheckbox, false );
}

else
// If there is no time
{
    // CH.6 Update the hour
    CtlSetValue( hourButton, false );
    CtlSetLabel( hourButton, "" );

    // CH.6 Update the minute tens
    CtlSetValue( minuteTensButton, false );
    CtlSetLabel( minuteTensButton, "" );

    // CH.6 Update the minute ones
    CtlSetValue( minuteOnesButton, false );
    CtlSetLabel( minuteOnesButton, "" );

    // CH.6 Update AM
    CtlSetValue( amButton, false );

    // CH.6 Update PM
    CtlSetValue( pmButton, false );
```

```
            // CH.6 Uncheck the no time checkbox
            CtlSetValue( noTimeCheckbox, true );
        }

    // CH.6 We're done
    return;
}


// CH.7 This function is called by Palm OS to sort records
static Int sortFunc( CharPtr precord1, CharPtr precord2, Int sortBy )
{
    Int sortResult;

    // CH.7 Switch based on sort criteria
    switch( sortBy )
    {
        // CH.7 Sort by date and time
        case SORTBY_DATE_TIME:
        {
            DateTimePtr pdateTime1;
            DateTimePtr pdateTime2;
            Long lDiff;

            pdateTime1 = (DateTimePtr)(precord1 + DB_DATE_TIME_START);
            pdateTime2 = (DateTimePtr)(precord2 + DB_DATE_TIME_START);

            // CH.7 Compare the dates and times
            lDiff = (Long)(TimDateTimeToSeconds( pdateTime1 ) / 60 ) -
                    (Long)(TimDateTimeToSeconds( pdateTime2 ) / 60 );

            // CH.7 Date/time #1 is later
            if( lDiff > 0 )
                sortResult = 1;

            else
            // CH.7 Date/time #2 is later
            if( lDiff < 0 )
                sortResult = -1;

            else
            // CH.7 They are equal
                sortResult = 0;
        }
        break;

        // CH.7 Sort by first name
```

8

```
        case SORTBY_FIRST_NAME:
        {
            sortResult = StrCompare( precord1 + DB_FIRST_NAME_START,
                    precord2 + DB_FIRST_NAME_START );
        }
        break;

        // CH.7 Sort by last name
        case SORTBY_LAST_NAME:
        {
            sortResult = StrCompare( precord1 + DB_LAST_NAME_START,
                    precord2 + DB_LAST_NAME_START );
        }
        break;
    }

    // CH.7 We're done
    return( sortResult );
}

// CH.8 Draw our list of choices using a table object
static void drawTable( void )
{
    FormPtr    form;
    TablePtr   table;
    Int        column;
    Int        count;
    ControlPtr upArrow;
    ControlPtr downArrow;

    // CH.8 Get the form pointer
    form = FrmGetActiveForm();

    // CH.8 Get the table pointer
    table = getObject( form, ContactListTableTable );

    // CH.8 For all columns
    for( column = 0; column < TABLE_NUM_COLUMNS; column++ )
    {
        // CH.8 Set the draw routine
        TblSetCustomDrawProcedure( table, column, drawCell );

        // CH.8 Make the column visible
        TblSetColumnUsable( table, column, true );
    }
```

```
// CH.8 Initialize the table styles
for( count = 0; count < TABLE_NUM_ROWS; count++ )
{
    // CH.8 If there is data
    if( count < numRecords )
    {
        // CH.8 Show the row
        TblSetRowUsable( table, count, true );

        // CH.8 Set the cell styles
        for( column = 0; column < TABLE_NUM_COLUMNS; column++ )
        {
            TblSetItemStyle( table, count, column,
            customTableItem );
        }
    }

    else
    // CH.8 Hide unused rows if any
        TblSetRowUsable( table, count, false );
}

// CH.8 Draw the table
TblDrawTable( table );

// CH.8 Get pointers to the arrow buttons
upArrow = getObject( form, ContactListRecordUpRepeating );
downArrow = getObject( form, ContactListRecordDownRepeating );

// CH.8 Update the arrow buttons and scrollbars
if( numRecords > TABLE_NUM_ROWS )
{
    // CH.8 Show the up arrow
    if( cursor > 0 )
    {
        CtlSetLabel( upArrow, BLACK_UP_ARROW );
        CtlSetEnabled( upArrow, true );
    }
    else
    {
        CtlSetLabel( upArrow, GRAY_UP_ARROW );
        CtlSetEnabled( upArrow, false );
    }
    CtlShowControl( upArrow );
```

8

```
        // CH.8 Show the down arrow
        if( cursor >= numRecords - TABLE_NUM_ROWS )
        {
            CtlSetLabel( downArrow, GRAY_DOWN_ARROW );
            CtlSetEnabled( downArrow, false );
        }
        else
        {
            CtlSetLabel( downArrow, BLACK_DOWN_ARROW );
            CtlSetEnabled( downArrow, true );
        }
        CtlShowControl( downArrow );

        // CH.8 Show the scrollbar
        FrmShowObject( form, FrmGetObjectIndex( form,
                ContactListScrollbarScrollBar ) );
        SclSetScrollBar( getObject( form,
                ContactListScrollbarScrollBar ), cursor, 0,
                numRecords - TABLE_NUM_ROWS, TABLE_NUM_ROWS );
    }
    else
    {
        // CH.8 Hide the arrows
        CtlHideControl( upArrow );
        CtlHideControl( downArrow );

        // CH.8 Hide the scrollbar
        FrmHideObject( form, FrmGetObjectIndex( form,
                ContactListScrollbarScrollBar ) );
    }

    // CH.8 We're done
    return;
}


// CH.8 The custom drawing routine for a table cell
static void drawCell( VoidPtr table, Word row, Word column,
        RectanglePtr bounds )
{
    Int     record;
    CharPtr precord;
    Char    string[DB_FIRST_NAME_SIZE + DB_LAST_NAME_SIZE];
    SWord   width;
    SWord   len;
    Boolean noFit;
```

```
// CH.8 Calculate our record
record = cursor + row;

// CH.8 Get our record
hrecord = DmQueryRecord( contactsDB, record );
precord = MemHandleLock( hrecord );

// CH.8 Get the date and time
MemMove( &dateTime, precord + DB_DATE_TIME_START,
        sizeof( dateTime ) );

// CH.8 Switch on the column
switch( column )
{
    // CH.8 Handle dates
    case TABLE_COLUMN_DATE:
    {
        if( dateTime.year != NO_DATE )
        {
            DateToAscii( dateTime.month, dateTime.day,
                    dateTime.year,
                    (DateFormatType)PrefGetPreference(
                    prefDateFormat ), string );
        }
        else
            StrCopy( string, "-" );
    }
    break;

    // CH.8 Handle times
    case TABLE_COLUMN_TIME:
    {
        if( dateTime.hour != NO_TIME )
        {
            TimeToAscii( dateTime.hour, dateTime.minute,
                    (TimeFormatType)PrefGetPreference(
                    prefTimeFormat ), string );
        }
        else
            StrCopy( string, "-" );
    }
    break;

    // CH.8 Handle names
```

8

```
        case TABLE_COLUMN_NAME:
        {
            StrCopy( string, precord + DB_FIRST_NAME_START );
            StrCat( string, " " );
            StrCat( string, precord + DB_LAST_NAME_START );
        }
        break;
    }

    // CH.8 Unlock the record
    MemHandleUnlock( hrecord );

    // CH.8 Set the text mode
    WinSetUnderlineMode( noUnderline );
    FntSetFont( stdFont );

    // CH.8 Truncate the string if necessary
    width = bounds->extent.x;
    len = StrLen( string );
    noFit = false;
    FntCharsInWidth( string, &width, &len, &noFit );

    // CH.8 Draw the cell
    WinEraseRectangle( bounds, 0 );
    WinDrawChars( string, len, bounds->topLeft.x, bounds->topLeft.y
);

    // CH.8 We're done
    return;
}
```

CHAPTER 9

Categories and Find

In this chapter you'll add categories to the Contacts application. We'll use Categories to allow you to separate contacts into groups like Business and Personal. You'll be able to view these groups of contacts separately or together. You'll also be able to add, delete, and change category names for the Contacts application. You'll be able to assign each record a category.

We will also add code to Contacts that will allow you to find things in the Contacts database using Palm OS's own system Find. You'll be able to enter the short date or the person's full name and still get a match even though these values are stored in the database in separate fields and formats. You'll also be able to select any of the found items and go directly to the Contact Detail form displaying that record.

Save a Copy of Your Project

Before we start the fireworks, consider this yet another reminder to save a backup copy of your hard work up to this point. Here are the steps:

1. Launch Windows Explorer.
2. Find the folder that your project is stored in.
3. Select it and press CTRL-C to copy the folder.
4. Select a folder to save the copy in.
5. Press CTRL-V to paste a copy of your project into your backup folder.
6. Rename the project to something you will remember. I named mine Contacts CH.8.

Categories

If you have an application that lends itself to groupings of data, categories might be just the thing for it. You can have up to 15 categories defined for a given application, which is more than enough for most data that lends itself to categorization. On my Palm, I try not to go above six categories in any of my applications.

The Palm OS does most of the work regarding categories for you. Once you create the application information area in which its data lives, the Categories Manager maintains the data there. It creates and manages the category lists that pop up. It manages the creation, modification, and deletion of categories as well.

Our main challenge will be in separating and navigating through the records in a given category. Before this, we could treat the records all the same. Now we'll need to find out if a record belongs to the current category before we display it. This poses some problems for scrolling.

Additions to Contacts.rsrc

The work to be done over in Constructor falls into three categories:

◆ Add pop-up trigger and list objects to the Contact List form. These will be used to filter the list of contacts. These objects have to conform to the requirements of the Category Manager.

◆ Add pop-up trigger and list objects to the Contact Detail form. These will be used to select the category of the current record.

◆ Create an App Info String List resource that defines the initial categories your application will have.

Additions to the Contact List Form

Now it's time to add the stuff to the Contact List form that we'll use to allow people to look at a particular category.

1. Launch Metrowerks Constructor.

2. Open the resource file Contacts.rsrc. It is located in the Src folder inside your project folder.

3. Double-click on the Contact List form to open it.

4. Open the Catalog by selecting Window I Catalog from the menu.

5. Select a list object from the Catalog and drop it onto the form.

6. Give the list an Object Identifier of CategoryList. Give it a Left Origin of 86 and a Top Origin of 1. Make its Width 72. Uncheck Usable, because we don't want this list to show up when the form is drawn. Make the number of Visible Items 0. The Palm OS will build this list dynamically for us (upon our request) as part of the services it provides to support categories.

7. Select a pop-up trigger from the Catalog and drop it on the form.

8. Name the trigger CategoryPopup. Put its Left Origin at 160 and its Top Origin at 0. Give it a Width of 0. Uncheck Anchor Left; this (along with a Left Origin of 160) will make the trigger label right-justified against the right side of the screen. Wipe out the label or leave it there. We will be changing it programmatically at any rate.

9

NOTE: You don't need to set the list ID in this pop-up trigger like you do with a normal pop-up trigger, although it doesn't hurt anything if you do. As you'll see, we will end up circumventing the normal pop-up trigger behavior anyway in the way we swallow up the trigger's ctlSelectEvent events and call the special category functions instead.

9. When you're done, your Contact List form should look like Figure 9-1.

Additions to the Contact Detail Form

Now we modify the Contact Detail form to allow people to select the category of a particular item.

10. Open the Contact Detail form by double-clicking it in the Resource Type and Name list.

11. Drop a label from the Catalog onto the form. Change the text to Category: and make it bold. Put its Top Origin at 90. Line it up with the other right-justified labels by selecting them all (by SHIFT-clicking) and choosing Arrange | Align Right Edges.

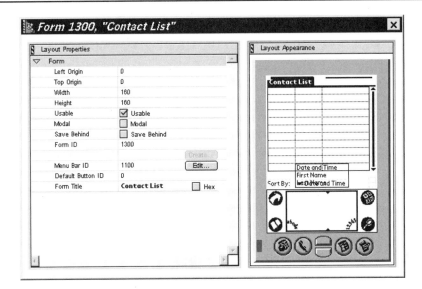

The modified Contact List form

Figure 9-1.

12. Select a list object from the Catalog and drop it onto the form.

13. Give the list an Object Identifier of CategoryList as before. Give it a Left Origin of 80 and a Top Origin of 90. Make its Width 80. Uncheck Usable, because we don't want this list to show up when the form is drawn. Make the number of Visible Items 0. As with the other category list, the Palm OS will end up building this list dynamically for us.

14. Select a pop-up trigger from the Catalog and drop it on the form.

15. Name the trigger CategoryPopup like the one on the Contact List form. Put its Left Origin at 80 and its Top Origin at 89. Give it a Width of 80. As before, you can leave the label text or wipe it out.

16. When you're done, your Contact Detail form should look like Figure 9-2.

17. Finally, we need to create an App Info String List resource for initializing our category names. Click on App Info String Lists in the Resource Type and Name list of Constructor and press CTRL-K to create a new one. Be careful not to create a regular old String List, which looks identical.

18. Name the App Info String List **Category Labels**. Double-click on it to open it.

19. Type in the first three items in the list: **Unfiled**, **Business**, and **Personal**.

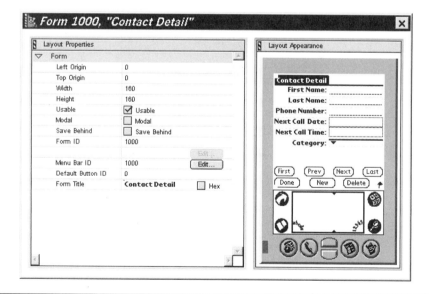

The modified
Contact
Detail form

Figure 9-2.

9

20. Press the ENTER key 12 more times to create a total of 16 entries. This will initialize the other categories as blank instead of as garbage. When you're done, your list should look like Figure 9-3. I reiterate: you must initialize all 16 entries with something; otherwise, bad and confusing things will happen.

This concludes the changes we need to make to the resource file to support Categories in our Contacts application. Close Constructor and save the resource file when prompted.

Changes to Contacts.c

There are four main tasks to perform to add category support to Contacts.c:

◆ Create the data structures that the Category Manager needs in order to work.

◆ Support the category pop-up list in the Contact Detail form.

◆ Support the category pop-up list in the Contact List form.

◆ Deal with scrolling through different categories of records in the Contact List form.

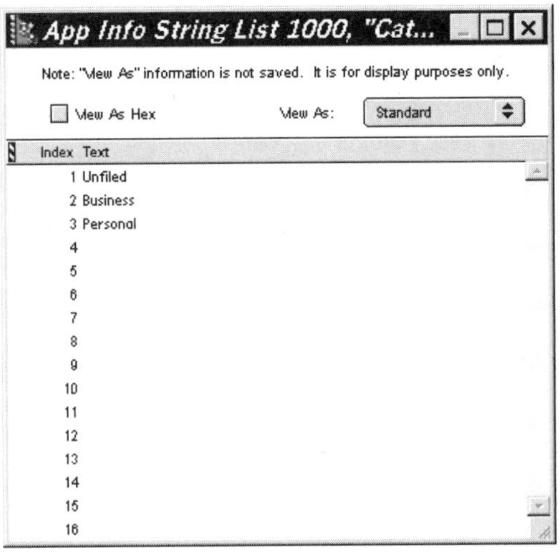

The App Info String List for initializing the category names

Figure 9-3.

Initializing the Categories

Category information is traditionally stored in the application information block of the application's main database. To do this, we need to add some code after we create our database in **PilotMain()**. We'll need some new variables at the top of the function:

```
LocalID    dbID;        // CH.9 Local ID of the database
UInt       cardNum;     // CH.9 Card number
LocalID    appInfoID;   // CH.9 Local ID of the app info block
VoidHand   hAppInfo;    // CH.9 Handle to the app info block
AppInfoPtr pAppInfo;    // CH.9 Points to the app info block
```

First, we look for our application's info block.

```
// CH.9 Get the ID and card number
   DmOpenDatabaseInfo( contactsDB, &dbID, NULL, NULL, &cardNum,
       NULL);

   // CH.9 Get the app info pointer if any
   DmDatabaseInfo( cardNum, dbID, NULL, NULL, NULL, NULL, NULL,
           NULL, NULL, &appInfoID, NULL, NULL, NULL );
```

IN DEPTH

9

App Info Blocks

Every Palm OS database has a special area in it called the *app info block*. You can use this area to store anything you like. Even if you're using it already for categories, you can just tack your special data onto the end of the category structures, and Palm OS will leave it alone. I often use this space for preferences or to specify global things about the database in question. For example, you can use it to store information about how the records in the database are structured so that generic database handling code can operate on many different kinds of databases.

TIP: Notice how we are careful to use the card number here instead of just specifying a card number of 0. Although a card number of 0 will always work in existing stock Palm Computing devices to date, some of the third-party hardware, most notably the Handspring Visor and TRGpro, can have more than one memory card. In supporting the wider range of Palm units and future units, handling the card number correctly everywhere in your code becomes vital.

If we don't find that we have already provided for categories by creating an application info block, we go ahead and create one.

```
// CH.9 If there is no application info block, create one
   if( appInfoID == 0 )
   {
       // CH.9 Allocate an application info block
       if( (hAppInfo = DmNewHandle( contactsDB,
               sizeof( AppInfoType ) )) == NULL )
           errorExit( MemoryErrorAlert );

       // CH.9 Translate the handle to a local ID
       appInfoID = MemHandleToLocalID( hAppInfo );

       // CH.9 Set the application info block
       DmSetDatabaseInfo( cardNum, dbID, NULL, NULL, NULL, NULL,
               NULL, NULL, NULL, &appInfoID, NULL, NULL, NULL );

       // CH.9 Translate the local ID to a pointer
       pAppInfo = MemLocalIDToLockedPtr( appInfoID, cardNum );

       // CH.9 Clear it
       DmSet( pAppInfo, 0, sizeof( AppInfoType ), 0 );

       // CH.9 Initialize the categories
       CategoryInitialize( pAppInfo, CategoryLabelsAppInfoStr );

       // CH.9 Unlock the application info block
       MemPtrUnlock( pAppInfo );
   }
```

The Palm OS will automatically initialize your categories when you call the Palm OS function **CategoryInitialize()**. You pass to this function the ID of the App Info String List resource you created in Constructor. Make sure you create this string exactly as described in the previous section. If you don't, the categories just won't appear or will appear as garbage, and you won't know why because **CategoryInitialize()** has no error return value.

TIP: You can store anything in an application info block. If you use categories, you just need to extend the application info block structure for categories, appending to it whatever data you want to store in there. Any data you add to the app info block must come after the category structures.

Supporting the Contact Detail Form

The Contact Detail form should show us the correct category for each record as we scroll through the records. It should also allow us to set the category for a record.

Unlike conventional pop-up triggers, to use the Category Manager to handle this, you must catch the initial tap on the category pop-up trigger as a *ctlSelectEvent* and then allow the special Palm OS function **CategorySelect()** do all the work from there. We return *true* from the event to prevent Palm OS from doing what it would normally do for a pop-up trigger, which is to try to pop up a list. In this case, the list is built, popped up, and destroyed all within the call to **CategorySelect()**, so we don't want Palm OS to handle this pop-up trigger like a normal pop-up trigger.

At the top of the file, we define three variables. The variable *detailCat* holds the category of the current record shown in the Contact Detail form. The *listCat* record holds the category that the Contact List is currently displaying. The third variable, *tableIndex*, is for the purpose of navigating through the records of a particular category and will be explained in the next section.

9

```
// CH.9 Category variables
static Word listCat = dmAllCategories;  // CH.9 The current cat ID
static Word detailCat;                   // CH.9 Cat ID for details
static UInt tableIndex[TABLE_NUM_ROWS];  // CH.9 Rec indexes for rows
```

At the top of **contactDetailHandleEvent()**, you need to allocate space to store the category name:

```
Char       catName[dmCategoryLength];  // CH.9 Category name
```

Here is the code, added to the switch statement for *ctlSelectEvent*, that does the job of handling the category pop-up trigger and list:

```
// CH.9 Catch a tap on the category trigger
case ContactDetailCategoryPopupPopTrigger:
{
    UInt    recAttrs;    // CH.9 The record attribs

    // CH.9 Palm OS will present the popup list.
    CategorySelect( contactsDB, form,
            ContactDetailCategoryPopupPopTrigger,
            ContactDetailCategoryListList,
            false, &detailCat, catName, 1, 0 );

    // CH.9 Get the record attributes
    DmRecordInfo( contactsDB, cursor, &recAttrs,
            NULL, NULL );

    // CH.9 Put in the category bits
    recAttrs &= ~dmRecAttrCategoryMask;
    recAttrs |= detailCat;

    // CH.9 Set the record attributes
    DmSetRecordInfo( contactsDB, cursor, &recAttrs,
            NULL );
}
// CH.9 Reattach fields and return true in this case
attachFields();
return( true );
```

Here, **CategorySelect()** does practically all the hard work, including creating and managing the list and potential edits of that list. Note the fifth parameter in **CategorySelect()** with the value of False. This parameter tells **CategorySelect()** that we are using the list for selecting the category for a single record rather than for sorting a list of items. This makes **CategorySelect()** leave out the All selection in the list.

The eighth parameter (the one after *catName*) in **CategorySelect()**, given the value 1, tells it that we always want to protect the first category, Unfiled, from being changed. You can keep as many categories as you want from being changed in this fashion.

You can use the last parameter to specify a string resource you want as the title to the category edit dialog instead of Edit Categories. This default title is fine in all the cases I've encountered so far, so I have always set this to 0.

NOTE: Palm OS 1.0 has its own version of **CategorySelect()** that can still be accessed using the call **CategorySelectV10()**. If you are interested in supporting original Pilot 1000 and 5000 units, you'll need to use this call instead.

After the call to **CategorySelect()** we set the category value in the current record's attribute bits. We accomplish this by getting the attribute bits with **DmRecordInfo()**, doing some bitwise math, and setting the new version of the attributes with **DmSetRecordInfo()**. This is all we need to do in the event handler.

In the **newRecord()** function we'll have to initialize the category of each record that's created. At the top of the function, we'll need a variable to store the record attributes in temporarily.

```
UInt    recAttrs;    // CH.9 The record's attributes
```

At the bottom of the function, we get and set the attributes of the record much as we did in the event handler. If the current category we have selected over in the contact list is All, we have no clue what might be the preferred starting category for this record, so we set the category to Unfiled. If we are viewing a specific category over in the list, we start this record off in that category.

9

```
// Ch.9 Get the record attribute bits
DmRecordInfo( contactsDB, cursor, &recAttrs, NULL, NULL );

// CH.9 Clear the category bits
recAttrs &= ~dmRecAttrCategoryMask;

// CH.9 Set the category to the appropriate category
if( listCat == dmAllCategories )
    recAttrs |= dmUnfiledCategory;
else
    recAttrs |= listCat;

// CH.9 Set the record attributes
DmSetRecordInfo( contactsDB, cursor, &recAttrs, NULL );
```

In **attachFields()**, we need to set the pop-up trigger label. First, we'll need some new variables at the top of the function.

```
UInt        recAttrs;    // CH.9 The record attribute bits
Char        catName[dmCategoryLength];   // CH.6 The category name
```

At the bottom of the function, we use some special category-manager function calls to set the label after retrieving it in the standard fashion.

```
// CH.9 Get the record attributes
DmRecordInfo( contactsDB, cursor, &recAttrs, NULL, NULL );

// CH.9 Get the category
detailCat = recAttrs & dmRecAttrCategoryMask;

// CH.9 Set the category popup trigger label
CategoryGetName( contactsDB, detailCat, catName );
CategorySetTriggerLabel( getObject( form,
        ContactDetailCategoryPopupPopTrigger ), catName );
```

This is everything we need to do to have categories working properly on the Contact Detail form, including putting specific records in categories.

Supporting the Contact List Form

Changes to the Contact List form are more extensive. Here we merely need to display the records in a given category or all categories. The problem with this is that our previous code depended heavily on every record in the database being displayed. Thus, we could count on the fact that the next record to display after *cursor* is *cursor + 1*, for example. With categories, we can no longer count on that. Some, all, or none of the records could belong to a given category we are asked to display.

One way to manage the problem of sifting the records for membership in the current category is to encapsulate it in functions we can then use to navigate through the records much as we did before. Here are three new functions whose prototypes appear at the top of the file:

```
static void     initIndexes( void );
static void     scrollIndexes( Int amount );
static UInt     findIndex( UInt scrollValue );
```

The function **initIndexes()** fills the array *tableIndex* with one table's worth of records from the currently selected category. Thus, we can scroll through the records as before by cross-referencing the table values instead of just blindly stepping through all the records. The function **scrollIndexes()** allows us to move this category-specific window up or down. The function **findIndex()** gives us the actual cursor position of a record given its position in the list of records in its category. We will see how these functions work in later sections. For now we'll just call them to handle the scrolling situations in the Contact List form's event handler and elsewhere.

Speaking of the Contact List form's event handler, **contactListHandleEvent()**, what to do? First, you'll need storage for a category name at the top of the function.

```
Char    catName[dmCategoryLength];  // CH.9 Category name
```

Modify the open event of the form to set the pop-up trigger label and call **initIndexes()** to initialize our list of acceptable records.

```
// CH.7 Form open event
    case frmOpenEvent:
    {
        // CH.7 Draw the form
        FrmDrawForm( form );

        // CH.9 Set the category popup trigger label
        CategoryGetName( contactsDB, listCat, catName );
        CategorySetTriggerLabel( getObject( form,
                ContactListCategoryPopupPopTrigger ),
                catName );

        // CH.8 The cursor starts at the beginning
        cursor = 0;

        // CH.9 Initialize the table indexes
        initIndexes();

        // CH.8 Populate and draw the table
        drawTable();
    }
    break;
```

9

When we go to the Contact Detail form by selecting a record, we look up the actual cursor location of the record that was selected in the *tableIndex* array.

```
// CH.7 Respond to a list selection
    case tblSelectEvent:
    {
        // CH.7 Set the database cursor to the selected contact
        cursor = tableIndex[event->data.tblSelect.row];

        // CH.7 Go to contact details
        FrmGotoForm( ContactDetailForm );
    }
    break;
```

In the *popSelectEvent* case, where we re-sort the records based on various criteria, we also now need to re-initialize the *tableIndex* structure with the records in the new sort order.

```
// CH.7 Sort the contact database by the new criteria
DmQuickSort( contactsDB, (DmComparF*)sortFunc, sortBy );

// CH.8 Cursor starts at zero
cursor = 0;

// CH.9 Initialize the table indexes
initIndexes();

// CH.8 Rebuild the table
drawTable();
```

We replace the simple math in the up and down arrow repeating buttons with calls to **scrollIndexes()**.

```
    // CH.8 Up arrow
    case ContactListRecordUpRepeating:
        scrollIndexes( -1 );
    break;

    // CH.8 Down arrow
    case ContactListRecordDownRepeating:
        scrollIndexes( 1 );
    break;
```

Similarly, we replace the cursor math done by the hard-key events with calls
to **scrollIndexes()**.

```
// CH.8 Up arrow hard key
case pageUpChr:
    scrollIndexes( -(TABLE_NUM_ROWS - 1) );
break;

// CH.8 Down arrow hard key
case pageDownChr:
    scrollIndexes( TABLE_NUM_ROWS - 1 );
break;
```

To handle the scrollbar, we do two things. First of all, updating the records
based on the scrollbar now takes longer, so we opt to update the table
when we are done scrolling by responding to the *sclExitEvent* instead of the
sclRepeatEvent. Secondly, here is where we use **findIndex()** to find the cursor
value of an arbitrary record in the subset of records in the category. We have
to manage the scrollbar based only on the records in the current category.
What it returns to us is a number between zero and the record that would
appear at the top of the table if the table was scrolled all the way down. We
use **findIndex()** to turn this number into a real cursor value. Once the
actual position of the record at the top of the table is known, we call
initIndexes() to fill the *tableIndex* array with the rest of the values.

```
// CH.8 Respond to scrollbar events
case sclExitEvent:
{
    //CH.9 Find the record in our category
    cursor = findIndex( event->data.sclExit.newValue );

    // CH.9 Initialize our index list
    initIndexes();

    // CH.8 Draw the table
    drawTable();
}
break;
```

9

Here is where we service the category pop-up trigger itself. As with the
Contact Detail form, we catch the *ctlSelectEvent* for the trigger and pass
control to **CategorySelect()**, returning True to the Palm OS afterwards to

prevent the default system behavior for pop-up triggers. Note that we pass True to this **CategorySelect()**, which tells it that it should put the All choice in the list. Once a new category is selected, we need to redo the indexes and redraw the table.

```
// CH.9 Catch a tap on the category trigger
case ctlSelectEvent:
{
    // CH.9 Palm OS will present the popup list for us.
    CategorySelect( contactsDB, form,
            ContactListCategoryPopupPopTrigger,
            ContactListCategoryListList,
            true, &listCat, catName, 1, 0 );

    // CH.9 Cursor starts at zero
    cursor = 0;

    // CH.9 Initialize the indexes
    initIndexes();

    // CH.9 Draw the table
    drawTable();
}
// CH.9 Don't let the OS generate other events from this
return( true );
```

Changes to **drawTable()** involve changing one line of code and chopping out a whole bunch of code. It's more convenient to manage the repeating buttons and the scrollbar in **initIndexes()** and **scrollIndex()**, where the information about what is coming next is more readily available. Similarly, we handle the problems of running off the end of the table and records in these functions because the information is available there.

Instead of disabling all the rows after you run out of records as you did in Chapter 8, look into the *tableIndex* array to see if the row has a record associated with it.

```
// CH.8 Initialize the table styles
for( count = 0; count < TABLE_NUM_ROWS; count++ )
{
    // CH.9 If there is data
    if( tableIndex[count] != 0xffff )
    {
        // CH.8 Show the row
        TblSetRowUsable( table, count, true );
```

Chop out all the code dealing with the up and down arrow buttons and the scrollbars and place it at the bottom of the file. When you're done, the **drawTable()** function will end abruptly after the call to **TblDrawTable()**.

```
// CH.8 Draw the table
TblDrawTable( table );

// CH.8 We're done
return;
}
```

We change only one line in **drawCell()**—the one at the top of the function that controls how we determine which record to use.

```
// CH.9 Calculate our record
record = tableIndex[row];
```

The Function initIndexes()

The function **initIndexes()** establishes the records we will display in the table. It creates an array, *tableIndex*, of records that are in the current category. We define some variables at the top of the function and get the active form as usual.

```
// CH.9 Initialize the row information by finding the right records
static void initIndexes( void )
{
    FormPtr     form;
    Int         count;
    UInt        index = cursor;
    ControlPtr  downArrow;
    ControlPtr  upArrow;
    UInt        numRecsInCategory;

    // CH.9 Get the current form
    form = FrmGetActiveForm();
```

9

Then loop through the rows, looking for the next record in the current category to put into that row. If we run out of records, we put the number 0xffff (65,535) in the array to signal that we don't have a record for that row. Finally, we set the cursor to a known good record instead of the record it was originally on, which may not even have been in the category. It could be that we're setting the cursor to 0xffff here, if there are no records in the category. This is okay because all the rows in the table will be turned off.

```
// CH.9 For each table row
for( count = 0; count < TABLE_NUM_ROWS; count++ )
{
    // CH.9 Find the next matching record
    if( DmSeekRecordInCategory( contactsDB, &index, 0,
            dmSeekForward, listCat ) )
    {
        // CH.9 No more records. Fill the rest of the array with
        // 0xffff
        for( ; count < TABLE_NUM_ROWS; count++ )
            tableIndex[count] = 0xffff;
        break;
    }

    // CH.9 Put the index number in the array
    tableIndex[count] = index;
    index++;
}

// CH.9 Set the cursor to a known category record
cursor = tableIndex[0];
```

Here is where our arrow button and scroll bar code went. It is largely unchanged from its original appearance in **drawTable()**. This time it uses **DmNumRecordsInCategory()** and **DmPositionInCategory()** to find out what to do with the buttons and the scrollbar.

```
// CH.8 Get pointers to the arrow buttons
upArrow = getObject( form, ContactListRecordUpRepeating );
downArrow = getObject( form, ContactListRecordDownRepeating );

// CH.8 Update the arrow buttons and scrollbars
numRecsInCategory = DmNumRecordsInCategory( contactsDB,
        listCat );
if( numRecsInCategory > TABLE_NUM_ROWS )
{
    UInt    position = DmPositionInCategory( contactsDB, cursor,
            listCat );

    // CH.8 Show the up arrow
    if( position > 0 )
    {
        CtlSetLabel( upArrow, BLACK_UP_ARROW );
        CtlSetEnabled( upArrow, true );
```

```
        }
        else
        {
            CtlSetLabel( upArrow, GRAY_UP_ARROW );
            CtlSetEnabled( upArrow, false );
        }
        CtlShowControl( upArrow );

        // CH.8 Show the down arrow
        if( position >= numRecsInCategory - TABLE_NUM_ROWS )
        {
            CtlSetLabel( downArrow, GRAY_DOWN_ARROW );
            CtlSetEnabled( downArrow, false );
        }
        else
        {
            CtlSetLabel( downArrow, BLACK_DOWN_ARROW );
            CtlSetEnabled( downArrow, true );
        }
        CtlShowControl( downArrow );

        // CH.9 Show the scrollbar
        SclSetScrollBar( getObject( form,
                ContactListScrollbarScrollBar ), position, 0,
                numRecsInCategory - TABLE_NUM_ROWS, TABLE_NUM_ROWS );
    }
    else
    {
        // CH.8 Hide the arrows
        CtlHideControl( upArrow );
        CtlHideControl( downArrow );

        // CH.8 Hide the scrollbar
        SclSetScrollBar( getObject( form,
                ContactListScrollbarScrollBar ), 0, 0, 0, 0 );
    }

    // CH.9 We're done
    return;
}
```

9

The Function scrollIndexes()

The function **scrollIndexes()** modifies the *tableIndex* array, knowing that we're probably only moving a short distance and that most of the values in

the table will therefore probably still be good. We start with some variable
definitions and the call to get the active form. We use the form pointer to get
pointers to the up and down repeating buttons.

```
// CH.9 Scroll a certain number of records in the current category
static void scrollIndexes( Int amount )
{
    FormPtr     form;
    UInt        count;
    UInt        index;
    ControlPtr  downArrow;
    ControlPtr  upArrow;
    UInt        numRecsInCategory;

    // CH.9 Get the current form
    form = FrmGetActiveForm();

    // CH.9 Get pointers to the arrow buttons
    upArrow = getObject( form, ContactListRecordUpRepeating );
    downArrow = getObject( form, ContactListRecordDownRepeating );
```

The rest of the function is split into two halves, one for scrolling up and one
for scrolling down. First, the scrolling-down version. We loop through until
we have scrolled down the desired amount.

```
// CH.9 If we're scrolling down
    if( amount > 0 )
    {
        // CH.9 While there is still an amount to scroll
        while( amount-- )
        {
```

Inside the loop, we look for the next record. If we don't find one, we gray out
the down arrow. We move the indexes up one place in the list and put our
newest index at the bottom.

```
            // CH.9 Get a new index after the last one
            index = tableIndex[TABLE_NUM_ROWS - 1];
            if( DmSeekRecordInCategory( contactsDB, &index, 1,
                    dmSeekForward, listCat ) )
            {
                // CH.9 No more records. We're done scrolling
                CtlSetLabel( downArrow, GRAY_DOWN_ARROW );
```

```
            CtlSetEnabled( downArrow, false );
            return;
        }

        // CH.9 Move current indexes up one
        for( count = 0; count < TABLE_NUM_ROWS - 1; count++ )
            tableIndex[count] = tableIndex[count + 1];

        // CH.9 Put the index number in the array
        tableIndex[count] = index;
    }
```

To really see for sure whether we should have a down arrow, we need to look one record farther. If there is another record down there, we should still have a down arrow. Also, if we're here, we know we should have a good up arrow.

```
        // CH.9 Disable the down arrow if needed
        if( DmSeekRecordInCategory( contactsDB, &index, 1,
                dmSeekForward, listCat ) )
        {
            CtlSetLabel( downArrow, GRAY_DOWN_ARROW );
            CtlSetEnabled( downArrow, false );
        }

        // CH.9 Enable the up arrow
        CtlSetLabel( upArrow, BLACK_UP_ARROW );
        CtlSetEnabled( upArrow, true );
    }
```

9

The code for the up direction is the same, but in the other direction.

```
    else
    // CH.9 If we're scrolling up
    if( amount < 0 )
    {
        // CH.9 While there is still an amount to scroll
        while( amount++ )
        {
            // CH.9 Get a new index before the first one
            index = tableIndex[0];
            if( DmSeekRecordInCategory( contactsDB, &index, 1,
                    dmSeekBackward, listCat ) )
            {
                // CH.9 No more records. We're done scrolling
```

```
            CtlSetLabel( upArrow, GRAY_UP_ARROW );
            CtlSetEnabled( upArrow, false );
            return;
        }

        // CH.9 Move current indexes down one
        for( count = TABLE_NUM_ROWS - 1; count > 0; count-- )
            tableIndex[count] = tableIndex[count - 1];

        // CH.9 Put the index number in the array
        tableIndex[count] = index;
    }

    // CH.9 Disable the up arrow if needed
    if( DmSeekRecordInCategory( contactsDB, &index, 1,
            dmSeekBackward, listCat ) )
    {
        CtlSetLabel( upArrow, GRAY_UP_ARROW );
        CtlSetEnabled( upArrow, false );
    }

    // CH.9 Enable the down arrow
    CtlSetLabel( downArrow, BLACK_DOWN_ARROW );
    CtlSetEnabled( downArrow, true );
}
```

After the two directions of scrolling are handled, we set the cursor to the top of the index and update the scrollbar.

```
// CH.9 Set the cursor
cursor = tableIndex[0];

// CH.9 Set the scrollbar
numRecsInCategory = DmNumRecordsInCategory( contactsDB,
        listCat );
SclSetScrollBar( getObject( form,
        ContactListScrollbarScrollBar ), DmPositionInCategory(
        contactsDB, cursor, listCat ), 0,
        numRecsInCategory - TABLE_NUM_ROWS, TABLE_NUM_ROWS );

// CH.9 We're done
return;
}
```

The Function findIndex()

The function **findIndex()** is fairly straightforward, thanks to the Palm OS call **DmSeekRecordInCategory()**. This function with the right parameters does basically the opposite of **DmPositionInCategory()**.

```
// CH.9 Find a particular index
static UInt findIndex( UInt scrollValue )
{
    UInt index = 0;

    // CH.9 Seek from zero to the scrollvalue
    DmSeekRecordInCategory( contactsDB, &index, scrollValue,
            dmSeekForward, listCat );

    // We're done
    return( index );
}
```

Debugging Categories

The main thing to remember here is to check the parameters going into Category Manager function calls. Many of these functions don't return error values, so the only way you'll find out what's wrong is by looking at the input and output of the functions. Trust that these functions work as advertised and look for mistakes in what you're sending them. The most common mistake I've made is not defining the App Info String List resource properly for **CategoryInitialize()**. This causes a host of ugly-looking problems. If you hand **CategoryInitialize()** a String List instead of an App Info String List, it will happily do nothing. Also remember to define 16 strings in this list, although most of them will probably be blank. Otherwise, you'll get garbage category names cropping up. If you fail to clear the application info block before handing it to **CategoryInitialize()**, watch out.

Figures 9-4 and 9-5 show the Contacts application running. Figure 9-4 shows the category list open in the Contact Detail form. Figure 9-5 shows the appearance of the pop-up trigger in the Contact List.

Secret Records

Secret records are handled very similarly to categories. There is a bit in the attributes of every record that defines whether it is secret or not. We could

9

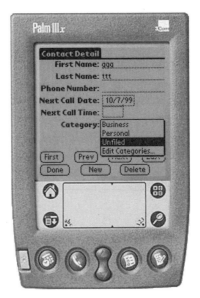

The category
list managed
by the
Palm OS

Figure 9-4.

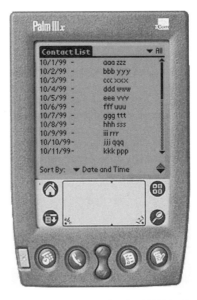

The category
pop-up trigger
on the Contact
List form

Figure 9-5.

add a checkbox to the Contact Detail form to set and clear this bit. Then, if you never scroll through the records using math but always use **DmSeekRecordInCategory()** or similar functions, the secret records will automatically be excluded.

The changes you would have to make to Contacts to support secret records are mainly in the Contacts form. You would have to add that checkbox and the code to set the bit in the record accordingly. You would then have to replace all the cursor math in the Contact Details form with function calls similar to the ones we made for the Contact List form. Otherwise, secret records could be scrolled to using the navigation buttons in the Contact Detail form.

Find

If there is stuff to find in your application, I highly recommend supporting Find. All well-behaved Palm OS applications should support Find to whatever degree makes sense for them.

In Contacts, we will turn our entire record into a text analog to facilitate finding information in our database by date, time, or full name. Although a net win (I think), this feature prevents us from highlighting the exact field where the match was made, another common feature of Find. In our case, the match might span fields.

Changes to Contacts.c

9

To support Find, we will add a single function. Here is the prototype that should appear near the top of the file.

```
static void     find( Ptr params );
```

This function, using no global variables, searches our database for instances of the search string.

Launch Codes

Up until now, we have only concerned ourselves with the situation where our application is started because someone has selected it from the application area. Our application is also invoked during Find. Also, if someone selects one of our found records, we are called to go to that record. We can tell these instances apart using launch codes.

For some of these new launch codes, we will need to look at more of the information passed to us by **PilotMain()**. Thus, we define the variable *params*.

IN DEPTH

Unused Parameters

We're still ignoring the last parameter of type Word. Some compilers that shall remain nameless give you a warning if you define a function parameter and don't use it. It helps me to see what I'm doing if I leave unused parameters unnamed as I've done here.

```
// CH.2 The main entry point
DWord PilotMain( Word cmd, Ptr params, Word )
{
```

The first type of launch we respond to is the good old launch we have always responded to.

```
// CH.9 Respond to launches
switch( cmd )
{
    // CH.2 Normal launch
    case sysAppLaunchCmdNormalLaunch:
    break;
```

If we are called due to a system Find, another application may be using the application area. Therefore, our global variables aren't available to us. We can only store things on the stack or allocate memory, both of which should be done sparingly. Because of this, it's a good idea to encapsulate the Find operation in its own function call.

```
// CH.9 System find
case sysAppLaunchCmdFind:
    find( params );
return( 0 );
```

We receive this launch flag if the user selects an item we provided as a Find result. In this case, our application is fully activated and we can use our global variables.

```
// CH.9 Go to item from find
case sysAppLaunchCmdGoTo:
break;
```

If we don't handle a particular launch code that was given, we just return.

```
// CH.2 We don't handle what's being asked for
default:
return( 0 );
}
```

IN DEPTH

There are several launch codes besides the ones we are dealing with here, but these are the most important ones. The other launch codes and what they do is described in *The Palm OS SDK Reference*, which is included in the version of CodeWarrior Lite on the CD at the back of the book.

Also in **PilotMain()** we need to handle the instance where we may already have been running when a Find and subsequent selection happened. In this case, system Find relaunches us on our previous stack. If we fail to detect this behavior, we can run off the end of our stack given enough subsequent calls to system Find. To protect against this, we can add a global variable that we can use to determine our state. We don't have access to global variables during the initial Find, but during the subsequent Goto launch we have full access to our globals.

```
// CH.9 Goto variable
static Boolean    upStack;
```

A sure-fire way for us to know that we are running on top of ourselves is to see if our database is open. If our database is open, we'd better not open it again. Furthermore, we should set the variable *upStack* to *true* so that we know we are running on top of ourselves.

9

```
// CH.9 Open the database if it isn't already open
if( contactsDB == NULL )
{
    contactsDB = DmOpenDatabaseByTypeCreator( 'ctct', 'PPGU',
            dmModeReadWrite );
}
else
    upStack = true;
```

Also, we need to specially direct ourselves to the Contact Detail form if someone has selected a specific item in the Find. To this end, we can add another instance to our logic of what form to start on. Here, if we are launched as the result of a Goto selection, we go to the corresponding record in our database and display it in the Contact Detail form. It is vitally important to first close all open forms in case our application is active when the user starts the system Find. Otherwise, our application will die when it tries to open a form that's already open. Also, if we are running on top of ourselves, we need to return to our original instance after setting the cursor and going to our details form. This code goes right between the existing two **FrmGotoForm()** calls in **PilotMain()**.

```
else
// CH.9 We are going to a particular record
if( cmd == sysAppLaunchCmdGoTo )
{
    // CH.9 In case our app was running before the find
    FrmCloseAllForms();

    // CH.9 Point the cursor to the found item
    cursor = ((GoToParamsPtr)params)->recordNum;

    // CH.9 Go to the details page
    FrmGotoForm( ContactDetailForm );

    // CH.9 If we are running on top of ourselves,
    // return to the original event loop
    if( upStack )
    {
        upStack = false;
        return( 0 );
    }
}
```

The Function find()

The **find()** function runs off its own separate set of variables that are listed at the top of the function.

```
// CH.9 Find something in our records
static void find( Ptr params )
{
    FindParamsPtr    findParams = (FindParamsPtr)params;// CH.9 Params
    DmOpenRef        contactsDB; // CH.9 Our local database ptr
    UInt             numRecords; // CH.9 Number of records in the db
    LocalID          dbID;       // CH.9 Local ID of the database
    UInt             cardNum;    // CH.9 Card number
    UInt             cursor;     // CH.9 The current record
    VoidHand         hrecord;    // CH.9 Handle to the record
    CharPtr          precord;    // CH.9 Pointer to the record
    DateTimeType     dateTime;   // CH.9 Date and time in this record
    Char             textRecord[dateStringLength + 1 +   // CH.9 We
                        timeStringLength + 1 +      // build
                        DB_FIRST_NAME_SIZE +        // text
                        DB_LAST_NAME_SIZE +         // rec here
                        DB_PHONE_NUMBER_SIZE];
    Char             lcText[dateStringLength + 1 +       // CH.9 Copy
                        timeStringLength + 1 +      // lower
                        DB_FIRST_NAME_SIZE +        // case
                        DB_LAST_NAME_SIZE +         // text here
                        DB_PHONE_NUMBER_SIZE];
    Word             offset;     // CH.9 Offset of the match
    RectangleType    bounds;     // CH.9 Bounding rect for text
    SWord            width;      // CH.9 Width of the bounds rect
    SWord            len;        // CH.9 Text length
    Boolean          noFit;      // CH.9 Does it fit
```

9

The first thing is to draw a title that separates our area of the Find from other applications.

```
// CH.9 Draw a title for our find items
// CH.9 If there's no more room, return
if( (FindDrawHeader( findParams, "Contacts" )) == true )
    return;
```

Next we open up our database and get a few bits of information about it that we will use later on. We should open our database in read-only mode because we are not going to change anything in there during a Find operation.

```
// CH.9 Open the database for reading
if( (contactsDB = DmOpenDatabaseByTypeCreator( 'ctct', 'PPGU',
```

```
        dmModeReadOnly )) == NULL )
    return;

// CH.9 Find out how many records we have
numRecords = DmNumRecords( contactsDB );

// CH.9 Get the ID and card number
DmOpenDatabaseInfo( contactsDB, &dbID, NULL, NULL, &cardNum,
        NULL);
```

Here we loop through the records looking for matches. Note that we may not start at record zero. It depends on whether the Find Manager is calling us for the first time or some subsequent time on subsequent pages of Find output. Each run of Find displays only one screen of data.

IN DEPTH

If we supported secret records, we would have to make sure that we weren't finding secret records that were supposed to be hidden. In this case, instead of stepping through every record, we would use a call like **DmSeekRecordInCategory()** instead. Hidden records are automatically excluded by this call.

Depending on the kind of information you have in a record, you may want to convert the data to find matches that wouldn't otherwise be apparent. For example, because I'm putting the first and last name into the same string to search, Find will now find John Smith in our database if the user put "John Smith" as the search string. If we had just searched record by record without putting the strings together, a search for John Smith in our database would turn up nothing even if our database contained a record for him. This is the reason for converting the date, time, and so on to text and putting it all in one big string. You'll note that the built-in applications are not capable of making such matches, because they search for matches on a field-by-field basis.

```
// CH.9 For each record
for( cursor = findParams->recordNum; cursor < numRecords;
```

```
                        cursor++ )
      {
          // CH.9 Get the record
          hrecord = DmQueryRecord( contactsDB, cursor );
          precord = MemHandleLock( hrecord );

          // CH.9 Get the date and time
          MemMove( &dateTime, precord + DB_DATE_TIME_START,
                  sizeof( dateTime ) );

           // CH.9 Start over
          *textRecord = '\0';

         // CH.9 Add the date string if any
         if( dateTime.year != NO_DATE )
         {
             DateToAscii( dateTime.month, dateTime.day,
                     dateTime.year,
                     (DateFormatType)PrefGetPreference(
                     prefDateFormat ), textRecord );
             StrCat( textRecord, " " );
         }

         // CH.9 Add the time string if any
         if( dateTime.hour != NO_TIME )
         {
             TimeToAscii( dateTime.hour, dateTime.minute,
                     (TimeFormatType)PrefGetPreference(
                     prefTimeFormat ), textRecord +
                     StrLen( textRecord ) );
             StrCat( textRecord, " " );
         }

         // CH.9 Append the first name
         StrCat( textRecord, precord + DB_FIRST_NAME_START );
         StrCat( textRecord, " " );

         // CH.9 Append the last name
         StrCat( textRecord, precord + DB_LAST_NAME_START );
         StrCat( textRecord, " " );

         // CH.9 Append the phone number
         StrCat( textRecord, precord + DB_PHONE_NUMBER_START );

         // CH.9 Unlock the record
         MemHandleUnlock( hrecord );
```

IN DEPTH

Cancelling Find
This is a simple find function that can't be cancelled, but it is fairly straightforward to add the ability to cancel your find. This way users won't have to wait if your find operation is taking too long for them. To do so you must add a call to **EvtSysEventAvail()** where you would run across it regularly. In this case it would be at the top of our **for()** loop.

We need to keep a regular version of our text record to show on the Find screen. We also need a lowercase version to use in the **find()** function. Use **FindStrInStr()** to match the strings. If you look at the parameters being passed, you'll notice that *strToFind* is not a regular lowercase string. If you use your own or a different function to make the comparison, you'll have to build your own match string as well unless you use this particular Palm OS call.

```
// CH.9 Copy and convert to lower case
StrToLower( lcText, textRecord );

// CH.9 If there's no match, move on
if( (FindStrInStr( lcText, findParams->strToFind,
        &offset )) == false )
    continue;
```

If we get a match, we send it to the Find Manager. If there is still room, we draw the text on the screen and continue to the next record.

```
// CH.9 Send it to find
// CH.9 If there's no more room, return
if( (FindSaveMatch( findParams, cursor, offset, 0,
        NULL, cardNum, dbID )) == true )
    break;

// CH.9 Get the rectangle for our line of text
FindGetLineBounds( findParams, &bounds );

// CH.9 Truncate the string if necessary
```

```
        width = bounds.extent.x;
        len = StrLen( textRecord );
        noFit = false;
        FntCharsInWidth( textRecord, &width, &len, &noFit );

        // CH.9 Draw the text
        WinEraseRectangle( &bounds, 0 );
        WinDrawChars( textRecord, len, bounds.topLeft.x,
                bounds.topLeft.y );

        // We used a line in the find dialog
        (findParams->lineNumber)++;
    }
```

When we're done with all records, we close the database.

```
// CH.9 Close the database
    DmCloseDatabase( contactsDB );

    // CH.9 We're done
    return;
}
```

Debugging Find

The main issues I've run into in debugging **find()** functions myself concern the parameters I'm passed as the result of a Find or how I'm supposed to modify them. For example, don't believe *strToFind* is actually the string to find. Also, be careful to increment *lineNumber* because the Palm OS won't. Figure 9-6 shows the **find()** function above in action.

9

What's Next?

This is the last of the chapters covering Palm OS basics. In the next several chapters we'll deal with many broader issues of software design. Chapter 10 deals with user interface design and what is expected of a Palm OS application. Chapter 11 talks all about the tools and solutions available to aid you in creating your own Palm OS solutions. Chapter 12 introduces a new way to organize and modularize your code so that you can reuse it in future Palm OS designs.

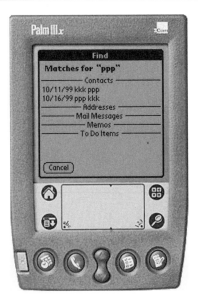

Contacts
participating in
a system Find
Figure 9-6.

Listing

Here is the latest version of Contacts.c including all the changes we made
this chapter.

```
// CH.2 The super-include for the Palm OS
#include <Pilot.h>

// CH.5 Added for the call to GrfSetState()
#include <Graffiti.h>

// CH.3 Our resource file
#include "Contacts_res.h"

// CH.4 Prototypes for our event handler functions
static Boolean  contactDetailHandleEvent( EventPtr event );
static Boolean  aboutHandleEvent( EventPtr event );
static Boolean  enterTimeHandleEvent( EventPtr event );
static Boolean  contactListHandleEvent( EventPtr event );
static Boolean  menuEventHandler( EventPtr event );
```

```
// CH.4 Constants for ROM revision
#define ROM_VERSION_2    0x02003000
#define ROM_VERSION_MIN ROM_VERSION_2

// CH.5 Prototypes for utility functions
static void     newRecord( void );
static VoidPtr  getObject( FormPtr, Word );
static void     setFields( void );
static void     getFields( void );
static void     setText( FieldPtr, CharPtr );
static void     getText( FieldPtr, VoidPtr, Word );
static void     setDateTrigger( void );
static void     setTimeTrigger( void );
static void     setTimeControls( void );
static Int      sortFunc( CharPtr, CharPtr, Int );
static void     drawTable( void );
static void     drawCell( VoidPtr table, Word row, Word column,
                RectanglePtr bounds );
static void     initIndexes( void );
static void     scrollIndexes( Int amount );
static UInt     findIndex( UInt scrollValue );
static void     find( Ptr params );

// CH.5 Our open database reference
static DmOpenRef    contactsDB;
static ULong        numRecords;
static UInt         cursor;
static Boolean      isDirty;
static VoidHand     hrecord;

// CH.5 Constants that define the database record
#define DB_ID_START              0
#define DB_ID_SIZE               (sizeof( ULong ))
#define DB_DATE_TIME_START       (DB_ID_START +\
                                 DB_ID_SIZE)
#define DB_DATE_TIME_SIZE        (sizeof( DateTimeType ))
#define DB_FIRST_NAME_START      (DB_DATE_TIME_START +\
                                 DB_DATE_TIME_SIZE)
#define DB_FIRST_NAME_SIZE       16
#define DB_LAST_NAME_START       (DB_FIRST_NAME_START +\
                                 DB_FIRST_NAME_SIZE)
#define DB_LAST_NAME_SIZE        16
#define DB_PHONE_NUMBER_START    (DB_LAST_NAME_START +\
                                 DB_LAST_NAME_SIZE)
#define DB_PHONE_NUMBER_SIZE     16
#define DB_RECORD_SIZE           (DB_PHONE_NUMBER_START +\
                                 DB_PHONE_NUMBER_SIZE)
```

9

```
// CH.6 Storage for the record's date and time in expanded form
static DateTimeType dateTime;
static Word        timeSelect;
#define NO_DATE     0
#define NO_TIME     0x7fff

// CH.7 The error exit macro
#define errorExit(alert) { ErrThrow( alert ); }

// CH.7 The sort order variable and constants
static Int sortBy;
// CH.7 NOTE: These items match the popup list entries!
#define SORTBY_DATE_TIME    0
#define SORTBY_FIRST_NAME   1
#define SORTBY_LAST_NAME    2

// CH.8 Table constants
#define TABLE_NUM_COLUMNS   3
#define TABLE_NUM_ROWS      11
#define TABLE_COLUMN_DATE   0
#define TABLE_COLUMN_TIME   1
#define TABLE_COLUMN_NAME   2
#define BLACK_UP_ARROW      "\x01"
#define BLACK_DOWN_ARROW    "\x02"
#define GRAY_UP_ARROW       "\x03"
#define GRAY_DOWN_ARROW     "\x04"

// CH.9 Category variables
static Word listCat = dmAllCategories;  // CH.9 The current cat ID
static Word detailCat;                   // CH.9 Cat ID for details
static UInt tableIndex[TABLE_NUM_ROWS]; // CH.9 Rec indexes for rows

// CH.9 Goto variable
static Boolean    upStack;

// CH.2 The main entry point
DWord PilotMain( Word cmd, Ptr params, Word )
{
    DWord        romVersion; // CH.4 ROM version
    LocalID      dbID;       // CH.9 Local ID of the database
    UInt         cardNum;    // CH.9 Card number
    LocalID      appInfoID;  // CH.9 Local ID of the app info block
    VoidHand     hAppInfo;   // CH.9 Handle to the app info block
    AppInfoPtr   pAppInfo;   // CH.9 Points to the app info block
    FormPtr      form;       // CH.2 A pointer to our form structure
    EventType    event;      // CH.2 Our event structure
    Word         error;      // CH.3 Error word
```

```
// CH.4 Get the ROM version
romVersion = 0;
FtrGet( sysFtrCreator, sysFtrNumROMVersion, &romVersion );

// CH.4 If we are below our minimum acceptable ROM revision
if( romVersion < ROM_VERSION_MIN )
{
    // CH.4 Display the alert
    FrmAlert( LowROMVersionErrorAlert );

    // CH.4 PalmOS 1.0 will continuously re-launch this app
    // unless we switch to another safe one
    if( romVersion < ROM_VERSION_2 )
    {
        AppLaunchWithCommand( sysFileCDefaultApp,
                sysAppLaunchCmdNormalLaunch, NULL );
    }
    return( 0 );
}

// CH.9 Respond to launches
switch( cmd )
{
    // CH.2 Normal launch
    case sysAppLaunchCmdNormalLaunch:
    break;

    // CH.9 System find
    case sysAppLaunchCmdFind:
        find( params );
    return( 0 );

    // CH.9 Go to item from find
    case sysAppLaunchCmdGoTo:
    break;

    // CH.2 We don't handle what's being asked for
    default:
    return( 0 );
}

// CH.5 Create a new database in case there isn't one
if( ((error = DmCreateDatabase( 0, "ContactsDB-PPGU", 'PPGU',
        'ctct', false )) != dmErrAlreadyExists) && (error != 0) )
{
    // CH.5 Handle db creation error
    FrmAlert( DBCreationErrorAlert );
    return( 0 );
}
```

```
// CH.9 Open the database if it isn't already open
if( contactsDB == NULL )
{
    contactsDB = DmOpenDatabaseByTypeCreator( 'ctct', 'PPGU',
            dmModeReadWrite );
}
else
    upStack = true;

// CH.9 Get the ID and card number
DmOpenDatabaseInfo( contactsDB, &dbID, NULL, NULL, &cardNum,
        NULL);

// CH.9 Get the app info pointer if any
DmDatabaseInfo( cardNum, dbID, NULL, NULL, NULL, NULL, NULL,
        NULL, NULL, &appInfoID, NULL, NULL, NULL );

// CH.9 If there is no application info block, create one
if( appInfoID == 0 )
{
    // CH.9 Allocate an application info block
    if( (hAppInfo = DmNewHandle( contactsDB,
            sizeof( AppInfoType ) )) == NULL )
        errorExit( MemoryErrorAlert );

    // CH.9 Translate the handle to a local ID
    appInfoID = MemHandleToLocalID( hAppInfo );

    // CH.9 Set the application info block
    DmSetDatabaseInfo( cardNum, dbID, NULL, NULL, NULL, NULL,
            NULL, NULL, NULL, &appInfoID, NULL, NULL, NULL );

    // CH.9 Translate the local ID to a pointer
    pAppInfo = MemLocalIDToLockedPtr( appInfoID, cardNum );

    // CH.9 Clear it
    DmSet( pAppInfo, 0, sizeof( AppInfoType ), 0 );

    // CH.9 Initialize the categories
    CategoryInitialize( pAppInfo, CategoryLabelsAppInfoStr );

    // CH.9 Unlock the application info block
    MemPtrUnlock( pAppInfo );
}

// CH.5 Get the number of records in the database
numRecords = DmNumRecords( contactsDB );

// CH.5 Initialize the record number
cursor = 0;
```

```
// CH.7 Choose our starting page
// CH.5 If there are no records, create one
if( numRecords == 0 )
{
    newRecord();
    FrmGotoForm( ContactDetailForm );
}

else
// CH.9 We are going to a particular record
if( cmd == sysAppLaunchCmdGoTo )
{
    // CH.9 In case our app was running before the find
    FrmCloseAllForms();

    // CH.9 Point the cursor to the found item
    cursor = ((GoToParamsPtr)params)->recordNum;

    // CH.9 Go to the details page
    FrmGotoForm( ContactDetailForm );

    // CH.9 If we are running on top of ourselves,
    // return to the original event loop
    if( upStack )
    {
        upStack = false;
        return( 0 );
    }
}

else
// CH.7 Display the list
    FrmGotoForm( ContactListForm );

// CH.7 Begin the try block
ErrTry {

// CH.2 Our event loop
do
{
    // CH.2 Get the next event
    EvtGetEvent( &event, -1 );

    // CH.2 Handle system events
    if( SysHandleEvent( &event ) )
        continue;

    // CH.3 Handle menu events
    if( MenuHandleEvent( NULL, &event, &error ) )
```

9

```
        continue;

    // CH.4 Handle form load events
    if( event.eType == frmLoadEvent )
    {
        // CH.4 Initialize our form
        switch( event.data.frmLoad.formID )
        {
            // CH.4 Contact Detail form
            case ContactDetailForm:
                form = FrmInitForm( ContactDetailForm );
                FrmSetEventHandler( form,
                        contactDetailHandleEvent );
            break;

            // CH.4 About form
            case AboutForm:
                form = FrmInitForm( AboutForm );
                FrmSetEventHandler( form, aboutHandleEvent );
            break;

            // CH.6 Enter Time form
            case EnterTimeForm:
                form = FrmInitForm( EnterTimeForm );
                FrmSetEventHandler( form, enterTimeHandleEvent );
            break;

            // CH.7 Contact List form
            case ContactListForm:
                form = FrmInitForm( ContactListForm );
                FrmSetEventHandler( form,
                        contactListHandleEvent );
            break;
        }
        FrmSetActiveForm( form );
    }

    // CH.2 Handle form events
    FrmDispatchEvent( &event );

// CH.2 If it's a stop event, exit
} while( event.eType != appStopEvent );

// CH.7 End the try block and do the catch block
}
ErrCatch( errorAlert )
{
    // CH.7 Display the appropriate alert
    FrmAlert( errorAlert );
} ErrEndCatch
```

```
        // CH.5 Close all open forms
        FrmCloseAllForms();

        // CH.5 Close the database
        DmCloseDatabase( contactsDB );

        // CH.2 We're done
        return( 0 );
    }

    // CH.4 Our Contact Detail form handler function
    static Boolean contactDetailHandleEvent( EventPtr event )
    {
        FormPtr form;        // CH.3 A pointer to our form structure
        VoidPtr precord;     // CH.6 Points to a database record
        Char    catName[dmCategoryLength]; // CH.9 Category name

        // CH.3 Get our form pointer
        form = FrmGetActiveForm();

        // CH.4 Parse events
        switch( event->eType )
        {
            // CH.4 Form open event
            case frmOpenEvent:
            {
                // CH.2 Draw the form
                FrmDrawForm( form );

                // CH.5 Draw the database fields
                setFields();
            }
            break;

            // CH.5 Form close event
            case frmCloseEvent:
            {
                // CH.5 Store away any modified fields
                getFields();
            }
            break;

            // CH.5 Parse the button events
            case ctlSelectEvent:
            {
                // CH.5 Store any field changes
                getFields();

                switch( event->data.ctlSelect.controlID )
                {
                    // CH.5 First button
                    case ContactDetailFirstButton:
                    {
```

```
        // CH.5 Set the cursor to the first record
        if( cursor > 0 )
            cursor = 0;
    }
    break;

    // CH.5 Previous button
    case ContactDetailPrevButton:
    {
        // CH.5 Move the cursor back one record
        if( cursor > 0 )
            cursor--;
    }
    break;

    // CH.5 Next button
    case ContactDetailNextButton:
    {
        // CH.5 Move the cursor up one record
        if( cursor < (numRecords - 1) )
            cursor++;
    }
    break;

    // CH.5 Last button
    case ContactDetailLastButton:
    {
        // CH.5 Move the cursor to the last record
        if( cursor < (numRecords - 1) )
            cursor = numRecords - 1;
    }
    break;

    // CH.5 Delete button
    case ContactDetailDeleteButton:
    {
        // CH.5 Remove the record from the database
        DmRemoveRecord( contactsDB, cursor );

        // CH.5 Decrease the number of records
        numRecords--;

        // CH.5 Place the cursor at the first record
        cursor = 0;

        // CH.5 If there are no records left, create one
        if( numRecords == 0 )
            newRecord();
    }
    break;
```

```
// CH.5 New button
case ContactDetailNewButton:
{
    // CH.5 Create a new record
    newRecord();
}
break;

// CH.7 Done button
case ContactDetailDoneButton:
{
    // CH.7 Load the contact list
    FrmGotoForm( ContactListForm );
}
break;

// CH.6 Date selector trigger
case ContactDetailDateSelTrigger:
{
    // CH.6 Initialize the date if necessary
    if( dateTime.year == NO_DATE )
    {
        DateTimeType currentDate;

        // CH.6 Get the current date
        TimSecondsToDateTime( TimGetSeconds(),
                &currentDate );

        // CH.6 Copy it
        dateTime.year = currentDate.year;
        dateTime.month = currentDate.month;
        dateTime.day = currentDate.day;
    }

    // CH.6 Pop up the system date selection form
    SelectDay( selectDayByDay, &(dateTime.month),
            &(dateTime.day), &(dateTime.year),
            "Enter Date" );

    // CH.6 Get the record
    hrecord = DmQueryRecord( contactsDB, cursor );

    // CH.6 Lock it down
    precord = MemHandleLock( hrecord );

    // CH.6 Write the date time field
    DmWrite( precord, DB_DATE_TIME_START, &dateTime,
            sizeof( DateTimeType ) );
```

9

```
        // CH.6 Unlock the record
        MemHandleUnlock( hrecord );

        // CH.6 Mark the record dirty
        isDirty = true;
    }
    break;

    // CH.6 Time selector trigger
    case ContactDetailTimeSelTrigger:
    {
        // CH.6 Pop up our selection form
        FrmPopupForm( EnterTimeForm );
    }
    break;

    // CH.9 Catch a tap on the category trigger
    case ContactDetailCategoryPopupPopTrigger:
    {
        UInt    recAttrs;    // CH.9 The record attribs

        // CH.9 Palm OS will present the popup list.
        CategorySelect( contactsDB, form,
                ContactDetailCategoryPopupPopTrigger,
                ContactDetailCategoryListList,
                false, &detailCat, catName, 1, 0 );

        // CH.9 Get the record attributes
        DmRecordInfo( contactsDB, cursor, &recAttrs,
                NULL, NULL );

        // CH.9 Put in the category bits
        recAttrs &= ~dmRecAttrCategoryMask;
        recAttrs |= detailCat;

        // CH.9 Set the record attributes
        DmSetRecordInfo( contactsDB, cursor, &recAttrs,
                NULL );
    }
    // CH.9 Set fields and return true in this case
    setFields();
    return( true );
}

// CH.5 Sync the current record to the fields
setFields();
}
break;
```

```
                // CH.5 Respond to field tap
                case fldEnterEvent:
                    isDirty = true;
                break;

                // CH.3 Parse menu events
                case menuEvent:
                    return( menuEventHandler( event ) );
                break;
        }

        // CH.2 We're done
        return( false );
}

// CH.4 Our About form event handler function
static Boolean aboutHandleEvent( EventPtr event )
{
    FormPtr form;    // CH.4 A pointer to our form structure

    // CH.4 Get our form pointer
    form = FrmGetActiveForm();

    // CH.4 Respond to the Open event
    if( event->eType == frmOpenEvent )
    {
        // CH.4 Draw the form
        FrmDrawForm( form );
    }

    // CH.4 Return to the calling form
    if( event->eType == ctlSelectEvent )
    {
        FrmReturnToForm( 0 );

        // CH.4 Always return true in this case
        return( true );
    }

    // CH.4 We're done
    return( false );
}

// CH.6 Our Enter Time form event handler function
static Boolean enterTimeHandleEvent( EventPtr event )
{
    FormPtr             form;       // CH.6 A form structure pointer
    static DateTimeType oldTime;    // CH.6 The original time
```

9

```
// CH.6 Get our form pointer
form = FrmGetActiveForm();

// CH.6 Switch on the event
switch( event->eType )
{
    // CH.6 Initialize the form
    case frmOpenEvent:
    {
        // CH.6 Store the time value
        oldTime = dateTime;

        // CH.6 Draw it
        FrmDrawForm( form );

        // CH.6 Set the time controls
        setTimeControls();
    }
    break;

    // CH.6 If a button was repeated
    case ctlRepeatEvent:
    // CH.6 If a button was pushed
    case ctlSelectEvent:
    {
        Word    buttonID;   // CH.6 The ID of the button

        // CH.6 Set the ID
        buttonID = event->data.ctlSelect.controlID;

        // CH.6 Switch on button ID
        switch( buttonID )
        {
            // CH.6 Hours button
            case EnterTimeHoursPushButton:
            // CH.6 Minute Tens button
            case EnterTimeMinuteTensPushButton:
            // CH.6 Minute Ones button
            case EnterTimeMinuteOnesPushButton:
            {
                // CH.6 If no time was set
                if( dateTime.hour == NO_TIME )
                {
                    // CH.6 Set the time to 12 PM
                    dateTime.hour = 12;
                    dateTime.minute = 0;

                    // CH.6 Set the controls
                    setTimeControls();
                }
```

```
        // CH.6 Clear the old selection if any
        if( timeSelect )
            CtlSetValue( getObject( form, timeSelect ),
                    false );

        // CH.6 Set the new selection
        CtlSetValue( getObject( form, buttonID ), true );
        timeSelect = buttonID;
    }
    break;

    // CH.6 Up button
    case EnterTimeTimeUpRepeating:
    {
        // CH.6 If there's no time, do nothing
        if( dateTime.hour == NO_TIME )
            break;

        // CH.6 Based on what push button is selected
        switch( timeSelect )
        {
            // CH.6 Increase hours
            case EnterTimeHoursPushButton:
            {
                // CH.6 Increment hours
                dateTime.hour++;

                // CH.6 If it was 11 AM, make it 12 AM
                if( dateTime.hour == 12 )
                    dateTime.hour = 0;

                // CH.6 If it was 11 PM, make it 12 PM
                if( dateTime.hour == 24 )
                    dateTime.hour = 12;
            }
            break;

            // CH.6 Increase tens of minutes
            case EnterTimeMinuteTensPushButton:
            {
                // CH.6 Increment minutes
                dateTime.minute += 10;

                // CH.6 If it was 5X, roll over
                if( dateTime.minute > 59 )
                    dateTime.minute -= 60;
            }
            break;

            // CH.6 Increase minutes
            case EnterTimeMinuteOnesPushButton:
            {
```

```
        // CH.6 Increment minutes
        dateTime.minute++;

        // CH.6 If it is zero, subtract ten
        if( (dateTime.minute % 10) == 0 )
            dateTime.minute -= 10;
    }
    break;
}

    // Revise the controls
    setTimeControls();
}
break;

// CH.6 Down button
case EnterTimeTimeDownRepeating:
{

    // CH.6 If there's no time, do nothing
    if( dateTime.hour == NO_TIME )
        break;

    // CH.6 Based on what push button is selected
    switch( timeSelect )
    {
        // CH.6 Decrease hours
        case EnterTimeHoursPushButton:
        {
            // CH.6 Decrement hours
            dateTime.hour--;

            // CH.6 If it was 12 AM, make it 11 AM
            if( dateTime.hour == -1 )
                dateTime.hour = 11;

            // CH.6 If it was 12 PM, make it 11 PM
            if( dateTime.hour == 11 )
                dateTime.hour = 23;
        }
        break;

        // CH.6 Decrease tens of minutes
        case EnterTimeMinuteTensPushButton:
        {
            // CH.6 Decrement minutes
            dateTime.minute -= 10;

            // CH.6 If it was 0X, roll over
            if( dateTime.minute < 0 )
                dateTime.minute += 60;
```

```
            }
            break;

            // CH.6 Decrease minutes
            case EnterTimeMinuteOnesPushButton:
            {
                // CH.6 Decrement minutes
                dateTime.minute--;

                // CH.6 If it is 9, add ten
                if( (dateTime.minute % 10) == 9 )
                    dateTime.minute += 10;

                // CH.6 If less than zero, make it 9
                if( dateTime.minute < 0 )
                    dateTime.minute = 9;
            }
            break;
        }

        // CH.6 Revise the controls
        setTimeControls();
    }
    break;

    // CH.6 AM button
    case EnterTimeAMPushButton:
    {
        // CH.6 If no time was set
        if( dateTime.hour == NO_TIME )
        {
            // CH.6 Set the time to 12 AM
            dateTime.hour = 0;
            dateTime.minute = 0;

            // CH.6 Set the controls
            setTimeControls();
        }

        // CH.6 If it is PM
        if( dateTime.hour > 11 )
        {
            // CH.6 Change to AM
            dateTime.hour -= 12;

            // CH.6 Set the controls
            setTimeControls();
        }
    }
    break;
```

```
// CH.6 PM button
case EnterTimePMPushButton:
{
    // CH.6 If no time was set
    if( dateTime.hour == NO_TIME )
    {
        // CH.6 Set the time to 12 PM
        dateTime.hour = 12;
        dateTime.minute = 0;

        // CH.6 Set the controls
        setTimeControls();
    }

    // CH.6 If it is AM
    if( dateTime.hour < 12 )
    {
        // CH.6 Change to PM
        dateTime.hour += 12;

        // CH.6 Set the controls
        setTimeControls();
    }
}
break;

// CH.6 No Time checkbox
case EnterTimeNoTimeCheckbox:
{
    // CH.6 If we are unchecking the box
    if( dateTime.hour == NO_TIME )
    {
        // CH.6 Set the time to 12 PM
        dateTime.hour = 12;
        dateTime.minute = 0;

        // CH.6 Set the controls
        setTimeControls();

        // CH.6 Set the new selection
        timeSelect = EnterTimeHoursPushButton;
        CtlSetValue( getObject( form, timeSelect ),
                true );
    }

    else
    // CH.6 If we are checking the box
        dateTime.hour = NO_TIME;

    // CH.6 Set the controls
    setTimeControls();
```

```
                    }
                    break;

                    // CH.6 Cancel button
                    case EnterTimeCancelButton:
                    {
                        // CH.6 Restore time
                        dateTime = oldTime;

                        // CH.6 Return to calling form
                        FrmReturnToForm( 0 );
                    }
                    // CH.6 Always return true
                    return( true );

                    // CH.6 OK button
                    case EnterTimeOKButton:
                    {
                        VoidPtr precord;    // CH.6 Points to the record

                        // CH.6 Lock it down
                        precord = MemHandleLock( hrecord );

                        // CH.6 Write the date time field
                        DmWrite( precord, DB_DATE_TIME_START, &dateTime,
                                sizeof( DateTimeType ) );

                        // CH.6 Unlock the record
                        MemHandleUnlock( hrecord );

                        // CH.6 Mark the record dirty
                        isDirty = true;

                        // CH.6 Return to the Contact Details form
                        FrmReturnToForm( 0 );

                        // CH.6 Update the field
                        setTimeTrigger();
                    }
                    // CH.6 Always return true
                    return( true );
                }
            }
            break;
    }

    // CH.6 We're done
    return( false );
}
```

9

```
// CH.7 Our Contact List form event handler function
static Boolean contactListHandleEvent( EventPtr event )
{
    FormPtr form;    // CH.7 A form structure pointer
    Char    catName[dmCategoryLength];  // CH.9 Category name

    // CH.7 Get our form pointer
    form = FrmGetActiveForm();

    // CH.7 Parse events
    switch( event->eType )
    {
        // CH.7 Form open event
        case frmOpenEvent:
        {
            // CH.7 Draw the form
            FrmDrawForm( form );

            // CH.9 Set the category popup trigger label
            CategoryGetName( contactsDB, listCat, catName );
            CategorySetTriggerLabel( getObject( form,
                    ContactListCategoryPopupPopTrigger ),
                    catName );

            // CH.8 The cursor starts at the beginning
            cursor = 0;

            // CH.9 Initialize the table indexes
            initIndexes();

            // CH.8 Populate and draw the table
            drawTable();
        }
        break;

        // CH.7 Respond to a list selection
        case tblSelectEvent:
        {
            // CH.7 Set the database cursor to the selected contact
            cursor = tableIndex[event->data.tblSelect.row];

            // CH.7 Go to contact details
            FrmGotoForm( ContactDetailForm );
        }
        break;

        // CH.7 Respond to a menu event
        case menuEvent:
            return( menuEventHandler( event ) );
```

```
// CH.7 Respond to the popup trigger
case popSelectEvent:
{
    // CH.7 If there is no change, we're done
    if( sortBy == event->data.popSelect.selection )
        return( true );

    // CH.7 Modify sort order variable
    sortBy = event->data.popSelect.selection;

    // CH.7 Sort the contact database by the new criteria
    DmQuickSort( contactsDB, (DmComparF*)sortFunc, sortBy );

    // CH.8 Cursor starts at zero
    cursor = 0;

    // CH.9 Initialize the table indexes
    initIndexes();

    // CH.8 Rebuild the table
    drawTable();
}
break;

// CH.8 Respond to arrows
case ctlRepeatEvent:
{
    switch( event->data.ctlRepeat.controlID )
    {
        // CH.8 Up arrow
        case ContactListRecordUpRepeating:
            scrollIndexes( -1 );
        break;

        // CH.8 Down arrow
        case ContactListRecordDownRepeating:
            scrollIndexes( 1 );
        break;
    }

    // CH.8 Now refresh the table
    drawTable();
}
break;

// CH.8 Respond to up and down arrow hard keys
case keyDownEvent:
{
    switch( event->data.keyDown.chr )
    {
        // CH.8 Up arrow hard key
```

```
            case pageUpChr:
                scrollIndexes( -(TABLE_NUM_ROWS - 1) );
            break;

            // CH.8 Down arrow hard key
            case pageDownChr:
                scrollIndexes( TABLE_NUM_ROWS - 1 );
            break;
        }

        // CH.8 Now refresh the table
        drawTable();
    }
    break;

    // CH.8 Respond to scrollbar events
    case sclExitEvent:
    {
        //CH.9 Find the record in our category
        cursor = findIndex( event->data.sclExit.newValue );

        // CH.9 Initialize our index list
        initIndexes();

        // CH.8 Draw the table
        drawTable();
    }
    break;

    // CH.9 Catch a tap on the category trigger
    case ctlSelectEvent:
    {
        // CH.9 Palm OS will present the popup list for us.
        CategorySelect( contactsDB, form,
                ContactListCategoryPopupPopTrigger,
                ContactListCategoryListList,
                true, &listCat, catName, 1, 0 );

        // CH.9 Cursor starts at zero
        cursor = 0;

        // CH.9 Initialize the indexes
        initIndexes();

        // CH.9 Draw the table
        drawTable();
    }
    // CH.9 Don't let the OS generate other events from this
    return( true );
```

```
        }       // CH.7 End of the event switch statement

        // CH.7 We're done
        return( false );
    }

    // CH.3 Handle menu events
    Boolean menuEventHandler( EventPtr event )
    {
        FormPtr       form;    // CH.3 A pointer to our form structure
        Word          index;   // CH.3 A general purpose control index
        FieldPtr      field;   // CH.3 Used for manipulating fields

        // CH.3 Get our form pointer
        form = FrmGetActiveForm();

        // CH.3 Erase the menu status from the display
        MenuEraseStatus( NULL );

        // CH.4 Handle options menu
        if( event->data.menu.itemID == OptionsAboutContacts )
        {
            // CH.4 Pop up the About form as a Dialog
            FrmPopupForm( AboutForm );
            return( true );
        }

        // CH.3 Handle graffiti help
        if( event->data.menu.itemID == EditGraffitiHelp )
        {
            // CH.3 Pop up the graffiti reference based on
            // the graffiti state
            SysGraffitiReferenceDialog( referenceDefault );
            return( true );
        }

        // CH.3 Get the index of our field
        index = FrmGetFocus( form );

        // CH.3 If there is no field selected, we're done
        if( index == noFocus )
            return( false );

        // CH.3 Get the pointer of our field
        field = FrmGetObjectPtr( form, index );

        // CH.3 Do the edit command
        switch( event->data.menu.itemID )
        {
            // CH.3 Undo
            case EditUndo:
```

9

```
            FldUndo( field );
        break;

        // CH.3 Cut
        case EditCut:
            FldCut( field );
        break;

        // CH.3 Copy
        case EditCopy:
            FldCopy( field );
        break;

        // CH.3 Paste
        case EditPaste:
            FldPaste( field );
        break;

        // CH.3 Select All
        case EditSelectAll:
        {
            // CH.3 Get the length of the string in the field
            Word length = FldGetTextLength( field );

            // CH.3 Sound an error if appropriate
            if( length == 0 )
            {
                SndPlaySystemSound( sndError );
                return( false );
            }

            // CH.3 Select the whole string
            FldSetSelection( field, 0, length );
        }
        break;

        // CH.3 Bring up the keyboard tool
        case EditKeyboard:
            SysKeyboardDialogV10();
        break;
    }

    // CH.3 We're done
    return( true );
}

// CH.5 This function creates and initializes a new record
static void newRecord( void )
{
    VoidPtr precord;    // CH.5 Pointer to the record
    UInt    recAttrs;   // CH.9 The record's attributes
```

```
// CH.7 Create the database record and get a handle to it
if( (hrecord = DmNewRecord( contactsDB, &cursor,
        DB_RECORD_SIZE )) == NULL )
    errorExit( MemoryErrorAlert );

// CH.5 Lock down the record to modify it
precord = MemHandleLock( hrecord );

// CH.5 Clear the record
DmSet( precord, 0, DB_RECORD_SIZE, 0 );

// CH.6 Initialize the date and time
MemSet( &dateTime, sizeof( dateTime ), 0 );
dateTime.year = NO_DATE;
dateTime.hour = NO_TIME;
DmWrite( precord, DB_DATE_TIME_START, &dateTime,
        sizeof( DateTimeType ) );

// CH.5 Unlock the record
MemHandleUnlock( hrecord );

// CH.5 Clear the busy bit and set the dirty bit
DmReleaseRecord( contactsDB, cursor, true );

// CH.5 Increment the total record count
numRecords++;

// CH.5 Set the dirty bit
isDirty = true;

// Ch.9 Get the record attribute bits
DmRecordInfo( contactsDB, cursor, &recAttrs, NULL, NULL );

// CH.9 Clear the category bits
recAttrs &= ~dmRecAttrCategoryMask;

// CH.9 Set the category to the appropriate category
if( listCat == dmAllCategories )
    recAttrs |= dmUnfiledCategory;
else
    recAttrs |= listCat;

// CH.9 Set the record attributes
DmSetRecordInfo( contactsDB, cursor, &recAttrs,
        NULL );

// CH.5 We're done
return;
}
```

```
// CH.5 A time saver: Gets object pointers based on their ID
static VoidPtr getObject( FormPtr form, Word objectID )
{
    Word     index;   // CH.5 The object index

    // CH.5 Get the index
    index = FrmGetObjectIndex( form, objectID );

    // CH.5 Return the pointer
    return( FrmGetObjectPtr( form, index ) );
}

// CH.5 Gets the current database record and displays it
// in the detail fields
static void setFields( void )
{
    FormPtr      form;         // CH.5 The contact detail form
    CharPtr      precord;      // CH.6 A record pointer
    Word         index;        // CH.5 The object index
    UInt         recAttrs;     // CH.9 The record attribute bits
    Char         catName[dmCategoryLength];   // CH.6 The category name

    // CH.5 Get the contact detail form pointer
    form = FrmGetActiveForm();

    // CH.5 Get the current record
    hrecord = DmQueryRecord( contactsDB, cursor );

    // CH.6 Initialize the date and time variable
    precord = MemHandleLock( hrecord );
    MemMove( &dateTime, precord + DB_DATE_TIME_START,
            sizeof( dateTime ) );

    // CH.6 Initialize the date control
    setDateTrigger();

    // CH.6 Initialize the time control
    setTimeTrigger();

    // CH.5 Set the text for the First Name field
    setText( getObject( form, ContactDetailFirstNameField ),
            precord + DB_FIRST_NAME_START );

    // CH.5 Set the text for the Last Name field
    setText( getObject( form, ContactDetailLastNameField ),
            precord + DB_LAST_NAME_START );

    // CH.5 Set the text for the Phone Number field
    setText( getObject( form, ContactDetailPhoneNumberField ),
            precord + DB_PHONE_NUMBER_START );
```

```
MemHandleUnlock( hrecord );

// CH.5 If the record is already dirty, it's new, so set focus
if( isDirty )
{
    // CH.3 Get the index of our field
    index = FrmGetObjectIndex( form,
            ContactDetailFirstNameField );

    // CH.3 Set the focus to the First Name field
    FrmSetFocus( form, index );

    // CH.5 Set upper shift on
    GrfSetState( false, false, true );
}

// CH.9 Get the record attributes
DmRecordInfo( contactsDB, cursor, &recAttrs, NULL, NULL );

// CH.9 Get the category
detailCat = recAttrs & dmRecAttrCategoryMask;

// CH.9 Set the category popup trigger label
CategoryGetName( contactsDB, detailCat, catName );
CategorySetTriggerLabel( getObject( form,
        ContactDetailCategoryPopupPopTrigger ), catName );

// CH.5 We're done
return;
}

// CH.5 Puts any field changes in the record
void getFields( void )
{
    FormPtr form;    // CH.5 The contact detail form

    // CH.5 Get the contact detail form pointer
    form = FrmGetActiveForm();

    // CH.5 Turn off focus
    FrmSetFocus( form, -1 );

    // CH.5 If the record has been modified
    if( isDirty )
    {
        CharPtr precord;    // CH.5 Points to the DB record

        // CH.7 Detach the record from the database
        DmDetachRecord( contactsDB, cursor, &hrecord );

        // CH.5 Lock the record
```

```
    precord = MemHandleLock( hrecord );

    // CH.5 Get the text for the First Name field
    getText( getObject( form, ContactDetailFirstNameField ),
            precord, DB_FIRST_NAME_START );

    // CH.5 Get the text for the Last Name field
    getText( getObject( form, ContactDetailLastNameField ),
            precord, DB_LAST_NAME_START );

    // CH.5 Get the text for the Phone Number field
    getText( getObject( form, ContactDetailPhoneNumberField ),
            precord, DB_PHONE_NUMBER_START );

    // CH.7 Find the proper position
    cursor = DmFindSortPosition( contactsDB, precord, NULL,
            (DmComparF*)sortFunc, sortBy );

    // CH.5 Unlock the record
    MemHandleUnlock( hrecord );

    // CH.7 Reattach the record
    DmAttachRecord( contactsDB, &cursor, hrecord, NULL );
    }

    // CH.6 Reset the dirty bit
    isDirty = false;

    // CH.5 We're done
    return;
}

// CH.5 Set the text in a field
static void setText( FieldPtr field, CharPtr text )
{
    VoidHand    hfield; // CH.5 Handle of field text
    CharPtr     pfield; // CH.5 Pointer to field text

    // CH.5 Get the current field handle
    hfield = FldGetTextHandle( field );

    // CH.5 If we have a handle
    if( hfield != NULL )
    {
        // CH.5 Resize it
        if( MemHandleResize( hfield, StrLen( text ) + 1 ) != 0 )
            errorExit( MemoryErrorAlert );
    }

    else
    // CH.5 Allocate a handle for the string
```

```
    {
        hfield = MemHandleNew( StrLen( text ) + 1 );
        if( hfield == NULL )
            errorExit( MemoryErrorAlert );
    }

    // CH.5 Lock it
    pfield = MemHandleLock( hfield );

    // CH.5 Copy the string
    StrCopy( pfield, text );

    // CH.5 Unlock it
    MemHandleUnlock( hfield );

    // CH.5 Give it to the field
    FldSetTextHandle( field, hfield );

    // CH.5 Draw the field
    FldDrawField( field );

    // CH.5 We're done
    return;
}

// CH.5 Get the text from a field
static void getText( FieldPtr field, VoidPtr precord, Word offset )
{
    CharPtr pfield; // CH.5 Pointer to field text

    // CH.5 Get the text pointer
    pfield = FldGetTextPtr( field );

    // CH.5 Copy it
    DmWrite( precord, offset, pfield, StrLen( pfield ) );

    // CH.5 We're done
    return;
}

// CH.6 Set the Contact Detail date selector trigger
static void setDateTrigger( void )
{
    FormPtr form;    // CH.5 The contact detail form

    // CH.6 Get the contact detail form pointer
    form = FrmGetActiveForm();

    // CH.6 If there is no date
    if( dateTime.year == NO_DATE )
    {
```

9

```
        CtlSetLabel( getObject( form, ContactDetailDateSelTrigger ),
                "           " );
    }

    else
    // CH.6 If there is a date
    {
        Char dateString[dateStringLength];

        // CH.6 Get the date string
        DateToAscii( dateTime.month, dateTime.day, dateTime.year,
                (DateFormatType)PrefGetPreference( prefDateFormat ),
                dateString );

        // CH.6 Set the selector trigger label
        CtlSetLabel( getObject( form, ContactDetailDateSelTrigger ),
                dateString );

    }

    // CH.6 We're done
    return;
}

// CH.6 Set the Contact Detail time selector trigger
static void setTimeTrigger( void )
{
    FormPtr form;    // CH.5 The contact detail form

    // CH.6 Get the contact detail form pointer
    form = FrmGetActiveForm();

    // CH.6 If there's no time
    if( dateTime.hour == NO_TIME )
    {
        CtlSetLabel( getObject( form, ContactDetailTimeSelTrigger ),
                "         " );
    }

    else
    // CH.6 If there is a time
    {
        Char timeString[timeStringLength];

        // CH.6 Get the time string
        TimeToAscii( dateTime.hour, dateTime.minute,
                (TimeFormatType)PrefGetPreference( prefTimeFormat ),
                timeString );
```

```
                // CH.6 Set the selector trigger label
                CtlSetLabel( getObject( form, ContactDetailTimeSelTrigger ),
                        timeString );

        }

        // CH.6 We're done
        return;
}

// CH.6 Set the controls in the Enter Time form based on dateTime
static void setTimeControls( void )
{
        FormPtr         form;
        ControlPtr      hourButton;
        ControlPtr      minuteTensButton;
        ControlPtr      minuteOnesButton;
        ControlPtr      amButton;
        ControlPtr      pmButton;
        ControlPtr      noTimeCheckbox;
        Char            labelString[3];
        SWord           hour;

        // CH.6 Get the form
        form = FrmGetActiveForm();

        // CH.6 Get the control pointers
        hourButton = getObject( form, EnterTimeHoursPushButton );
        minuteTensButton = getObject( form,
                EnterTimeMinuteTensPushButton );
        minuteOnesButton = getObject( form,
                EnterTimeMinuteOnesPushButton );
        amButton = getObject( form, EnterTimeAMPushButton );
        pmButton = getObject( form, EnterTimePMPushButton );
        noTimeCheckbox = getObject( form, EnterTimeNoTimeCheckbox );

        // CH.6 If there is a time
        if( dateTime.hour != NO_TIME )
        {
                // CH.6 Update the hour
                hour = dateTime.hour % 12;
                if( hour == 0 )
                        hour = 12;
                CtlSetLabel( hourButton,
                        StrIToA( labelString, hour ) );

                // CH.6 Update the minute tens
                CtlSetLabel( minuteTensButton,
                        StrIToA( labelString, dateTime.minute / 10 ) );
```

9

```
        // CH.6 Update the minute ones
        CtlSetLabel( minuteOnesButton,
                StrIToA( labelString, dateTime.minute % 10 ) );

        // CH.6 Update AM
        CtlSetValue( amButton, (dateTime.hour < 12) );

        // CH.6 Update PM
        CtlSetValue( pmButton, (dateTime.hour > 11) );

        // CH.6 Uncheck the no time checkbox
        CtlSetValue( noTimeCheckbox, false );
    }

    else
    // If there is no time
    {
        // CH.6 Update the hour
        CtlSetValue( hourButton, false );
        CtlSetLabel( hourButton, "" );

        // CH.6 Update the minute tens
        CtlSetValue( minuteTensButton, false );
        CtlSetLabel( minuteTensButton, "" );

        // CH.6 Update the minute ones
        CtlSetValue( minuteOnesButton, false );
        CtlSetLabel( minuteOnesButton, "" );

        // CH.6 Update AM
        CtlSetValue( amButton, false );

        // CH.6 Update PM
        CtlSetValue( pmButton, false );

        // CH.6 Uncheck the no time checkbox
        CtlSetValue( noTimeCheckbox, true );
    }

    // CH.6 We're done
    return;
}

// CH.7 This function is called by Palm OS to sort records
static Int sortFunc( CharPtr precord1, CharPtr precord2, Int sortBy )
{
    Int sortResult;

    // CH.7 Switch based on sort criteria
    switch( sortBy )
    {
```

```
        // CH.7 Sort by date and time
        case SORTBY_DATE_TIME:
        {
            DateTimePtr pdateTime1;
            DateTimePtr pdateTime2;
            Long lDiff;

            pdateTime1 = (DateTimePtr)(precord1 +
                    DB_DATE_TIME_START);
            pdateTime2 = (DateTimePtr)(precord2 +
                    DB_DATE_TIME_START);

            // CH.7 Compare the dates and times
            lDiff = (Long)(TimDateTimeToSeconds( pdateTime1 )
                    / 60 ) -
                    (Long)(TimDateTimeToSeconds( pdateTime2 ) / 60 );

            // CH.7 Date/time #1 is later
            if( lDiff > 0 )
                sortResult = 1;

            else
            // CH.7 Date/time #2 is later
            if( lDiff < 0 )
                sortResult = -1;

            else
            // CH.7 They are equal
                sortResult = 0;
        }
        break;

        // CH.7 Sort by first name
        case SORTBY_FIRST_NAME:
        {
            sortResult = StrCompare( precord1 + DB_FIRST_NAME_START,
                    precord2 + DB_FIRST_NAME_START );
        }
        break;

        // CH.7 Sort by last name
        case SORTBY_LAST_NAME:
        {
            sortResult = StrCompare( precord1 + DB_LAST_NAME_START,
                    precord2 + DB_LAST_NAME_START );
        }
        break;
    }

    // CH.7 We're done
    return( sortResult );
```

9

```
}

// CH.8 Draw our list of choices using a table object
static void drawTable( void )
{
    FormPtr     form;
    TablePtr    table;
    Int         column;
    Int         count;

    // CH.8 Get the form pointer
    form = FrmGetActiveForm();

    // CH.8 Get the table pointer
    table = getObject( form, ContactListTableTable );

    // CH.8 For all columns
    for( column = 0; column < TABLE_NUM_COLUMNS; column++ )
    {
        // CH.8 Set the draw routine
        TblSetCustomDrawProcedure( table, column, drawCell );

        // CH.8 Make the column visible
        TblSetColumnUsable( table, column, true );
    }

    // CH.8 Initialize the table styles
    for( count = 0; count < TABLE_NUM_ROWS; count++ )
    {
        // CH.9 If there is data
        if( tableIndex[count] != 0xffff )
        {
            // CH.8 Show the row
            TblSetRowUsable( table, count, true );

            // CH.8 Set the cell styles
            for( column = 0; column < TABLE_NUM_COLUMNS; column++ )
            {
                TblSetItemStyle( table, count, column,
                    customTableItem );
            }
        }

        else
        // CH.8 Hide unused rows if any
            TblSetRowUsable( table, count, false );
    }

    // CH.8 Draw the table
    TblDrawTable( table );
```

```
            // CH.8 We're done
            return;
    }


    // CH.8 The custom drawing routine for a table cell
    static void drawCell( VoidPtr table, Word row, Word column,
            RectanglePtr bounds )
    {
        Int     record;
        CharPtr precord;
        Char    string[DB_FIRST_NAME_SIZE + DB_LAST_NAME_SIZE];
        SWord   width;
        SWord   len;
        Boolean noFit;

        // CH.9 Calculate our record
        record = tableIndex[row];

        // CH.8 Get our record
        hrecord = DmQueryRecord( contactsDB, record );
        precord = MemHandleLock( hrecord );

        // CH.8 Get the date and time
        MemMove( &dateTime, precord + DB_DATE_TIME_START,
                sizeof( dateTime ) );

        // CH.8 Switch on the column
        switch( column )
        {
            // CH.8 Handle dates
            case TABLE_COLUMN_DATE:
            {
                if( dateTime.year != NO_DATE )
                {
                    DateToAscii( dateTime.month, dateTime.day,
                            dateTime.year,
                            (DateFormatType)PrefGetPreference(
                            prefDateFormat ), string );
                }
                else
                    StrCopy( string, "-" );
            }
            break;

            // CH.8 Handle times
            case TABLE_COLUMN_TIME:
            {
                if( dateTime.hour != NO_TIME )
                {
                    TimeToAscii( dateTime.hour, dateTime.minute,
                            (TimeFormatType)PrefGetPreference(
```

9

```
                           prefTimeFormat ), string );
            }
            else
                StrCopy( string, "-" );
        }
        break;

        // CH.8 Handle names
        case TABLE_COLUMN_NAME:
        {
            StrCopy( string, precord + DB_FIRST_NAME_START );
            StrCat( string, " " );
            StrCat( string, precord + DB_LAST_NAME_START );
        }
        break;
    }

    // CH.8 Unlock the record
    MemHandleUnlock( hrecord );

    // CH.8 Set the text mode
    WinSetUnderlineMode( noUnderline );
    FntSetFont( stdFont );

    // CH.8 Truncate the string if necessary
    width = bounds->extent.x;
    len = StrLen( string );
    noFit = false;
    FntCharsInWidth( string, &width, &len, &noFit );

    // CH.8 Draw the cell
    WinEraseRectangle( bounds, 0 );
    WinDrawChars( string, len, bounds->topLeft.x,
            bounds->topLeft.y );

    // CH.8 We're done
    return;
}

// CH.9 Initialize the row information by finding the right records
static void initIndexes( void )
{
    FormPtr     form;
    Int         count;
    UInt        index = cursor;
    ControlPtr  downArrow;
    ControlPtr  upArrow;
    UInt        numRecsInCategory;

    // CH.9 Get the current form
    form = FrmGetActiveForm();
```

```
// CH.9 For each table row
for( count = 0; count < TABLE_NUM_ROWS; count++ )
{
    // CH.9 Find the next matching record
    if( DmSeekRecordInCategory( contactsDB, &index, 0,
            dmSeekForward, listCat ) )
    {
        // CH.9 No more records. Fill the rest of the array with
        // 0xffff
        for( ; count < TABLE_NUM_ROWS; count++ )
            tableIndex[count] = 0xffff;
        break;
    }

    // CH.9 Put the index number in the array
    tableIndex[count] = index;
    index++;
}

// CH.9 Set the cursor to a known category record
cursor = tableIndex[0];

// CH.8 Get pointers to the arrow buttons
upArrow = getObject( form, ContactListRecordUpRepeating );
downArrow = getObject( form, ContactListRecordDownRepeating );

// CH.8 Update the arrow buttons and scrollbars
numRecsInCategory = DmNumRecordsInCategory( contactsDB,
        listCat );
if( numRecsInCategory > TABLE_NUM_ROWS )
{
    UInt    position = DmPositionInCategory( contactsDB, cursor,
            listCat );

    // CH.8 Show the up arrow
    if( position > 0 )
    {
        CtlSetLabel( upArrow, BLACK_UP_ARROW );
        CtlSetEnabled( upArrow, true );
    }
    else
    {
        CtlSetLabel( upArrow, GRAY_UP_ARROW );
        CtlSetEnabled( upArrow, false );
    }
    CtlShowControl( upArrow );

    // CH.8 Show the down arrow
    if( position >= numRecsInCategory - TABLE_NUM_ROWS )
    {
        CtlSetLabel( downArrow, GRAY_DOWN_ARROW );
```

```
                CtlSetEnabled( downArrow, false );
        }
        else
        {
            CtlSetLabel( downArrow, BLACK_DOWN_ARROW );
            CtlSetEnabled( downArrow, true );
        }
        CtlShowControl( downArrow );

        // CH.9 Show the scrollbar
        SclSetScrollBar( getObject( form,
                ContactListScrollbarScrollBar ), position, 0,
                numRecsInCategory - TABLE_NUM_ROWS, TABLE_NUM_ROWS );
    }
    else
    {
        // CH.8 Hide the arrows
        CtlHideControl( upArrow );
        CtlHideControl( downArrow );

        // CH.8 Hide the scrollbar
        SclSetScrollBar( getObject( form,
                ContactListScrollbarScrollBar ), 0, 0, 0, 0 );
    }

    // CH.9 We're done
    return;
}

// CH.9 Scroll a certain number of records in the current category
static void scrollIndexes( Int amount )
{
    FormPtr     form;
    UInt        count;
    UInt        index;
    ControlPtr  downArrow;
    ControlPtr  upArrow;
    UInt        numRecsInCategory;
    .

    // CH.9 Get the current form
    form = FrmGetActiveForm();

    // CH.9 Get pointers to the arrow buttons
    upArrow = getObject( form, ContactListRecordUpRepeating );
    downArrow = getObject( form, ContactListRecordDownRepeating );

    // CH.9 If we're scrolling down
    if( amount > 0 )
    {
        // CH.9 While there is still an amount to scroll
        while( amount- )
```

9

```
    {
        // CH.9 Get a new index after the last one
        index = tableIndex[TABLE_NUM_ROWS - 1];
        if( DmSeekRecordInCategory( contactsDB, &index, 1,
              dmSeekForward, listCat ) )
        {
            // CH.9 No more records. We're done scrolling
            CtlSetLabel( downArrow, GRAY_DOWN_ARROW );
            CtlSetEnabled( downArrow, false );
            return;
        }

        // CH.9 Move current indexes up one
        for( count = 0; count < TABLE_NUM_ROWS - 1; count++ )
            tableIndex[count] = tableIndex[count + 1];

        // CH.9 Put the index number in the array
        tableIndex[count] = index;
    }

    // CH.9 Disable the down arrow if needed
    if( DmSeekRecordInCategory( contactsDB, &index, 1,
          dmSeekForward, listCat ) )
    {
        CtlSetLabel( downArrow, GRAY_DOWN_ARROW );
        CtlSetEnabled( downArrow, false );
    }

    // CH.9 Enable the up arrow
    CtlSetLabel( upArrow, BLACK_UP_ARROW );
    CtlSetEnabled( upArrow, true );
}

else
// CH.9 If we're scrolling up
if( amount < 0 )
{
    // CH.9 While there is still an amount to scroll
    while( amount++ )
    {
        // CH.9 Get a new index before the first one
        index = tableIndex[0];
        if( DmSeekRecordInCategory( contactsDB, &index, 1,
              dmSeekBackward, listCat ) )
        {
            // CH.9 No more records. We're done scrolling
            CtlSetLabel( upArrow, GRAY_UP_ARROW );
            CtlSetEnabled( upArrow, false );
            return;
        }
```

```
            // CH.9 Move current indexes down one
            for( count = TABLE_NUM_ROWS - 1; count > 0; count- )
                tableIndex[count] = tableIndex[count - 1];

            // CH.9 Put the index number in the array
            tableIndex[count] = index;
        }

        // CH.9 Disable the up arrow if needed
        if( DmSeekRecordInCategory( contactsDB, &index, 1,
                dmSeekBackward, listCat ) )
        {
            CtlSetLabel( upArrow, GRAY_UP_ARROW );
            CtlSetEnabled( upArrow, false );
        }

        // CH.9 Enable the down arrow
        CtlSetLabel( downArrow, BLACK_DOWN_ARROW );
        CtlSetEnabled( downArrow, true );
    }

    // CH.9 Set the cursor
    cursor = tableIndex[0];

    // CH.9 Set the scrollbar
    numRecsInCategory = DmNumRecordsInCategory( contactsDB,
            listCat );
    SclSetScrollBar( getObject( form,
            ContactListScrollbarScrollBar ), DmPositionInCategory(
            contactsDB, cursor, listCat ), 0,
            numRecords - TABLE_NUM_ROWS, TABLE_NUM_ROWS );

    // CH.9 We're done
    return;
}

// CH.9 Find a particular index
static UInt findIndex( UInt scrollValue )
{
    UInt index = 0;

    // CH.9 Seek from zero to the scrollvalue
    DmSeekRecordInCategory( contactsDB, &index, scrollValue,
            dmSeekForward, listCat );

    // We're done
    return( index );
}

// CH.9 Find something in our records
static void find( Ptr params )
```

```
{
    FindParamsPtr    findParams = (FindParamsPtr)params;// CH.9 Params
    DmOpenRef        contactsDB;     // CH.9 Our local database ptr
    UInt             numRecords;     // CH.9 Number of recs in the db
    LocalID          dbID;           // CH.9 Local ID of the database
    UInt             cardNum;        // CH.9 Card number
    UInt             cursor;         // CH.9 The current record
    VoidHand         hrecord;        // CH.9 Handle to the record
    CharPtr          precord;        // CH.9 Pointer to the record
    DateTimeType     dateTime;       // CH.9 Date and time in this record
    Char             textRecord[dateStringLength + 1 +    // CH.9 We
                          timeStringLength + 1 +          // build
                          DB_FIRST_NAME_SIZE +            // text
                          DB_LAST_NAME_SIZE +             // record here
                          DB_PHONE_NUMBER_SIZE];
    Char             lcText[dateStringLength + 1 +        // CH.9 Copy
                          timeStringLength + 1 +          // lower
                          DB_FIRST_NAME_SIZE +            // case
                          DB_LAST_NAME_SIZE +             // text here
                          DB_PHONE_NUMBER_SIZE];
    Word             offset;         // CH.9 Offset of the match
    RectangleType    bounds;         // CH.9 Bounding rect for text
    SWord            width;          // CH.9 Width of the bounds rect
    SWord            len;            // CH.9 Text length
    Boolean          noFit;          // CH.9 Does it fit

    // CH.9 Draw a title for our find items
    // CH.9 If there's no more room, return
    if( (FindDrawHeader( findParams, "Contacts" )) == true )
        return;

    // CH.9 Open the database for reading
    if( (contactsDB = DmOpenDatabaseByTypeCreator( 'ctct', 'PPGU',
            dmModeReadOnly )) == NULL )
        return;

    // CH.9 Find out how many records we have
    numRecords = DmNumRecords( contactsDB );

    // CH.9 Get the ID and card number
    DmOpenDatabaseInfo( contactsDB, &dbID, NULL, NULL, &cardNum,
            NULL);

    // CH.9 For each record
    for( cursor = findParams->recordNum; cursor < numRecords;
            cursor++ )
    {
        // CH.9 Get the record
        hrecord = DmQueryRecord( contactsDB, cursor );
        precord = MemHandleLock( hrecord );
```

9

```
// CH.9 Get the date and time
MemMove( &dateTime, precord + DB_DATE_TIME_START,
        sizeof( dateTime ) );

// CH.9 Start over
*textRecord = '\0';

// CH.9 Add the date string if any
if( dateTime.year != NO_DATE )
{
    DateToAscii( dateTime.month, dateTime.day,
            dateTime.year,
            (DateFormatType)PrefGetPreference(
            prefDateFormat ), textRecord );
    StrCat( textRecord, " " );
}

// CH.9 Add the time string if any
if( dateTime.hour != NO_TIME )
{
    TimeToAscii( dateTime.hour, dateTime.minute,
            (TimeFormatType)PrefGetPreference(
            prefTimeFormat ), textRecord +
            StrLen( textRecord ) );
    StrCat( textRecord, " " );
}

// CH.9 Append the first name
StrCat( textRecord, precord + DB_FIRST_NAME_START );
StrCat( textRecord, " " );

// CH.9 Append the last name
StrCat( textRecord, precord + DB_LAST_NAME_START );
StrCat( textRecord, " " );

// CH.9 Append the phone number
StrCat( textRecord, precord + DB_PHONE_NUMBER_START );

// CH.9 Unlock the record
MemHandleUnlock( hrecord );

// CH.9 Copy and convert to lower case
StrToLower( lcText, textRecord );

// CH.9 If there's no match, move on
if( (FindStrInStr( lcText, findParams->strToFind,
        &offset )) == false )
    continue;

// CH.9 Send it to find
// CH.9 If there's no more room, return
```

```
            if( (FindSaveMatch( findParams, cursor, offset, 0,
                    NULL, cardNum, dbID )) == true )
                break;

            // CH.9 Get the rectangle for our line of text
            FindGetLineBounds( findParams, &bounds );

            // CH.9 Truncate the string if necessary
            width = bounds.extent.x;
            len = StrLen( textRecord );
            noFit = false;
            FntCharsInWidth( textRecord, &width, &len, &noFit );

            // CH.9 Draw the text
            WinEraseRectangle( &bounds, 0 );
            WinDrawChars( textRecord, len, bounds.topLeft.x,
                    bounds.topLeft.y );

            // We used a line in the find dialog
            (findParams->lineNumber)++;
        }

        // CH.9 Close the database
        DmCloseDatabase( contactsDB );

        // CH.9 We're done
        return;
    }
```

9

PART II

Stratosphere

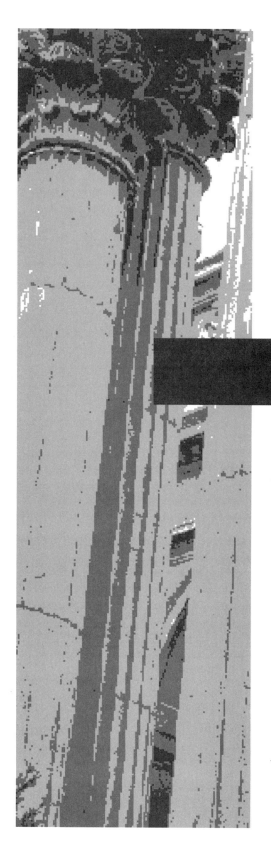

CHAPTER 10

Creating Effective User Interfaces

In this chapter I'll talk about user interface design and testing. First I'll be talking about general user interface design considerations as they pertain to Palm devices. Then I'll go through specific design principles put forward by Palm Computing and others that will help your user interface be more effective and consistent with other Palm OS user interfaces. Finally, I'll talk about user interface and general application design cycles and testing, because great user interfaces aren't designed in a vacuum—they're the result of an effective process.

Design Considerations

Where to begin? In the case of Palm devices, the design angle to choose seems to be a functional one, sharply focused on exactly what the user wants at the moment of use. I always like to imagine my user flipping up the lid of a Palm III while driving through heavy traffic (not a place where I'd recommend using your Palm device, but, nevertheless, a place where it can get used). The user at this point has a very limited ability to figure out how to get the required information, and just a brief second to glance at the screen to see what's going on there. If my app is easy enough and focused enough to use in that situation, it stands a good chance of passing muster anywhere else.

Let's break down the heavy traffic scenario some more. Well, to start with, the need is immediate. Perhaps I'm looking up driving directions someone has given me. I need to see those directions before I miss the turnoff! Maybe I need to look up someone's number in order to dial it on my cell phone. I'd better find it quickly or they won't know what I need to tell them right this second.

Second, the heavy traffic situation underscores the critical need for ease of use in Palm OS application design. To be useful in heavy traffic, the application would have to follow many simplicity and ease-of-use principles that we'll delve into as this chapter unfolds. The application would also have to work in the way the user expects it to. In other words, it would have to "feel" like a Palm OS application. It would use a minimal number of taps to get to the required information. The information would be easily visible on the screen when it is reached. If the user must respond to the information or enter data, this process would be made as easy and intuitive as possible.

Standing in the User's Shoes

In any software application interface design, a good place to start is to imagine yourself in your user's shoes. In this case, make sure you look at them as Palm device user shoes, not as PC or Mac user or some other kind of shoes. In other words, this user has chosen to use a Palm device, and has probably figured out the way around the Palm OS standard applications. Therefore, your users have the right to expect that other applications will use the same operating conventions. Given this precept, we can create unlimited new and interesting applications, certainly, but we want to strongly resist doing established things in a radically different way. It's a pitfall to get so creative that your user can't figure out how your variation on the Palm OS style is supposed to work.

Face it: If you're capable of reading this book, you are not a typical computer or PDA user. To put yourself in your user's shoes you must first climb out of your own. Resist user-interface decisions based on ease of programming. Resist user-interface ideas that are complex or don't have a basis in the real world of your users, no matter how cool they look. Use the opinions of others to make yourself more objective.

The heavy-traffic analogy is one way to visualize what your user needs in terms of ease and immediacy, but there are others, too. Who is the typical Palm device user? Usually, this is a busy person. This is a person with lots of priorities. This is a person on the go. We know this, of course, because this is the kind of person who can benefit most from what Palm devices do. Most likely, this person also uses a personal computer of some kind daily, so some degree of computer familiarity can be assumed. Based on marketing surveys, Palm device users have tended to like technology and technology gadgets, and are therefore used to fiddling with new technical wonders. Thus, they may also enjoy fiddling with applications and being able to customize them to their liking.

10

You can find good design ideas in popular Palm OS applications. The applications we are building together in this book are generally poor examples of user-interface design. This is because their intention is to illustrate some internal truth or technology regarding Palm OS, not to satisfy a customer base. When you look at other applications for design ideas, consider the popularity of the application you're looking at. If users aren't using that cool-looking gadget in that obscure application, chances are they won't enjoy using that cool-looking gadget in your application. Additionally, consider whether the users of an application fit the profile of your likely users. You can use these user profile insights to see what parts of another Palm application solves problems that are truly similar to parts of the problem you're solving.

Immediacy Is Everything

We established, back in heavy traffic, that immediacy of information is critical to any Palm OS application. One might make an exception in the case of games, which aren't likely to be pulled out in a traffic jam, I hope. By and large, immediacy is one of the user's top priorities. But what does immediacy mean, anyway? To me, immediacy means that what you need is at your fingertips, effortlessly. Design-wise, my experience of immediacy is the result of taking many small things into account in your design and execution. Some of these things are

◆ Logical, minimum-tap application flow design

◆ Carefully laid-out screens that present information in a way that is easy to see

◆ Appropriate, sparing use of visual design elements to make the application easy to use

The Tap Factor

I've mentioned above that "the fewer taps, the better." But what does that mean? If you analyze the standard Palm OS applications, you will find that they require the following number of taps to perform standard operations:

◆ Zero to three taps to view information, depending on frequency of use

◆ Zero or one tap to start entering new records

◆ One to three taps to edit existing records

◆ Three taps to delete existing records

This seems like a good place to set our goals, then. All but the most obscure information should be visible in three taps, preferably fewer. Deletes are acceptable at three taps. Adding records should be as quick as possible—zero taps if this is feasible. The "tap factor" must be taken into consideration at every point in development, as it will drive usability.

It may be stating the obvious at this point, but the more often a feature is used, the fewer taps it should take—zero or one tap for common functions. Viewing detail screens and deleting records are probably less-frequent operations in most applications than are viewing and adding information, and, therefore, the former are allowed more taps than the latter. This principle does not give permission, however, to have less-used features hidden down a deep hole of menus and taps; everything should be within three taps of the "main" application screen, if possible.

The Rule of Seven

Let's get quantitative about how many controls a screen can handle before things get too cluttered. Many psychological studies have shown that people generally are incapable of considering more than seven or so items at any given time. This scale varies depending on the complexity of the items involved, so we could also be talking about three complex controls or nine very simple controls. So the general rule is three to nine controls on a form.

Considering the Screen

The screen of the Palm device can be your 160×160-pixel friend, but you must treat it gently. If you're used to the bloated, large screens of PCs, you'll need to adjust down a little and get out of the habit of just throwing everything you might need onto the screen.

In the most general of cases, you have a black-and-white screen, and only four shades of gray in the case of Palm III and above. This means that your user interface design can't depend on lots of subtle shading and highlighting to get the message across.

10

Given the tight space and the need for clear readability, laying out all of your forms beforehand with lots of care is an indispensable step. Before you put each word or construct into your screen layout, consider the following:

◆ Is this piece of information adding value to the user?

◆ Is this piece of information making the screen easier to use?

◆ Is this piece of information placed where the user can see it easily?

◆ Is the screen too cluttered for easy use; in other words, is this really the right screen for this information to reside in?

◆ Is this information used frequently or infrequently? (If infrequently, you may want to consider making it part of a "details" screen that requires more taps to get to, in the interest of keeping the frequently used screen uncluttered and optimally useful.)

You could think of the design of a PC application a little like arranging stuff in a house, and a Palm application like arranging stuff in a tiny boat cabin. When setting up the boat cabin, you must think about the purpose of your voyage, then critically examine each thing you're tempted to bring along to see if it's really necessary, and then carefully consider where to stow it so it will be easy to find and use. Similarly, in a Palm application, there won't be room for all the information you're likely to be tempted to put there, so you need to carefully consider what information is used frequently, which is used infrequently but still necessary, and which to jettison from the application entirely. Next, the information must be "stowed" on logical, minimum-tap screen layouts that are easy to use.

The Importance of Space

It's a good idea to put as much blank white space around important information as possible. It tends to accentuate it and make it easier for the eye to find. On the Palm screen, this is especially true, and can add a great deal of usability to your applications. You very definitely want to space information wherever possible to make it easier for the eye to pick out. Face it, the Palm screen is not the largest, most effortless viewing surface there is, especially the earlier lower-contrast models. We want to do everything we can to bring to users just what they're looking for and put it right where they will see it, rather than making them hunt for it in a crowded visual field.

The human eye can pick out even very tiny visual inconsistencies. To take good care of your users, do take the trouble to line up objects on the screen so that they are spaced evenly. Also, do make sure your display or data entry fields are all left- or right-justified and don't stagger down the screen. These may seem like small things, but they make a great difference in the visual impact of an application. If you have avoided "clogging" your screen with too much information, as suggested above, you should end up with enough white space between fields to make them readable to the user.

Sometimes the strict spacing of controls just doesn't look right. In these cases, you need to trust your eye and the eyes of your friends to determine what will be the easiest arrangement of controls.

Considering the Stylus, or Its Lack

The stylus is also your little buddy, but if you've always designed for the keyboard and are used to having the user type everything, you'll have to kick that keyboard habit. In Palm OS land, entering text is a last resort. The last thing we want our user to do is to have to pull off the road in heavy traffic to graffiti or type something in that could have been selected with a list or a radio button. There will be some situations where typing is necessary, but limit them to places where new text information must truly be entered and put it on detail screens, so that the user can look up existing information in just a tap or two.

Ditto on gratuitous stylus taps. Taps on the Palm are analogous to mouse-clicks on the PC/Mac, but the difference is that you don't want your users to have to tap more than three times to see what they need. Just say this mantra to yourself: Tapping not typing, and the fewer taps the better.

Double taps are a bad idea. Instead, consider a pop-up menu if you need to fit those choices into that screen area. It takes the same number of taps but is more intuitive.

The ideal situation is to leave out the stylus altogether. After all, what's going to happen in heavy traffic is that during that near-collision or coffee spill, the stylus is going to fall and roll to that mysterious place under the seat, never to be seen again. Then what? Ideally, your application should use controls that have size and spacing sufficient to allow someone to use it with finger taps. Take note that much of the built-in applications can be used without a stylus.

Considering the Processor

10

The Palm device is not designed for powerhouse computing. Don't get me wrong—it does what it does faster than the rest, thank you, mostly due to the efficiency of Palm OS, but it just isn't designed for heavy-duty processing. I bring this up to add one more general user interface consideration: Before you choose to show any calculated values, think carefully about whether the user needs this information. As with screen display and mouse taps, in a PC application it wouldn't even be a question, but in our little boat cabin, any calculations will slow down the boat!

One good example I can think of using this kind of restraint is in the Expense application; the designers wisely did not include a running total of expenses, although it would have been easy to include one. They quite accurately reasoned that the traveler wouldn't really need to know their expense totals until after they arrived home, synched with their PC, and copied their expenses onto their expense report or log. The designers thus avoided one more little slowdown for the users of their application.

A general area where calculation slowdowns can occur is in translating dates to and from the Palm OS internal date and time structures to a text representation of the date and time, as we did in our Contacts application. Given enough records, these calculations can slow down your application. One way to combat this kind of problem is to trade storage space for performance—for example, by storing the text representations of dates and times in the record as well as the numeric representation.

Design Principles

Now that we've considered general principles of design as they apply to Palm devices, let's get more specific about advice. In this section we will discuss today's commonly used design principles for all Palm OS applications, divided into rules (which are enforced by Palm Computing's testing partners to obtain certification) and suggestions.

Fields, Graffiti, and the Clipboard

It's critical to carefully examine the methods by which you allow users to enter data into your Palm OS application. Consistency and appropriateness with other applications are important here because learning graffiti, to give one example, is a time investment on the part of the user which you wouldn't want to lose or confuse with an inconsistent user interface.

Rules

◆ For editable fields, make sure that the standard Edit menu (Cut, Copy, Paste, and so on) is available, as well as the associated shortcuts.

◆ Allow people to copy or cut data out of your application. Make sure that you leave things in the Clipboard intact unless the user explicitly orders a copy or cut.

◆ Wherever graffiti can be used, make sure graffiti help is available via an Edit menu and shortcut.

◆ If graffiti can be used on a particular form, supply a graffiti shift indicator in the lower right-hand corner. On these forms, never use the lower-right corner for anything else.

◆ If graffiti is used on the form, support graffiti navigation (that is, downstroke-upstroke equals next field).

◆ Writable fields should always take graffiti input. Never just supply the keyboard.

◆ If a field has focus, you should always be able to bring up the system keyboard via an Edit menu and shortcut.

◆ Never place anything in the Clipboard without the user clearly understanding that this will happen. Never corrupt the Clipboard if you're not using it.

◆ Make sure that fields chirp when selected.

◆ Make sure that the error sound accompanies bad Edit menu selections or shortcuts, such as choosing Copy when there is nothing selected.

◆ Make sure invalid data cannot be entered.

Suggestions

◆ Generally, in the absence of previous state information, set the focus to the top-left field.

◆ Do not pop up alerts for Edit menu or shortcut errors. Just use the error sound.

◆ Use graffiti to streamline the use of your application for power users wherever possible.

Menus

10

If you use menus at all in your application, it is worth it for you to adhere to the standard design rules for these under Palm OS. Menus feel much more fundamentally a part of the OS than other parts of your application due to the silkscreen button, and due to their very consistent look. Other kinds of look and feel for the menu would be startling.

Rules

◆ Don't gray out unusable menu items or other UI elements like buttons. Remove them or hide them instead.

◆ Always have shortcut strokes for menu items other than About.

◆ Make sure the standard menus—Edit, Options, and Record—match or are a subset of the menus shown in Figure 10-1.

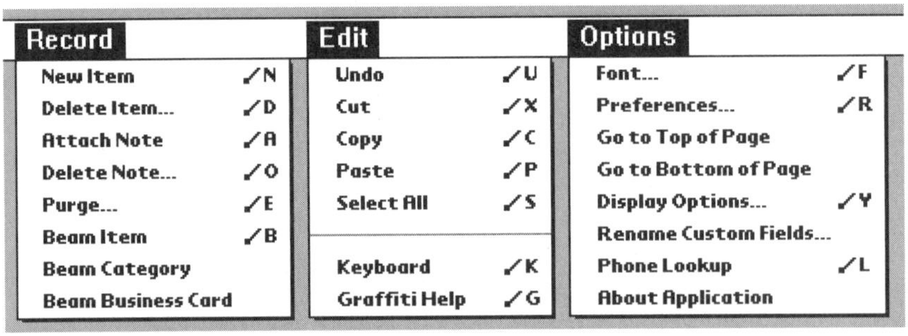

Record		Edit		Options	
New Item	⁄N	Undo	⁄U	Font...	⁄F
Delete Item...	⁄D	Cut	⁄X	Preferences...	⁄R
Attach Note	⁄A	Copy	⁄C	Go to Top of Page	
Delete Note...	⁄O	Paste	⁄P	Go to Bottom of Page	
Purge...	⁄E	Select All	⁄S	Display Options...	⁄Y
Beam Item	⁄B			Rename Custom Fields...	
Beam Category		Keyboard	⁄K	Phone Lookup	⁄L
Beam Business Card		Graffiti Help	⁄G	About Application	

The standard menus

Figure 10-1.

◆ Sounds should not accompany a valid menu selection or shortcut. The button that brings up the menu bar can chirp.

◆ Use the error sound when a menu command that cannot be executed is selected.

◆ Do not pop up alerts in response to Edit menu errors.

Suggestions

◆ Provide shortcuts for every menu item.

◆ Pop up alerts in response to menu errors unless the cause of the failure is obvious.

◆ On Palm OS 3.0 and above, support beaming and make sure there is a beam menu option and shortcut in the Record menu.

Buttons and Controls

Here are some rules that will help you to stay out of trouble when designing your forms.

Rules

◆ Don't change the behavior of the silk-screened icons Application/Home, Menu, or Find.

◆ Don't override the calculator button with an application that doesn't incorporate the original functionality of the calculator.

◆ If you use the Date Book, Address, To Do List, or Memo Pad buttons for anything in your application, make sure they are restored to their original use after exit.

◆ In non-modal forms, align buttons at the bottom of the screen as far down as they can go.

◆ Leave plenty of space, two pixels at least, between text and the edges of rounded buttons.

Suggestions

◆ If you have more than one row of buttons, put the most important buttons right at the bottom.

General

Here are a bunch of things that are easy to forget about. If you go through this list as you are polishing your application, you'll be glad you did.

Rules

◆ Respond to changes in system preferences for date, time, number, and week formats.

◆ If you use categories, prevent the user from defining more than 15 categories.

◆ If you support private records, hide private records if Hide is selected in the Security application.

◆ Support Global Find by handling the launch code for Find and searching your records.

◆ Provide your own About box.

◆ If appropriate, restore your application to its previous state when it is relaunched.

◆ Make sure your application and all of its databases have the same unique creator ID.

◆ Make sure that your application can be backed up and restored properly.

◆ Your applications should not be significantly slower than the built-in applications with regard to launching, switching, or finding records.

10

◆ Make sure you have created a small icon for your application.

Suggestions

◆ Don't just sit in modal forms during normal operation. If the user is in a modal form, the Palm OS can't pop up alarms or low battery warnings. Modal forms should be used for situations where the user will go in, change something, and get back out.

◆ Don't nest modal forms more than three levels deep.

◆ When at all possible, use the standard user-interface elements that people are already familiar with in Palm OS.

◆ Use custom gadgets only when your users would have no previous expectations or the control has unquestionable advantages in terms of speed (fewer taps) or clarity (easier to see or understand the information).

◆ Provide help for modal dialogs.

The Layout of Forms

Here are a few easy rules that you can follow to make your forms fit in seamlessly with the standard applications.

Rules

◆ All major application forms should cover the entire screen.

◆ Every form should have a title bar containing the application name or critical information about the application.

◆ Make sure all forms can be reached with just finger taps, without having to resort to a stylus.

◆ Modal forms must come up full width (borders showing) and aligned with the bottom of the screen.

◆ See Figure 10-2 for the proper layout of controls on non-modal forms.

◆ See Figure 10-3 for the proper layout of controls on modal forms.

◆ For non-modal forms, use the entire screen. Don't leave space between controls and the edge of the screen.

◆ For modal forms, leave at least three pixels between all controls and the border of the modal form.

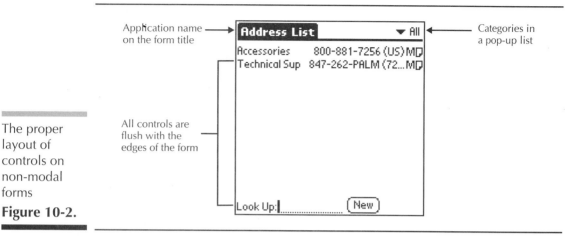

Application name on the form title

Categories in a pop-up list

The proper layout of controls on non-modal forms

Figure 10-2.

All controls are flush with the edges of the form

◆ On forms where labels and controls for different items are listed in columnar fashion but are not in a table, make the labels bold and right-justified.

Suggestions

◆ Put your most-used controls in the top left and your least-used controls in the bottom right. The exception to this is buttons, which should go along the bottom of a form. The rationale is that people naturally scan a

10

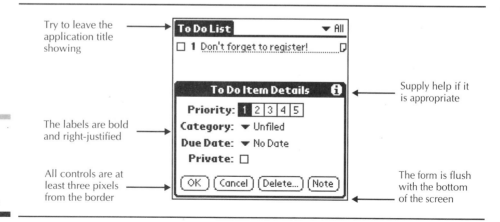

Try to leave the application title showing

Supply help if it is appropriate

The proper layout of controls on modal forms

Figure 10-3.

The labels are bold and right-justified

All controls are at least three pixels from the border

The form is flush with the bottom of the screen

page the way they would read it. If you're designing an application for a culture that doesn't read left to right and top to bottom, you might want to consider a different arrangement, after determining how familiar the users might be by now with other Palm applications written left to right and top to bottom.

◆ Show just the information that users need on the screen. Don't clutter it up with stuff they don't absolutely need. If there is more related information that users are less likely to need to see, relegate it to a details form, which users can view with an extra tap if they choose to, rather than trying to stuff it all on one form.

◆ Use labeling wherever possible to make the use of your controls obvious.

Application Flow

In this section, we will discuss good application flow design for the Palm. Application flow design goes closely with the "tap factor," discussed earlier. If the application flows properly, users will not have to tap much at all to do the operations they use most in the application. Correct design with an eye to the number of taps things take and the other eye pointed towards good application flow will create an application that can be used effectively and conveniently even by the most hurried user. See Figure 10-4.

Categories

If your application deals with database records and it makes sense to differentiate these records into 15 or fewer groups, you should consider using the built-in database categories for this job. This is not only a comfortable concept for Palm device users, it is also quick and easy to do, as we saw in earlier chapters.

If you support categories, you should display the pop-up list allowing your user to display categories. This pop-up list should live in the upper-right corner of the screen, next to the form title.

The built-in applications scroll through their categories when you push the hard case button for the application while it is already the active application. I encourage you to mimic this behavior if you use categories. If your application is launched normally and the launch flags tell you that you are already the active application, change to the next category in the list instead.

Scrolling

There are three common types of scrolling in Palm OS: repeating buttons with up and down arrows, scrollbars (in version 2.0 or later), and the up and down buttons on the case.

Generally, up and down buttons on the screen should move up or down one line or record, while the hard buttons should scroll up or down one page. The scrollbar of course has the added ability to respond to a pen drag to reposition the view.

Prioritizing Objectives

To design Palm applications, one must carefully consider what the user wants to accomplish using the application, in an 80%/20% fashion. That is, what does the user want to do with it most of the time? Here's an example. When the people at Palm Computing went to create the phone list app, they thought about the functions that users would want to do with regard to their phone lists: add new entries, edit entries, delete entries, and look up entries—the standard list of database functions. Then they dug a little deeper and considered what users would do more than any other function. Looking up entries is by far a more common function than adding, editing, or deleting entries. They must have also decided that deleting entries was least common of the four functions, because they hid it in a subscreen beyond the edit screen. Hence, we have a design that looks something like the following, with the arrows representing a tap between screens, and the rectangles representing screens.

10

Phone list
application
flow

Figure 10-4.

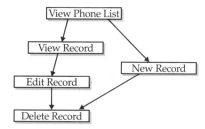

Note that this flow is very different than that of a well-designed PC application, where navigation is mostly done via menus. Menus exist on the Palm, but mostly for the purpose of including lesser-used functions that are available anywhere in the application (such as Keyboard, Cut, Copy, Paste, Preferences, About, and so on) and not very much for navigational purposes. Most navigation is correctly accomplished through tappable buttons on the screen, which is much more direct (fewer taps) and clear (a button is always there) from the Palm user interface standpoint.

The Main Form

As you consider an application, one of the first things to determine is what the major function of the app is. This is the part your user will be using for the large majority of the time. It may even be the only screen of your application, if it is a simple one. Try to think in terms of the structure of the standard Palm OS applications, in terms of having a detail screen or a New record screen or an Edit screen in addition to the main screen, and this may make it easier to allocate different functions to the screens.

If it seems to you that there are multiple main parts, you may have bitten off too big a set of functions for just one Palm OS application. Palm OS apps are best implemented if their functions are distinct and not too many. For example, consider how much better it works to have one app for the date book, another for the calendar, and yet another for to-do lists than it would to combine these into one application. On the PC platform, it very well might have made more sense to integrate them, and this is one very distinct example of a programming problem whose best solution would be very different on the two different platforms.

One reliable danger sign of a bloated Palm OS application is if any function in your application takes more than three taps to get to. If this is the case, consider splitting the application into a pair or suite of smaller applications that interrelate.

What's Next?

In this chapter we've taken a careful look at the outside functional interface of Palm OS applications and how they can be made effective. In the next chapter we'll take a look at all the tools available for the Palm OS and what they provide. In the chapters following that, we will use the creation of a calculator application to examine methods for good application design in terms of coding, organizing, and user interface design.

CHAPTER 11

A Survey of Tools and Solutions

Now that you know enough to be dangerous, it's time to discuss all the tools and solutions that are out there to help you be an even more dangerous Palm OS solution provider. Perhaps you have a specific Palm OS application that requires hardware you're not even sure exists. Or perhaps your solution must synchronize to Linux boxes. Here is where you will find the information to do that sort of stuff.

Because links go bad so quickly on our rapidly changing World Wide Web, I'd like to first offer you this link:

www.mykland.com/palmosbook/

This link to my Web site will provide you with a wealth of information, including book addenda, other articles I've written, sample code and applications, and so forth. Most importantly for this chapter, I'll keep live and up-to-date versions of links to all the Web sites mentioned in this chapter.

Palm OS Application Development Tools

This section covers all the major tools, free and unfree, that allow you to develop applications for Palm OS. Table 11-1 describes these tools in a nutshell. Longer descriptions of each tool follow.

Name	Description
CodeWarrior	The most popular IDE for Palm OS development. MacOS and Win32 only.
GCC/PRC-Tools	Free compiler and linker for Palm OS. Very high quality but hard to use. The only real solution for UNIX users.
Palm OS Emulator	A free tool that completely emulates a wide selection of Palm OS devices under Win32, MacOS, and UNIX. More useful for development purposes than an actual device. You must have this tool.
Palm OS SDK	A free kit from Palm Computing that contains all the latest support code and documentation.

Useful
Application
Development
Tools for the
Palm OS

Table 11-1.

Name	Description
Pendragon Forms	A non-C development environment for Palm apps. Difficult to use compared to Satellite Forms. Builds cumbersome apps with poor user interfaces. Docs and tutorial are of poor quality.
PilRC	A free resource compiler for Palm OS. Many think it's a better tool overall than Constructor.
Satellite Forms	The perfect tool for non-programmers. Good for rapid development. You would need to be a developer to do conduits with this, however. You also need to buy a license for every Palm device you deploy on, making this an expensive solution.

Useful Application Development Tools for the Palm OS *(continued)*

Table 11-1.

CodeWarrior

This is the premier development tool for Palm OS and the fastest way to write and debug Palm OS applications in C. If you are a serious Palm OS developer, you should own this tool even if you don't use it all the time. There are versions for Windows and for MacOS. This is the development tool used throughout this book.

Maintainer:	Metrowerks, Inc.
URL:	www.metrowerks.com/
Price:	Full professional version is $369 or less.
Test Drive:	CodeWarrior 6 Lite is on the CD at the back of the book and is available for free download at www.palm.com/devzone/tools/cw/.

11

GCC/PRC-Tools

Originally developed by the Free Software Foundation and now managed by the EGCS Steering Committee, the GCC compiler is pretty much acknowledged to be the finest 68K linker ever written, producing code that is significantly faster and tighter than any of the tools that cost money.

That said, this tool takes significant amounts of time and effort to set up if you are not familiar with it. You can usually find someone in the newsgroups who will have mercy on a newbie and answer your installation dilemmas. There also used to be restrictions on the use of this compiler that caused regular for-profit corporations to shy away from its use. These have been eliminated, but you should still check GCC's licensing policy carefully to make sure you can live with it before investing too much time in this tool.

This is not a complete solution for Palm OS development. At the very least, you'll need a resource compiler such as PilRC as well.

GCC is really the only way to go if you are a UNIX person. However, if you are a UNIX person, there's a good chance that you are already familiar with GCC.

Maintainer:	Palm Computing, Inc.
URL:	www.palm.com/devzone/tools/gcc/
Price:	Free, and built to stay that way
Test Drive:	N/A

Palm OS Emulator

For quite some time only Mac developers had a useful version of Palm OS Emulator (or POSE for short), but now the Windows version is excellent, and I hear that the UNIX version is coming along nicely. This application emulates all the inner workings of a Palm device right on your desktop.

You need to obtain a ROM image to make it work. You can copy the ROM image from your own Palm device with a ROM image copier that is included. If you sign agreements with Palm Computing, you can download ROM images of various incarnations of Palm OS from their Web site, including debug versions that are particularly helpful.

This emulator is actually better for debugging than a device. The debugger comes up faster. Stepping through code is faster. And there is this neat feature called Gremlins. Gremlins sends quasi-random events to your Palm OS application. Gremlins knows about controls and operates them fully. It even knows about Gadgets. This doesn't replace thorough functional testing, but it tends to find many crash problems you may have otherwise missed. All the examples in this book have run over 1,000,000 Gremlin events.

You'll still find a device useful for debugging conduits and other communications things, but I bet you'll be using Palm OS Emulator for everything else once you have it set up. To use POSE with CodeWarrior:

1. Select Edit | Preferences.
2. In the left tree list, select Palm Connection S under Debugger.
3. Change the Target combo box to read Palm OS Emulator.
4. Check Always Launch Emulator.
5. Click the Choose button and find the path to your desired copy of Emulator.exe.
6. Click the Save button.
7. Shut down the IDE. Make sure the emulator is not running.
8. Launch the IDE. The emulator should come up after the IDE.

Maintainer:	Palm Computing, Inc.
URL:	www.palm.com/devzone/pose/pose.html
Price:	Free
Test Drive:	N/A

Palm OS SDK

This is the standard documentation and tools put out by Palm Computing for all developers. In order to get the latest versions of this kit you'll probably have to join Palm Computing's Solution Provider Program, which is free.

Maintainer:	Palm Computing, Inc.
URL:	www.palm.com/devzone/tools/
Price:	Free
Test Drive:	N/A

11

Pendragon Forms

This application is a non-C development environment for Palm applications. What I have had the opportunity to look at is their free demo, which works with Access 97.

I would expect non-programmers to find this development environment difficult to use and non-intuitive compared to Satellite Forms. Programmers will find this development environment lacking in features and usability compared to something like CodeWarrior. Furthermore, the applications that can be built with it have poor and cumbersome user interfaces.

The documentation and tutorial were of poor quality.

Maintainer:	Pendragon Software Corporation
URL:	www.pendragon-software.com/
Price:	$149
Test Drive:	Yes, a free download is available at www.pendragon-software.com/forms3/downloads.html

PilRC

PilRC is a tool that sucks in a script file and spits out a binary image that can be used with the GCC/PRC-Tools package to make a complete Palm OS application. This is a nice tool, some say better than Constructor. It is not a graphical tool, but includes a viewer called PilRCUI that allows you to see what you are doing. It is a must if you are running on UNIX or if you have an SCCS-like source control system that doesn't version binary files well.

Maintainer:	Aaron Ardiri
URL:	www.hig.se/~ardiri/development/palmIII/pilrc/
Price:	Free
Test Drive:	N/A

Satellite Forms

This is the perfect tool for non-programmers. Fairly non-technical people should be able to bash out a reasonable Palm OS application with this tool. It is fun to use and the documentation is well written. It is also useful as an extremely rapid development environment for knocking together prototypes.

There are two downsides to this most excellent tool. For anything beyond the straightforward and standard, you really do have to be a developer to get it done with this package. This goes especially for the conduit portion of the toolkit. Even worse, you need to buy a license for every Palm device you deploy your Palm OS application onto. These limitations rule it out for more complex or widely distributed applications.

Maintainer:	Puma Technology
URL:	www.pumatech.com/
Price:	$795 for Standard Edition, $995 for Enterprise Edition, plus a per-user license fee
Test Drive:	Yes, a free download is available at www.pumatech.com/trial-sf.html.

Windows Conduit Development Tools

Here's a review of the relevant tools for developing conduits for Windows 95, 98, and NT. The following table gives a summary of this information:

Name	Description
CDK	Free standard conduit development kit from Palm Computing.
CDK Java Edition	Java version of the free standard conduit development kit from Palm Computing.
Insider	A handy shareware utility that helps you examine databases on Palm devices.
VisualCafé Professional	The Java IDE from Symantec used by Palm Computing's CDK.
Visual C/C++	The C++ IDE from Microsoft used by Palm Computing's CDK.

11

CDK

This is the free standard conduit development kit that Palm Computing puts out. It uses Microsoft's Visual C/C++ and particularly the MFC class library.

You can get away with a minimum of MFC chicanery, but you must do considerable work if you want to entirely avoid linking with MFC.

Maintainer:	Palm Computing, Inc.
URL:	www.palm.com/devzone/cdkwin/cdkwin.html
Price:	Free
Test Drive:	N/A

CDK Java Edition

This is a Java version of the free standard conduit development kit that Palm Computing puts out. It uses Symantec's Visual Café Pro for Java. Although I have not tried it, the documentation says it has not been tested with Sun's free version of Java, although I expect you could get it to work with this tool with a little sweat.

Maintainer:	Palm Computing, Inc.
URL:	www.palm.com/devzone/cdkjava/cdkjava.html
Price:	Free
Test Drive:	N/A

Insider

This is a handy little tool that allows you to examine databases on the Palm. This way, you don't even need a working application on the Palm in order to ensure you are creating the database correctly there.

Maintainer:	Sylvain Beaulis
URL:	www.iro.umontreal.ca/~beaulis/pilot.html
Price:	$10
Test Drive:	Yes, a free download is available at www.iro.umontreal.ca/~beaulis/pilot.html.

VisualCafé Professional

This is a good Java IDE. You'll enjoy using it.

Maintainer:	Symantec
URL:	www.symantec.com/domain/cafe/index.html
Price:	$749.95 for Expert Edition at Programmer's Paradise
Test Drive:	No

Visual C/C++

This is the industry standard development environment for Windows at this point. This is not the greatest IDE ever made, but lots of people know how to use it. Especially maddening is the MFC class library, which is difficult to employ in a bug-free, leak-free manner. You should seriously consider a memory debug tool like NuMega BoundsChecker if you make much use of MFC.

Maintainer:	Microsoft
URL:	msdn.microsoft.com/visualc/
Price:	$95.95 for Standard Edition at Programmer's Paradise
Test Drive:	No

Macintosh Conduit Development Tools

Here is a review of the relevant tools for developing conduits on the Macintosh. This table contains a summary of these items:

11

Name	Description
CDK	A free kit from Palm Computing that allows you to develop conduits for MacOS.
CodeWarrior for MacOS	The most popular IDE for MacOS development.

CDK

This is the standard bunch of stuff for developing conduits for MacOS.

Maintainer:	Palm Computing, Inc.
URL:	www.palm.com/devzone/cdkmac/cdkmac.html
Price:	Free
Test Drive:	N/A

CodeWarrior for MacOS

This is a well-known and loved tool for developing software for MacOS.

Maintainer:	Metrowerks
URL:	www.metrowerks.com/desktop/mac_os/
Price:	$404.95 for Professional Edition at Programmer's Paradise
Test Drive:	No

Peripherals

There are a number of Palm OS peripherals under development. Here are the interesting products that are available as of this printing.

Cards for the TRGpro

Check at **www.trgpro.com/support/cf_compatible.html** for a list of CompactFlash cards that are recommended for use with the TRGpro. There are a slew of memory cards, and a few others, including the Pretec Compact Modem 56K, the Socket Communications Serial I/O CF+ Card, and the Socket Communications Bar Code Wand CF+ Card.

Cards for the Visor

Check at **www.handspring.com/products/modules.asp** for new springboard modules. Currently available are an 8MB flash memory module, a modem, a backup module, and some games.

General Purpose Hardware

Palm Computing markets its own peripherals, keyboards, and modems. In addition, you can get keyboards for Palm devices from LandWare (**www.landware.com/**) and iBiz (**www.ibizcorp.com/**).

TRG markets memory expansion for the Palm IIIx and a few other Palm devices (**www.superpilot.com/**).

Corex Technologies makes CardScan, a card scanner for Palm devices (**www.cardscan.com/**).

DeLorme makes a GPS receiver that plugs into the modem port of a Palm device. It's called the Earthmate. You can find it at **www.delorme.com/gps.htm**.

The last and probably most interesting peripherals are Novatel Wireless' wireless modems for Palm devices (**www.novatelwireless.com/**). Their wireless modems cover the range of standard Palm devices, including the IIIc, and are supported by some of the best wireless networks such as AT&T.

Web Sites

The Web sites below should get you started on the way to obtaining up-to-date information on a number of topics.

eScribe

This site (**www.escribe.com/computing/**) currently carries four useful developer forums about various aspects of Palm OS and conduit development:

◆ Palm Computing Platform Conduit Developer Forum

◆ Palm Computing Platform Emulator Forum

◆ Development Questions About the Palm Computing Platform

◆ Palm Computing Platform PQA Developers Forum

11

Handspring

This is the Web site (**www.handspring.com/**) of the people who make the Visor Palm OS device. It has useful information for developers intent on making use of their proprietary Springboard slot.

J. Marshall

This site (**homepages.enterprise.net/jmarshall/palmos/**) is the best one I've found to connect you with all the tools you want to have to program Palm OS applications using GCC.

Massena.com

There are lots of helpful links and unique development tools at this site (**www.massena.com/darrin/pilot/index.html**). Ever heard of Jump?

Palm Computing

As you might imagine, this site (**www.palm.com/**) is packed with useful information and links. Make sure to check out the Developer Zone. If you are serious about programming for the Palm, join Palm's free Solutions Provider program to gain access to a Provider Pavilion containing all kinds of useful prototype and beta hardware and software from Palm Computing.

Qualcomm/Kyocera

Qualcomm (**www.qualcomm.com/**) recently sold its division in charge of the pdQ phone to Kyocera (**www.kyocera.com/**). Some information on the pdQ lingers at the Qualcomm site. There is as yet no information to be found on Kyocera's site.

Quality Partners

The documents available on this site (**www.qpqa.com/palm/index.html**) tell you everything you ever wanted to know about thoroughly testing your Palm OS application and getting it certified.

Roadcoders

This site (**www.developer.com/roadcoders/**) has some interesting articles and sample code regarding various Palm OS topics.

Symbol

This is the maker of the Palm devices with built-in bar code scanners (**www.symbol.com/products/mobile_computers/mobile_palm.html**).

The SPT1740 also has a wireless LAN interface. You can find information on how to interface with this unique hardware at the URL just mentioned.

TRG

These people make the TRGpro Palm device and also memory expansion units for some Palm Computing devices. Information on the TRGpro use of the CompactFlash slot is at this site (**www.trgpro.com/**).

11

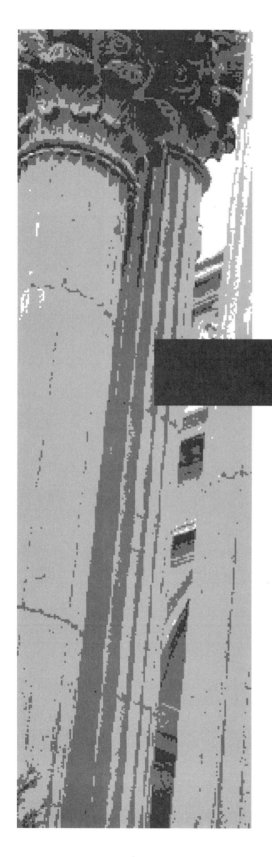

CHAPTER 12

Programming Tricks of the Professionals

As your applications get larger, you'll find that many things that were not problems when you were dealing with a few thousand lines of code start to become major problems when you have 10,000 or more lines of code or multiple programmers working on the same piece of software.

This is where carefully considered structure, commenting, and notation pay off. There are two main concerns with creating big applications or even many related small applications:

◆ How easy is the code to maintain?

◆ How easy is the code to reuse?

Ideally, you want to create code that is easy for anyone to read and maintain and that is as reusable as possible. Especially with regard to the Palm OS, with its many similar forms, such tactics can have enormous benefits in productivity. Because processor speed and memory size are always growing, these are rarely as important as these first two points. Compared to PCs, though, current Palm devices do require wise use of the processor and memory. But it always comes back to maintainability. Code that is easy to maintain is also easier to optimize.

In this chapter we'll investigate many strategies professional programmers use. As our investigation proceeds, you'll build a few reusable building blocks using these principles, and hopefully get a taste of some of these benefits yourself.

The result of your work this chapter will be a solid and reusable foundation you can add to for creating your own Palm OS applications.

Type-Safe Variables and Portability

Portability is one of the keys to code reusability. Code that is portable can be compiled with different compilers with few modifications. Code that is portable has its user-interface portions (which are invariably operating system–dependent) separate from other code that might be reused on other platforms.

The calculator program coming up in the next few chapters is an example of this latter exercise. The user interface of the calculator is in separate modules from the generic guts of the application code that responds to events and runs the calculator. These guts could therefore easily be reused in calculator programs for Windows or the Macintosh.

Type-safe variables are one of the major ways that professional programmers insure that code will still work even if you switch compilers or operating systems. You may not know it, but you've been using type-safe variables all along in this book—at least the Palm OS's version of them. *Type-safe variables* are variables that, instead of using standard C data types like *int* and *char*, use data types created using the *typedef* command.

Why are type-safe variables useful? Consider the standard C type *int*. In the CodeWarrior C compiler we're using, *int* is 16 bits in length, but in many other popular compilers, including GCC, *int* is 32 bits in length. If you used just *int* everywhere and changed from CodeWarrior to GCC, you would introduce bugs into your code everywhere your code assumed a particular size for *int*. Data structures would change size. Database records might change in size, with disastrous results. Numeric calculations would break.

The type *int* is not the only type that can cause you portability problems. Even types as innocuous as *char* can become problems in many common circumstances. In Japan, characters take up 16 bits instead of 8 bits. If you want to internationalize your code and use *char* everywhere, you'll have a lot of reworking to do.

Here's my advice with regard to type-safe variables and the Palm OS. If you are writing user interface code that is Palm OS–dependent, use the Palm OS type-safe variables. The people at Palm Computing will take care to manage those type-safe variables carefully as the Palm OS continues to grow in power. You will almost certainly find it easiest to upgrade your code to future versions of the Palm OS by being scrupulous about your correct use of Palm OS types.

If you are writing code for the Palm OS that could be used in other operating systems as well, use your own set of type-safe data types. Also, do not call Palm OS functions directly in this code. Call functions of your own definition that call these functions, or use #define statements in an include file to change function names of your own devising into Palm OS function calls.

Hungarian Notation

When you're looking at a big piece of code, it's easy to forget the exact data types of variables that were defined at the top of a long function. One way to fight this problem and make it easier for you and other people to read your code is to use Hungarian Notation. In Hungarian Notation, you start every variable name with some letters that remind you what type of variable it is. For example, "c" stands for *char* and "p" stands for pointer, so *cpBuffer* represents a *char** to some buffer.

12

There are many different flavors of Hungarian Notation. In Table 12-1, I present my own version, which I have found works well coding both C and C++ on the Mac, Windows, UNIX, and, of course, Palm OS. I'll be using this notation throughout the rest of the book.

Letter	Type	Description and Example
a	[ ]	An array: Char caBuffer[20];
b	Byte	An 8-bit variable used as a number: Byte bFlags;
c	Char	A character of text: char c;
d	DWord	A 32-bit variable used as a number: DWord dCounter;
e	enum	A member of an enumerated type: spEvent->eType;
f	float	A 32-bit floating point number: float fResult;
g	global	A global variable, that is, one accessible to all modules: app_t gsApp;
h	handle	In some OS's, a void*; in others, an Int: VoidHand hRecord;
i	int	An integer: Int iCounter;
j		unused
k	const	For C++ style const definitions or return values
l	long	A long integer: long lValue;
m	member	Member of a structure or class: char mcaBuffer[20];
n	double	A 64-bit floating point number: double nBigNum;
o	Boolean	A Boolean value, true or false: Boolean oFirstPass;
p	pointer	A pointer to a type: void* vpPointer;
q		unused
r	raw	Raw binary data class (C++)
s	struct	A structure or class: sEvent;
t	text	Text string class (C++)
u	unsigned	An unsigned number: unsigned long ulNumber;
v	void	Void data type: void* vpPointer;
w	Word	A word, usually 16-bits: Word wNumber;
x		unused
y		unused
z		unused

Robert's Rules
of Hungarian
Notation

Table 12-1.

A Reusable Main Module

Pardon me while we reinvent the wheel, but it will pay off. Our first step is to create an application that works pretty much like your old Hello application did in Chapter 2, except the code will be organized in a way that will make it easier for us to reuse it and add to it as our applications get larger. This new framework represents how I would code a major Palm OS application, no holds barred.

First let's create a new application in the CodeWarrior IDE and call it Calculator. Remove the source file and the resource file from the project. Go and erase everything in the Src folder of Calculator.

Go into Constructor and create a new resource project. Save it as Calculator.rsrc in the Src folder for your Calculator project. Use CTRL-K to create a form. Name it calc. This will eventually become the form for our calculator front panel. Open the form and put a button in the middle of it. We'll use this button to make sure our new code is alive. We'll create a real user interface for our calculator later. Right now it should look like Figure 12-1.

Let's also add an alert called LowROMVersionError. This alert will pop up if users try to run our app on a Palm device that is too old to support the functions we're using. Your alert should look something like Figure 12-2.

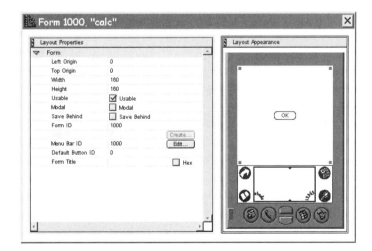

The test version of the calc form

Figure 12-1.

12

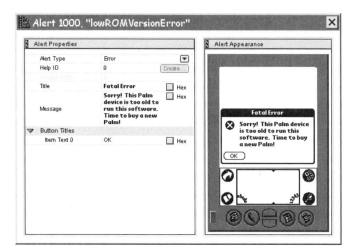

Now let's put some source code into the project.

1. Go into the CodeWarrior IDE and select Project | Create New Group.
2. Name the new group AppIncludes. This is where we will put all our include files. Your new resource project created a file named Calculator_res.h by default.
3. Add Calculator_res.h to your project and put it in this new group.

The main.c Module

Now create a new file and save it as main.c. Put it in your AppSource group. We'll make this file a reusable building block that contains a main entry point for our application and an event loop. Let's take a look at it.

```
/////////////////////////////////////////////////////////////////
// main.c
// Main entry point and event loop.
// Copyright (c) 1999-2000, Robert Mykland.  All rights reserved.
/////////////////////////////////////////////////////////////////
```

Commenting your code is a very good idea. In fact, it's the key to maintainability. As a professional programmer, if you write a lot of code and don't comment it, you'll never get promoted and you'll go crazy. You'll never get promoted because nobody else will ever be able to figure out the code that you've written well enough to maintain it. You'll go crazy because you'll spend the rest of your career babysitting the same valuable piece of code you've written. Don't let this happen to you. Comment your code.

I feel lucky (in a sense) because I spent the first several years of my career programming in assembly language for the most part. If you don't comment your assembly language, it can take you enormous amounts of time to figure out what you were up to even a few weeks later. The effect is the same but on a different scale for C. Once you get together with 12 other programmers and write a few hundred thousand lines of C together, you'll be right there, cursing your younger self for leaving out that critical comment about what the heck you were thinking at the time.

It used to be hard for me to think of things to say in my comments. Now I've developed structures that work for me and tend to inspire me to say something. For example, I have the habit of putting a comment block like the one you see above at the top of every module I write. It contains the name of the file, what it is, and my copyright information. Some people like to put revision history here, too. This works well if you can build it into your source control system. If not, I've found it's awfully hard to make the history comments trustworthy enough to be useful.

NOTE: What is a source control system? It's a system of special tools that allow you to store and retrieve multiple revisions of your source code. If you introduce a bad bug into your program, you can look at all the changes you made between the time it was working and the time it broke to zero in on the problem. You can create custom versions of your code for different uses and keep them all well organized. If you get together with other programmers and start writing really big applications, a source control system will keep two programmers from editing a file at the same time, thus losing one programmer's changes. All in all, a source control system is an essential tool for professional programmers.

12

```
/////////////
// Includes //
/////////////

#include "app.h"    // The definitions for this application
```

You may be asking yourself, "Where is Pilot.h?" This include file, "app.h," is an include file we're going to create. It will have all the definitions we need for our entire application, including Pilot.h, and we'll include it everywhere. It will be sort of a customized Pilot.h, with stuff added for our use. I've found that this is a good method even for very large applications. If your program and include file get so big that your builds are taking a long time, you can use CodeWarrior to pre-compile the information in this file to make your code build faster.

```
////////////////////////
// Global Prototypes //
////////////////////////

DWord PilotMain( Word, Ptr, Word ); // Main entry point.
Boolean processEvent( Long );       // Processes the next event.
```

These are prototype definitions for the functions in this module. We've been using prototypes all along, but we haven't really discussed why they're a valuable and good thing. Prototypes help maintainability. You put these here to make sure that you don't make the mistake of calling the function and passing it parameters that don't match those of the actual function call. If this happens, you can cause bugs that are sometimes bizarre and difficult to find. Unfortunately, in C it's possible to call functions without prototypes or with prototypes that leave out the parameters. To make sure these functions are used correctly everywhere, we'll put another copy of these in an include file that will end up in app.h. The prototypes at the top of your file assure you that the prototypes in the include files match and completely define the parameters.

```
//////////////////////
// Local Variables //
//////////////////////

// The event handler list defined in app.h
EVENT_HANDLER_LIST
```

Here are the local variables. This local variable, EVENT_HANDLER_LIST, looks like a syntax error. EVENT_HANDLER_LIST is defined in app.h and will be fully explained later on. This is the thing that will define what the event handler functions are for the forms in your application. Actually, this #define statement defines a function, although you could serve the purpose of generically defining these event handler functions in several different ways. You want to use capital letters or something distinctive in your code when you do things like this so that people (including you in the distant future) know to look for the definition of the thing in some include file in order to figure out what's going on.

```
/////////////////////
// Global Functions //
/////////////////////


//------------------------------------------------------------
DWord PilotMain(
//------------------------------------------------------------
// The main entry point for this application.
// Always returns zero.
//------------------------------------------------------------
Word wCmd,   // The launch code
Ptr,         // The launch parameter block
Word )       // The launch flags
//------------------------------------------------------------
{
```

Here's another standard comment block that I use to elicit comments from myself. I like this kind of block because it's very distinctive, so it's easy to find the tops of functions in a long module. In the first part of the comment is the name of the function and its return value. The next part describes what the function does and what it returns. The last part contains the parameters and what they mean. Some people add a part with a revision history for the function, but I've never been able to get myself or other people to do this reliably enough for it to be useful to me.

```
    DWord dROMVersion;

    // Get the ROM version
    dROMVersion = 0;
    FtrGet( sysFtrCreator, sysFtrNumROMVersion, &dROMVersion );

    // Alert and bail if the ROM version is too low
    if( dROMVersion < ROM_VERSION_MIN )
    {
        FrmAlert( LowROMVersionErrorAlert );

        // Palm OS 1.0 will continuously re-launch this app unless we
        // switch to another safe one
        if( dROMVersion < ROM_VERSION_2 )
        {
```

12

```
            AppLaunchWithCommand( sysFileCDefaultApp,
                  sysAppLaunchCmdNormalLaunch, NULL );
      }
      return( 0 );
}
```

You've seen this code before. This block of code prevents users from
running your code on Palm devices that don't support the functionality
you're using. In the case of our calculator, we'll be using floating-point
libraries that only exist for Palm OS 2.0 and above, so we will define the
constant ROM_VERSION_MIN as ROM_VERSION_2 in app.h. This way we
can reuse main.c for other applications that support a different set of Palm
platforms by having a different app.h for each of those other applications.
The glue that holds our generic building blocks together will be in app.h.

```
      // If this is not a normal launch, don't launch
      if( wCmd != sysAppLaunchCmdNormalLaunch )
          return( 0 );

      // Initialize all parts of the application
      appInit();
```

The bit of code at the top here also looks familiar. Here we're making sure that
we are being launched by being selected by the user. The call to **appInit()** is
defined in app.h. It is intended to allow all the pieces of the application to
initialize their data and get ready to run. For example, in our Contacts
application, we would do that work with opening the databases in a function
called by **appInit()**. You'll see exactly how it works when we get there.

```
      // Go to the starting form
      FrmGotoForm( StartForm );
```

This puts events in the event queue that cause the StartForm to be loaded.
As you know, we don't have a form called StartForm. StartForm is defined as
CalcForm in app.h. This is another technique that makes main.c generic
and reusable. If we want to change the starting form, we just change app.h
instead of having to have a bunch of different copies of main.c for different
applications.

```
      // Wait indefinitely for events
      ErrTry
      {
          while( true )
```

```
                    processEvent( -1 );
        }

        // Stop the application
        ErrCatch( lError )
        {
        } ErrEndCatch

        // Clean up before exit
        appStop();

        // We're done
        return( 0 );
}
```

This code is a reiteration of the event loops we have done before, except the function calls in the loop are off in a separate function **processEvent()**. This is so that we can control how events are processed in other areas of the program if we need to. You'll see why this is useful when we get to later chapters.

After the **ErrCatch()** block is our call to **appStop()**. Like the call to **appInit()**, this function is defined in app.h to incorporate anything from the various program modules that need to get cleaned up before we exit our program. As you'll see, even regular program termination ends up in this catch block, so **appStop()** always gets called on the way out.

Next comes our event handler function.

```
//-----------------------------------------------------------------
Boolean processEvent(
//-----------------------------------------------------------------
// Waits for and processes the next event.
// Returns false if the queue is empty.
//-----------------------------------------------------------------
Long    lTimeout )  // Time to wait in 100ths of a second, -1 = forever
//-----------------------------------------------------------------
{
```

12

Note the parameter to control the time to wait for an event to come in. This will be very useful in future programs that control animation or sound, among other things. Since the Palm OS is a single-tasking operating system from our standpoint, we need to be able to carefully control how often the Palm OS allows our program to execute in order to produce smooth effects.

You might rightfully ask why we return a Boolean value from **processEvent()** when we ignore that return value in **PilotMain()**. In future applications there will be times (while we're doing animations, for example) when we want to control how events are being processed so that we can do smooth animations. In these cases we will call **processEvent()** elsewhere in our application to handle or flush events in various ways.

```
EventType    sEvent; // Our event
Word         wError; // The error word for the menu event handler

// Get the next event
EvtGetEvent( &sEvent, lTimeout );
```

Here we define a few familiar variables, and follow it with a call to **EvtGetEvent()**. Notice that **EvtGetEvent()** is where we pass our timing parameter to the operating system.

```
// If it's a stop event, exit
if( sEvent.eType == appStopEvent )
{
    // Exit
    ErrThrow( 0 );
}
```

Our stop event handler has changed. Instead of just returning like it did in the earlier examples, our stop event handler does an **ErrThrow()** back to the **ErrCatch()** block in **main()**. Why don't we have it just return to main much like it did before? If we call **processEvent()** elsewhere in our program and receive an *appStopEvent* during that call, control would return somewhere locally instead of to **main()**. We need a mechanism for returning to **main()** no matter where we received the *appStopEvent*, and the Error Manager provides this functionality about as safely as it can be provided in C.

```
// If it's a nil event, return queue empty
if( sEvent.eType == nilEvent )
    return( false );
```

This is a new check in our event loop. Palm OS sends a *nilEvent* when the event queue is empty. Since we always told the Palm OS to wait forever in our earlier programs, we could never receive one. Now receiving *nilEvent* tells us the event queue is empty. This is useful to know if we're using *processEvent* to flush the event queue periodically while performing some time-consuming task. This is why it's important to give this case a special return value.

```
// Handle system events
if( SysHandleEvent( &sEvent ) )
    return( true );

// Handle menu events
if( MenuHandleEvent( NULL, &sEvent, &wError ) )
    return( true );
```

Here are a few familiar calls. We handle system events and menu events just like before.

```
// Load a form
if( sEvent.eType == frmLoadEvent )
{
    Word    wFormID;     // The form ID
    FormPtr spForm;      // Points to the form
    // Get the ID
    wFormID = sEvent.data.frmLoad.formID;
    // Initialize the form
    spForm = FrmInitForm( wFormID );

    // Establish the event handler
    FrmSetEventHandler( spForm, getEventHandler( wFormID ) );

    // Point events to our form
    FrmSetActiveForm( spForm );

    // Draw the form
    FrmDrawForm( spForm );
```

12

Here is our generic form-loading code. These function calls are all pretty familiar. First we get the ID of the form we're supposed to load out of the event structure. After that come the familiar calls to initialize and draw a form. Notice, however, the call to **getEventHandler()** inside **FrmSetEventHandler()**. The function **getEventHandler()** is defined inside app.h, and matches form IDs with their corresponding event handlers using information from the various modules that support those forms. This allows us to treat all forms the same in main.c, so this code doesn't have to explicitly know about all the forms in the application. We can reuse this code in applications with many different assortments of forms as a result.

```
    // Handle form events
    FrmDispatchEvent( &sEvent );

    // We're done
    return( true );
}
```

Here is the last bit of **processEvent()**. We dispatch remaining events to the specific active form. We return true to indicate that there may be other events in the queue.

The main.h Module

The include file main.h has definitions that support main.c. The definitions found in main.h also support the customization we have to do in app.h for the benefit of main.c. Create a new file, save it as main.h in your source directory. Add it to the Calculator project and save it in AppIncludes. Here it is in its entirety:

```
#ifndef MAIN_H
#define MAIN_H
//////////////////////////////////////////////////////////////////////
// main.h
// Definitions for the main entry point.
// Copyright (c) 1999, Robert Mykland.  All rights reserved.
//////////////////////////////////////////////////////////////////////

///////////////////////////
// Global Prototypes //
///////////////////////////

DWord PilotMain( Word, Ptr, Word ); // Main entry point.
Boolean processEvent( Long );        // Processes the next event.

///////////////////
// Constants //
///////////////////
```

```
// The different versions of Palm OS
// Pilot 1000 and Pilot 5000
#define ROM_VERSION_1    0x01003001
// PalmPilot and PalmPilot Professional
#define ROM_VERSION_2    0x02003000
// Palm III, IIIx, IIIe and V
#define ROM_VERSION_3    0x03003000

#endif  // MAIN_H
```

At the top of the file are two preprocessor directives: #ifndef MAIN_H and #define MAIN_H. A preprocessor directive at the end of the file matches these: #endif. The #ifndef #endif pair causes everything in the file to be skipped if the constant MAIN_H is defined. Inside this pair MAIN_H is defined. This has the effect of causing the whole file to be skipped if the compiler has seen it before.

Often in larger and more complex programs, include files get included in the same file more than once, usually just for convenience. This way the code can be split and recombined in various ways without the need to worry whether the things in the include file will be undefined. Putting these preprocessor directives at the top and bottom of your include files will prevent needless time tracking down multiple definitions or repairing things that become undefined when you reuse code.

Below the standard module comment header are the same function prototypes in main.c. Since they are in both the source and include file, the compiler will flag an error if they differ in the smallest detail.

At the bottom of the file the version constants that are returned by the Palm OS are defined. It is better to define constants like these in the include file for the source file (if they aren't already defined by the operating system) to further reduce the chances of mistyping them in some future revision. A raw hexadecimal number in code is generally a red flag that something is not being properly documented or explained. Such code will often become a maintenance hassle in the future.

12

The fcalc.c Module

The source file fcalc.c contains one function, an event handler function. Create a new source file and save it as fcalc.c in the Src folder of your Calculator project. Add it to the project and put it under AppSource.

Below you see a complete listing of fcalc.c. At the top is the familiar directive to include app.h, followed by a prototype for the event handler function.

```
///////////////////////////////////////////////////////////////
// fcalc.c
// Code for the "calc" form.
// Copyright (c) 1999, Robert Mykland.  All rights reserved.
///////////////////////////////////////////////////////////////


//////////////
// Includes //
//////////////

#include "app.h"     // The definitions for this application

////////////////////////
// Global Prototypes //
////////////////////////

Boolean calcFormEventHandler( EventPtr spEvent );

//////////////////////////
// Global Functions //
//////////////////////////

//-------------------------------------------------------------
Boolean calcFormEventHandler(
//-------------------------------------------------------------
// Handles events for this form.
// Returns true if it fully handled the event.
//-------------------------------------------------------------
EventPtr spEvent )
//-------------------------------------------------------------
{
    // Handle the event
    switch( spEvent->eType )
    {
        // A control was selected
        case ctlSelectEvent:

            // Sound an alarm
            SndPlaySystemSound( sndAlarm );
            return( false );

        // A menu item was selected
        case menuEvent:
```

```
                    // Handle the menu event
                    calcFormMenuEventHandler( spEvent );
                    return( true );
            }

            // We're done
            return( false );
    }
```

If a button is pressed, the function plays the alarm sound. If a menu item or shortcut is selected, we call **calcFormMenuEventHandler()**. This is actually a macro that is defined in app.h. Having the menu event handler defined as a macro in app.h allows us to potentially reuse the fcalc.c form in other applications where a different menu layout or different selections might be appropriate.

Note that we return false in the situation where the button is pressed. This is because we need the Palm OS to further handle the button-pressing graphics. Remember, the general rule is to return false unless you specifically want the event to be ignored elsewhere. The exception to this rule is *menuEvent*. If you return false after servicing a menu event, the Palm OS will beep as if there has been an error.

Once we have this modular code in hand, we can add a calculator as a seamless tool to any other Palm OS application we write. For example, we can add it as a pop-up form to a financial information package so that people can pop it up to make a calculation and then have the result appear in the current field of the main form.

The fcalc.h Module

The include file for fcalc.c is fcalc.h. Create a new file and save it as fcalc.h in the Src folder of your Calculator project. Add it to the project. Put it under AppIncludes.

Just like main.h, fcalc.h contains the standard #ifndef #define #endif logic that prevents it from being included multiple times. There is also the prototype we saw in fcalc.c, which insures that the compiler will complain unless this function is defined and called in exactly the same way wherever it appears.

12

```
#ifndef FCALC_H
#define FCALC_H
/////////////////////////////////////////////////////////////////
// fcalc.h
// Definitions for the "calc" form.
// Copyright (c) 1999, Robert Mykland.  All rights reserved.
```

```
//////////////////////////////////////////////////////////////

/////////////////////
// Global Prototypes //
/////////////////////

Boolean calcFormEventHandler( EventPtr spEvent );

#endif    // FCALC_H
```

You might ask, "Why have an include file at all to define only one function?" The thing is, it's only one function *right now*. But one thing that's worth being careful about in your code is the beginning structure. Plan for expansion. Make room for comments. If it never expands, there's no harm done. The definition is still easy to find.

The app.h Module

The include file app.h is the module that "glues together" all the previous modules we've discussed. Start by creating a new file and saving as app.h in the Src folder under your Calculator project. Then add it to the project. Put it under AppIncludes.

Let's go through app.h line by line:

```
#ifndef APP_H
#define APP_H
//////////////////////////////////////////////////////////////
// app.h
// Definitions for the application.
// Copyright (c) 1999, Robert Mykland.  All rights reserved.
//////////////////////////////////////////////////////////////

//////////////
// Includes //
//////////////

#include <Pilot.h>            // All the Palm OS includes
#include "Calculator_res.h" // Resource definitions
#include "fcalc.h"            // Definitions for the "calc" form
#include "main.h"             // Definitions for the main entry point
```

So far, app.h looks similar to other include files we've gone through. The #ifndef #define construct appears at the top, followed by the module comment block and some include file definitions. First there is the include statement for Pilot.h. Since we're including app.h in all of our source files, this is the only place where it has to appear. Next comes our resource include file followed by the other two include files we've created. Note that Pilot.h is enclosed in <> symbols as befits a system include file, whereas our include files are enclosed in quotes.

Next come all the definitions for fcalc.c. Note that app.h is split into sections dealing with each of the source files. This will make it easier in the future for you to come back and steal code from this application. It will be easy to look in app.h and steal everything that's necessary and sufficient to supply a given module you steal with definitions.

```
/////////////////////////////
// Definitions for fcalc.c //
/////////////////////////////

// The menu event handler macro for the "calc" form
#define calcFormMenuEventHandler(spEvent)
```

Here is the definition of the menu handler function for our calc form. Right now it is defined as nothing and will be replaced with nothing in the code. The calc form doesn't have a menu yet. I've left the characteristic white space out of the parenthesis of the function call on purpose. Macro bodies start after the first white space after the macro name, so you must pack your macro parameters in like sardines with no white space in order to make the macro compile properly.

NOTE: Use macros only when necessary in your code. They are dangerous to use. Unlike regular function calls whose parameters can be checked using prototyping, no prototypes are available for macros, so if you pass something wrong into a macro, it will get used anyway. Macros are used in app.h because they allow for quick and easy "functions" that don't take up code space except where they are referred to in the source modules. You don't want to write functions in an include file because the code will be duplicated in every source file in which that include file appears.

12

Next come the definitions for main.c. First is a prototype for the **getEventHandler()** function followed by a definition for the strange thing we saw in main.c: EVENT_HANDLER_LIST.

```
/////////////////////////////
// Definitions for main.c //
/////////////////////////////
```

```
// The prototype for getEventHandler()
static FormEventHandlerPtr getEventHandler( Word );

// This creates the function getEventHandler,
// which returns the event handler for a given form
// in this application.
#define EVENT_HANDLER_LIST \
FormEventHandlerPtr getEventHandler( Word wFormID )\
{\
    switch( wFormID )\
    {\
        case CalcForm:\
            return( calcFormEventHandler );\
    }\
    return( NULL );\
}
```

EVENT_HANDLER_LIST actually turns out to be a #define statement that creates the function **getEventHandler()**. The preprocessor replaces the label in main.c with this code. You can use the #define this way to replace anything. It's just like using a search-and-replace command in a text editor. The backslashes at the end of each line cause the preprocessor to ignore the line breaks that directly follow them. A #define statement ends when it encounters a line break. This is why the last line of **getEventHandler()** has no backslash at the end.

Right now, **getEventHandler()** only correlates the function **calcFormEventHandler()** with the form CalcForm. As we add forms and event handler functions, **getEventHandler()** will expand to include definitions for each form we add.

```
// This defines the macro that initializes the app
#define appInit()

// This defines the macro that cleans up the app
#define appStop()

// This application works on Palm OS 2.0 and above
#define ROM_VERSION_MIN ROM_VERSION_2

// Define the starting form
#define StartForm CalcForm

#endif  // APP_H
```

Next the **appInit()** and **appStop()** macros are defined. For now they do nothing. The file ends by defining the minimum acceptable version of the Palm OS for our application as version 2.0. Note that this uses the version definitions from main.h. Also, we define our starting form to be CalcForm. Finally comes our #endif statement. Don't forget this, or you'll get some very strange compiler errors.

The main purpose of setting up a glue file like app.h is that it saves time and effort to change things in include files rather than in source files. There are several reasons why this is a good idea. Whenever you modify code, there is always a chance of introducing a bug. On the other hand, changing constants rarely introduces bugs into code. Whenever you touch a file at all, there is a chance of introducing a bug. Concentrating changes in a few include files reduces the chance that files with code that worked successfully in the past will be edited and inadvertently polluted with bugs.

Even programmers who never introduce bugs into code (yeah, sure) can benefit from this kind of archtecture. Even if code is well commented, it takes time to understand it and make prudent changes. Concentrating changes in well-documented include files saves you the time of relearning the details of the modules themselves in order to modify them.

Debugging It

Now you have all the pieces. Time to debug your code. When you are done, the program should operate like our old Hello application. It should look like this:

12

The program starts execution at **PilotMain()**. It does its initial stuff: checking the ROM version and checking the launch code. It does a **FrmGotoForm()** call that specifies the CalcForm and puts two messages in the queue: a frmLoadEvent and a frmOpenEvent. Then it goes into its infinite event loop.

The frmLoadEvent gets picked up in **processEvent()**, which gets the form ID from the event structure and proceeds to initialize the calc form. Then the program sits there and waits for something to happen.

If you touch the OK button, it rings the alarm. That's it.

Listings

Here's all of app.h:

```
#ifndef APP_H
#define APP_H
//////////////////////////////////////////////////////////////////////
// app.h
// Definitions for the application.
// Copyright (c) 1999, Robert Mykland.  All rights reserved.
//////////////////////////////////////////////////////////////////////


//////////////
// Includes //
//////////////

#include <Pilot.h>              // All the Palm OS includes
#include "Calculator_res.h" // Resource definitions
#include "fcalc.h"              // Definitions for the "calc" form
#include "main.h"               // Definitions for the main entry point

///////////////////////////////
// Definitions for fcalc.c //
///////////////////////////////

// The menu event handler macro for the "calc" form
#define calcFormMenuEventHandler(spEvent)

///////////////////////////////
// Definitions for main.c //
///////////////////////////////

// The prototype for getEventHandler()
static FormEventHandlerPtr getEventHandler( Word );
```

```
// This creates the function getEventHandler,
// which returns the event handler for a given form
// in this application.
#define EVENT_HANDLER_LIST \
static FormEventHandlerPtr getEventHandler( Word wFormID )\
{\
    switch( wFormID )\
    {\
        case CalcForm:\
            return( calcFormEventHandler );\
    }\
    return( NULL );\
}

// This defines the macro that initializes the app
#define appInit()

// This defines the macro that cleans up the app
#define appStop()

// This application works on Palm OS 2.0 and above
#define ROM_VERSION_MIN ROM_VERSION_2

// Define the starting form
#define StartForm CalcForm

#endif  // APP_H
```

Here's all of main.c:

```
///////////////////////////////////////////////////////////////////
// main.c
// Main entry point and event loop.
// Copyright (c) 1999, Robert Mykland.  All rights reserved.
///////////////////////////////////////////////////////////////////

/////////////////
// Includes //
/////////////////

#include "app.h"    // The definitions for this application

/////////////////////////
// Global Prototypes //
```

12

```
/////////////////////////

DWord PilotMain( Word, Ptr, Word ); // Main entry point.
Boolean processEvent( Long );        // Processes the next event.

//////////////////////
// Local Variables //
//////////////////////

// The menu bar pointer
static MenuBarPtr spMenuBar;

// The event handler list
EVENT_HANDLER_LIST

//////////////////////
// Global Functions //
//////////////////////

//-----------------------------------------------------------------
DWord PilotMain(
//-----------------------------------------------------------------
// The main entry point for this application.
// Always returns zero.
//-----------------------------------------------------------------
Word wCmd,  // The launch code
Ptr,        // The launch parameter block
Word )      // The launch flags
//-----------------------------------------------------------------
{
    DWord dROMVersion;

    // Get the ROM version
    dROMVersion = 0;
    FtrGet( sysFtrCreator, sysFtrNumROMVersion, &dROMVersion );

    // Alert and bail if the ROM version is too low
    if( dROMVersion < ROM_VERSION_MIN )
    {
        FrmAlert( LowROMVersionErrorAlert );

        // Palm OS 1.0 will continuously re-launch this app
        // unless we switch to another safe one
        if( dROMVersion < ROM_VERSION_2 )
        {
```

```
                AppLaunchWithCommand( sysFileCDefaultApp,
                        sysAppLaunchCmdNormalLaunch, NULL );
        }
        return( 0 );
    }

    // If this is not a normal launch, don't launch
    if( wCmd != sysAppLaunchCmdNormalLaunch )
        return( 0 );

    // Initialize all parts of the application
    appInit();

    // Go to the starting form
    FrmGotoForm( StartForm );

    // Wait indefinitely for events
    ErrTry
    {
        while( true )
            processEvent( -1 );
    }

    // Stop the application
    ErrCatch( lError )
    {
    } ErrEndCatch

    // Clean up before exit
    appStop();

    // We're done
    return( 0 );
}


//------------------------------------------------------------------
Boolean processEvent(
//------------------------------------------------------------------
// Waits for and processes the next event.
// Returns false if the queue is empty.
//------------------------------------------------------------------
Long    lTimeout )  // Time to wait in 100ths of a second, -1=forever
//------------------------------------------------------------------
{
    EventType   sEvent; // Our event
```

```
Word        wError; // The error word for the menu event handler

// Get the next event
EvtGetEvent( &sEvent, lTimeout );

// If it's a stop event, exit
if( sEvent.eType == appStopEvent )
{
    // Exit
    ErrThrow( 0 );
}

// If it's a nil event, return queue empty
if( sEvent.eType == nilEvent )
    return( false );

// Handle system events
if( SysHandleEvent( &sEvent ) )
    return( true );

// Handle menu events
if( MenuHandleEvent( spMenuBar, &sEvent, &wError ) )
    return( true );

// Load a form
if( sEvent.eType == frmLoadEvent )
{
    Word    wFormID;    // The form ID
    FormPtr spForm;     // Points to the form

    // Get the ID
    wFormID = sEvent.data.frmLoad.formID;

    // Initialize the form
    spForm = FrmInitForm( wFormID );

    // Establish the event handler
    FrmSetEventHandler( spForm, getEventHandler( wFormID ) );

    // Point events to our form
    FrmSetActiveForm( spForm );

    // Draw the form
    FrmDrawForm( spForm );
}
```

```
     // Handle form events
     FrmDispatchEvent( &sEvent );

     // We're done
     return( true );
}
```

A Reusable About Form

In this section we will add two forms to our resource file and our new code structure: an about form, which we will eventually turn into an about box, and a prefs form, which we will turn into a preferences dialog. In this chapter we'll just put OK buttons on them to verify their aliveness.

Additions to Calculator.rsrc

We will start by adding an about form, a preferences form, and a menu bar to our resource file.

1. Launch Constructor and open Calculator.rsrc.
2. Create the skeleton of the about form. We're going to do this by copying the calc form and making a few small modifications.
3. Select the calc form.
4. Select Edit | Copy or press CTRL-C to copy the calc form.
5. Choose Edit | Paste or press CTRL-V to paste the copy back into Constructor. A dialog will come up giving the choice of replacing the original calc or copying the form to a unique ID.
6. Choose Unique ID.
7. Change the name of the form to "about."
8. Double-click on the about form to open it. Go to the form attributes.
9. Check Save Behind. Fill in a title of About Calculator.
10. Move the button down 20 pixels so that it doesn't fall on top of the button on the calc form. This, along with the title, will help you tell the forms apart when you're switching between them. When you're done, your about form resource should look like the one shown in Figure 12-3.

12

Now create the prefs form. Cut and paste the about form to create the prefs form. Rename the form "prefs." Change the title to Calculator Preferences.

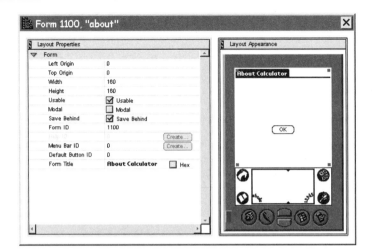

What the about form resource should look like

Figure 12-3.

Move the button down another 20 pixels. When you're done, the prefs form resource should look like the one shown in Figure 12-4.

We'll add a menu bar to the calc form to allow us to navigate to these two new forms. First, create a menu bar resource by selecting a menu bar resource

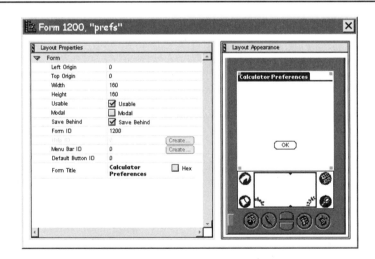

What the prefs form resource should look like

Figure 12-4.

type in the list and pressing CTRL-K. Name the new menu bar resource "calc."
Create a menu resource by selecting that resource type and pressing CTRL-K.
Name the new menu resource "options." Open the menu bar resource with a
double-click. Then drag and drop the menu resource into the menu bar
window. Entitle the menu Options. Add an entry to the menu by pressing
CTRL-K. Name it Preferences... and give it a shortcut key of "R." Add another
entry and name it About Calculator. When you're done, your menu bar
resource should look like this:

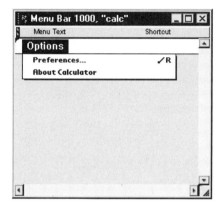

The fabout.c Module

Now we are ready to create the source code that supports our new forms and
menu. Below is the fabout.c source file. All it contains is an event handler
function for the about form and the prototype for that function. It is
extremely similar at this point to fcalc.c, so I recommend making a copy of
that file and modifying it from there. Don't forget to add your resulting
fabout.c file into the project under AppSource.

```
/////////////////////////////////////////////////////////////////////
// fabout.c
// Code for the "about" form.
// Copyright (c) 1999, Robert Mykland.  All rights reserved.
/////////////////////////////////////////////////////////////////////

//////////////
// Includes //
//////////////

#include "app.h"     // The definitions for this application
```

12

```
/////////////////////////
// Global Prototypes //
/////////////////////////

Boolean aboutFormEventHandler( EventPtr spEvent );

/////////////////////////
// Global Functions //
/////////////////////////

//-------------------------------------------------------------
Boolean aboutFormEventHandler(
//-------------------------------------------------------------
// Handles events for this form.
// Returns true if it fully handled the event.
//-------------------------------------------------------------
EventPtr spEvent )
//-------------------------------------------------------------
{
    // Handle the event
    switch( spEvent->eType )
    {
        // A control was selected
        case ctlSelectEvent:

            // Return to the calling form
            FrmReturnToForm( 0 );
            return( false );

        // A menu item was selected
        case menuEvent:

            // Handle the menu event
            aboutFormMenuEventHandler( spEvent );
            return( true );
    }

    // We're done
    return( false );
}
```

In **aboutFormEventHandler()** we handle two types of events. If any button is pressed we call **FrmReturnToForm()** to return control to the form that popped us up. By using this function we establish this form as a pop-up form that can only be invoked by a call to **FrmPopupForm()** rather than the more general **FrmGotoForm()**. Since about forms are invariably pop-up forms, this shouldn't limit our ability to reuse this code in future applications.

For menu events, we call the function **aboutFormEventHandler()**. This is actually a macro that we will add to app.h. Having the menu event handler defined as a macro in our glue file allows us to potentially reuse fabout.c and fabout.h in other applications with different menus.

The fabout.h Module

This include file is identical in nature to the include file for the calc form. Copy fcalc.h and rename it to fabout.h. Add it to the project and put it under AppIncludes. Modify it to match the file shown below.

```
#ifndef FABOUT_H
#define FABOUT_H
/////////////////////////////////////////////////////////////////
// fabout.h
// Definitions for the "about" form.
// Copyright (c) 1999, Robert Mykland.  All rights reserved.
/////////////////////////////////////////////////////////////////


//////////////////////////
// Global Prototypes //
//////////////////////////

Boolean aboutFormEventHandler( EventPtr spEvent );

#endif  // FABOUT_H
```

The fprefs.c Module

Below is the fprefs.c source file. At present, it is identical to the fabout.c source file except that "about" has been changed to "prefs" everywhere. Copy fabout.c into fprefs.c and make the necessary changes. Add it to the Calculator project under AppSource.

12

```
/////////////////////////////////////////////////////////////////
// fprefs.c
// Code for the "prefs" form.
// Copyright (c) 1999, Robert Mykland.  All rights reserved.
/////////////////////////////////////////////////////////////////
```

```
/////////////
// Includes //
/////////////

#include "app.h"     // The definitions for this application

//////////////////////
// Global Prototypes //
//////////////////////

Boolean prefsFormEventHandler( EventPtr spEvent );

//////////////////////
// Global Functions //
//////////////////////

//-----------------------------------------------------------
Boolean prefsFormEventHandler(
//-----------------------------------------------------------
// Handles events for this form.
// Returns true if it fully handled the event.
//-----------------------------------------------------------
EventPtr spEvent )
//-----------------------------------------------------------
{
    // Handle the event
    switch( spEvent->eType )
    {
        // A control was selected
        case ctlSelectEvent:

            // Return to the calling form
            FrmReturnToForm( 0 );
            return( false );

        // A menu item was selected
        case menuEvent:

            // Handle the menu event
            prefsFormMenuEventHandler( spEvent );
            return( true );
    }

    // We're done
    return( false );
}
```

The fprefs.h Module

This include file is identical in nature to the include file for the calc and about forms. Copy fabout.h and rename it to fprefs.h. Add it to the project and put it under AppIncludes. Modify it to match the file shown below.

```
#ifndef FPREFS_H
#define FPREFS_H
////////////////////////////////////////////////////////////////
// fprefs.h
// Definitions for the "prefs" form.
// Copyright (c) 1999, Robert Mykland.  All rights reserved.
////////////////////////////////////////////////////////////////

////////////////////////
// Global Prototypes //
////////////////////////

Boolean prefsFormEventHandler( EventPtr spEvent );

#endif  // FPREFS_H
```

The moptions.c Module

The Options menu source file moptions.c has a single event handler function in it as well. Copy it from any of the form source files. Add it to the project under AppSource. Make the necessary changes to have it match the listing below.

```
////////////////////////////////////////////////////////////////
// moptions.c
// Code for the "options" menu.
// Copyright (c) 1999, Robert Mykland.  All rights reserved.
////////////////////////////////////////////////////////////////

///////////////
// Includes //
///////////////

#include "app.h"     // The definitions for this application

////////////////////////
// Global Prototypes //
////////////////////////
```

12

```
Boolean optionsMenuEventHandler( EventPtr spEvent );

/////////////////////////
// Global Functions //
/////////////////////////

//------------------------------------------------------------
Boolean optionsMenuEventHandler(
//------------------------------------------------------------
// Handles events for this form.
// Returns true if it fully handled the event.
//------------------------------------------------------------
EventPtr spEvent )  // The menu event to look at.
//------------------------------------------------------------
{
    switch( spEvent->data.menu.itemID )
    {
        // The about menu item was selected
        case OptionsAbout:
            FrmPopupForm( AboutForm );
            return( true );

        // The prefs menu item was selected
        case OptionsPreferences:
            FrmPopupForm( PrefsForm );
            return( true );
    }

    // We're done
    return( false );
}
```

In the case of these menu items being selected, we call **FrmPopupForm()** to pop up the appropriate form. We return true if there is a menu item that matches the ID we were passed and false otherwise.

The moptions.h Module

This include file is very similar to those used by the forms. It just contains a prototype for the event handler function. Copy one of the form include files and rename it moptions.h. Add it to the project under the AppIncludes group. Change the file as shown in the listing below.

```
#ifndef MOPTIONS_H
#define MOPTIONS_H
```

```
//////////////////////////////////////////////////////////////
// moptions.h
// Definitions for the "options" menu.
// Copyright (c) 1999, Robert Mykland.  All rights reserved.
//////////////////////////////////////////////////////////////


////////////////////////
// Global Prototypes //
////////////////////////


Boolean optionsMenuEventHandler( EventPtr spEvent );

#endif        // MOPTIONS_H
```

Additions to app.h

In order to glue in the other modules we've created, we'll add some code to
app.h. First add the new include files.

```
//////////////
// Includes //
//////////////


#include <Pilot.h>             // All the Palm OS includes
#include "Calculator_res.h"    // Resource definitions
#include "fabout.h"            // Definitions for the "about" form
#include "fcalc.h"             // Definitions for the "calc" form
#include "fprefs.h"            // Definitions for the "prefs" form
#include "main.h"              // Definitions for the main entry point
#include "moptions.h"          // Definitions for the "options" menu
```

Add a new section for each of the added modules. I usually do this in
alphabetical order. This makes them easier to find as the number of modules
in the application climbs.

```
////////////////////////////////
// Definitions for fabout.c //
////////////////////////////////


// The menu event handler macro for the "about" form
#define aboutFormMenuEventHandler(spEvent)


////////////////////////////////
// Definitions for fcalc.c //
////////////////////////////////
```

12

```
// The menu event handler macro for the "calc" form
#define calcFormMenuEventHandler(spEvent) \
{ \
    optionsMenuEventHandler( spEvent ); \
}


/////////////////////////////
// Definitions for fprefs.c //
/////////////////////////////

// The menu event handler macro for the "prefs" form
#define prefsFormMenuEventHandler(spEvent)
```

What's needed for fabout.c and fprefs.c resembles the existing entry for fcalc.c. You add a macro definition for their respective menu event handler functions. Additionally, the menu event handler macro for fcalc.c should now evaluate to something, since we added a menu bar for it. Put in a call to **optionsMenuEventHandler()** so that events for that menu will be handled when the calc form is showing.

Next, add code to the **getEventHandler()** function so that the event handlers for the forms we added can be found.

```
// This creates the function getEventHandler,
// which returns the event handler for a given form
// in this application.
#define EVENT_HANDLER_LIST \
static FormEventHandlerPtr getEventHandler( Word wFormID ) \
{ \
    switch( wFormID ) \
    { \
        case AboutForm: \
            return( aboutFormEventHandler ); \
        case CalcForm: \
            return( calcFormEventHandler ); \
        case PrefsForm: \
            return( prefsFormEventHandler ); \
    } \
    return( NULL ); \
}
```

The new entries for the about form and the prefs form follow the same pattern established by the calc form. Nothing else in the section for main.c needs changing.

Add a section for the Options menu just as you would for a form.

```
///////////////////////////////
// Definitions for moptions.c //
///////////////////////////////

// Menu ID name conversions
#define OptionsAbout      OptionsAboutCalculator
```

Since the constants defined in Calculator_res.h are based on the actual text of the menu items, we should abstract these constants into more generic names when they contain application-dependent words like "Calculator" so that moptions.c is potentially reusable.

Listing

Here is a complete listing of the new version of app.h:

```
#ifndef APP_H
#define APP_H
///////////////////////////////////////////////////////////////////////
// app.h
// Definitions for the application.
// Copyright (c) 1999, Robert Mykland.  All rights reserved.
///////////////////////////////////////////////////////////////////////

//////////////
// Includes //
//////////////

#include <Pilot.h>            // All the Palm OS includes
#include "Calculator_res.h"  // Resource definitions
#include "fabout.h"           // Definitions for the "about" form
#include "fcalc.h"            // Definitions for the "calc" form
#include "fprefs.h"           // Definitions for the "prefs" form
#include "main.h"             // Definitions for the main entry point
#include "moptions.h"         // Definitions for the "options" menu

////////////////////////////////
// Definitions for fabout.c //
////////////////////////////////

// The menu event handler macro for the "about" form
#define aboutFormMenuEventHandler(spEvent)
```

12

```
/////////////////////////////
// Definitions for fcalc.c //
/////////////////////////////

// The menu event handler macro for the "calc" form
#define calcFormMenuEventHandler(spEvent) \
{ \
    optionsMenuEventHandler( spEvent );\
}


/////////////////////////////
// Definitions for fprefs.c //
/////////////////////////////

// The menu event handler macro for the "prefs" form
#define prefsFormMenuEventHandler(spEvent)

/////////////////////////////
// Definitions for main.c //
/////////////////////////////

// The prototype for getEventHandler()
static FormEventHandlerPtr getEventHandler( Word );

// This creates the function getEventHandler,
// which returns the event handler for a given form
// in this application.
#define EVENT_HANDLER_LIST \
static FormEventHandlerPtr getEventHandler( Word wFormID )\
{ \
    switch( wFormID )\
    { \
        case AboutForm:\
            return( aboutFormEventHandler );\
        case CalcForm:\
            return( calcFormEventHandler );\
        case PrefsForm:\
            return( prefsFormEventHandler );\
    } \
    return( NULL );\
}

// This defines the macro that initializes the app
#define appInit()
```

```
// This defines the macro that cleans up the app
#define appStop()

// This application works on Palm OS version 2.0 or later
#define ROM_VERSION_MIN ROM_VERSION_2

// Define the starting form
#define StartForm CalcForm

////////////////////////////////
// Definitions for moptions.c //
////////////////////////////////

// Menu ID name conversions
#define OptionsAbout      OptionsAboutCalculator

#endif  // APP_H
```

Debugging It

It's time to debug again. Your calc screen should look and work as it did before. Your prefs and about forms should pop up if you select their items from the menu. They should return to the calc form when you press their OK buttons.

As before, the program starts execution at **PilotMain()** and goes through its regular routine. When the frmLoadEvent gets picked up in **processEvent()**, it initializes the calc form's new menu bar. Then the program sits there and waits for something to happen.

If you touch the OK button, it rings the alarm. That's it.

Object-Oriented Programming

12

The purpose of object-oriented principles is to make code easier to maintain and reuse. Basically, they are ways of isolating and abstracting code depending on other pieces of code or on the variables used by that code. This makes code more maintainable because it often localizes bugs in obvious ways. Also, you can find and fix problems after only having to learn how a relatively small section of code works. It makes code more reusable because, with less dependencies between sections of code, you have a better chance of cleanly and easily stealing useful code out of any given object-oriented application to use in your next project.

Considering all that's been said about object-oriented programming in the last decade, your opinion about it may range from considering it to be dangerous hype to considering it to be the only way to code. And you may be right. That said, I might as well add my not-so-humble opinion to the millions of reams out there about object-oriented programming, for whatever it's worth.

First of all, object-oriented programming has less to do with the language you're coding in and more to do with the design principles you use to create code no matter what language you're using. Sure, languages like C++ and Java are easier to use in an object-oriented way, but ease of use is really all they provide. After well over a decade of heavily using object-oriented languages like Smalltalk, C++, and Java for all kinds of things, I'm clear that just because someone knows the syntax of Java doesn't mean they know anything about how to apply objects in useful or valuable ways.

What is really required is an understanding of object-oriented concepts and design patterns and why these concepts and design patterns are useful and valuable. Object-oriented programming is a tool like anything else, and when used indiscriminately, it can do just as much damage as any misused tool. Nobody would start whacking everything in their house with a hammer just because it was the latest tool in their collection. Yet I've seen countless times the indiscriminate use of object syntax applied in ways that do more harm than good.

C++, Java, and the Palm OS

Generally, I prefer working in C++ and Java. I don't favor them on the Palm OS because I haven't seen any implementations of either of these languages whose class libraries make any sense for Palm OS. So far, what we've gotten is bigger, slower applications and not much other benefit from these tools.

When there is a small, clean shared class library for Palm OS for C++ or Java, I'll be the first to make use of it. Perhaps I'll write one.

Luckily, you can employ and derive value from object-oriented principles in your Palm OS applications without necessarily resorting to C++ or Java. The key, as I said before, is understanding the principles themselves. In the sections that follow, I'll explain some of the most popular concepts in object-oriented programming and give advice on how you can write C programs that make use of these principles.

Data Encapsulation

The basic principle of object-oriented programming is that data structures and all the code that uses those data structures travel together in a composite entity called an *object*. The idea of data encapsulation is that the data structures in an object need to be protected from being modified by code outside the object. If you enforce this principle, you can be sure that if one of these data structures gets corrupted, the bug that did the corrupting is inside the same object, unless the culprit is a so-called "wild pointer."

Wild pointer bugs happen when pointers get set to some number that doesn't point to anything in particular. For example, this code would probably cause such a bug:

```
char* cpBuffer = 2000;
```

In the case of a wild pointer, an unrelated object's data structures might be the unlucky target of any writes done using that pointer, thereby getting corrupted and causing a bug. It's best to use pointers sparingly and carefully for this reason.

Data encapsulation in C is straightforward. Break up the code for each object into separate files and declare all variables outside function calls as static. This prevents them from being explicitly referred to by other objects in other files.

If objects need access to a data structure in another object, you can manage that access by creating global functions that expose this data only as much as it needs to be. Don't pass pointers to your data to functions outside the module. Instead, have the caller pass you a data structure that you fill in, or create a copy of your original data that you manage on behalf of the caller (trickier).

Data Abstraction

Data abstraction is the principle that code in one object does not depend on the structure of the data in any other object. Thus, any object could be rewritten and its underlying variables entirely changed without affecting the validity of code or data in any other object.

Data abstraction is useful because objects become replaceable building blocks that are easy to reuse and easy to maintain without affecting the rest of the system.

12

Obviously, don't make use of "inside information" about other objects' data structures. Treat them as black boxes. Don't assume the size of other objects' data structures. Use **sizeof()**. Don't assume you know where a variable is located within a structure.

Inheritance

Inheritance is the principle that you can have objects that consist of only specialized additions to other more general-purpose objects. This is good because you don't have to reinvent the wheel every time you create an object that is similar in many respects to objects you've already written.

One way to do inheritance in C is to use #define statements. Say you have an object that is a simple list and you want to create another object that has all the capabilities of that simple list plus the ability to iterate through the list items. Here are the prototypes for the simple list:

```
VoidHand slCreateList( void );
void slDestroyList( VoidHand );
void slAddToList( VoidHand, listitem_t* );
void slSaveList( VoidHand, FILE* );
void slLoadList( VoidHand, FILE* );
```

In the include file of the iterated list, you could have something like:

```
#define ilCreateList slCreateList
#define ilDestroyList slDestroyList
#define ilAddToList slAddToList
#define ilSaveList slSaveList
#define ilLoadList slLoadList
void ilGetFirst( VoidHand, listitem_t* );
void ilGetNext( VoidHand, listitem_t* );
```

Polymorphism

Polymorphism is the ability of objects to treat another group of objects generically. For example, say I wanted to be able to delete a list item without having to know whether the list was a simple list or an iterated list.

You can do this in C by carefully employing function pointers. Be careful, as with all pointers. You would store a pointer to the correct delete function in the data structure that represents the object at the time the list is created.

When the generic function **DeleteListItem()** is called, you would dereference and call the function pointed to by this variable.

What's Next?

In the next two chapters we will use the new framework we created in this chapter and apply it to the design of a calculator program for the Palm OS. This will allow you to take the framework for a major spin.

In the next chapter, we will apply user-interface design principles from Chapter 10 to design the calculator. We will discuss how to use shared libraries, MathLib in particular, and why these libraries can be advantageous.

12

CHAPTER 13

More About Creating User Interfaces

In this chapter and the next we'll create a complete working calculator application. Along the way we'll learn about how to use shared libraries, especially MathLib, as well as many details of application and user interface development.

Designing the Calculator

Next we're going to design and create our calculator form. It will have

◆ A field for displaying its number

◆ Ten buttons for the ten digits

◆ A decimal point (.) button

◆ A button to change the sign

◆ An Exponent button

◆ Plus (+), minus (–), multiply(×), and divide (÷) buttons

◆ An equals (=) button

◆ A Clear button

◆ A "Done" button that copies the result of your calculations to the Clipboard and closes the calculator.

The calculator will be able to add, subtract, multiply, and divide numbers up to $99,999,999 \times 10^{99}$.

In this chapter we will talk about the visual design of the calculator form and user-interface elements. We will talk about the functional design of the calculator in the next chapter.

The Visual Design

In this section we'll go through the visual design of this particular user interface. I'll sort of think out loud about the things I would consider in this specific case. Hopefully, my musings will give you some more ideas about how to constructively approach user-interface designs in a general sense. These musings are mostly based on the user interface design discussion in Chapter 7 and the Palm OS SDK documentation.

In designing this user interface, I would take into account that people are used to certain things when it comes to a calculator. For example, the digit buttons are organized a certain way. Also, there are some practical requirements that are also conventions, like having the field at the top of the form so that the user's hand does not block the field when pushing buttons. Also, there are needs based on the mechanical limitations of Palm Computing devices, like having buttons that are big enough to push easily with a finger so that the user doesn't need to pull out the stylus. These considerations yield a user interface that looks like a calculator: regular rows of buttons beneath a field displaying a number.

I'm happy bowing to tradition in this case because people generally don't complain too much about calculators (at least not around me). It seems to have been a fairly successful design. Don't be too incredibly quick to bow to tradition, however, especially if there is compelling evidence that the current conventions are unsatisfactory. For example, if we were designing a virtual VCR, I would question whether my design should be anything like most VCRs, because of all the complaints I've heard about them.

The next step is to get more specific about where the buttons should be with respect to one another. One thing that's helpful to look at is how often each of the buttons gets used. I'm sure that authoritative studies have been done on this. Instead, I will use my best guess. I want to point out that in real life this is probably the worst thing you can do with regard to good user interface design. Developers like you and me tend to be poor models for how most people want to use technology, and so we also tend to be poor guessers in this regard. In real life, I would do the research, or do a study, and generally make sure I understood what real users really want.

Anyway, here's my guess as to how often these buttons get used:

◆ **Digit Buttons**   Less than once per calculation on the average.

◆ **Decimal Point Button**   Maybe half the calculations.

◆ **Button to Change the Sign**   Probably about once per calculation.

◆ **Exponent Button**   Fairly rarely.

◆ **Plus, Minus, Multiply, and Divide Buttons**   One-fourth the calculations.

◆ **Equals Button**   Every calculation.

◆ **Clear Button**   Probably about every calculation.

◆ **"Done" Button**   Less than once every calculation.

Another thing worth looking at is the cost of a mis-press of a button. There's a high cost to pressing Clear or Done by accident, so they should probably be farther away from the major action than their frequency of use would warrant.

13

We have 20 buttons in this design. Based on the above considerations, my design is a grid five down by four across, as shown in Figure 13-1.

The next step is to calculate exactly where these controls should be placed on the form. The most important thing to know when placing this many buttons on a form is that the borders of Palm OS buttons are drawn around the buttons and take up one extra pixel on each side of the button (two if the button is bold). Thus, the closest to the upper-left of the form that you can place a button with a border is 1 across and 1 down.

We can use a field as our calculator display. There are several advantages in this over a label. We can have our field be a no-underline, uneditable, right-justified field. We can use a button to create a border around it so that it's not just raw numbers hanging out at the top of the screen. Fooling around in Constructor and displaying the form using my Hello code, I found that a field 20 pixels high works pretty well.

Given that a maximum size Palm Computing device form is (for now) 160 by 160 pixels, there are many ways to fit the buttons on. Here is what I came up with. I used a field 20 pixels high and buttons 23 pixels high and 35 pixels wide. I came to a decision about the height and width of the buttons by looking at how the pixels added up across the screen and down the screen. With this button height and width, the pixels count out across the form like this:

1 + 35 + 1 + 4 + 1 + 35 + 1 + 4 + 1 + 35 + 1 + 4 + 1 + 35 + 1
1   36   37 41 42 77   78 82 83 118 119 123 124 159 160

The pixels count out down the form like this:

20 + 3 + 1 + 23 + 1 + 3 + 1 + 23 + 1 + 3 + 1 + 23 + 1 + 3 + 1 + 23 + 1 + 3 + 1 + 23 + 1
20   23 24 47   48 51 52 75   76 79 80   103 104 107 108 131 132 135 136 159 160

7	8	9	/
4	5	6	*
1	2	3	–
+/–	.	0	+
Done	C	Exp	=

My particular button design

Figure 13-1.

This means that for the purposes of button placement, we have columns at 1, 42, 83, and 124, and we have rows at 24, 52, 80, 108, and 136.

Creating the Calculator

Now we will begin adding resources and code to create the calculator. First, you may want to save a copy of your current version of Calculator that we made last chapter. This will give you known working code to back up to if you need to.

On the CD there are four Calculator projects. Calculator CH. 12 is the first version that just had one OK button very much like the Hello application. Calculator 2 is the version as of the end of Chapter 8, with three forms and a menu bar. The version you'll have at the end of this chapter is Calculator CH. 13.

Additions to Calculator.rsrc

Now we will go into the resource file for our Calculator project and add the field and buttons to implement the user interface. We will add the field first, then all the buttons from left to right and from the top down. Here are the steps:

1. Launch Constructor. You do this by clicking the Start button and selecting Programs | CodeWarrior Lite for Palm OS | Constructor for Palm OS.

2. Edit Calculator's resource file. You do this by selecting File | Open Project File in Constructor. This brings up a file selection dialog box. Navigate to the Src folder of your Calculator project and select the file Calculator.rsrc.

3. Bring up the calc form by double-clicking on its entry in the Resource Type and Name list.

4. Delete the OK button that is there by selecting the button and pressing the DELETE key. You know the button is selected when there are four dots surrounding it and its attributes appear in the Layout Properties pane of the form editor control.

5. Create the field. You can do this by selecting Windows | Catalog, grabbing a field control off of the Catalog palette, and dropping it onto the form's Layout Appearance pane.

6. Edit the field's attributes in the following manner:
   Object Identifier = number
   Left Origin = 5
   Top Origin = 4

13

Width = 150
Height = 18
Editable = no check
Underline = no check
Left Justified = no check

All other attributes have their default value. You can change attributes by clicking on the field in the form's Layout Appearance pane. The field's attributes will appear in the Layout Properties pane. Click on the current value of an attribute to edit it.

7. Create the button that borders the field by dragging a button from the Catalog and dropping it on the form.

8. Edit the button's attributes as follows:

Object Identifier = fieldborder
Left Origin = 1
Top Origin = 1
Width = 158
Height = 18

Delete the word "OK" from the Label attribute. All other attributes stay at their default values.

9. Create the 7 button by dragging a button from the Catalog and dropping it on the form.

10. Edit the button's attributes as follows:

Object Identifier = seven
Left Origin = 1
Top Origin = 24
Width = 35
Height = 23
Font = Large
Label = 7

All other attributes stay at their default values.

11. To create the 8 button, select the 7 button. Press CTRL-C to copy it. Click on the form to select the form itself. Press CTRL-V to paste the copy of the 7 button.

12. Edit the button's attributes as follows:

Object Identifier = eight
Left Origin = 42
Top Origin = 24
Label = 8

All other attributes stay as they were for the 7 button.

13. Create the 9 button by clicking on the form to select the form. Then press CTRL-V to paste another copy of the 7 button. Edit the button's attributes as follows:

Object Identifier = nine
Left Origin = 83
Top Origin = 24
Label = 9

14. Create all the other buttons just like you created the 9 button. Make the following attribute changes to them:

Object Identifier	Left Origin	Top Origin	Label
Divide	124	24	/
Four	1	52	4
Five	42	52	5
Six	83	52	6
Multiply	124	52	*
One	1	80	1
Two	42	80	2
Three	83	80	3
Subtract	124	80	–
Changesign	1	108	+/–
Point	42	108	.
Zero	83	108	0
Add	124	108	+
Done	1	136	Done
Clear	42	136	C
Exponent	83	136	exp
Equals	124	136	=

15. Your form should look like the one in Figure 13-2.

Some people like the 0 button below the 2 button. Remember that this is your calculator and that you should put the buttons where you want them.

13

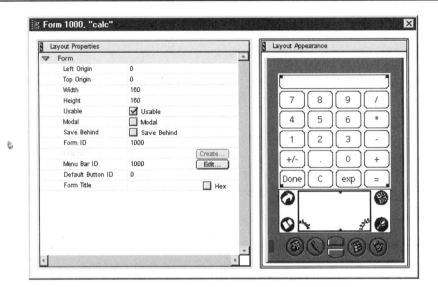

What your
calc form
should look
like now

Figure 13-2.

As long as you've given them the names in the table above, everything else
will work out.

I'm not completely happy with the name of the Done button. Ideally, your
user should know for sure whether something is going to displace what's on
the Clipboard. Perhaps "Clip 'n' Die" would be a more descriptive label.

Once you have added all the buttons, save your calculator form.

Creating an Alert

Select Alerts from the resource types list. Press CTRL-K to create a new alert.
Name it MathLibError. Double-click it to open it. Modify the Alert Type
attribute to Error and the Title attribute to Error also. For the message, write
something like "This application requires the free shared library MathLib to
be installed on your Palm device. Please install it." When you are done your
alert should look like the one in Figure 13-3.

Creating Application Icons

Follow the directions in Chapter 4 for creating large and small application
icons for your calculator. When you're done, save Calculator.rsrc and exit
Constructor.

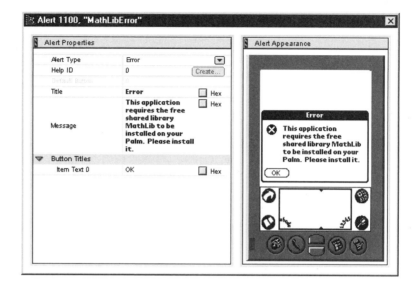

Figure 13-3.

Additions to fcalc.c

Now it's time to add code to fcalc.c to handle the new events from all those
new buttons. Launch the CodeWarrior IDE by clicking Start and selecting
Programs | CodeWarrior Lite for Palm OS | CodeWarrior IDE. Open your
Calculator project by selecting File | Open Recent | Calculator. Double-click
on fcalc.c in the project's file list to open it for editing.

Change your version of fcalc.c to match the new version described below. I'll
go through the new code line by line, pointing out and explaining additions
and changes.

```
//////////////////////////////////////////////////////////////////////
// fcalc.c
// Code for the "calc" form.
// Copyright (c) 2000, Robert Mykland.  All rights reserved.
//////////////////////////////////////////////////////////////////////
```

13

```
/////////////
// Includes //
/////////////

#include "app.h"     // The definitions for this application
#include "calc.h"    // Calculator guts
```

Here we see a new include file, calc.h. It contains the definitions for another module, calc.c, which handles the calculation operations of the calculator in a platform-independent manner. Since this module is only used by fcalc.c, the include file is placed here instead of in app.h. This underscores the fact that fcalc.c is the only module using calc.c's functions.

```
/////////////////////
// Global Prototypes //
/////////////////////

void    calcInit( void );
void    calcStop( void );
Boolean calcFormEventHandler( EventPtr spEvent );
void    calcDisplay( char* cpNumber );
void    calcSignalError( void );
```

Joining **calcFormEventHandler()** are four new global functions. The functions **calcInit()** and **calcStop()** set up and destroy new resources local to fcalc.c. When we get to app.h you will see how these are placed in the **appInit()** and **appStop()** macros that are called in **PilotMain()**. The function **calcDisplay()** allows callers to modify the contents of the calculator display. The function **calcSignalError()** allows callers to signal an error via the user interface. Note that the user interface is encapsulated but provided to the application as a whole with these two functions.

```
/////////////////////
// Local Variables //
/////////////////////

static char    cComma;    // The comma symbol we're using
static char    cPoint;    // The decimal point we're using
static Handle  hNumber;   // Handle to the number in our edit
                          // field
```

Here are the variables shared by the functions in this module. Note that they are declared static so that code outside this module cannot touch them. This significantly reduces the number of places you'll have to look if one of these variables is getting modified unexpectedly. The char variables *cComma* and *cPoint* will contain the characters we should use for the thousands separator and the decimal point. Users can adjust these settings in the Formats form of the Palm device's system preferences. Below you will see how we read these preferences and respond to them in our user interface.

The other variable is the handle to the chunk of memory holding the number for our calculator display. This is similar in nature and use to the handle *hText* that you saw in the FieldToy application.

The Function calcInit()

```
////////////////////////
// Global Functions //
////////////////////////

//------------------------------------------------------------------
void calcInit(
//------------------------------------------------------------------
// Initializes this module.
//------------------------------------------------------------------
void )
//------------------------------------------------------------------
{
    DWord   dChoice;
    char*   cpNumber;
```

Here is the beginning of the first global function in the module, **calcInit()**. It takes no parameters and returns nothing. The variable *dChoice* will be used to store the choice of thousands separator and decimal point provided by Palm OS. The variable will be used to initialize the chunk of memory we allocate for our field.

Finding and Loading a Dynamic Library

```
// Find MathLib
if( (SysLibFind( MathLibName, &MathLibRef ) == 0) ||
        SysLibLoad( LibType, MathLibCreator, &MathLibRef ) ||
        MathLibOpen( MathLibRef, MathLibVersion ) )
{
    FrmAlert( MathLibErrorAlert );
    hardStop( 0 );
}
```

13

The guts of the calculator will use a free shared library called MathLib to do floating point mathematics. We will talk more about MathLib later. Here in this code you see how we find, load, and initialize MathLib. You can use **SysLibFind()** to find any shared library that has been installed. Right now MathLib is the most popular shared library you might want to find. **SysLibLoad()** creates a connection to the library. **MathLibOpen()** is a function call provided by MathLib that it uses to initialize itself. **SysLibFind()** and **SysLibLoad()** are Palm OS functions. You can find their definitions in the System Manager section of the Palm OS reference Reference.pdf.

If MathLib can't be successfully found, loaded, or opened for some reason, we pop up our MathLibError alert using a call to **FrmAlert()**. We then bail out of our application by calling **hardStop()**, which puts us back in **PilotMain()**. The function **FrmAlert()** is part of the Form Manager (Ref1.pdf).

Initializing a Memory Chunk

```
// Allocate our field chunk
hNumber = MemHandleNew( HNUMBER_SIZE );

// Lock the memory, get the pointer
cpNumber = MemHandleLock( hNumber );

// Initialize it
StrCopy( cpNumber, "0" );

// Unlock the field's memory
MemHandleUnlock( hNumber );
```

Here are four function calls familiar to us from FieldToy. Here we use three Memory Manager functions (Ref3.pdf) to allocate and initialize the memory chunk we will use for the calculator display field. The function **MemHandleNew()** allocates the memory. The function **MemHandleLock()** keeps Palm OS from relocating it while we're using it. The function **StrCopy()** (from the String Manager) is used to copy an initial zero into the display chunk. Finally, we unlock the chunk with a call to **MemHandleUnlock()**.

Getting and Manipulating System Preferences

```
// Get the number format
dChoice = PrefGetPreference( prefNumberFormat );
```

```
    // Handle the number format
    switch( dChoice )
    {
        default:
            cComma = ',';
            cPoint = '.';
        break;

        case nfPeriodComma:
            cComma = '.';
            cPoint = ',';
        break;

        case nfSpaceComma:
            cComma = ' ';
            cPoint = ',';
        break;

        case nfApostrophePeriod:
            cComma = '\'';
            cPoint = '.';
        break;

        case nfApostropheComma:
            cComma = '\'';
            cPoint = ',';
        break;
    }

    // We're done
    return;
}
```

At the end of our initialization routine is the code that reads the system preferences that describe how numbers should be displayed. We call **PrefGetPreference()** to get the system preference we're after and then use a switch statement to fill in our local static variables *cComma* and *cPoint* with the appropriate values. **PrefGetPreference()** is one of the system preferences functions.

The Function calcStop(): Cleaning Up After MathLib

```
//------------------------------------------------------------------
void calcStop(
```

13

```
//-----------------------------------------------------------------
// Cleans up stuff from this module.
//-----------------------------------------------------------------
void )
//-----------------------------------------------------------------
{
    UInt uiUseCount;

    // Close MathLib
    MathLibClose( MathLibRef, &uiUseCount );
    if( uiUseCount == 0 )
        SysLibRemove( MathLibRef );

    // Free the number field chunk
    MemHandleFree( hNumber );

    // We're done
    return;
}
```

Next, add the function **calcStop()**, the companion function to **calcInit()**. First, we close our connection to MathLib. MathLib keeps track of how many applications are sharing it. You use the count it returns to you to decide whether you should remove this shared resource. Since Palm OS is pretty much a single-tasking operating system at the moment, you will almost always make this call. **SysLibRemove()** is a reserved function, but the maker of MathLib recommends that you call it in this case.

After this we use **MemHandleFree()** (from the Memory Manager) to free the chunk we use for our calculator display.

Modifications to calcFormEventHandler

```
//-----------------------------------------------------------------
Boolean calcFormEventHandler(
//-----------------------------------------------------------------
// Handles events for this form.
// Returns true if it fully handled the event.
//-----------------------------------------------------------------
EventPtr spEvent )
//-----------------------------------------------------------------
{
    // Handle the event
```

```
switch( spEvent->eType )
{
```

Here is our good old **calcFormEventHandler()** function. Nothing changes from last chapter up to this point in the call. From here on the function is completely rewritten.

Initializing a Field

```
// The form is opened
case frmOpenEvent:
{
    FormPtr       spForm;
    Word          wIndex;
    FieldPtr      spField;
    ControlPtr    spButton;
    char          caPoint[2];

    // Get the field
    spForm = FrmGetActiveForm();
    wIndex = FrmGetObjectIndex( spForm, calcNumberField );
    spField = FrmGetObjectPtr( spForm, wIndex );

    // Draw the field
    FldSetTextHandle( spField, hNumber );
    FldDrawField( spField );
```

The event frmOpenEvent happens right after a form is loaded. We tap into the event here to initialize our form at a point after we know it has been loaded. First, we get a pointer to the field using the three Form Manager calls **FrmGetActiveForm()**, **FrmGetObjectIndex()**, and **FrmGetObjectPtr()**. Then we set the text handle and display the field using the Field Manager calls **FldSetTextHandle()** and **FldDrawField()**. Note that every time you draw a field, you must call **FldSetTextHandle()** even if you're using the same chunk, because Palm OS recalculates the size and positioning of the field text in this call.

For example, if you enter **123** into the finished calculator and had no intervening calls to **FldSetTextHandle()**, only a 1 would show up on your display in place of the original 0. This is because the field's display length was originally one digit long and it won't get recalculated until you call **FldSetTextHandle()** or a similar function.

13

Changing a Button Label

```
        // Get the decimal point button
        wIndex = FrmGetObjectIndex( spForm, calcPointButton );
        spButton = FrmGetObjectPtr( spForm, wIndex );

        // Draw the decimal point button
        caPoint[0] = cPoint;
        caPoint[1] = '\0';
        CtlSetLabel( spButton, caPoint );
    }
    break;
```

Since Palm OS allows you to change the look of numbers on the fly, we are compelled in the ideal case to dynamically modify our user interface to reflect these changes. This extends to the character we use to represent the decimal point on the decimal point button.

To initialize the button face, we first get the pointer to the button's structure using the now familiar calls to **FrmGetObjectIndex()** and FrmGetObjectPtr() (Form Manager, Ref1.pdf). Form a string using the character for the decimal point. Call **CtlSetLabel()** to change the label and redraw the button (Control Manager, Ref1.pdf).

Handling Events for Multiple Buttons on a Form

```
        // A control was selected
        case ctlSelectEvent:
        {
            // Handle the different buttons
            switch( spEvent->data.ctlSelect.controlID )
            {
                case calcAddButton:
                    calcAdd();
                break;

                case calcChangesignButton:
                    calcChangeSign();
                break;

                case calcClearButton:
                    calcClear();
                break;
```

```
case calcDivideButton:
    calcDivide();
break;

case calcEightButton:
    calcAppend( 8 );
break;

case calcEqualsButton:
    calcEquals();
break;

case calcExponentButton:
    calcExponent();
break;

case calcFieldborderButton:
    // Ignore this button
    return( true );

case calcFiveButton:
    calcAppend( 5 );
break;

case calcFourButton:
    calcAppend( 4 );
break;

case calcMultiplyButton:
    calcMultiply();
break;

case calcNineButton:
    calcAppend( 9 );
break;

case calcOneButton:
    calcAppend( 1 );
break;

case calcPointButton:
    calcPoint();
break;
```

13

```
        case calcSevenButton:
            calcAppend( 7 );
        break;

        case calcSixButton:
            calcAppend( 6 );
        break;

        case calcSubtractButton:
            calcSubtract();
        break;

        case calcThreeButton:
            calcAppend( 3 );
        break;

        case calcTwoButton:
            calcAppend( 2 );
        break;

        case calcZeroButton:
            calcAppend( 0 );
        break;
```

To determine which button we're looking at, we look at the controlID
member variable of the event structure. The event structure is defined
in the Palm OS include file Events.h. Constructor defines the ID numbers
in our own Calculator_res.h file. In response to these button selections,
we call a number of functions. These are functions that appear in the
platform-independent module calc.c. The calcFieldborderButton is an
exception because we just want to ignore it. Using this method, it will
beep but not flash when selected. If we wanted to get rid of the beep, we
would have to put code into main.c that would filter out the event before
it got to the **FrmDispatchEvent()** call.

Leaving Results on the Clipboard

```
        case calcDoneButton:
        {
            FormPtr     spForm;
            Word        wIndex;
            FieldPtr    spField;
```

```
                                // Get the field
                                spForm = FrmGetActiveForm();
                                wIndex = FrmGetObjectIndex( spForm,
                                        calcNumberField );
                                spField = FrmGetObjectPtr( spForm, wIndex );

                                // Select all
                                FldSetSelection( spField, 0,
                                        FldGetTextLength( spField ) );

                                // Copy to clipboard
                                FldCopy( spField );

                                // Exit the application
                                softStop();
                        }
                        break;
                }
        }
        break;
```

In the case of the Done button, we want to exit and leave the number on the
display on the Clipboard. To do this, we get the field pointer as before. We
use **FldSetSelection()** and **FldGetTextLength()** (Field Manager) to select
the entire contents of the field. We then call another Field Manager function,
FldCopy(), to copy the selection to the Clipboard. Finally we use **softStop()**
to put a stop event on the event queue and exit our application.

```
                // A menu item was selected
                case menuEvent:

                        // Handle the menu event
                        calcFormMenuEventHandler( spEvent );
                        return( true );
        }

        // We're done
        return( false );
}
```

13

Menu events are handled as before. This ends our new version of
calcFormEventHandler().

The Function calcDisplay()

```
//--------------------------------------------------------------
void calcDisplay(
//--------------------------------------------------------------
// Displays the number in the field.
// IMPORTANT: A leading + or - sign is assumed for all numbers passed
// to this function!
//--------------------------------------------------------------
char* cpNumber )
//--------------------------------------------------------------
{
    char*       cpSrc;
    Word        wIntSize;
    char*       cpDest;
    char        caNumber[40];
    char*       cpText;
    FormPtr     spForm;
    Word        wIndex;
    FieldPtr    spField;
```

Here is the beginning of **calcDisplay()**. The function accepts a floating-point number in conventional C string form, something like +123456.78e-4. It puts in thousands separators and a decimal point of the correct type. There is a Palm OS String Manager function, **StrLocalizeNumber()**, which changes the regular commas and decimal point to their correct values, but it requires the number to already have thousands separators in it. Since we have to put thousands separators in, we might as well do the whole job and have that much more control of the display of the number.

The function **calcDisplay()** has two parts. The first part reconstructs in exactly the way we desire the number we are passed in string form. The second part actually displays the string we produce.

Inserting Thousands Separators in a Floating-point Number

The top half of **calcDisplay()** reconstructs the floating-point number we are given, adding thousands separators and other small details.

```
// Find the end of the number and determine exponent and decimal
wIntSize = -1;  // To account for leading sign
for( cpSrc = cpNumber; *cpSrc != '\0'; cpSrc++ )
{
```

```
        if( (*cpSrc == '.') || (*cpSrc == 'e') )
            break;
        wIntSize++;
    }
```

This first loop counts the number of integer digits so that we know how many thousands separators to add and where to add them. Note that a leading + or – sign is assumed for all numbers passed to this function.

```
    // Start source and destination
    cpSrc = cpNumber;
    cpDest = caNumber;

    // Handle the leading sign
    if( *cpSrc++ == '-' )
        *cpDest++ = '-';
```

Here we start out the char pointers that will serve as our source and destination pointers for copying characters from the old string to our new, improved string. Next we copy the leading sign if it is negative.

```
    // Copy the integer part
    while( wIntSize )
    {
        do
        {
            *cpDest++ = *cpSrc++;
            wIntSize--;
        } while( (wIntSize % 3) != 0 );
        if( wIntSize == 0 )
            break;
        *cpDest++ = cComma;
    }
```

In this tricky bit of code we count down through the integer digits, inserting thousands separators in front of every group of three digits. With zero digits left, we jump out before adding another thousands separator.

13

```
    // Do the decimal point
    if( *cpSrc == '.' )
    {
        cpSrc++;
        *cpDest++ = cPoint;
```

```
    }

    // Copy the decimal part
    while( *cpSrc && (*cpSrc != 'e') )
        *cpDest++ = *cpSrc++;
```

In this part of the function we copy the correct decimal point symbol in place of ".". After that, we copy the fractional part of the number straight across.

```
    // Build up the exponent if any
    if( *cpSrc == 'e' )
    {
        *cpDest++ = ' ';
        while( *cpSrc )
            *cpDest++ = *cpSrc++;
    }

    // Zero delimit the string
    *cpDest = '\0';
```

Next, we copy the exponent over, leading it with a space. Finally, we zero delimit the string. This concludes the string-building part of the function.

Changing the Text in a Field

```
    // Change the string in the handle
    // Lock the memory, get the pointer
    cpText = MemHandleLock( hNumber );

    // Initialize it
    StrCopy( cpText, caNumber );

    // Unlock the field's memory
    MemHandleUnlock( hNumber );

    // Get the field pointer
    spForm = FrmGetActiveForm();
    wIndex = FrmGetObjectIndex( spForm, calcNumberField );
    spField = FrmGetObjectPtr( spForm, wIndex );

    // Refresh the field
    FldSetTextHandle( spField, hNumber );
```

```
    FldDrawField( spField );

    // We're done
    return;
}
```

Here we perform the familiar task of copying a new string into the memory chunk we're using for the field. After that we retrieve the field pointer and refresh the field pretty much as we did in response to the frmOpenEvent.

The Function calcSignalError()

```
//-------------------------------------------------------------
void calcSignalError(
//-------------------------------------------------------------
// Signals an error.
//-------------------------------------------------------------
void )
//-------------------------------------------------------------
{
    SndPlaySystemSound( sndError );
    return;
}
```

To signal an error, we play the system error sound using a call to **SndPlaySystemSound()**. This Sound Manager function is documented in Ref2.pdf.

Additions to fcalc.h

Since we have added global functions to fcalc.c, we need to add them to fcalc.h so that they can be used everywhere. A complete listing of the modified fcalc.h appears below.

```
#ifndef FCALC_H
#define FCALC_H
////////////////////////////////////////////////////////////////
// fcalc.h
// Definitions for the "calc" form.
// Copyright (c) 1999, Robert Mykland.  All rights reserved.
////////////////////////////////////////////////////////////////
```

13

```
//////////////////////
// Global Prototypes //
//////////////////////

void calcInit( void );
void calcStop( void );
Boolean calcFormEventHandler( EventPtr spEvent );
void calcDisplay( char* cpNumber );
void calcSignalError( void );

#endif      // FCALC_H
```

As usual, this file contains a copy of the prototypes for fcalc.c's global functions.

The calc.h Module

In the next chapter we will add a generic bit of code that runs the calculator. For now, create an include file named calc.h to stub out these functions. Function stubs allow you to compile, link, and debug what you've written so far even if your application is not complete. The stubs below are replacing soon-to-be function calls with macros that just display a certain number. Another way to stub out functions that is quite popular is to create the new module (in our case calc.c) and functions, but just put test code in them (like our calls to **calcDisplay()**).

```
#ifndef CALC_H
#define CALC_H
////////////////////////////////////////////////////////////////////////////
// calc.h
// Definitions for the generic calculation routines.
// Copyright (c) 1999, Robert Mykland.  All rights reserved.
////////////////////////////////////////////////////////////////////////////

//////////////////////
// Global Prototypes // to be...
//////////////////////

#define calcAdd()               calcDisplay( "+1.2345678e+90" )
#define calcAppend(x)           calcDisplay( "-12.345678e+90" )
#define calcChangeSign()        calcDisplay( "+123.45678e-90" )
#define calcClear()             calcDisplay( "-1234.5678e-90" )
```

```
#define calcDivide()        calcDisplay( "+12345.678e+90" )
#define calcEquals()        calcDisplay( "-123456.78e+90" )
#define calcExponent()      calcDisplay( "+1234567.8e-90" )
#define calcMultiply()      calcDisplay( "-12345678.e-90" )
#define calcPoint()         calcDisplay( "+1.2345678e+90" )
#define calcSubtract()      calcDisplay( "-12.345678e+90" )


//////////////////////
// Global Constants //
//////////////////////


#define MAX_NUMBER_SIZE 40

#endif          // CALC_H
```

All the functions to be contained in calc.c are stubbed out in this version. Instead, they contain a variety of calls that will allow us to test the **calcDisplay()** function.

Additions to app.h

```
//////////////
// Includes //
//////////////

#include <Pilot.h>              // All the Palm OS includes
#include "MathLib.h"            // Definitions for MathLib
#include "Calculator_res.h"     // Resource definitions
#include "fabout.h"             // Definitions for the "about" form
#include "fcalc.h"              // Definitions for the "calc" form
#include "fprefs.h"             // Definitions for the "prefs" form
#include "main.h"               // Definitions for the main entry point
#include "moptions.h"           // Definitions for the "options" menu
```

Here we additionally include MathLib.h, which contains definitions for the MathLib math functions.

```
// This defines the macro that initializes the app
#define appInit() \
{ \
    calcInit(); \
}
```

13

```
// This defines the macro that cleans up the app
#define appStop() \
{\
    calcStop();\
}
```

Here we add macro functions to the previously empty definitions for
appInit() and **appStop()**. Any modules that need to have initialization or
cleanup code called will add function calls into these macros.

Adding MathLib

MathLib is in self-extracting executable form on the CD (MathLib.exe).
Extract it into a convenient folder by double-clicking on the icon and
following the instructions.

In the folder you extracted you'll find everything you need to use MathLib,
including documentation in HTML form. Copy MathLib.c and MathLib.h
into the Src folder of your Calculator project. Add MathLib.c to your project
and put it with your libraries, considering it is basically an import library.

You'll also have to install MathLib.prc on to your Palm device. Use your Palm
Install Tool and HotSync to do this. Check to make sure it has been transferred
by selecting App | Info and looking in the list of items.

The first time you test your app, you may want to leave MathLib off your
Palm device in order to test the MathLibError alert.

Debugging

Download and run your application. You can test **calcDisplay()** by pressing
various buttons. Check to see that the Done button exits the application,
leaving the number currently displayed on the Clipboard. Change the values
of the thousands separator and the decimal point in the system preferences
and make sure these changes are reflected in the number and on the face of
the decimal point button. Lastly, make sure you can still bring up the about
form and the prefs form.

What's Next?

In the next chapter we'll design and build the guts of the calculator, learning
how to port generic C code over to Palm devices in the process.

Listings

Here's an uninterrupted copy of the new fcalc.c:

```c
////////////////////////////////////////////////////////////////////
// fcalc.c
// Code for the "calc" form.
// Copyright (c) 1999, Robert Mykland.  All rights reserved.
////////////////////////////////////////////////////////////////////


//////////////
// Includes //
//////////////

#include "app.h"     // The definitions for this application
#include "calc.h"    // Calculator guts

//////////////////////
// Global Prototypes //
//////////////////////

void    calcInit( void );
void    calcStop( void );
Boolean calcFormEventHandler( EventPtr spEvent );
void    calcDisplay( char* cpNumber );
void    calcSignalError( void );

////////////////////
// Local Variables //
////////////////////

static char     cComma;     // The comma symbol we're using
static char     cPoint;     // The decimal point we're using
static Handle   hNumber;    // Handle to the number in our edit field

////////////////////
// Global Functions //
////////////////////

//-----------------------------------------------------------------
void calcInit(
//-----------------------------------------------------------------
// Initializes this module.
//-----------------------------------------------------------------
void )
//-----------------------------------------------------------------
```

13

```
{
    Dword    dChoice;
    char*    cpNumber;

    // Find MathLib
    if( (SysLibFind( MathLibName, &MathLibRef ) == 0) ||
            SysLibLoad( LibType, MathLibCreator, &MathLibRef ) ||
            MathLibOpen( MathLibRef, MathLibVersion ) )
    {
        FrmAlert( MathLibErrorAlert );
        hardStop();
    }

    // Allocate our field chunk
    hNumber = MemHandleNew( MAX_NUMBER_SIZE );

    // Lock the memory, get the pointer
    cpNumber = MemHandleLock( hNumber );

    // Initialize it
    StrCopy( cpNumber, "0" );

    // Unlock the field's memory
    MemHandleUnlock( hNumber );

    // Get the number format
    dChoice = PrefGetPreference( prefNumberFormat );

    // Handle the number format
    switch( dChoice )
    {
        default:
            cComma = ',';
            cPoint = '.';
        break;

        case nfPeriodComma:
            cComma = '.';
            cPoint = ',';
        break;

        case nfSpaceComma:
            cComma = ' ';
            cPoint = ',';
        break;
```

```
            case nfApostrophePeriod:
                cComma = '\'';
                cPoint = '.';
            break;

            case nfApostropheComma:
                cComma = '\'';
                cPoint = ',';
            break;
    }

    // We're done
    return;
}

//-------------------------------------------------------------------
void calcStop(
//-------------------------------------------------------------------
// Cleans up stuff from this module.
//-------------------------------------------------------------------
void )
//-------------------------------------------------------------------
{
    UInt uiUseCount;

    // Close MathLib
    MathLibClose( MathLibRef, &uiUseCount );
    if( uiUseCount == 0 )
        SysLibRemove( MathLibRef );

    // Free the number field chunk
    MemHandleFree( hNumber );

    // We're done
    return;
}

//-------------------------------------------------------------------
Boolean calcFormEventHandler(
//-------------------------------------------------------------------
// Handles events for this form.
// Returns true if it fully handled the event.
//-------------------------------------------------------------------
EventPtr spEvent )
//-------------------------------------------------------------------
{
```

13

```
// Handle the event
switch( spEvent->eType )
{
    // The form is opened
    case frmOpenEvent:
    {
        FormPtr      spForm;
        Word         wIndex;
        FieldPtr     spField;
        ControlPtr   spButton;
        char         caPoint[2];

        // Get the field
        spForm = FrmGetActiveForm();
        wIndex = FrmGetObjectIndex( spForm, calcNumberField );
        spField = FrmGetObjectPtr( spForm, wIndex );

        // Draw the field
        FldSetTextHandle( spField, hNumber );
        FldDrawField( spField );

        // Get the decimal point button
        wIndex = FrmGetObjectIndex( spForm, calcPointButton );
        spButton = FrmGetObjectPtr( spForm, wIndex );

        // Draw the decimal point button
        caPoint[0] = cPoint;
        caPoint[1] = '\0';
        CtlSetLabel( spButton, caPoint );
    }
    break;

    // A control was selected
    case ctlSelectEvent:
    {
        // Handle the different buttons
        switch( spEvent->data.ctlSelect.controlID )
        {
            case calcAddButton:
                calcAdd();
            break;

            case calcChangesignButton:
                calcChangeSign();
            break;
```

```
case calcClearButton:
    calcClear();
break;

case calcDivideButton:
    calcDivide();
break;

case calcDoneButton:
{
    FormPtr      spForm;
    Word         wIndex;
    FieldPtr     spField;

    // Get the field
    spForm = FrmGetActiveForm();
    wIndex = FrmGetObjectIndex( spForm,
            calcNumberField );
    spField = FrmGetObjectPtr( spForm, wIndex );

    // Select all
    FldSetSelection( spField, 0,
            FldGetTextLength( spField ) );

    // Copy to clipboard
    FldCopy( spField );

    // Exit the application
    softStop( 0 );
}
break;

case calcEightButton:
    calcAppend( 8 );
break;

case calcEqualsButton:
    calcEquals();
break;

case calcExponentButton:
    calcExponent();
break;
```

13

```
case calcFieldborderButton:
    // Ignore this button
    return( true );

case calcFiveButton:
    calcAppend( 5 );
break;

case calcFourButton:
    calcAppend( 4 );
break;

case calcMultiplyButton:
    calcMultiply();
break;

case calcNineButton:
    calcAppend( 9 );
break;

case calcOneButton:
    calcAppend( 1 );
break;

case calcPointButton:
    calcPoint();
break;

case calcSevenButton:
    calcAppend( 7 );
break;

case calcSixButton:
    calcAppend( 6 );
break;

case calcSubtractButton:
    calcSubtract();
break;

case calcThreeButton:
    calcAppend( 3 );
break;

case calcTwoButton:
    calcAppend( 2 );
break;
```

```
                        case calcZeroButton:
                            calcAppend( 0 );
                        break;
                }
            }
            break;

            // A menu item was selected
            case menuEvent:

                // Handle the menu event
                calcFormMenuEventHandler( spEvent );
                return( true );
        }

        // We're done
        return( false );
    }

    //-----------------------------------------------------------------
    void calcDisplay(
    //-----------------------------------------------------------------
    // Displays the number in the field.
    // IMPORTANT: A leading + or - sign is assumed for all numbers passed
    // to this function!
    //-----------------------------------------------------------------
    char* cpNumber )
    //-----------------------------------------------------------------
    {
        char*       cpSrc;
        Word        wIntSize;
        char*       cpDest;
        char        caNumber[40];
        char*       cpText;
        FormPtr     spForm;
        Word        wIndex;
        FieldPtr    spField;

        // Find the end of the number and determine exponent and decimal
        wIntSize = -1;  // To account for leading sign
        for( cpSrc = cpNumber; *cpSrc != '\0'; cpSrc++ )
        {
            if( (*cpSrc == '.') || (*cpSrc == 'e') )
                break;
            wIntSize++;
        }
```

13

```
// Start source and destination
cpSrc = cpNumber;
cpDest = caNumber;

// Handle the leading sign
if( *cpSrc++ == '-' )
    *cpDest++ = '-';

// Copy the integer part
while( wIntSize )
{
    do
    {
        *cpDest++ = *cpSrc++;
        wIntSize--;
    } while( (wIntSize % 3) != 0 );
    if( wIntSize == 0 )
        break;
    *cpDest++ = cComma;
}

// Do the decimal point
if( *cpSrc == '.' )
{
    cpSrc++;
    *cpDest++ = cPoint;
}

// Copy the decimal part
while( *cpSrc && (*cpSrc != 'e') )
    *cpDest++ = *cpSrc++;

// Build up the exponent if any
if( *cpSrc == 'e' )
{
    *cpDest++ = ' ';
    while( *cpSrc )
        *cpDest++ = *cpSrc++;
}

// Zero delimit the string
*cpDest = '\0';

// Change the string in the handle
// Lock the memory, get the pointer
```

```
        cpText = MemHandleLock( hNumber );

        // Initialize it
        StrCopy( cpText, caNumber );

        // Unlock the field's memory
        MemHandleUnlock( hNumber );

        // Get the field pointer
        spForm = FrmGetActiveForm();
        wIndex = FrmGetObjectIndex( spForm, calcNumberField );
        spField = FrmGetObjectPtr( spForm, wIndex );

        // Refresh the field
        FldSetTextHandle( spField, hNumber );
        FldDrawField( spField );

        // We're done
        return;
    }


    //-------------------------------------------------------------------
    void calcSignalError(
    //-------------------------------------------------------------------
    // Signals an error.
    //-------------------------------------------------------------------
    void )
    //-------------------------------------------------------------------
    {
        SndPlaySystemSound( sndError );
        return;
    }
```

Here's an uninterrupted version of the current app.h:

```
#ifndef APP_H
#define APP_H
///////////////////////////////////////////////////////////////////////
// app.h
// Definitions for the application.
// Copyright (c) 1999, Robert Mykland.  All rights reserved.
///////////////////////////////////////////////////////////////////////


/////////////////
// Includes //
/////////////////
```

13

```
#include <Pilot.h>          // All the Palm OS includes
#include "MathLib.h"        // Definitions for MathLib
#include "Calculator_res.h" // Resource definitions
#include "fabout.h"         // Definitions for the "about" form
#include "fcalc.h"          // Definitions for the "calc" form
#include "fprefs.h"         // Definitions for the "prefs" form
#include "main.h"           // Definitions for the main entry point
#include "moptions.h"       // Definitions for the "options" menu


////////////////////////////
// Definitions for fabout.c //
////////////////////////////

// The menu event handler macro for the "about" form
#define aboutFormMenuEventHandler(spEvent)


////////////////////////////
// Definitions for fcalc.c //
////////////////////////////

// The menu event handler macro for the "calc" form
#define calcFormMenuEventHandler(spEvent) \
{ \
    optionsMenuEventHandler( spEvent ); \
}


////////////////////////////
// Definitions for fprefs.c //
////////////////////////////

// The menu event handler macro for the "prefs" form
#define prefsFormMenuEventHandler(spEvent)


////////////////////////////
// Definitions for main.c //
////////////////////////////

// The prototype for getEventHandler()
static FormEventHandlerPtr getEventHandler( Word );

// This creates the function getEventHandler,
// which returns the event handler for a given form
// in this application.
#define EVENT_HANDLER_LIST \
static FormEventHandlerPtr getEventHandler( Word wFormID )\
{ \
```

```
        switch( wFormID )\
        {\
            case AboutForm:\
                return( aboutFormEventHandler );\
            case CalcForm:\
                return( calcFormEventHandler );\
            case PrefsForm:\
                return( prefsFormEventHandler );\
        }\
        return( NULL );\
}

// This defines the macro that initializes the app
#define appInit() \
{\
    calcInit();\
}

// This defines the macro that cleans up the app
#define appStop() \
{\
    calcStop();\
}

// This application works on Palm OS 2.0 and above
#define ROM_VERSION_MIN ROM_VERSION_2

// Define the starting form
#define StartForm    CalcForm

/////////////////////////////////
// Definitions for moptions.c //
/////////////////////////////////

// Menu ID name conversions
#define OptionsAbout     OptionsAboutCalculator

#endif       // APP_H
```

CHAPTER 14

Porting to the Palm OS

In this chapter we will design and implement the number-crunching guts of the calculator. I will then describe a fairly non-portable ANSI C standard version of these guts. Then we will go through techniques for getting code like this to run under the Palm OS.

Designing the Calculator Guts

Before we write the code to work the calculator, we have to decide what the thing is going to do. A good way that I have found to think about these kinds of problems is to make a diagram containing the states of the program as boxes or bubbles and the events as arrows. The calculator problem is good practice for this kind of problem solving because it has far more states and state transitions than you would normally want in a user interface.

You can also make these diagrams in outline form, which might be clearer for you. Usually, I start out on paper and then put the states of the program in outline form once I start to understand how I want it to work. You should do this however it works best for you. I encourage you to make your own diagram and then compare it to mine. Figure 14-1 shows one possible state diagram for the calculator.

My original state diagram had a few other states like the Clear State and the Enter Second Number State, but once I had it all drawn out, I saw that these states could easily be collapsed into other states. This is very good stuff to figure out before you start coding, which is why I recommend state diagrams. For most user interfaces they are (or at least should be!) far simpler and quicker than this example.

The Rest of the Code

I've written my example code for the calculator guts in a way that will help me illustrate issues involving porting code that's written to the ANSI standard onto Palm devices. As such, there are portability mistakes I'm making throughout. See if you can spot them before we get to the section on porting the code.

For all states:

    Operator → Change –0 to +0 →
        Perform any pending operations and display the result → Store this operation →
        Ready State

    Equals → Change –0 to +0 → Perform any pending operations and display the result →
        Ready State

    Clear → Clear numbers and operators → Ready State

    Done → Copy the current display to the clipboard → Exit the application

Ready State: Displays the previous number.

    Zero → Display Zero → Ready State

    Other Number → Display the digit → Integer State

    Change Sign → Display negative zero → Ready State

    Decimal Point → Display zero point → Decimal State

    Exponent → Error beep → Ready State

Integer State: Displays an integer

    Number → If max number digits, just beep → Put this digit on the end → Integer State

    Change Sign → Reverse the sign of the integer → Integer State

    Decimal Point → Add a decimal point to the end → Decimal State

    Exponent → Add an e+0 to the end → Exponent Ready State

Decimal State: Displays a number with a decimal fraction

    Number → If max number digits, just beep → Put the digit on the end → Decimal State

    Change Sign → Change the sign of the number → Decimal State

    Decimal Point → Error beep → Decimal State

    Exponent → Add an e+0 to the end → Exponent Ready State

Exponent Ready State: Displays a number with the exponent e+0

    Zero → Exponent Ready State

    Other Number → Display the digit as the exponent → Exponent Entry State

    Change Sign → Change exponent to e–0 → Exponent Ready State

    Decimal Point → Error beep → Exponent Ready State

    Exponent → Error beep → Exponent Ready State

Exponent Entry State: Displays a number with an exponent

    Number → If max exponent digits, just beep → Put the digit on the exponent →
        Exponent Entry State

    Change Sign → Change the sign of the exponent → Exponent Entry State

    Decimal Point → Error beep → Exponent Entry State

    Exponent → Error beep → Exponent Entry State

One possible state diagram for the calculator

Figure 14-1.

14

A New calc.h

This calc.h will replace the dummy file we created in the last chapter so that we could test out the code we had written so far.

```c
#ifndef CALC_H
#define CALC_H
////////////////////////////////////////////////////////////////////
// calc.h
// Definitions for the generic calculation routines.
// Copyright (c) 1999, Robert Mykland.  All rights reserved.
////////////////////////////////////////////////////////////////////


/////////////////////////
// Global Prototypes //
/////////////////////////

void calcAdd( void );           // Queue an addition operation
void calcAppend( int );         // Append a digit
void calcChangeSign( void );    // Change the sign of the entry
void calcClear( void );         // Clear/reset the calculator
void calcDivide( void );        // Queue a division operation
void calcEquals( void );        // Finish the current operation
void calcExponent( void );      // Start gathering the exponent
void calcMultiply( void );      // Queue a multiplication operation
void calcPoint( void );         // Start gathering the fraction
void calcSubtract( void );      // Queue a subtraction operation

/////////////////////////
// Global Constants //
/////////////////////////

#define MAX_NUMBER_SIZE     40

#endif  // CALC_H
```

Now the file has turned into a number of pretty conventional prototypes.

Generic Code: calc.c

The file calc.c implements the functions prototyped in calc.h. I will breeze through a description of this code pretty quickly because none of it illustrates anything about Palm OS. In fact, this is all generic code that would run on any platform that supported ANSI C.

```c
////////////////////////////////////////////////////////////////////
// calc.c
// Implements a generic calculator.
// Copyright (c) 1999, Robert Mykland.  All rights reserved.
```

```
///////////////////////////////////////////////////////////////////

/////////////
// Includes //
/////////////

#include "app.h"    // The definitions for this application
#include "calc.h"   // The definitions for this module

////////////////////////
// Global Prototypes //
////////////////////////

void calcAdd( void );          // Queue an addition operation
void calcAppend( int );        // Append a digit
void calcChangeSign( void );   // Change the sign of the entry
void calcClear( void );        // Clear/reset the calculator
void calcDivide( void );       // Queue a division operation
void calcEquals( void );       // Finish the current operation
void calcExponent( void );     // Start gathering the exponent
void calcMultiply( void );     // Queue a multiplication operation
void calcPoint( void );        // Start gathering the fraction
void calcSubtract( void );     // Queue a subtraction operation

//////////////////////
// Local Prototypes //
//////////////////////

static double ca2n( char* );        // Converts ascii str to double
static void n2ca( double, char* );  // Changes a double to a string

//////////////////////
// Local Constants //
//////////////////////

#define MAX_DIGITS      8
#define MAX_EXP_DIGITS  2

enum {
    OPERATION_NONE = 0,
    OPERATION_ADD,
    OPERATION_DIVIDE,
    OPERATION_MULTIPLY,
    OPERATION_SUBTRACT
};

#define CALC_INITIAL_NUMBER    "+0"
#define CALC_INITIAL_EXPONENT  "e+0"
#define CALC_ZERO_SYMBOL       0x30

//////////////////////
// Local Variables //
//////////////////////
```

14

```
static char caNumber[MAX_NUMBER_SIZE] = CALC_INITIAL_NUMBER;
static int iDigitCount;
static int iOperator;
static double nOperand;
static int oExponent;
static int oFraction;
```

Above are the include files, prototypes, variable declarations, and so forth that are used in the functions below.

```
////////////////////////
// Global Functions //
////////////////////////

//------------------------------------------------------------------
void calcAdd(
//------------------------------------------------------------------
// Queues an add operation.
//------------------------------------------------------------------
void )
//------------------------------------------------------------------
{
    // Resolve any pending operations
    calcEquals();

    // Queue the operation
    iOperator = OPERATION_ADD;

    // We're done
    return;
}
```

This function does the state work for the add operator. The **calcEquals()** function internally handles any pending calculations, so we need not even check the state of the calculator here to handle the states the add operation travels to and from.

```
//------------------------------------------------------------------
void calcAppend(
//------------------------------------------------------------------
// Appends a digit to the entry.
//------------------------------------------------------------------
int iDigit )     // The digit to append
//------------------------------------------------------------------
{
    char caDigit[2];

    // If we are entering the exponent part
    if( oExponent )
    {
```

```
        // If the exponent digit count is at maximum, signal an error
        if( iDigitCount >= MAX_EXP_DIGITS )
        {
            calcSignalError();
            return;
        }
    }

    else
    // If we are entering the number part
    {
        // If the digit count is at maximum, then signal an error
        if( iDigitCount >= MAX_DIGITS )
        {
            calcSignalError();
            return;
        }
    }

    // Destroy leading zeroes
    if( (oFraction == false) && (iDigitCount < 2) &&
            (caNumber[1] == '0') )
        caNumber[1] = '\0';

    // Append the digit
    caDigit[0] = iDigit + CALC_ZERO_SYMBOL;
    caDigit[1] = '\0';
    strcat( caNumber, caDigit );

    // Increase the digit count if it wasn't a leading zero
    if( (oFraction == true) || (iDigitCount == 0) ||
            (caNumber[1] != '0') )
        iDigitCount++;

    // Display the new number
    calcDisplay( caNumber );
    return;
}
```

The function **calcAppend()** is one of the most complicated functions. It keeps track of whether we are entering a regular number or an exponent and acts accordingly.

```
//-------------------------------------------------------------------
void calcChangeSign(
//-------------------------------------------------------------------
// Changes the sign of the number or exponent.
//-------------------------------------------------------------------
void )
//-------------------------------------------------------------------
{
```

```
    int iPlace;

    // Find the last sign in the number
    for( iPlace = strlen( caNumber ) - 1; iPlace >= 0; iPlace-- )
    {
        // If it's a plus, change to minus
        if( caNumber[iPlace] == '+' )
        {
            caNumber[iPlace] = '-';
            break;
        }

        // If it's a minus, change to plus
        if( caNumber[iPlace] == '-' )
        {
            caNumber[iPlace] = '+';
            break;
        }
    }

    // Display the new number
    calcDisplay( caNumber );
    return;
}
```

This function, **calcChangeSign()**, is another one that keeps track of whether we are in the regular number or in the exponent. It is easiest here to just backtrack through the number to find the most recently entered sign. This is why a + or – is always stored in the number wherever a sign can be.

```
//----------------------------------------------------------------
void calcClear(
//----------------------------------------------------------------
// Clears/resets the calculator.
//----------------------------------------------------------------
void )
//----------------------------------------------------------------
{
    // Set our local variables in a default state
    strcpy( caNumber, CALC_INITIAL_NUMBER );
    iDigitCount = 0;
    iOperator = OPERATION_NONE;
    nOperand = 0.0;
    oExponent = false;
    oFraction = false;

    // Display the new number
    calcDisplay( caNumber );
    return;
}
```

This function puts us back in a known good state. This is a good function to debug first.

```
//----------------------------------------------------------------
void calcDivide(
//----------------------------------------------------------------
// Queues a divide operation.
//----------------------------------------------------------------
void )
//----------------------------------------------------------------
{
    // Resolve any pending operations
    calcEquals();

    // Queue the operation
    iOperator = OPERATION_DIVIDE;

    // We're done
    return;
}
```

This function is virtually identical to **calcAdd()**. All these operator functions look alike.

```
//----------------------------------------------------------------
void calcEquals(
//----------------------------------------------------------------
// Resolves a math operation.
//----------------------------------------------------------------
void )
//----------------------------------------------------------------
{
    double nOperand2;

    // If there is an entry
    if( iDigitCount > 0 )
        // Convert the entry to floating point
        nOperand2 = ca2n( caNumber );

    else
    // If there is no entry
        // The entry is the last operand
        nOperand2 = nOperand;

    // Perform the operation
    switch( iOperator )
    {
        case OPERATION_ADD:
            nOperand = nOperand + nOperand2;
```

14

```
        break;

        case OPERATION_DIVIDE:
            nOperand = nOperand / nOperand2;
        break;

        case OPERATION_MULTIPLY:
            nOperand = nOperand * nOperand2;
        break;

        case OPERATION_SUBTRACT:
            nOperand = nOperand - nOperand2;
        break;

        default:
            nOperand = nOperand2;
        break;
    }

    // Clear the operator
    iOperator = OPERATION_NONE;

    // Convert the result from floating point for display
    n2ca( nOperand, caNumber );

    // Display the new number
    calcDisplay( caNumber );

    // Reset the entry
    iDigitCount = 0;
    strcpy( caNumber, CALC_INITIAL_NUMBER );
    oExponent = false;
    oFraction = false;

    // We're done
    return;
}
```

Here's where the actual math operation takes place.

```
//------------------------------------------------------------------
void calcExponent(
//------------------------------------------------------------------
// Starts gathering the exponent.
//------------------------------------------------------------------
void )
//------------------------------------------------------------------
{
    // If we're not already doing the exponent
    if( (oExponent == false) &&
            // and if the number is nonzero
            (ca2n( caNumber ) != 0.0) )
```

```
    {
        // Set up the exponent part
        oExponent = true;
        iDigitCount = 0;
        strcat( caNumber, CALC_INITIAL_EXPONENT );

        // Display the new number
        calcDisplay( caNumber );
    }

    else
        // This was done in error
        calcSignalError();

    // We're done
    return;
}
```

This function responds to the exponent key. The modal variables set here mostly affect the operation of **calcAppend()**.

```
//----------------------------------------------------------------
void calcMultiply(
//----------------------------------------------------------------
// Queues a multiply operation.
//----------------------------------------------------------------
void )
//----------------------------------------------------------------
{
    // Resolve any pending operations
    calcEquals();

    // Queue the operation
    iOperator = OPERATION_MULTIPLY;

    // We're done
    return;
}
```

This looks just like add and divide above.

```
//----------------------------------------------------------------
void calcPoint(
//----------------------------------------------------------------
// Appends a decimal point to the entry.
//----------------------------------------------------------------
void )
//----------------------------------------------------------------
{
    // If we are not collecting the fractional part already
```

14

```
        if( (oFraction == false) &&
                // If we are not doing the exponent
                (oExponent == false) &&
                // If we are not maxed out on digits
                (iDigitCount != MAX_DIGITS) )
        {
            // If no digit has been entered, enter a zero
            if( iDigitCount == 0 )
                calcAppend( 0 );

            // Now we will have a fractional part
            oFraction = true;

            // Append the decimal point
            strcat( caNumber, "." );
        }

        else
            // This was done in error
            calcSignalError();

        // Display the new number
        calcDisplay( caNumber );
        return;
}
```

This function has a lot of the complexity **calcAppend()** had because it is also dealing with all the different states of entering numbers.

```
//------------------------------------------------------------------
void calcSubtract(
//------------------------------------------------------------------
// Queues a subtract operation.
//------------------------------------------------------------------
void )
//------------------------------------------------------------------
{
    // Resolve any pending operations
    calcEquals();

    // Queue the operation
    iOperator = OPERATION_SUBTRACT;

    // We're done
    return;
}
```

This function looks like add, divide, and multiply above.

```
/////////////////////////
// Local Functions //
```

```
//////////////////////

//-----------------------------------------------------------------
static double ca2n(
//-----------------------------------------------------------------
// Converts a decimal ascii string to a double.
//-----------------------------------------------------------------
char*    cpNumber )    // The string to convert
//-----------------------------------------------------------------
{
    double  nSign;
    int     oDecimal;
    int     iDivisor;
    int     iCount;
    char    caInt[MAX_DIGITS + 1];
    int     iNumber;
    double  nNumber;

    // Get any leading sign
    nSign = 1.0;
    if( *cpNumber == '+' )
        cpNumber++;
    if( *cpNumber == '-' )
    {
        nSign = -1.0;
        cpNumber++;
    }

    // Convert to an integer string
    oDecimal = false;
    iDivisor = 0;
    for( iCount = 0; (iCount <= MAX_DIGITS) && *cpNumber &&
            (*cpNumber != 'e'); iCount++ )
    {
        // Do the decimal point thing
        if( *cpNumber == '.' )
        {
            oDecimal = true;
            iCount--;
            cpNumber++;
            continue;
        }

        // If we are gathering the fraction
        if( oDecimal )
            iDivisor++;

        // Otherwise, copy the digit
        caInt[iCount] = *cpNumber++;
    }

    // Zero delimit the string
    caInt[iCount] = '\0';
```

14

```
    // Use atoi
    iNumber = atoi( caInt );

    // Convert to a double
    nNumber = nSign * (double)iNumber * pow( 10.0,
            -(double)iDivisor );

    // If there is an exponent
    if( *cpNumber == 'e' )
    {
        cpNumber++;

        // Get any leading sign
        nSign = 1.0;
        if( *cpNumber == '+' )
            cpNumber++;
        if( *cpNumber == '-' )
        {
            nSign = -1.0;
            cpNumber++;
        }

        // Convert to an integer string
        for( iCount = 0; (iCount <= MAX_EXP_DIGITS) && *cpNumber;
                iCount++ )
            caInt[iCount] = *cpNumber++;

        // Zero delimit the string
        caInt[iCount] = '\0';

        // Use atoi
        iNumber = atoi( caInt );

        // Multiply the number
        nNumber *= pow( 10.0, nSign * (double)iNumber );
    }

    // Return the number
    return( nNumber );
}
```

The above function converts an ASCII string number in our internal always-signed format to a double float. This is not the least math-intensive way to do this operation. This method is comparatively easy to follow. Understanding exactly how this function works is not essential to our future discourses.

```
//------------------------------------------------------------------
static void n2ca(
//------------------------------------------------------------------
```

```
// Converts a double to an ascii string.
//----------------------------------------------------------------
double    nNumber,     // The number to convert
char*     cpNumber )    // Storage for the converted number
//----------------------------------------------------------------
{
    double  nExp;
    int     iExp;
    int     iNumber;
    char    caInt[9];
    int     iZeroes;

    // Handle zero
    if( nNumber == 0.0 )
    {
        strcpy( cpNumber, CALC_INITIAL_NUMBER );
        return;
    }

    // Grab the sign
    *cpNumber = '+';
    if( nNumber < 0.0 )
    {
        nNumber = -nNumber;
        *cpNumber = '-';
    }
    cpNumber++;

    // Normalize
    nExp = log10( nNumber );
    iExp = (int)nExp;
    if( nExp < 0 )
        iExp--;
    iExp -= MAX_DIGITS - 1;
    nNumber /= pow( 10.0, (double)iExp );

    // Convert to an integer
    iNumber = (int)(nNumber + 0.5);

    // Convert to an integer string
    itoa( caInt, iNumber );

    // Count trailing zeroes
    for( iZeroes = 0; caInt[strlen( caInt ) - 1 - iZeroes] == '0';
            iZeroes++ )
        ;

    // Handle decimal notation
    if( (iExp <= 0) && (iExp > -MAX_DIGITS) )
    {
        // Integer part
        strncpy( cpNumber, caInt, MAX_DIGITS + iExp );
        cpNumber[MAX_DIGITS + iExp] = '\0';
```

14

```
    // Decimal point
    strcat( cpNumber, "." );

    // Mantissa part
    strcat( cpNumber, caInt + MAX_DIGITS + iExp );

    // Eliminate trailing zeroes
    while( cpNumber[strlen( cpNumber ) - 1] == '0' )
        cpNumber[strlen( cpNumber ) - 1] = '\0';
}

// Handle decimal notation with leading zeroes
else if( (iExp <= -MAX_DIGITS) && (iExp > -(MAX_DIGITS +
        iZeroes)) )
{
    // Integer part and decimal point
    strcpy( cpNumber, "0." );
    iExp += MAX_DIGITS;

    // Other zeroes
    for( ; iExp; iExp++ )
        strcat( cpNumber, "0" );

    // Eliminate trailing zeroes
    while( caInt[strlen( caInt ) - 1] == '0' )
        caInt[strlen( caInt ) - 1] = '\0';

    // The rest of the number
    strcat( cpNumber, caInt );
}

else
// Handle exponential notation
{
    // Build the number part
    *cpNumber++ = *caInt;
    *cpNumber++ = '.';
    strcpy( cpNumber, caInt + 1 );

    // Convert the exponent to ascii
    iExp += MAX_DIGITS - 1;
    itoa( caInt, iExp );

    // Build the exponent part
    strcat( cpNumber, "e" );
    if( iExp > 0 )
        strcat( cpNumber, "+" );
    else
        strcat( cpNumber, "-" );
    strcat( cpNumber, caInt );
```

```
        // Eliminate trailing zeroes
        while( cpNumber[strlen( cpNumber ) - 1] == '0' )
            cpNumber[strlen( cpNumber ) - 1] = '\0';
    }

    // We're done
    return;
}
```

The above function translates a floating point double back into an ASCII string. Again, the algorithm I'm using is an attempt at clarity over efficiency.

Porting Problems

There are two problems with the above code from a portability standpoint. First of all, the type int is used freely throughout the code despite my warnings to this effect in earlier chapters. Won't I ever learn? But now let's say this code is already running on two other platforms. The last thing we want to do is rip into this code and fix the data types. Especially, we don't want to rip into those ugly conversion functions. Even if we did, we're still using ANSI standard functions like **atoi()** in them that require the use of ints.

Is the use of int really a problem in this code? If you look carefully, or even run the code at this point and step through it, you'll see that it is. Oh, that's right. Some of those ANSI function calls are still undefined at this point. But take my word for it, or go back and do this when you get done with the chapter. There are several places, especially in the conversion functions, where int is definitely, but not so clearly, assumed to be 32 bits in length. The problem is that in the CodeWarrior compiler, int is 16 bits by default.

Changes to the Project

Luckily, you can change the settings of the project to make the type int 32 bits in length. This is an expedient solution you should know about. Now, you didn't use int anywhere else in your copy of the calculator program, did you? If you did, and if you assumed a 16-bit int, you will introduce bugs by changing this setting—yet another reason to *always* use type-safe variables.

Launch the CodeWarrior IDE and open your calculator project. I assume here that you have previously saved off a clean copy of your project so that you won't go mad at the end of the chapter trying to debug all these changes. Anyway, select Edit | Calculator Settings and go to Code Generation, 68K Processor. Check the box labeled "4 byte ints." This will make the type int 32 bits in length to the compiler.

14

Additions to app.h

When you make this code, you'll notice the second portability problem. The Palm OS doesn't support all the ANSI standard C function calls! Luckily, you can usually get around this restriction using a couple of methods. We replaced all those wickedly difficult math functions by bringing in MathLib in the previous chapter. We wrote a couple of our own functions for converting doubles to ASCII and back. The last accommodation we need to make appears in app.h:

```
///////////////////////////
// Definitions for calc.c //
///////////////////////////

#define atoi    StrAToI
#define itoa    StrIToA
#define strcat  StrCat
#define strcpy  StrCopy
#define strlen  StrLen
#define strncpy StrNCopy
```

Many of the ANSI string functions are fairly faithfully represented in the Palm OS string manager library. To apply them to ANSI standard C code you need only put the following define statements in a strategic location.

Debugging

I recommend you copy calc.c off of the CD because there's not a lot of Palm OS learning value in typing in this generic code. However, you might learn a few cool things about floating point conversion. It's your choice.

To debug calc.c, I recommend you step through **calcAppend()** and **calcExponent()** first and get the number entry stuff working. From there you can tackle **calcEquals()**, which will probably force you to step through the conversion routines **n2ca()** and **ca2n()**.

Index

References to figures and illustrations are in italics.

About the CD

Dear Reader,

This CD contains all the example code from all the chapters. The folder titles indicate which chapter the example is from. The CD also contains CodeWarrior Lite for Windows and for the Macintosh.

◆ **Windows People**   Double-click on the **cw_lite_palm_win.exe** file to begin installing CodeWarrior Lite. Follow the directions given by the install program to complete the installation.

◆ **Macintosh People**   You need a free utility called StuffIt Expander to install CodeWarrior Lite. This utility is made by my good friends at Aladdin Systems. If you don't already have this utility, you can download it from their website:

http://www.aladdinsys.com/expander/index.html

Enjoy, Robert Mykland

Technical support from Metrowerks is available by acquiring any of Metrowerks' commercial products. For more information on upgrading from this limited version of CodeWarrior to a commercial product, contact Metrowerks at 1-800-377-5416, or via email at sales@metrowerks.com.

METROWERKS AND METROWERKS' LICENSOR(S), AND THEIR DIRECTORS, OFFICERS, EMPLOYEES OR AGENTS (COLLECTIVELY METROWERKS) MAKE NO WARRANTIES, EXPRESS OR IMPLIED, INCLUDING WITHOUT LIMITATION THE IMPLIED WARRANTIES OF MERCHANTABILITY AND FITNESS FOR A PARTICULAR PURPOSE, REGARDING THE SOFTWARE. METROWERKS DOES NOT WARRANT, GUARANTEE OR MAKE ANY REPRESENTATIONS REGARDING THE USE OR THE RESULTS OF THE USE OF THE SOFTWARE IN TERMS OF ITS CORRECTNESS, ACCURACY, RELIABILITY, CURRENTNESS OR OTHERWISE. THE ENTIRE RISK AS TO THE RESULTS AND PERFORMANCE OF THE SOFTWARE IS ASSUMED BY YOU. THE EXCLUSION OF IMPLIED WARRANTIES IS NOT PERMITTED BY SOME JURISDICTIONS. THE ABOVE EXCLUSION MAY NOT APPLY TO YOU.

IN NO EVENT WILL METROWERKS AND METROWERKS' LICENSOR(S), AND THEIR DIRECTORS, OFFICERS, EMPLOYEES OR AGENTS (COLLECTIVELY METROWERKS) BE LIABLE TO YOU FOR ANY CONSEQUENTIAL, INCIDENTAL OR INDIRECT DAMAGES (INCLUDING DAMAGES FOR LOSS OF BUSINESS PROFITS, BUSINESS INTERRUPTION, LOSS OF BUSINESS INFORMATION, AND THE LIKE) ARISING OUT OF THE USE OR INABILITY TO USE THE SOFTWARE EVEN IF METROWERKS HAS BEEN ADVISED OF THE POSSIBILITY OF SUCH DAMAGES. BECAUSE SOME JURISDICTIONS DO NOT ALLOW THE EXCLUSION OR LIMITATION OF LIABILITY FOR CONSEQUENTIAL OR INCIDENTAL DAMAGES, THE ABOVE LIMITATIONS MAY NOT APPLY TO YOU. Metrowerks' liability to you for actual damages from any cause whatsoever, and regardless of the form of the action (whether in contract, tort (including negligence), product liability or otherwise), will be limited to the cost of the replacement of the media on which the software is distributed.

Metrowerks CodeWarrior Lite Disclaimer and End-User Software License Agreement

METROWERKS DOES NOT PROVIDE ANY TECHNICAL SUPPORT FOR CODEWARRIOR LITE.

IN ORDER TO RECEIVE TECHNICAL SUPPORT YOU MUST UPGRADE TO THE COMMERCIAL VERSION OF CODEWARRIOR. PLEASE USE THE ORDER FORM IN THE DOCUMENT NAMED 'HOW TO ORDER'.

PLEASE READ THIS LICENSE CAREFULLY BEFORE USING THE SOFTWARE. BY USING THE SOFTWARE, YOU ARE AGREEING TO BE BOUND BY THE TERMS OF THIS LICENSE. IF YOU DO NOT AGREE TO THE TERMS OF THIS LICENSE, PROMPTLY RETURN THE UNUSED SOFTWARE TO THE PLACE WHERE YOU OBTAINED IT AND YOUR MONEY WILL BE REFUNDED.

1. License. The application and other software accompanying this License, whether on disk, in read only memory, or on any other media (the "Software") and the related documentation and fonts are licensed to you by Metrowerks and its Licensors. You own the disc on which the Software and documentation are recorded but Metrowerks and/or Metrowerks' Licensors retain title to the Software, related documentation and fonts. This License allows you to use the Software and fonts on a single computer. You may use a copy of the software on a home or a portable computer, as long as the extra copy is never loaded at the same time the software is loaded on the primary computer on which you use the Software. You may make one copy of the Software and fonts in machine-readable form for backup purposes. You must reproduce on such copy the Metrowerks copyright notice and any other proprietary legends that were on the original copy of the Software and fonts. You may also transfer all your license rights in the Software and the fonts, the backup copy of the Software and fonts, the related documentation and a copy of this license to another party, provided the other party reads and agrees to accept the terms and conditions of this License.

2. Restrictions. The Software contains copyrighted material, trade secrets and other proprietary material. In order to protect them, and except as permitted by applicable legislation, you may not decompile, reverse engineer, disassemble or otherwise reduce the Software to a human-perceivable form. You may not modify, rent, lease, loan, distribute or create derivative works based upon the Software in whole or in part. You may not electronically transmit the Software from one computer to another or over a network. You may not use the Software to produce software that is distributed for sale or resale or as shareware or freeware.

3. Termination. This License is effective until terminated. You may terminate this License at any time by destroying the Software and related documentation and all copies thereof. This License will terminate immediately without notice from Metrowerks if you fail to comply with any provision of this License. Upon termination you must destroy the Software and related documentation and all related copies thereof.

4. Export Law Assurances. You agree and certify that neither the Software nor any technical data received from Metrowerks, nor the direct product thereof, will be exported outside the United States except as authorized and as permitted by the laws and regulations of the United States. If the Software has been rightfully obtained by you outside of the United States, you agree that you will not re-export the Software nor any other technical data received from Metrowerks, nor the direct product thereof, except as permitted by the laws and regulations of the United States and the laws and regulations of the jurisdiction in which you obtained the Software.

5. Government End Users. If you are acquiring the Software and fonts on behalf of any unit or agency of the United States Government, the following provisions apply. The Government agrees that the Software and fonts shall be classified as "commercial computer software" as that term is defined in the applicable provisions of the Federal Acquisition Regulation ("FAR") and supplements thereto, including the Department of Defense ("DoD") FAR Supplement ("DFARS"). If the Software and fonts are supplied for use by DoD, it is delivered subject to the terms of this Agreement and either (i) in accordance with DFARS 227.7202-1(a) and 227.7202-3(a), or (ii) with restricted rights in accordance with DFARS 252.227-7013(c)(1)(ii) (OCT 1988), as applicable. If the Software and fonts are supplied for use by any other Federal agency, it is restricted computer software delivered subject to the terms of this Agreement and (i) FAR 12.212(a); (ii) FAR 52.227-19; or (iii) FAR 52.227-14(ALT III), as applicable.

6. Disclaimer of Warranty on Metrowerks Software. You expressly acknowledge and agree that use of the Software and fonts is at your sole risk. Except as is stated above, the Software, related documentation and fonts are provided "AS IS" and without warranty of any kind and Metrowerks and Metrowerks' Licensor(s) (for the purposes of provisions 6 and 7, Metrowerks and Metrowerks' Licensor(s) shall be collectively referred to as "Metrowerks") EXPRESSLY DISCLAIM ALL OTHER WARRANTIES, EXPRESS OR IMPLIED, INCLUDING, BUT NOT LIMITED TO, THE IMPLIED WARRANTIES OF MERCHANTABILITY, FITNESS FOR A PARTICULAR PURPOSE AND NONINFRINGEMENT. METROWERKS DOES NOT WARRANT THAT THE FUNCTIONS CONTAINED IN THE SOFTWARE WILL MEET YOUR REQUIREMENTS, OR THAT THE OPERATION OF THE SOFTWARE WILL BE UNINTERRUPTED OR ERROR-FREE, OR THAT DEFECTS IN THE SOFTWARE AND THE FONTS WILL BE CORRECTED. FURTHERMORE, METROWERKS DOES NOT WARRANT OR MAKE ANY REPRESENTATIONS REGARDING THE USE OR THE RESULTS OF THE USE OF THE SOFTWARE AND FONTS OR RELATED DOCUMENTATION IN TERMS OF THEIR CORRECTNESS, ACCURACY, RELIABILITY, OR OTHERWISE. NO ORAL OR WRITTEN INFORMATION OR ADVICE GIVEN BY METROWERKS OR A METROWERKS AUTHORIZED REPRESENTATIVE SHALL CREATE A WARRANTY OR IN ANY WAY INCREASE THE SCOPE OF THIS WARRANTY. SHOULD THE SOFTWARE PROVE DEFECTIVE, YOU (AND NOT METROWERKS OR A METROWERKS AUTHORIZED REPRESENTATIVE) ASSUME THE ENTIRE COST OF ALL NECESSARY SERVICING, REPAIR OR CORRECTION. SOME JURISDICTIONS DO NOT ALLOW THE EXCLUSION OF IMPLIED WARRANTIES, SO THE ABOVE EXCLUSION MAY NOT APPLY TO YOU.

7. Limitation of Liability. UNDER NO CIRCUMSTANCES INCLUDING NEGLIGENCE, SHALL METROWERKS BE LIABLE FOR ANY INCIDENTAL, SPECIAL OR CONSEQUENTIAL DAMAGES THAT RESULT FROM THE USE OR INABILITY TO USE THE SOFTWARE OR RELATED DOCUMENTATION, EVEN IF METROWERKS OR A METROWERKS AUTHORIZED REPRESENTATIVE HAS BEEN ADVISED OF THE POSSIBILITY OF SUCH DAMAGES. SOME JURISDICTIONS DO NOT ALLOW THE LIMITATION OR EXCLUSION OF LIABILITY FOR INCIDENTAL OR CONSEQUENTIAL DAMAGES SO THE ABOVE LIMITATION OR EXCLUSION MAY NOT APPLY TO YOU.

In no event shall Metrowerks' total liability to you for all damages, losses, and causes of action (whether in contract, tort (including negligence) or otherwise) exceed that portion of the amount paid by you which is fairly attributable to the Software and fonts.

8. Controlling Law and Severability. This License shall be governed by and construed in accordance with the laws of the United States and the State of California, as applied to agreements entered into and to be performed entirely within California between California residents. If for any reason a court of competent jurisdiction finds any provision of this License, or portion thereof, to be unenforceable, that provision of the License shall be enforced to the maximum extent permissible so as to effect the intent of the parties, and the remainder of this License shall continue in full force and effect.

9. Complete Agreement. This License constitutes the entire agreement between the parties with respect to the use of the Software, the related documentation and fonts, and supersedes all prior or contemporaneous understandings or agreements, written or oral, regarding such subject matter. No amendment to or modification of this License will be binding unless in writing and signed by a duly authorized representative of Metrowerks.

Should you have any questions or comments concerning this license, please do not hesitate to write to Metrowerks Corp., 9801 Metric Boulevard, Suite 100, Austin, TX, 78758, USA. Attn: Warranty Information.